PIKS Foundation
C Programmer's Guide

William K. Pratt

PixelSoft

MANNING

Greenwich

This book is dedicated to my late uncle, Howard Welsh. When I was twelve, my uncle, an electrician, introduced me to the magical world of electricty. I was enthralled then by the simple circuits of bells and buzzers, and I remain enthralled by the wonders of electronics, computers, and especially image processing. I will be forever grateful to my uncle for his interest and encouragement in my career.

The publisher offers discounts on this book when ordered in quantity. For more information please contact:

Special Sales Department
Manning Publications Co.
3 Lewis Street
Greenwich, CT 06830
or
73150,1431@compuserve.com
Fax: (203) 661-9018

Recognizing the importance of preserving what has been written, it is the policy of Manning Publications to have the books they publish printed on acid-free paper, and we exert our best efforts to that end.

Library of Congress Cataloging in Publication Data

Pratt, William K.
    PIKS foundation C programmer's guide / William K. Pratt
      p. cm.
    Includes index.
    ISBN 1-884777-03-1
    1. Image processing—Digital techniques.   2. C (Computer program language) I. Title.
TK5102.9.P75   1994
621.36'7'02855133—dc20   94-31833
                                              CIP

1 2 3 4 5 6 7 8 9 10 — BB — 98 97 96 95 94

Printed in the United States of America

Contents

Preface   vii

Acknowledgements   xi

Prologue   xiii

PART 1   PIKS Imaging Model   1

1   PIKS Imaging Model   3

    1.1   Image Data Object   4

      Image Array   5, Image Structure   6, Image Colour Spaces   7, Pixel Data Types   8

    1.2   Nonimage Data Objects   9

      Tuple   9, Matrix   9, Neighbourhood Array   10, Histogram   12, Lookup Table   12, Region-of-Interest   14, Data Object Creation   15, Data Object Repository   15

    1.3   Elements   16

      Operators   16, Tools   16, Utilities   18, Mechanisms   18

    1.4   Basic Operator Model   18

      Point Operators   20, Ensemble Operators   20, Neighbourhood Operators   21, Geometric Operators   22

    1.5   Region-of-Interest Control   22

      ROI Data Object Creation   22, Image to Nonimage ROI Control   23, Image to Image ROI Control   23, ROI Data Object Manipulation   25

    1.6   PIKS to Application Interface   26

    1.7   Error Reporting   26

PART 2   Semantic Description of PIKS Elements   29

2   PIKS Operators   32

    2.1   Point Operators   32

      Bit Shift   32, Complement   34, Lookup   35, Monadic, Arithmetic   38, Monadic, Logical   41, Threshold   42, Unary, Integer   45, Window-Level   46

2.2   Ensemble Operators   48

Alpha Blend, Constant   48, Dyadic, Arithmetic   49, Dyadic, Logical   51, Dyadic Predicate   54, Split Image   58

2.3   Filtering and Morphological Operators   59

Convolve, Two-dimensional   59, Morphic Processor   67

2.4   Geometric Operators   69

Flip, Spin, Transpose   69, Flip, Spin, Transpose ROI   72, Rescale   73, Rescale ROI   75, Resize   77, Resize ROI   78, Rotate   81, Subsample   84, Translate   85, Translate ROI   87, Zoom   88, Zoom ROI   90

2.5   Presentation Operators   92

Diffuse   92, Dither   94

2.6   Colour Operators   96

Colour Conversion, Linear   95, Colour Conversion, Subtractive   97, Luminance Generation   98

2.7   Pixel Modification Operator   102

Draw Pixels   102

2.8   Analysis Operators   103

Accumulator   103, Extrema   104, Histogram, One-dimensional   106, Moments   108

3   PIKS Tools   109

3.1   Image and ROI Generation Tools   109

Image Constant   109, ROI Rectangular   110

3.2   Nonimage Object Generation Tools   112

Array to Lookup Table   112, Colour Conversion Matrix   113, Impulse Rectangular   115

4   PIKS Mechanisms   117

4.1   Control Mechanisms   117

Close PIKS   117, Close PIKS Emergency   117, Open PIKS   117

4.2   Allocation and Deallocation Mechanisms   118

Allocate Histogram   118, Allocate Image   119, Allocate Lookup Table   122, Allocate Matrix   123, Allocate Neighbourhood Array   123, Allocate Region of Interest   125, Allocate Tuple   126, Deallocate Data Object   127

4.3   Inquiry Mechanisms   127

Inquire Elements   127, Inquire Image   128, Inquire Nonimage Object   130, Inquire PIKS Implementation   132, Inquire PIKS Status   133, Inquire Repository   134, Inquire Resampling   135

	4.4	Management Mechanisms	136

Bind ROI   136, Define Sub Image   137, Return Repository
Identifier   139, Set Globals   139, Set Image Attribuutes   140

	4.5	Error Mechanisms	141

Error Handler   141, Error Logger   143, Error Test   143, Set Error
Handler   144

5	PIKS Utilities		145

	5.1	Internal Utilities	145

Convert Array to Image   145, Convert Image Data Type   146, Convert
Image to Array   147, Convert ROI to Image   147, Copy Window   148,
Create Tuple   149, Extract Pixel Plane   150, Insert Pixel Plane   151

	5.2	Import Utilities	152

Import Histogram   152, Import Image   153, Import Lookup Table   154,
Import Matrix   155, Import Neighbourhood Array   156, Import
Tuple   158, Put Colour Pixel   159, Put Pixel   160, Put Pixel Array   160

	5.3	Export Utilities	161

Export Histogram   162, Export Image   162, Export Lookup Table   163,
Export Matrix   164, Export Neighbourhood Array   165, Export
Tuple   165, Get Colour Pixel   166, Get Pixel   167, Get Pixel ROI   168,
Get Pixel Array   169, Get Pixel Array ROI   170

PART 3	**Syntactical Description of PIKS Elements**		171

6	PIKS C Language Binding		173

	6.1	Binding Notation	173
	6.2	Header Information	179
	6.3	Memory Management	180
	6.4	Convenience Functions	181
	6.5	Implementation-specific Utilities	181

File Reading and Writing   181, Window Manipulation   182,
Image Display   182

	6.6	Program Structure	183
	6.7	ROI Complement Example	184
	6.8	Image Histogram Example	189
	6.9	Unsharp Mask Example	192

7	PIKS C Language Element Prototypes		197

8	PIKS C Language Convenience Function and PixelSoft Utility Prototypes		309

Appendices

A PIKS Mathematical Functions Definitions 333

    A.1 Conventional Mathematical Symbols 333

    A.2 Mathematical Functions 334

B PIKS Header 336

    B.1 External Physical Image Data Types 336

    B.2 Parameter Data Types 336

    B.3 Data Object Identifiers 337

    B.4 Enumerated Type Definitions 337

    B.5 Data Type Union Definitions 339

    B.6 Structure Type Definitions 340

    B.7 Macro Definitions 342

    B.8 Element Designaters 346

    B.9 Convenience Function Designaters 347

    B.10 Impulse Response Array Repository Entry Designaters 348

    B.11 Dither Array Repository Entry Designaters 349

    B.12 Colour Conversion Matrix Repository Entry Designaters 349

    B.13 Error Code Designaters 351

C Program Examples 354

    C.1 roi_complement.c 354

    C.2 histogram.c 357

    C.3 unsharp_mask.c 360

  Index 364

  PixelSoft, Inc. Software 371

Preface

During the past thirty years, the field of digital image processing has experienced phenomenal growth. Today, image processing plays a vital role in a multitude of scientific, industrial, medical, and governmental applications.

In the early years of image processing, most of the processing was performed on special purpose hardware operating under microcode control. As general purpose computers, workstations, and personal computers have become more powerful in terms of processing speed and memory capacity, there has been a shift away from special purpose hardware and software implementations to general purpose hardware using standard computer languages. This, in turn, has led to the desire by many application writers and end users for a common Application Program Interface (API) for image processing. Such an API would permit the portability of image processing computer programs between various computing platforms and computer operating systems.

In the United States, in early 1988, work on an image processing API, called the Programmer's Imaging Kernel (PIK) began under the direction of the American National Standards Institute (ANSI). During this time period, the German national standards body, Deutsches Institut für Normung (DIN), was developing an imaging API, called the Iconic Kernel System (IKS). Discussions began in 1989 to merge the two standards development efforts under the joint auspices of the International Organization for Standardization (ISO) and the International Electrotechnical Commission (IEC). A new work item was approved by the ISO/IEC in 1991 to develop a three part standard, called Image Processing and Interchange (IPI). Part 1 of this standard, named a Common Architecture for Imaging (CAI), provides an architectural framework for the Image Processing and Interchange standard. It also specifies an abstract description of image data objects and nonimage objects related to images. Part 2, called the Programmer's Imaging Kernel System (PIKS), is an API for image processing. Part 3, entitled the Image Interchange Facility (IIF), specifies means for transporting images and image-related data objects between an application and PIKS or between two general applications. Parts 2 and 3 of the IPI standard are stand-alone in the sense that conformant implementations may exist for PIKS functionality only, or for IIF capability only, or for combined PIKS-IIF functionality.

The IPI standard is published as a three part Functional Specification. It describes the image processing and interchange functionality in general terms, independent of any particular computer language. In 1991, ISO/IEC undertook the development of a C programming language binding for IPI. It specifies the syntactical usage of PIKS and IFF for the C language.

In July 1993, Parts 1, 2, and 3 of the IPI functional specification were formally approved to become international standards subject to directed editorial revisions. These standards were formally issued in 1994 and 1995. The C language binding document is under international review. It should be published as an international standard in 1995.

The PIKS standard provides several nested levels of standardized functionality, called profiles. They are:

PIKS Foundation   Basic image processing functionality for monochrome and color images whose pixels are represented as Boolean values or as nonnegative or signed integers.

PIKS Technical   Intermediate image processing functionality for monochrome, color, volume, temporal, and spectral images whose pixels are represented, as Boolean, nonnegative and signed integers, real arithmetic values, and complex arithmetic values. PIKS Technical is a superset of PIKS Foundation functionality.

PIKS Scientific   Complete set of image processing functionality for all image structures and pixel data types. PIKS Scientific is a superset of PIKS Technical functionality.

PIKS Full   Complete set of image processing functionality for all image structures and pixel data types plus the capability to chain together PIKS elements.

This book is a C language programmer's guide for the PIKS Foundation profile. It abstracts sufficient information from the IPI functional specification documents and the IPI C binding document to enable end users and application writers to write PIKS-based image processing programs without the need to access the ISO/IEC documents.

The guide is intended for readers who are familiar with the theory and practice of image processing. It is also intended for readers who are knowledgable of the C programming language.

Chapter 1 of this guide is an overview of the PIKS imaging model. It defines PIKS data objects in abstract terms, introduces the four types of PIKS processing elements—operators, tools, utilities, and mechanisms, and it discusses PIKS system control. Chapters 2 to 5 specify the usage of the PIKS operators, tools, mechanisms, and utilities, respectively. Each element is mathematically defined whenever possible. Chapter 2 provides several photographic examples of the functionality of PIKS operators.

The material in the first five chapters is based upon the IPI functional specification draft international standards of Part 1 edited by Adrian Clark and Part 2 edited by William K. Pratt. Their formal references are:

International Standard IS 12087-1
Information Technology
Computer Graphics and Image Processing
Image Processing and Interchange
Functional Specification
Part 1: Common Architecture for Imaging
1 November 1993

International Standard IS 12087-2
Information Technology

Computer Graphics and Image Processing
Image Processing and Interchange
Functional Specification
Part 2: Programmer's Imaging Kernel System Application Program Interface
1 August 1994

Chapter 6 discusses the notation and structure of the PIKS C language binding. This chapter also presents three complete C programs with explanations of their functionality. Chapter 7 provides an alphabetical listing of all of the PIKS Foundation element prototypes as well as C code snippets of their usage. The PIKS C language convenience functions and the PixelSoft utilities are defined in Chapter 8.

Chapters 6 to 8 are based upon the ISO C language binding draft international standard document edited by Gerard A. Paquette entitled:

Draft International Standard of IS 12088-4
Information Technology
Computer Graphics and Image Processing
Image Processing and Interchange
Application Program Interface Language Bindings
Part 4: C
10 November 1993

The appendices present definitions of mathematical functions, a complete listing of PIKS header information, and program listings of the PIKS examples.

ISO/IEC standards are based upon British spelling conventions, which differ from American spelling conventions for some words in the C Binding. For example, the word colour is used as part of the name of several PIKS operators. For consistency, British spelling conventions have been used in the remainder of this guide.

WILLIAM K. PRATT

Acknowledgements

The development of an international software standard is a formidable task, much more so than most participants envisage when they first volunteer for its development. The Image Processing and Interchange (IPI) standard has had a lengthy development period, about six years, partially because of the formalism of the international standards process itself, and partially because of the complexity of the standard in its complete form. Hopefully, the time and effort devoted to its development will prove worthwhile. For the first time, the image processing industry has available an internationally accepted API for image processing and a companion image interchange facility.

Five countries, over 50 organizations, and well over 100 individuals have participated in the development of the IPI standard directly or indirectly. I will not attempt to list all of the individuals. The following are the principal organizations, leaders, and document editors associated with the Image Processing and Interchange standard during the course of its development.

International Organization for Standardization (ISO)

Subcommittee SC24, Computer Graphics and Imaging Director: Barry Shepherd

Working Group WG1 Convener: Peter Bono

Working Group WG7 Convener: Detlef Kroemker

Part 1 Functional Specification Document Editor: Adrian Clark

Part 2 Functional Specification Document Editor: William K. Pratt

Part 3 Functional Specification Document Editors: G. Rainer Hoffman and Christof Blum

C Language Binding Document Editor: Gerard A. Paquette

American National Standards Institute, ANSI Computer Graphics and Image Processing Techniques Committee, X3H3

X3H3 Chairman: Peter Bono

X3H3 International Representative: Barbara Lurvey

X3H3.8 Chair: Patrick Krolak

X3H3.8 Vice Chair: Marty Deacutis

X3H3.8 Heads of Delegation: Keith Andress, Timothy Butler, Gerard A. Paquette, and William Puckett

British Standards Institute, BSI

Heads of Delegation: Robert Maybury and Andrew Rydz

Deutsches Institut für Normung, DIN

Head of Delegation: Ingwer Carlsen

Oesterreichisches Norumunes Institute, ON

Head of Delegation: Heimo Mueller-Seelich

Japanese Industrial Standards Committee, JISC

Head of Delegation: Koreaki Fujimura

Over its period of development, many individuals have made key contributions to the PIKS standard in terms of technical discussions, text contributions, and document reviews. Reluctantly, I have decided not to create a list of individual acknowledgements because it is impossible to draw the line in determining who should be mentioned. I simply wish to thank everyone who contributed.

For this guide, I wish to offer special thanks to Gerry Paquette, with whom I worked quite closely on reconciling conflicts between the PIKS functional specification and the C binding. I also wish to thank Gerry Paquette and Tim Butler for their constructive reviews of the manuscript of this book. I have worked closely with these individuals on a project to prototype PIKS Foundation. This work has helped to debug the PIKS functional specification, the C binding, and this guide.

I also wish to thank Matt Perez of SunSoft, Inc., who provided several Sun workstations to prototype PIKS Foundation. And, I wish to thank the management of Sun Microsystems, Inc. for their support over the many years of the IPI standard development.

Finally, I most sincerely thank my wife, Shelly, for her forebearance in the writing of this book.

WILLIAM K. PRATT

Prologue

The Programmer's Imaging Kernel System (PIKS) is an Application Program Interface (API) for image processing software developers. PIKS provides a rich set of both low-level and high-level software services, which can serve as building blocks for creating imaging applications in a wide variety of fields including animation, electronic publishing, graphic arts, industrial vision, medical imaging, photo-intelligence, remote sensing, and scientific visualization.

The following are the major features of PIKS.

International standard   PIKS is the only national or international standard API for image processing. There are no other "popular" imaging APIs that are considered to be defacto APIs. As a consequence, the imaging industry has had to suffer with multiple, usually proprietary APIs, many of which are limited to a particular computer. With a standard API that is made available on multiple computing platforms, it is possible for developers to create imaging applications that are truly portable between platforms.

Wide range of processing capability   PIKS provides over 250 processing elements ranging from low-level functions, such as convolution and histogram generation, to high-level functions, such as edge detection, morphology, and image warping. In addition, PIKS contains a repository of commonly used data objects, including convolution impulse response arrays, dither arrays, and colour conversion matrices.

Mathematical definitions   Unlike many other APIs, the PIKS processing operators are specified in complete mathematical detail. A PIKS developer can determine precisely the functionality of each operator.

Object oriented imaging model   PIKS provides a level of programming abstraction that frees the developer from many programming details, such as memory management and data structure generation. Images and data extracted from images, e.g., an image histogram, are treated as objects that can be manipulated by PIK operators without regard to their physical means of storage.

Multilevel functionality   PIKS has been subdivided into four nested levels of functionality ranging from basic operations required by virtually all applications to the full set of capabilites needed for specific applications. This guide is for the basic functionality profile called PIKS Foundation. An important feature of this functionality profiling is that there is no programming inconsistency between profiles.

Simple, self-describing programming interface　　Each PIKS element has an easily understood one line program interface that is self-describing in terms of data types. For example, the two-dimensional convolution operator is invoked by the call

```
InConvolve2D(nSrc, nDst, nArray, ICONVOLVE_ENCLOSED);
```

where the first three arguments specify the source image, destination image, and impulse response array by user-supplied identifiers, and the last argument specifies one of the four image boundary options.

These features, which are not provided by any single proprietary API, will appeal to two classes of users: application developers who desire portability of their application software, and research scientists and development engineers who will appreciate the imaging model and richness of the API.

PART 1

PIKS Imaging Model

Part 1 consists of a single chapter, the first chapter of this guide. Chapter 1 presents an architectural overview of the PIKS imaging model. It defines the image and nonimage data objects that are utilized by PIKS. The chapter also presents definitions of the PIKS processing elements, and provides a user-centric taxonomy for their classification by functionality.

The reader is advised not to skim this chapter, but rather to attempt to thoroughly grasp the principles presented before moving to the remainder of the guide.

1

PIKS Imaging Model

PIKS is based upon the imaging model shown in Figure 1-1. This model consists of four major parts:

- Data objects
- Operators, tools, and utilities
- System mechanisms
- Import and export

The PIKS data objects include image data objects (multidimensional arrays of pixels) and nonimage data objects (objects that contain image-related data, e.g., an image histogram). The operators, tools, and utilities are functional elements that are used to process image and nonimage data objects. The system mechanisms manage and control the processing. PIKS receives application calls to invoke its system mechanisms, operators, tools, and utilities. PIKS returns status and error information to the application. The import and export facility provides the means for accepting source image and nonimage data objects from the application for processing by PIKS, and for returning processed image and nonimage data objects to the application.

The following sections describe each of the major parts of the PIKS imaging model.

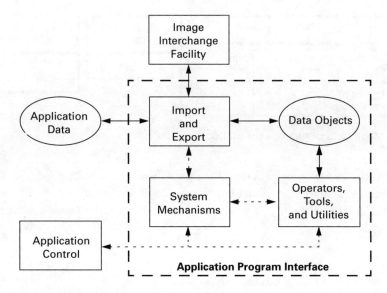

Figure 1-1 PIKS imaging model

1.1 Image Data Object

A PIKS image data object, as shown in Figure 1-2, is a hierarchical collection of image attributes, element control, and image array objects. The conceptual data structure of the upper level of Figure 1-2 is shown below.

Entry name	Description
Attributes	Image attributes public identifier
Control	Element control public identifier
Image	Image array private identifier

The key phrase of the previous sentence is "conceptual data structure." The PIKS imaging model is based upon an object-oriented design paradigm whereby the physical data structures of PIKS objects are not made available to the application. The philosophy of this design is that access by the application to the physical data structures is not necessary to exploit PIKS functionality. Furthermore, indirect access results in a simpler programming model. The identifiers provide the necessary indirect access to data objects. The image attributes and element control objects are accessed by public identifiers, which can be determined by the application through inquiry mechanisms. The image array identifier is private in the sense that it is not available to the application. However, an application can gain access to the image array data indirectly by the image export utility.

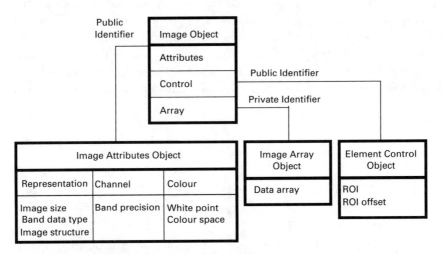

Figure 1-2   Image data object conceptual data structure

The image attributes object contains three parts: the representation, channel, and colour attributes. The representation attribute contains information regarding the image size, colour band data type, and semantic image structure. The conceptual data structure of the representation attribute is:

Entry name	Description
Image size	Image size 5-tuple public identifier
Band data type	Band data type 5-tuple public identifier
Image structure	Image structure code

PIKS makes extensive use of tuples as a convenient means of representing multidimensional data parameters. Section 1.2.1 describes the conceptual data structure of a tuple. Tuples are referenced by public identifiers.

The channel attribute contains information about the pixel storage precision of each band of an image. In the PIKS Foundation profile, all bands are homogeneous, and therefore, each band has the same precision. The conceptual data structure of the channel attribute is:

Entry name	Description
Band precision	Bits per pixel B-tuple public identifier

The colour attribute contains information regarding the colour space representation and the white point of a colour image. The conceptual data structure of the colour attribute is:

Entry name	Description
Colour space	Colour space code
White point	White point values

The control attribute contains information regarding the region-of-interest (ROI) control of PIKS image processing elements. The conceptual data structure is:

Entry name	Description
ROI	ROI public identifier
ROI offset	ROI offset tuple public identifier

Higher level PIKS profiles provide match point control capability in addition to ROI control. The following sections provide more detailed information about PIKS image objects.

1.1.1 Image Array

A PIKS image object references a five-dimensional array of pixels whose dimensions are either semantically or generically defined. The semantic index structure is:

x Horizontal space index
y Vertical space index
z Depth index
t Temporal index
b Colour or spectral band index

The generic ranges of the indices are:

$0 \leq x \leq X - 1$
$0 \leq y \leq Y - 1$
$0 \leq z \leq Z - 1$

$$0 \le t \le T - 1$$
$$0 \le b \le B - 1$$

where X, Y, Z, T, B represent the maximum sizes of the image indices x, y, z, t, b, respectively.

The PIKS Foundation profile supports usage of the x, y, and b indices only. However, all PIKS operations are defined for the general five-dimensional image model.

A single source image is expressed notationally as

$$SRC(x, y, z, t, b)$$

and the pth source images of a set of P images, where $1 \le p \le P$, is expressed as

$$SRC_p(x, y, z, t, b)$$

Similarly, a single destination image is expressed notationally as

$$DST(x, y, z, t, b)$$

PIKS Foundation does not provide any operators that create multiple destination images.

Figure 1-3 contains a geometric interpretation of a PIKS Foundation image array. As noted in the following sections, for a monochrome image, $B = 1$, and for a colour image $B = 3$ or $B = 4$. For geometric operations, such as individual band rotation, the directional sense of the indexing along each image array coordinate axis must be specified. For each band, the image origin is at the upper left corner of the band array. The x index increments positively from left to right. The y index increments positively from top to bottom. The b index increments positively from front to back.

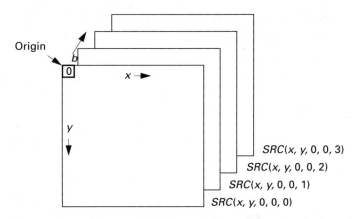

Figure 1-3 Geometric interpretation of PIKS image array

1.1.2 *Image Structure*

PIKS gives semantic meaning to certain dimensional subsets of the general five-dimensional image array. The image structures supported in the PIKS Foundation profile are:

Code	Image structure
MON	Monochrome
COLR	Colour

Some PIKS operators only apply to certain structured image representations.

1.1.3 Image Colour Spaces

PIKS supports a number of commonly-used colour spaces. The following is a taxonomy of PIKS colour spaces.

Nonstandardized:

Additive red, green, blue (RGB)
Subtractive cyan, magenta, yellow (CMY)
Subtractive cyan, magenta, yellow, black (CMYK)
Intensity, hue, saturation (IHS)

Standardized:

Point-linear, inter-component-linear:

Linear CCIR RGB, Illuminant D65 white reference
Linear CIE RGB, Illuminant E white reference
Linear EBU RGB, Illuminant C white reference
Linear EBU RGB, Illuminant D65 white reference
Linear NTSC RGB, Illuminant C white reference
Linear NTSC RGB, Illuminant D65 white reference
Linear SMPTE RGB, Illuminant D65 white reference
CIE XYZ
CIE UVW

Point-linear, inter-component-nonlinear:

CIE Yxy
CIE Yuv
CIE L*a*b*
CIE L*u*v*

Point-nonlinear, inter-component-linear:

Gamma CCIR RGB, Illuminant D65 white reference
Gamma EBU RGB, Illuminant C white reference
Gamma EBU RGB, Illuminant D65 white reference
Gamma NTSC RGB, Illuminant C white reference
Gamma NTSC RGB, Illuminant D65 white reference
Gamma SMPTE RGB, Illuminant D65 white reference
Luminance/chrominance EBU YUV, Illuminant C white reference
Luminance/chrominance EBU YUV, Illuminant D65 white reference
Luminance/chrominance NTSC YIQ, Illuminant C white reference
Luminance/chrominance NTSC YIQ, Illuminant D65 white reference
Luminance/chrominance SMPTE YCbCr, Illuminant D65 white reference

The term standardized means that the image is assumed to have been acquired by a calibrated scanner with known standard primary chromaticity coordinates and white point reference tristimulus values. The term nonstandardized means that the image is not assumed to have been acquired by a scanner calibrated to a standard colour reference.

The point-linear, inter-component-linear category of colour spaces represents images whose components are physical tristimulus values—e.g., RGB or nonphysical tristimulus values, e.g.,

XYZ. For such colour spaces, it is possible to convert from one colour space to another by an inter-component, 3×3 matrix multiplication conversion between colour components.

The point-linear, inter-component-nonlinear category represents images that have undergone a nonlinear transformation between the tristimulus components. Inverse nonlinear transformations exist for this colour space category.

The point-nonlinear, inter-component-linear category represents images, which are typically obtained from a video camera. Such images have colour components that are not linearly proportional to ambient light. Their colour components are said to be "gamma corrected." The luminance/chrominance colour spaces are one-to-one, inter-component linear transformations of the corresponding RGB colour spaces. For example, the YIQ components for an illuminant C white reference are obtained by a 3×3 matrix multiplication of the NTSC RGB components for illuminant C, and vice versa. It should be noted that there is no luminance/chrominance definition for gamma CCIR RGB. Transformations between gamma RGB colour spaces are not "legal." The proper operation is to "linearize" the gamma components, perform an inter-component linear transformation, and then perform a point nonlinear gamma correction.

Table 1-1 lists the white points of the standard illuminants in the XYZ coordinate system.

Table 1-1.   White point tristimulus values

Illuminant	X_0	Y_0	Z_0
C	0.981	1.000	1.182
E	1.000	1.000	1.000
D65	0.950	1.000	1.089

1.1.4 Pixel Data Types

The PIKS Foundation profile supports three pixel data types:

Data type	Code
Boolean	BD
Nonnegative integer	ND
Signed integer	SD

The PIKS functional specification does not mandate the internal physical storage mechanism of an implementation. However, PIKS implementations are required to provide the following minimum arithmetic pixel storage precisions:

ND   8-bit unsigned integer
SD   16-bit signed integer

This guide assumes the ND and SD precisions stated above for the programming examples in Chapter 6. For this assumption, the ND data type provides pixel amplitudes over the range of 0 to 255. The SD data type provides pixel amplitudes over the range of −32,768 to 32,767. The guide also assumes that a BD data type image is stored as a one-bit array in which the Boolean TRUE state is represented as an unsigned integer of value one, and the Boolean FALSE state is represented as an unsigned integer of value zero.

1.2 Nonimage Data Objects

The following sections define the PIKS nonimage data objects.

1.2.1 *Tuple*

A PIKS tuple (TUPLE) data object is a collection of data values of the same elementary data type combined with tuple object attributes that specify the tuple size and the data type of its data values. Tuples are widely used by PIKS to define other data object attributes and to specify input parameters for PIKS elements. The conceptual data structure of a PIKS tuple is shown below.

Entry name	Description
Tuple data size	Number of values
Data type code	CHOICE{BD, ND, SD, RD, CS}
Tuple	Data array private identifier

The function CHOICE indicates the selection of one of the five possible data types for the tuple data values:

Data type	Code
Boolean	BD
Nonnegative integer	ND
Signed integer	SD
Real arithmetic	RD
Character string	CS

As an example, the following is the conceptual data structure of a PIKS tuple that specifies the size of a PIKS nonnegative, trichromatic (3 band) colour image in PIKS five-dimensional space. Each image band contains 512 rows and 1024 columns of pixels.

5
ND
1024
512
1
1
3

1.2.2 *Matrix*

A PIKS matrix (MATRIX) data object is a two-dimensional array of matrix elements plus matrix object attributes. A matrix data object is used by operators that perform vector-matrix multiplication. The general form of a PIKS matrix data object is shown below.

Entry name	Description
Column size	Value
Row size	Value
Matrix data type	CHOICE{ND, SD, RD}
Matrix	Data array private identifier

The ND, SD, and RD codes denote nonnegative integer, signed integer, and real data type matrix elements, respectively.

The private array identifier references a two-dimensional array of the general form

$$
\begin{bmatrix}
M(1, 1) & M(1, 2) & \ldots & M(1, C) \\
\cdot & \cdot & & \cdot \\
M(r, 1) & M(r, 2) & \ldots & M(r, C) \\
\cdot & \cdot & & \cdot \\
M(R, 1) & M(R, 2) & \ldots & M(R, C)
\end{bmatrix}
$$

where the elements, $M(r,c)$, are ND, SD, or RD data types. Matrix indexing follows the common mathematical convention of specifying the row index before the column index. This is opposite to the indexing of an image array. As an example, the following is the conceptual data structure of a PIKS matrix data object, which can be used to convert a linear NTSC Illuminant D65 RGB colour space image to XYZ colour space.

3
3
RD
id

The private identifier, id, references the two-dimensional array:

$$
\begin{bmatrix}
0.58806226 & 0.17914326 & 0.18319448 \\
0.28964261 & 0.60567484 & 0.10468256 \\
0.00000000 & 0.06824505 & 1.02065495
\end{bmatrix}
$$

1.2.3   Neighbourhood Array

A PIKS neighbourhood array (NBHOOD_ARRAY) data object is a collection of object attributes and an array of up to five dimensions that can be used by PIKS operators that perform pixel neighbourhood manipulations. In PIKS Foundation, all neighbourhood arrays are two-dimensional. The general form of a PIKS neighbourhood array is shown below.

Entry name	Description
Neighbourhood size	Neighbourhood size 5-tuple public identifier
Key pixel	Key pixel 5-tuple public identifier
Scale factor	Value
Semantic label	CHOICE{GL, DL, IL, ML, SL}

Entry name	Description
Array data type	CHOICE{BD, ND, SD, RD}
Neighbourhood	Data array private identifier

The neighbourhood size 5-tuple has the following conceptual data structure:

5
ND
x index array size value
y index array size value
z index array size value
t index array size value
b index array size value

The key pixel 5-tuple has the following conceptual data structure:

5
ND
x index key pixel value
y index key pixel value
z index key pixel value
t index key pixel value
b index key pixel value

The key pixel establishes the origin of the neighbourhood array with respect to the first row and column element of the array. See Section 1.4.3.

The semantic label codes are defined as follows.

Code	Definition
GL	Generic array
DL	Dither array
IL	Impulse response array
ML	Mask array
SL	Structuring element array

In PIKS Foundation, the private array identifier references a two-dimensional array of the general form

$$\frac{1}{S}\begin{bmatrix} H(0,0) & H(2,1) & \ldots & H(C-1,1) \\ \cdot & \cdot & & \cdot \\ H(1,r) & H(2,r) & \ldots & H(C-1,r) \\ \cdot & \cdot & & \cdot \\ H(1,R-1) & H(2,R-1) & \ldots & H(C-1,R-1) \end{bmatrix}$$

where the array elements, $H(c,r)$ are specified as BD, ND, SD, or RD data type values. The scale factor, S, is a signed integer data type. It must be unity for BD, ND, and RD array element data types. For signed integer array elements, the nonunity data type scale factor can be used as an indirect means of specifying neighbourhood arrays with fractional elements. It should be noted that the neighbourhood array indexing is the same as the indexing of a two-dimensional image array.

As an example, the following is the conceptual data structure of a signed integer impulse response neighbourhood array, which can be used for high-pass filtering of an image by convolution to enhance image detail:

Neighbourhood size 5-tuple identifier
Key pixel 5-tuple identifier
1
IL
SD
id

The private identifier, id, references the two-dimensional array:

$$\begin{bmatrix} 0 & -1 & 0 \\ -1 & 5 & -1 \\ 0 & -1 & 0 \end{bmatrix}$$

1.2.4 Histogram

A PIKS histogram (HIST) data object is a one-dimensional array of unsigned integers that stores the histogram of an image, combined with histogram object attributes. The general form of a PIKS histogram data object is shown below.

Entry name	Description
Array size	Value
Lower amplitude bound	Value
Upper amplitude bound	Value
Histogram	Data array private identifier

The array size is a nonnegative integer. It specifies the number of histogram image amplitude bins. The lower and upper amplitude bounds are real arithmetic values that specify the limits of the pixel amplitude range over which the histogram data is collected. The histogram array stores the number of pixels of an image whose amplitudes lie in each amplitude bin.

The following is the conceptual data structure of the histogram of a signed integer image taken over the amplitude range of -100.0 to 100.0 (There are 256 histogram bins):

256
−100.0
100.0
id

1.2.5 Lookup Table

A PIKS lookup table (LUT) data object is a collection of object attributes combined with a two-dimensional array that stores the lookup table data. The table is accessed by a one-dimensional entry index. The general form of a PIKS lookup table is shown below.

Entry name	Description
Table entries	Value
Table bands	Value
Table input data type	CHOICE{ND, SD}
Table output data type	CHOICE{BD, ND, SD}
Table	Data array private identifier

The table identifier references a two-dimensional table of the general form shown below.

Entry	Bands 0		b		$B-1$
0	$T(0, 0)$	...	$T(b, 0)$	...	$T(B-1, 0)$
e	$T(0, e)$	...	$T(b, e)$	...	$T(B-1, e)$
$E-1$	$T(0, E-1)$	...	$T(b, E-1)$	...	$T(B-1, E-1)$

A positive integer, e, is the index to the LUT. The LUT output is a one-dimensional array

$$a(e) = [T(0, e) \dots T(b, e) \dots T(B-1, e)]$$

In the PIKS operator model, the LUT input index, e, is derived from a source image pixel by the assignment

$$e = SRC(x, y, z, t, b)$$

PIKS Foundation provides lookup table usage for two cases: the source and destination images are of the same band dimension, or the source image is a monochrome image and the destination image is a colour image. In the former case, when the source and destination images are of the same band size, i.e., both are monochrome or colour images, then for $0 \leq b \leq B-1$

$$DST(x, y, 0, 0, b) = T(0, SRC(x, y, 0, 0, b))$$

In the latter case, when the source image is a monochrome image, and the destination image is a colour image, then for $0 \leq b \leq B-1$

$$DST(x, y, 0, 0, b) = T(b, SRC(x, y, z, t, 0))$$

As an example, the following is the conceptual data structure for a 256 entry, single band lookup table where the source image is of nonnegative data type and the destination image is of Boolean data type:

256
1
ND
BD
id

1.2.6 Region-of-Interest

A PIKS Foundation region-of-interest (ROI_RECT) data object consists of region-of-interest object attributes and a conceptual two-dimensional array that contains Boolean values that are used to control operator processing. Higher PIKS profiles permit the ROI to be a conceptual array of up to five dimensions. The general form of a PIKS rectangular region-of-interest object is shown below.

Entry name	Description
ROI size	ROI virtual array size 5-tuple public identifier
Start	Start position 5-tuple public identifier
End	End position 5-tuple public identifier
Dimension	CHOICE{1D, 2D]
Polarity	CHOICE{TRUE, FALSE}
ROI	Conceptual ROI array private identifier

Notationally, a PIKS Foundation ROI is expressed as a two-dimensional array, $R(x, y)$.

The ROI size 5-tuple has the following conceptual data structure:

```
5
ND
X virtual array size value
Y virtual array size value
1
1
1
```

The start position 5-tuple specifies the upper left corner coordinates of the rectangle. Its conceptual data structure is:

```
5
ND
x start position
y start position
0
0
0
```

The end position 5-tuple specifies the lower right corner coordinates of the rectangle. Its conceptual data structure is:

```
5
ND
x end position
y end position
0
0
0
```

In PIKS Foundation, the y start position is zero and the y end position is $Y-1$ for a one-dimensional ROI. A two-dimensional ROI may have arbitrary start and end positions within the bounds of the virtual array. The polarity choice of TRUE specifies that the interior of the rectangular ROI consists of Boolean TRUE pixels and the exterior has Boolean FALSE pixels. A FALSE polarity choice provides a reversed logical state.

1.2.7 Data Object Creation

PIKS image and nonimage data objects referenced by a PIKS operator, tool, or utility must be allocated by a PIKS system management mechanism prior to their first usage. There exist three classes of allocated data objects:

- *Class A* identified with all object attributes and data;
- *Class B* identified with all object attributes, but no data;
- *Class C* identified with partial or no object attributes, but no data.

When a data object is allocated, an identifier is assigned to the data object. Data object allocation mechanisms allow the application to specify certain object attributes, e.g., image size and structure, or to leave the attributes to be unspecified. When a Class C data object is specified as a destination of an operator, tool, or utility, many of the operators, tools, and utilities are able to supply the "missing" data object attributes.

Typically, the attributes of a source image are completely specified at the time of its allocation by the *allocate_image* mechanism. The source image then becomes a Class B image object. Upon import of the source image data by the *import_image* utility, the source image becomes a Class A image. If the attributes of a source image are not completely specified at the time of its allocation, it is a Class C image. Class C images are often used as destination images for geometric operators that change the size of a source image. The size of the destination image in such cases is dependent upon the operator parameters. The preceding discussion for image objects applies for nonimage objects as well. The object parameters for nonimage objects can be specified upon allocation, import, or object creation.

1.2.8 Data Object Repository

PIKS contains a data object repository containing several hundred "built-in" impulse response function arrays, dither arrays, and colour conversion matrices, which are commonly used in image processing operations. These data objects can be referenced by their PIKS identifiers.

In PIKS Foundation, impulse response function arrays are two-dimensional neighbourhood array data objects, which are used by the two-dimensional convolution operator. Dither arrays are two-dimensional neighbourhood array data objects. They are used by the dither operator to reduce the number of bits per pixel required to render an image. Colour conversion matrices are 3×3 matrix data objects. They are used by the PIKS linear colour conversion operator.

1.3 Elements

This subsection describes the four types of PIKS elements: operators, tools, utilities, and mechanisms.

1.3.1 Operators

PIKS operators are elements that manipulate images or manipulate data objects extracted from images in order to enhance or restore images, or to assist in the extraction of information from images. Operators can be classified as being primitive or high-level. Primitive operators comprise a small set of low-level operators, fundamental to image processing, which can be used to implement high-level operators. Examples are image convolution and image histogram generation. The PIKS Foundation profile contains a set of primitive operators.

PIKS operators can also be classified by the types of source and destination objects supported by an operator:

Source	Destination
Image	Nonimage
Image	Image

Another form of operator classification is by image processing functionality as listed below.

Analysis Image to nonimage operators that extract numerical information from an image.

Colour Image to image operators that convert a colour image from one colour space to another.

Ensemble Image to image operators that perform arithmetic (e.g., add, subtract), extremal (e.g., maximum, minimum), and logical (e.g., AND, OR) combination of a pair of images.

Filtering Image to image operators that perform neighbourhood combinations of pixels (e.g., two-dimensional convolution).

Geometric Image to image and ROI to ROI operators that perform geometric manipulations (e.g., translation, magnification, rotation).

Morphological Image to image operators that perform morphological operations (e.g., erosion, dilation).

Pixel modification Image to image operators that modify an image by pixel drawing or painting.

Point Image to image operators that perform point manipulation on a pixel-by-pixel basis (e.g., magnitude, threshold).

Presentation Image to image operators that prepare an image for display (e.g., dither).

Exhibit 1-1 lists the PIKS Foundation operators by functional class.

1.3.2 Tools

PIKS tools are elements that create data objects to be used by PIKS operators. An example is a tool to create a uniform amplitude impulse response neighbourhood array to be used by the convolution operator. Exhibit 1-2 lists the PIKS Foundation tools according to the following functional classes.

PIKS IMAGING MODEL   CHAPTER 1

Image generation   Tools that create test images.

Impulse response function array generation   Tools that create impulse response function neighbourhood array data objects.

Lookup table generation   Tools that creates entries of a lookup table data object.

Matrix generation   Tools that create matrix data objects.

Region-of-interest generation   Tools that create region-of-interest data objects from a mathematical description of the region-of-interest.

■**Exhibit 1-1:** PIKS foundation operators listed by functional class:

Analysis
    Accumulator
    Extrema
    Histogram, one-dimensional
    Moments

Colour
    Colour conversion, linear
    Colour conversion, subtractive
    Luminance generation

Ensemble
    Alpha blend, constant
    Dyadic, arithmetic
    Dyadic, logical
    Dyadic predicate
    Split image

Filtering
    Convolve, two-dimensional

Geometric
    Flip, spin, transpose
    Flip, spin, transpose ROI
    Rescale
    Rescale ROI
    Resize

    Resize ROI
    Rotate
    Subsample
    Translate
    Translate ROI
    Zoom
    Zoom ROI

Morphological
    Morphic processor

Pixel Modification
    Draw pixels

Point
    Bit shift
    Complement
    Lookup
    Monadic, arithmetic
    Monadic, logical
    Threshold
    Unary, integer
    Window-level

Presentation
    Diffuse
    Dither

■**Exhibit 1-2:** PIKS Foundation tools listed by functional class.

Image Generation
    Image, constant

Impulse Response Function Array Generation
    Impulse, rectangular

Lookup Table Generation
    Array to lookup table

Matrix Generation
    Colour conversion matrix

Region-of-Interest Generation
    ROI, rectangular

1.3.3 *Utilities*

PIKS utilities are elements that perform basic mechanical image manipulation tasks. Examples are utilities that insert pixels into an image or extract pixels from an image. Exhibit 1-3 lists the PIKS Foundation utilities according to the following functional classes.

Export from PIKS   Utilities that export image and nonimage data objects from PIKS to an application.

Import to PIKS   Utilities that import image and nonimage data objects to PIKS from an application.

Internal   Utilities that perform manipulation and conversion of PIKS internal image and nonimage data objects.

1.3.4 *Mechanisms*

PIKS mechanisms are elements that perform control and management tasks. Examples are mechanisms that open a PIKS session and allocate an image. Exhibit 1-4 lists the PIKS Foundation mechanisms according to the following functional classes.

Allocation and deallocation   Mechanisms that allocate and deallocate data objects.

Control   Mechanisms that control the basic PIKS operational functionality.

Error   Mechanisms that provide means of reporting operational errors.

Inquiry   Mechanisms that return information to an application regarding PIKS data objects, status, and implementation.

Management   Mechanisms that bind and set attributes of data objects and that set global variables.

1.4 Basic Operator Model

There are two fundamental types of PIKS Foundation operators: those that create a nonimage object (e.g., a histogram, from a single source image) and those that create a single destination image from one or two source images. Figure 1-4 illustrates the basic operator model for these two cases. The following sections discuss special cases of the basic operator model.

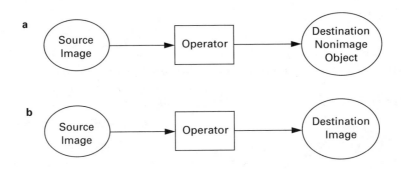

Figure 1-4   PIKS basic operator model: (a) Image to nonimage operators ; (b) Image to image operators

■Exhibit 1-3: PIKS Foundation utilities listed by functional class.

Export from PIKS

    Export histogram
    Export image
    Export lookup table
    Export matrix
    Export neighbourhood array
    Export tuple
    Get colour pixel
    Get pixel
    Get pixel ROI
    Get pixel array
    Get pixel array ROI

Import to PIKS

    Import histogram
    Import image
    Import lookup table

    Import matrix
    Import neighbourhood array
    Import tuple
    Put colour pixel
    Put pixel
    Put pixel array

Internal

    Convert array to image
    Convert image data type
    Convert image to array
    Convert ROI to image
    Copy window
    Create tuple
    Extract pixel plane
    Insert pixel plane

■Exhibit 1-4: PIKS Foundation mechanisms listed by functional class.

Control

    Close PIKS
    Close PIKS, emergency
    Open PIKS

Error

    Error handler
    Error logger
    Error test
    Set error handler

Inquiry

    Inquire elements
    Inquire image
    Inquire nonimage object
    Inquire PIKS implementation
    Inquire PIKS status
    Inquire repository
    Inquire resampling

Allocation and Deallocation

    Allocate histogram
    Allocate image
    Allocate lookup table
    Allocate matrix
    Allocate neighbourhood array
    Allocate ROI
    Allocate tuple
    Deallocate data object

Management

    Bind ROI
    Define sub image
    Return repository identifier
    Set globals
    Set image attributes

1.4.1 Point Operators

Point operators perform pixel manipulations independently, pixel-by-pixel on a single source image to produce a single destination image. For this class of operators, the source and destination spatial image sizes need not be the same. Prior to execution, the source and destination images are, conceptually, aligned at their origins. As shown in Figure 1-5, for a monochrome image, the point operation on the source image is recorded in the destination image over the spatial overlap of the source and destination images. Any pixels in the destination image that are not overlapped by the source are left unchanged.

For the mathematical definition of point operators, it is convenient to conceptually consider the operation as a three step process:

(a) An $X \times Y \times 1 \times 1 \times B$ operator input image $S(x, y, 0, 0, b)$ is extracted from the source image $SRC(x, y, 0, 0, b)$. The spatial extent of $S(x, y, 0, 0, b)$ is limited to that part of $SRC(x, y, 0, 0, b)$ that can be processed and recorded in the destination image $DST(x, y, 0, 0, b)$.

(b) An operator output image

$$D(x, y, 0, 0, b) = P\{S(x, y, 0, 0, b)\}$$

is generated by the point operator over the spatial limits $0 \le x \le X - 1$ and $0 \le y \le Y - 1$ for all bands $0 \le b \le B - 1$, where $P\{\cdot\}$ denotes the point transformation.

(c) The operator output image $D(x, y, 0, 0, b)$ is recorded in the destination image $DST(x, y, 0, 0, b)$.

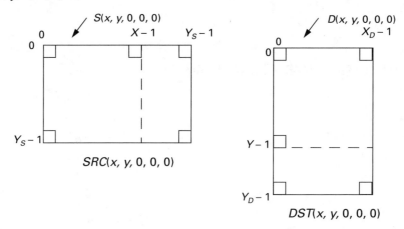

Figure 1-5 Relationship of source and destination images for a point processing operator

1.4.2 Ensemble Operators

Ensemble operators perform independent pixel-by-pixel combinations of a pair of source images to produce a single destination image. All images may be of different spatial extent. Prior to execution, the two source images and the destination image are spatially aligned, conceptually, at their origins and the pixel-by-pixel combination is generated over the spatial overlap of the three images.

The basic operator model for ensemble operators is again a three step process:

(a) Operator input images $S_1(x, y, 0, 0, b)$ and $S_2(x, y, 0, 0, b)$ are extracted from the source image pair $SRC_1(x, y, 0, 0, b)$ and $SRC_2(x, y, 0, 0, b)$, respectively. The spatial extent of $S_1(x, y, 0, 0, b)$ and $S_2(x, y, 0, 0, b)$ is limited to that which can be processed and recorded in $DST(x, y, 0, 0, b)$.

(b) An operator output image

$$D(x, y, 0, 0, b) = S_1(x, y, 0, 0, b) \; \text{O} \; S_2(x, y, 0, 0, b)$$

is generated by the ensemble operator over the spatial and band limits $0 \le x \le X - 1$, $0 \le y \le Y - 1$, and $0 \le b \le B - 1$, where O denotes the ensemble combination, e.g., addition.

(c) The operator output image $D(x, y, 0, 0, b)$ is recorded in the destination image $DST(x, y, 0, 0, b)$.

1.4.3 Neighbourhood Operators

The PIKS filtering and morphological neighbourhood operators perform linear and nonlinear spatial combinations, respectively, of source image pixels within a neighbourhood of a reference source pixel to produce a single destination image pixel. For such operators, the neighbourhood is specified by a neighbourhood array data object. It has an associated key pixel $(x_k, y_k, z_k, t_k, b_k)$, which is a five-dimensional index offset measured with respect to the first row and column element of the neighbourhood array. For the PIKS Foundation profile, z_k, t_k, and b_k are restricted to be zero. As shown in Figure 1-6, for a monochrome image, the key pixel is sequentially translated over all source image pixels, the linear or nonlinear spatial combination is computed for each reference source pixel, and the computed result is recorded in the destination pixel corresponding, spatially, to the reference source pixel. The default operation is that if the neighbourhood extends beyond the boundary of the source image, the "missing" source pixels are assumed to be of zero value for arithmetic combinations or of FALSE value for Boolean combinations. Some operators, for example the two-dimensional convolution operator, override the default operation with special boundary conditions.

The basic operator model for neighbourhood operators is the same as point operators except that the spatial extent of the operator output image is dependent upon the specific operator.

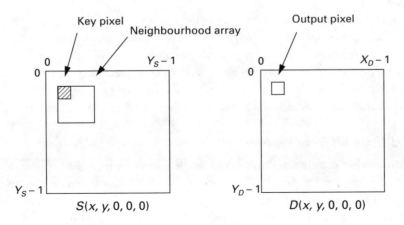

Figure 1-6 Relationship of source and destination images for a neighbourhood operator

1.4.4 Geometric Operators

Geometric operators change the size and shape of images, and consequently, operator input and output images are typically of different spatial extent. Many geometric operators attempt to access source image pixels outside the bounds of a source image. In such cases, the "missing" source pixels are assumed to be of zero value for an arithmetic data type image or of FALSE value for a Boolean data type image. Figure 1-7 is an example of the rotation of a monochrome source image about its centre. In this example, the destination image is forced to be of the same spatial extent as the source image.

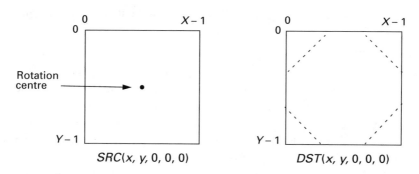

Figure 1-7   Relationship of source and destination images for a rotate operator

1.5   Region-of-Interest Control

The PIKS region-of-interest (ROI) control mechanism is a means to select those pixels of a source image that will be processed by an element, and to select those processed pixels that will be recorded in a destination image. The selection is governed by a ROI control object.

The ROI control object, conceptually, is a Boolean array of the same spatial and band size as its associated image. It is in spatial and band registration with the image with respect to the image origin. The ROI control object array assumes one of two logical states at each pixel. If a ROI pixel is in the logical TRUE state, the corresponding image pixel is said to be "inside" the ROI. Conversely, an image pixel is said to be "outside" the ROI if its ROI pixel is in the logical FALSE state.

A ROI control object is created, conceptually, by the ROI binding mechanism, which binds a PIKS ROI data object to an image. The ROI binding mechanism creates a ROI data object identifier reference in the image attribute collection of each image. If an image attribute collection makes no reference to a ROI data object, i.e., its entry is created as a NULL parameter, a default ROI control object is assumed to exist and to be logically TRUE for each pixel of the image. A ROI data object can be bound to more than one image.

1.5.1   ROI Data Object Creation

The PIKS Foundation profile only supports a single form of a ROI data object, a spatial rectangle replicated across image bands. The rectangular ROI can be created as logical TRUE within the rectangle and logical FALSE outside or vice versa. This rectangular ROI can be conceptually considered to be a two-dimensional Boolean array with an origin and defined

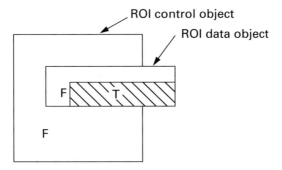

Figure 1-8 Relationship between a rectangular ROI data object and a ROI control object

spatial extent along x and y coordinates. Associated with each image is a key point 5-tuple $(x_k, y_k, z_k, t_k, b_k)$. In the PIKS Foundation profile, z_k, t_k, and b_k are restricted to be zero. When a ROI data object is bound to an image, conceptually, the ROI data object is translated within each band along each spatial coordinate such that the origin of the ROI data object is aligned with the key point in the image to which the ROI data object is bound. The ROI control object is conceptually formed by clipping the ROI control object to the extent of the image. If the ROI data object does not cover an image pixel, the corresponding ROI control object pixel is assumed to be FALSE. Figure 1-8 illustrates the binding of a rectangular ROI data object to a monochrome image to generate a ROI control object. The ROI TRUE state pixels are shown crosshatched.

1.5.2 Image to Nonimage ROI Control

Figure 1-9a shows the PIKS operator model for the processing of a source image to generate a destination nonimage object under ROI control. In this model, each source image pixel that is inside its ROI is processed by the operator to create the nonimage data object. Source image pixels outside the ROI are not included in the operator manipulation. An example of this usage is to generate the histogram of pixels lying within a rectangular region of an image.

1.5.3 Image to Image ROI Control

Figure 1-9b describes the PIKS operator model for the processing of a source image to generate a destination image under ROI control. In this model, each source image pixel that is inside its ROI is processed by the operator to create an operator output pixel. Operator output pixels are recorded in the destination image if and only if the corresponding destination pixel is inside its ROI. Each destination pixel outside a ROI is left in its state prior to the processing operation. In this sense, the destination image ROI control object acts as a write control mask for a destination image. Another way to consider the ROI control mechanism for source and destination images is that destination pixels are only recorded in the destination image in the region corresponding, spatially, to the logical intersection of the source and destination ROIs.

Examples of rectangular ROI operation are shown in Figure 1-10 for a monochrome image. In Case 1, the destination ROI control object is in a TRUE state over the entire image; the source ROI TRUE state pixels are indicated by the rectangular region. The processed source pixels recorded in the image are indicated by the crosshatching. All other pixels in the destination are unchanged. For Case 2, the source ROI is TRUE over the extent of the source image, and the destination ROI is TRUE within the indicated rectangle. Although all source pixels are,

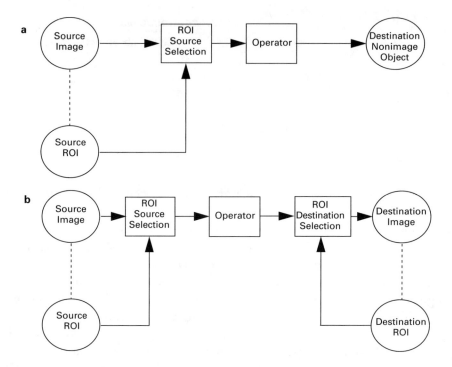

Figure 1-9 PIKS basic operator model under ROI control: (a) Image to nonimage operators, (b) Image to image operators

conceptually, processed, only those shown in the crosshatched region are recorded in the destination image. Finally, for Case 3, only those pixels in the intersection of the source and destination ROIs are both processed and recorded, as indicated by the double crosshatched region.

The ROI control concept applies to PIKS operators that combine two source images to produce a destination image. For example, if a pair of images is alpha-blended to create a destination image, only those source pixels lying within the logical intersection of the source images are sent to the destination for recording.

For neighbourhood operators, such as two-dimensional convolution, if the key pixel of a neighbourhood object lies over a TRUE state source ROI control object, the spatial combination of source pixels within the neighbourhood is formed; otherwise there is no source output. The combination is formed even if some pixels within the neighbourhood, other than at the key pixel location, lie within FALSE state regions of the source ROI.

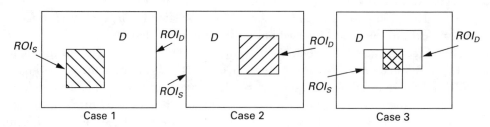

Figure 1-10 Examples of ROI operation

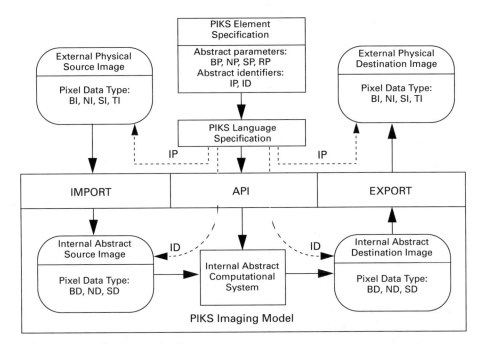

Figure 1-11 PIKS application interface

1.5.4 ROI Data Object Manipulation

In the PIKS Foundation profile, a rectangular ROI data object can be manipulated in the same sense that a Boolean image can be manipulated by an operator provided that the manipulated ROI data object can be represented as a rectangular ROI. Thus, in PIKS Foundation, it is possible to translate a ROI, but it is not possible to rotate a ROI.

1.6 PIKS to Application Interface

Figure 1-11 describes the interface between PIKS and an application. The interface has three points of contact: API calls, data import functions, and data export functions. PIKS makes a deliberate notational distinction between internal and external data types for both element parameters and data values.

Table 1-2 lists the PIKS data type codes for internal and external parameter data types. API calls that provide Boolean, nonnegative integer, signed integer, and real arithmetic parameters utilize the codes BP, NP, SP, and RP. The corresponding codes for the internal data types are BD, ND, SD, and RD. This distinction is made to permit different data type parameter representations for a general purpose computer that passes parameter information to a PIKS implementation, which employs an internal compute engine that uses a different computational precision than the general purpose computer. There is also a notational distinction between object identifiers, IP, of objects created by an application and passed to PIKS, and object identifiers, ID, of objects created within the PIKS domain.

Some PIKS elements provide options for the selection of specific functionality among two or more choices. Options that are not capable of extension are specified by an enumerated (nonnegative) data type parameter, EP. Options that are capable of being extended are specified

Table 1-2.   PIKS parameter data type codes

Data type	Internal	External
Boolean	BD	BP
Nonnegative integer	ND	NP
Signed integer	SD	SP
Real arithmetic	RD	RP
Character string	CS	CS
Data object identifier	ID	IP
Enumerated	*	EP
Null	NULL	NULL

* Not applicable

by a signed integer data type parameter, SP. For such options, negative integers are reserved for implementation-specific options. Positive integers beyond the range specified in the standard may be assigned by an ISO registration authority for future extensions of the standard.

As indicated in Table 1-3, there is a notational difference between the internal and external data types for pixels. A PIKS implementation may provide a different internal storage precision for pixels than that employed by the application. Upon import or export of an image, there is a physical conversion between the internal and external data types, which must be of the same data type class, e.g., SI and SD, but need not be of the same precision.

Table 1-3   PIKS pixel data type codes

Data type	Internal	External
Boolean	BD	BI
Nonnegative integer	ND	NI
Signed integer	SD	SI
Fixed point integer	*	TI

* Not applicable

1.7   Error Reporting

During the execution of a program containing PIKS calls there are three potential error situations:

   A. Errors detected within PIKS element calls;

   B. Errors detected in functions called from a PIKS implementation (underlying libraries, driver functions, operating system functions);

   C. Errors detected in nonPIKS parts of an application program.

There are two possible outcomes of these error situations:

I. Precisely defined reaction;

II. Unpredictable results, possibly including loss of data.

If errors are detected in nonPIKS functions (Situation C), either the application will regain control over the execution, or program execution will be terminated prematurely. In the latter case, results are unpredictable (Outcome II). In the former case, the application may attempt to close PIKS properly with the *close_piks* mechanism, or at least attempt an emergency closure with the *close_piks_emergency* mechanism.

If errors are detected in functions called by the PIKS implementation (Situation C), and control is passed back to PIKS, the result for a conformant PIKS implementation is Outcome I. But, unpredictable results (Outcome II) may occur if PIKS cannot regain program control.

PIKS provides an error handling mechanism that reports errors (Situation A) to an application if an element is improperly used. If an element is invoked, and more than one error condition is applicable, at least the first error encountered is reported. The PIKS error handler invokes an error logger mechanism that performs the following functions:

> Records an error message and PIKS element identification in an error file;
> Returns to the calling element.

All PIKS elements execute the following steps upon detecting an error condition:

> Set the error state to ON;
> Call the *error_handler* mechanism with appropriate parameters;
> Set the error state to OFF;
> Perform built-in error reaction.

The error codes are listed in Appendix B.

An application may provide its own error handler in place of the PIKS error handler. It is expected that such an error handler will accept the following information from PIKS:

> Identification of the error condition;
> Identification of the PIKS element that called the error handler;
> Designation of error file.

PART 2

Semantic Description of PIKS Elements

Chapters 2 to 5 provide semantic descriptions of the usage of PIKS elements. These chapters describe the PIKS elements in natural language, as opposed to a computer language. The chapters detail the information that must be provided to each element, the data to be returned from an executing element, and a definition of the element functionality.

The four chapters present semantic descriptions of the PIKS operators, tools, mechanisms, and utilities in that order. Within each chapter, the element descriptions are subdivided by the class taxonomy presented in Exhibits 1 to 4 of Chapter 1. Finally, within each section, the elements are presented in alphabetical order according to their functional specification name. For example, *bit_shift* is the name of the bit shift operator described in Chapter 2. The C Language binding name for this operator is InBitShift. As an aid in bridging the gap between the semantic and the syntactic description of each element, the binding name is printed at the right side of each section heading.

Part 2 has been written in the style of a reference book. Upon first encounter, the reader is advised to skim through the descriptions to obtain a grasp of the style and the material depth. Later, the definitions can be studied to determine exactly how each element functions.

The description style in each chapter of Part 2 is to:

- Provide the functional specification and binding names of an element;
- Provide a short verbal description of an element;
- Specify the element input parameters;
- Specify the element output parameters;
- Specify the object restrictions;

- Provide remarks about element functionality;
- Define the nomenclature to be used in the element definition;
- Present a definition of the element functionality;
- Specify input tuple structures, if applicable;
- Present examples of the element usage as appropriate.

The following is a a template, in italics, of the information provided for each element in Chapters 2 to 5 along with an example, in roman font, for the complement operator.

Element specification name	Element binding name
Complement	InComplement

Brief nonmathematical description of the functionality of the element.

The *complement* operator performs a logical complement of a Boolean or integer image.

Element input parameters

In general, this is a list of parameters necessary to specify source images, a destination image, nonimage data objects, and element data parameters. The data type of each entry is specified along with its semantic description. In this example, the source and destination images are specified by their unique identifiers that were named when the images were allocated.

Description	Data type
Source image	ID
Destination image	ID

Element output parameters

This is a list of identifiers and scalar values returned directly to an application by an element. The complement operator does not have any output parameters.

Object restrictions

This is a specification of the restrictions imposed on the choice of data objects in terms of their structure and data type. In this example, the source image may be monochrome, MON, *or colour,* COLR. *The destination image structure is required to be the same as the source image. The pixel data types of the source image may be Boolean,* BD, *nonnegative integer,* ND, *or signed integer,* SD. *The data type of the destination image must be the same as the source image data type.*

Source image structure	MON, COLR
Destination image structure	Same as source image structure
Source image data type	BD, ND, SD
Destination image data type	Same as source image data type

Remark

Information regarding element utilization and its limitations.

Bitwise operations apply to ND or SD data type images; Boolean operations apply to BD data type images.

Nomenclature

Mathematical nomenclature used in the mathematical definition of an element. In this example, the operator input and output images are of the same size.

$S(x, y, 0, 0, b)$ $X \times Y \times 1 \times 1 \times B$ source image
$D(x, y, 0, 0, b)$ $X \times Y \times 1 \times 1 \times B$ destination image

Definition

Definition of a PIKS element. A mathematical definition is provided whenever possible. Algorithmic or textual definitions are provided for some elements. Mathematical functions, such as the NOT function, are used in the definition of many elements. Such functions are defined in Appendix A.

For all x, y, b

Boolean complement:

$$D(x, y, 0, 0, b) = \text{NOT}\{S(x, y, 0, 0, b)\}$$

where the NOT function denotes the Boolean complement operation defined in Appendix A.

Integer bitwise complement:

Let $s(p)$ and $d(p)$ denote the pth bit of an integer data type pixel of $S(x, y, 0, 0, b)$ and $D(x, y, 0, 0, b)$, respectively. Then, for all x, y, b, p

$$d(p) = \overline{s(p)}$$

where the overbar denotes the logical complement operation defined in Appendix A.

Tuple specification

Some elements accept data from previously generated data parameter tuples. The conceptual data structure of such tuples is described here. The complement operator does not utilize tuples.

Example

Photographic example of the element functionality.

Figure 2-1 illustrates the complement operation on a Boolean and an 8-bit, ND data type, monochrome image. For display purposes, the Boolean image is represented as an unsigned integer image for which logical TRUE is integer value 255 and logical FALSE is integer value 0.

2

PIKS Operators

Chapter 2 describes the functionality of PIKS operators.

2.1   Point Operators

The following sections describe the PIKS point operators. Point operators perform processing of an image on an independent pixel-by-pixel basis.

2.1.1   *Bit Shift*   `InBitShift`

The *bit_shift* operator performs bit shifting of the bits of an integer data type image.

Element input parameters

Description	Data type
Source image	ID
Destination image	ID
Number of bits to be shifted	NP

Bit shift option
   left overflow shift
   right overflow shift
   left barrel shift
   right barrel shift
   left arithmetic shift
   right arithmetic shift
	SP

Object Restrictions

Source image structure	MON, COLR
Destination image structure	Same as source image structure
Source image data type	ND, SD
Destination image data type	Same as source image data type

Remarks

1. The "left" bit of a SD integer is its sign bit.
2. The "left" bit of a ND integer is its most significant bit.
3. The "right" bit of a ND or SD integer is its least significant bit.

Nomenclature

$S(x, y, 0, 0, b)$ $\quad X \times Y \times 1 \times 1 \times B$ source image
$D(x, y, 0, 0, b)$ $\quad X \times Y \times 1 \times 1 \times B$ destination image
n_b $\quad$ Number of bits to be shifted, $n_b \geq 0$

Definition

For all x, y, b

$$D(x, y, 0, 0, b) = P\{S(x, y, 0, 0, b)\}$$

where the point transformation, $P\{\cdot\}$, is defined as follows.

Left overflow shift, ND or SD:

Bits of integer pixel are translated left by n_b bit positions. Missing bits on the right are filled with zeros.

Right overflow shift, ND or SD:

Bits of integer pixel are translated right by n_b bit positions. Missing bits on the left are filled with zeros.

Left barrel shift, ND or SD:

Bits of integer pixel are translated left by n_b bit positions. Missing bits on the right are filled with overflow bits from the left.

Right barrel shift, ND or SD:

Bits of integer pixel are translated right by n_b bit positions. Missing bits on the left are filled with overflow bits from the right.

Left arithmetic shift, ND or SD:

Same as left overflow shift.

Right arithmetic shift, ND:

Same as right overflow shift.

Right arithmetic shift, SD:

Bits of integer pixel are translated right by n_b bit positions. Missing bits on the left are filled with the sign bit.

Examples

The following tables list the source and destination pixel values, for shifting by three bits, for 8-bit, ND and 16-bit, SD data type pixel images. The pixel amplitudes are represented in binary and hexadecimal notation.

ND data type pixels

Option	SRC (binary)	SRC (hex)	DST (binary)	DST (hex)
1	01011011	5b	11011000	d8
2	01011011	5b	0000 1101	0b
3	01011011	5b	11011010	da
4	01011011	5b	01101011	6b
5	01011011	5b	11011000	d8
6	01011011	5b	00001011	0b

SD data type pixels

Option	SRC (binary)	SRC (hex)	DST (binary)	DST (hex)
1	0101101100000000	5b00	1101100000000000	d800
2	0101101100000000	5b00	0101110101100000	0b60
3	0101101100000000	5b00	1101101000000010	d802
4	0101101100000000	5b00	0000101101100000	0b60
5	0101101100000000	5b00	1101100000000000	d800
5	1101101100000000	db00	1101100000000000	d800
6	0101101100000000	5b00	0000010110110000	0b60
6	1101101100000000	db00	1111101101100000	fb60

2.1.2   Complement   `InComplement`

The *complement* operator performs a logical complement of a Boolean or integer image.

Element input parameters

Description	Data type
Source image	ID
Destination image	ID

Object Restrictions:

Source image structure	MON, COLR
Destination image structure	Same as source image structure
Source image data type	BD, ND, SD
Destination image data type	Same as source image data type

Remark

Bitwise operations apply to ND or SD data type images; Boolean operations apply to BD data type images.

Nomenclature

$S(x, y, 0, 0, b)$ $X \times Y \times 1 \times 1 \times B$ source image

$D(x, y, 0, 0, b)$ $X \times Y \times 1 \times 1 \times B$ destination image

Definition

For all x, y, b

Boolean complement:

$$D(x, y, 0, 0, b) = \text{NOT}\{S(x, y, 0, 0, b)\}$$

where the NOT function denotes the Boolean complement operation defined in Appendix A.

Integer bitwise complement:

Let $s(p)$ and $d(p)$ denote the pth bit of an integer data type pixel of $S(x, y, 0, 0, b)$ and $D(x, y, 0, 0, b)$, respectively. Then, for all x, y, b, p

$$d(p) = \overline{s(p)}$$

where the overbar denotes the logical complement operation defined in Appendix A.

Example

Figure 2-1 illustrates the complement operation on a Boolean image and an 8-bit, ND data type, monochrome image. For display purposes, the Boolean image is represented as an unsigned integer image for which logical TRUE is integer value 255 and logical FALSE is integer value 0.

2.1.3   *Lookup*   InLookup

The *lookup* operator performs a lookup table manipulation of an image.

Element input parameters

Description	Data type
Source image	ID
Destination image	ID
Lookup table	ID
Source offset entry	NP

Lookup table mode option
   1D
   2D
	SP

Object Restrictions

Source image structure	MON, COLR
Destination image structure	See Remarks
Source image data type	ND, SD
Destination image data type	Same as lookup table output data type
Lookup table input data type	Same as source image data type
Lookup table output data type	BD, ND, SD

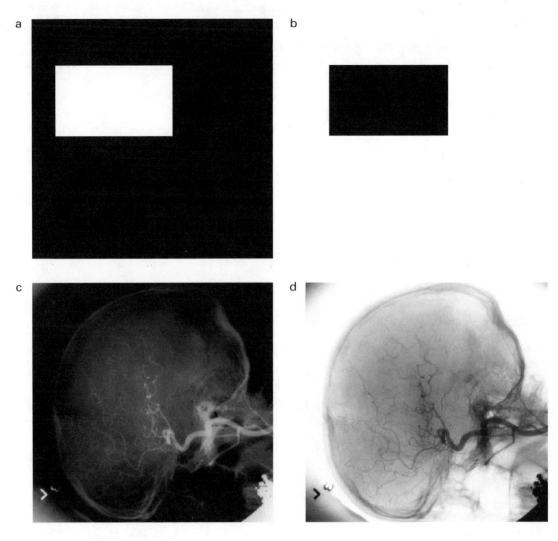

Figure 2-1   Examples of complement operation: (a) Boolean source, "rectangle"; (b) destination, complement of Boolean source; (c) Integer source, "brain"; (d) destination, complement of integer source.

Remarks

1. The destination image data type need not be the same as the source image data type.

2. In the 1D mode, the source image may be MON or COLR; the destination image structure must match the source image structure. In the 2D mode, the source image structure
must be MON; the destination image structure may be MON or COLR.

Nomenclature

$S(x, y, 0, 0, b)$ $X \times Y \times 1 \times 1 \times B$ source image
$D(x, y, 0, 0, b)$ $X \times Y \times 1 \times 1 \times B$ destination image
id   Lookup table identifier

Definition

1D table mode, MON to MON or COLR to COLR:

For all x, y, b

$$D(x, y, 0, 0, b) = \text{LOOK}\{W(x, y, 0, 0, b), f, b, \text{id}\}$$

where f is the source offset entry and LOOK is the lookup function defined in Appendix A.

2D table mode, MON to COLR:

For all x, y, z, b

$$D(x, y, 0, 0, b) = \text{LOOK}\{W(x, y, 0, 0, 0), f, 0, \text{id}\}$$

If the source image is of ND data type

$$W(x, y, 0, 0, b) = S(x, y, 0, 0, b)$$

If the source image is of SD data type

$$W(x, y, 0, 0, b) = S(x, y, 0, 0, b) - I$$

where I denotes the most negative integer value of the SD representation. For example, for a 16-bit SD integer representation, $I = -32, 768$.

The lookup table referenced by the LUT identifier has E entries and B cells per entry. Section 1.2.5 describes the structure of a PIKS lookup table. The unsigned integer entry to the LOOK function, $W(x, y, 0, 0, b)$, is biased negatively by the table offset, f, where $f \geq 0$, to form the lookup table entry cell index

$$e = W(x, y, 0, 0, b) - f$$

The content of the lookup table cell, $T(b, e)$, for $0 \leq b \leq B - 1$ and $0 \leq e \leq E - 1$ is assigned to the operator output image $D(x, y, 0, 0, b)$.

The purpose of the source offset entry parameter is to allow for the use of smaller tables when the amplitude range of source pixels is known to be restricted. For example, if a source image is of SD data type, but it is known that all source pixels are zero or positive, then by setting the source offset to $-I$ (32, 768 for a 16-bit SD representation), the size of the lookup table can be reduced by a factor of two.

Example

Figure 2-2 presents an example of lookup table manipulation of an 8-bit, ND data type, monochrome image in which the lookup table contains cells that are the normalized square root of each entry as defined below.

$$T(0, e) = \frac{255.0\sqrt{e}}{\sqrt{255.0}}$$

a  b

Figure 2-2   Example of lookup table operation: (a) source, "Oswald"; (b) destination, square root lookup table

2.1.4   *Monadic, Arithmetic*   `InMonadicArith`

The *monadic_arithmetic* operator performs a monadic arithmetic combination of an integer image and an integer constant.

Element input parameters

Description	Data type
Source image	ID
Destination image	ID
Value of constant	NP, SP

Combination option
    addition by constant
    addition by constant, scaled
    division by constant
    division of constant
    maximum with constant
    minimum with constant
    multiplication by constant
    subtraction by constant
    subtraction by constant, scaled
    subtraction of constant
    subtraction of constant, scaled
	SP

Object Restrictions

Source image structure	MON, COLR
Destination image structure	Same as source image structure
Source image data type	ND, SD
Destination image data type	Same as source image data type

Nomenclature

$S(x, y, 0, 0, b)$ $X \times Y \times 1 \times 1 \times B$ source image
$D(x, y, 0, 0, b)$ $X \times Y \times 1 \times 1 \times B$ destination image
c   Integer constant

Definition

For all x, y, b

Addition by constant:

$$D(x, y, 0, 0, b) = S(x, y, 0, 0, b) + c$$

Addition by constant, scaled:

$$D(x, y, 0, 0, b) = \frac{S(x, y, 0, 0, b) + c}{2}$$

Division by constant:

$$D(x, y, 0, 0, b) = \frac{S(x, y, 0, 0, b)}{c}$$

Division of constant:

$$D(x, y, 0, 0, b) = \frac{c}{S(x, y, 0, 0, b)}$$

Maximum with constant:

$$D(x, y, 0, 0, b) = \text{MAX}\{S(x, y, 0, 0, b), c\}$$

where the maxima function, MAX, is defined in Appendix A.

Minimum with constant:

$$D(x, y, 0, 0, b) = \text{MIN}\{S(x, y, 0, 0, b), c\}$$

where the minima function, MIN, is defined in Appendix A.

Subtraction by constant:

$$D(x, y, 0, 0, b) = S(x, y, 0, 0, b) - c$$

Subtraction by constant, scaled:

$$D(x, y, 0, 0, b) = \frac{S(x, y, 0, 0, b) - c}{2}$$

Subtraction of constant:

$$D(x, y, 0, 0, b) = c - S(x, y, 0, 0, b)$$

a
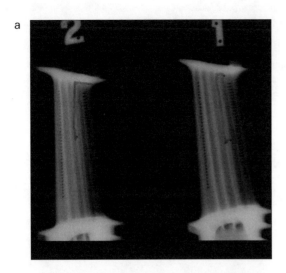

b
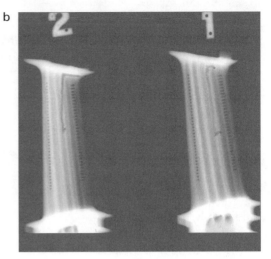

c
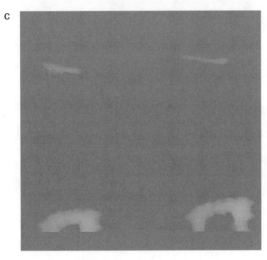

Figure 2-3. Examples of monadic, arithmetic operation: (a) source, "parts"; (b) destination, addition by constant, c = 100; (c) destination, maximum with constant option, c = 100

Subtraction of constant, scaled:

$$D(x, y, 0, 0, b) = \frac{c - S(x, y, 0, 0, b)}{2}$$

Example

Figure 2-3 illustrates the monadic, arithmetic operation for two options on an 8-bit, ND data type, monochrome image with a constant value of 100. In the addition by constant example, the sum pixel range exceeds the storage range, 0 to 255, of the ND representation. PIKS does not specify the result of underflow or overflow; the result is implementation dependent. In this example, potential overflow is clipped to 255.

The *monadic_logical* operator performs a monadic logical combination of a Boolean or integer image and a Boolean or integer constant.

Element input parameters

Description	Data type
Source image	ID
Destination image	ID
Value of constant	BP, NP, SP

Combination option
    bitwise AND
    bitwise NAND
    bitwise NOR
    bitwise OR
    bitwise XOR
    Boolean intersection
    Boolean union
	SP

Object Restrictions

Source image structure	MON, COLR
Destination image structure	Same as source image structure
Source image data type	BD, ND, SD
Destination image data type	Same as source image data type

Remark

Bitwise operations apply to ND or SD data type images; Boolean operations apply to BD data type images.

Nomenclature

$S(x, y, 0, 0, b)$	$X \times Y \times 1 \times 1 \times B$ source image
$D(x, y, 0, 0, b)$	$X \times Y \times 1 \times 1 \times B$ destination image
c	Boolean or integer constant
$s(p)$	pth bit of integer pixel of source image
$d(p)$	pth bit of integer pixel of destination image
$c(p)$	pth bit of integer pixel of constant

Definition

For all x, y, b, and, for integer operations, for all p

Integer bitwise AND:

$$d(p) = [s(p)] \oplus [c(p)]$$

where $\oplus$ denotes the AND operator defined in Appendix A.

Integer bitwise NAND:

$$d(p) = \overline{[s(p)] \oplus [c(p)]}$$

where the overbar denotes the complement operation defined in Appendix A.

Integer bitwise NOR:

$$d(p) = \overline{[s(p)] \ominus [c(p)]}$$

where $\ominus$ denotes the OR operation defined in Appendix A.

Integer bitwise OR:

$$d(p) = [s(p)] \ominus [c(p)]$$

Integer bitwise XOR:

$$d(p) = [s(p)] \otimes [c(p)]$$

where $\otimes$ denotes the exclusive-or, XOR, operation defined in Appendix A.

Boolean intersection:

$$D(x, y, 0, 0, b) = [S(x, y, 0, 0, b)] \cap [c]$$

where $\cap$ denotes the intersection operation defined in Appendix A.

Boolean union:

$$D(x, y, 0, 0, b) = [S(x, y, 0, 0, b)] \cup [c]$$

where $\cup$ denotes the union operation defined in Appendix A.

Example

Figure 2-4 provides examples of AND and OR options of the monadic, logical operator with a constant of value 128 for an 8-bit, ND data type, monochrome image.

2.1.6   *Threshold*   `InThreshold`

The *threshold* operator performs pixel amplitude thresholding of an image.

Element input parameters

Description	Data type
Source image	ID
Destination image	ID
Above threshold clip value	BP, NP, SP
Below threshold clip value	BP, NP, SP
Threshold value	NP, SP

Object Restrictions

Source image structure	MON, COLR
Destination image structure	Same as source image structure
Source image data type	ND, SD
Destination image data type	BD, ND, SD

a

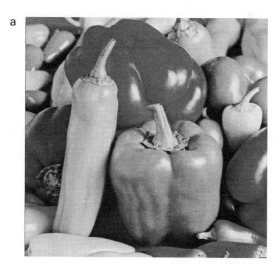

b

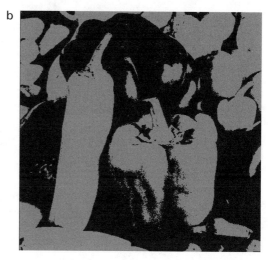

c

Figure 2-4 Examples of monadic, logical operation: (a) source, ND image; (b) destination, bitwise AND; (c) destination, bitwise OR; (d) destination, bitwise NOR

Remarks

1. The destination image data type need not be the same as the source image data type.
2. The threshold value must be of the same data type class as the source image data type.
3. The clip values must be of the same data type class as the destination image data type.

Nomenclature

$S(x, y, 0, 0, b)$ $X \times Y \times 1 \times 1 \times B$ source image
$D(x, y, 0, 0, b)$ $X \times Y \times 1 \times 1 \times B$ destination image
t_h Threshold value
a_c Above threshold output value
b_c Below threshold output value

Definition

As shown in the transfer function of Figure 2-5, for all x, y, b

$$D(x, y, 0, 0, b) = a_c \qquad \text{if } S(x, y, 0, 0, b) \geq t_h$$

$$D(x, y, 0, 0, b) = b_c \qquad \text{if } S(x, y, 0, 0, b) < t_h$$

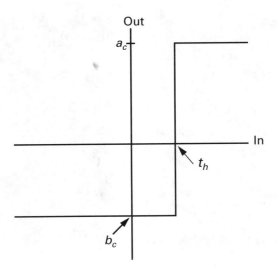

Figure 2-5   Threshold transfer function

Example

Figure 2-6 shows an example of thresholding for an 8-bit, ND data type, monochrome image at a threshold value of 135. Source image pixels above the threshold are set to value 255 in the destination image, and source image pixels below the threshold are set to value 0 in the destination image.

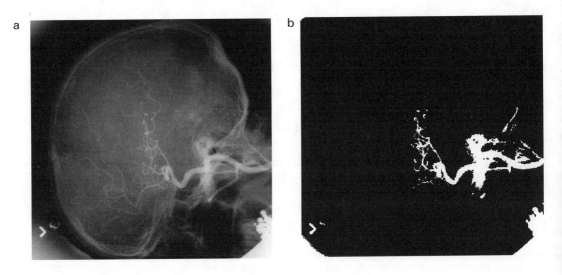

Figure 2-6   Example of threshold operation: (a) source, "brain"; (b) destination, threshold, $t_h = 135$, $a_c = 255$, $b_c = 0$

PIKS OPERATORS   CHAPTER 2

2.1.7   *Unary, Integer*   InUnaryInteger

The *unary_integer* operator performs unary point conversion of pixels of an integer data type image.

Element input parameters

Description	Data type
Source image	ID
Destination image	ID
Conversion option absolute value cube negative square	SP

Object Restrictions

Source image structure	MON, COLR
Destination image structure	Same as source image structure
Source image data type	ND, SD
Destination image data type	Same as source image data type

Nomenclature

$S(x, y, 0, 0, b)$ $X \times Y \times 1 \times 1 \times B$ source image
$D(x, y, 0, 0, b)$ $X \times Y \times 1 \times 1 \times B$ destination image

Definition

For all x, y, b

Absolute value:

$$D(x, y, 0, 0, b) = S(x, y, 0, 0, b) \qquad \text{if } S(x, y, 0, 0, b) \geq 0$$

$$D(x, y, 0, 0, b) = -S(x, y, 0, 0, b) \qquad \text{if } S(x, y, 0, 0, b) < 0$$

Cube:

$$D(x, y, 0, 0, b) = [S(x, y, 0, 0, b)]^3$$

Negative:

$$D(x, y, 0, 0, b) = -S(x, y, 0, 0, b)$$

Square:

$$D(x, y, 0, 0, b) = [S(x, y, 0, 0, b)]^2$$

The *window_level* operator performs window-level point scaling of an image.

Element input parameters

Description	Data type
Source image	ID
Destination image	ID
Above window clip value	NP, SP
Below window clip value	NP, SP
Window width	NP, SP
Window level	NP, SP

Remarks

The clip and window parameters must be of the same data type class as the source image data type.

Nomenclature

$S(x, y, 0, 0, b)$	$X \times Y \times 1 \times 1 \times B$ source image
$D(x, y, 0, 0, b)$	$X \times Y \times 1 \times 1 \times B$ destination image
a_c	Above window clip value
b_c	Below window clip value
W	Window width
L	Window level

Definition

As shown in the transfer function of Figure 2-7, for all x, y, b

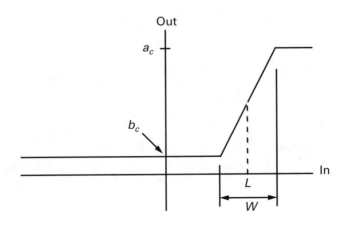

Figure 2-7   Window-level transfer function

If

$$S(x, y, 0, 0, b) < L - \frac{W}{2}$$

then

$$D(x, y, 0, 0, b) = b_c$$

If

$$L - \frac{W}{2} < S(x, y, 0, 0, b) \leq L + \frac{W}{2}$$

then

$$D(x, y, 0, 0, b) = \left[\frac{a_c - b_c}{W}\right] S(x, y, 0, 0, b) \left[\frac{(a_c)(W - 2L) + (b_c)(W + 2L)}{2W}\right]$$

If

$$L + \frac{W}{2} < S(x, y, 0, 0, b)$$

then

$$D(x, y, 0, 0, b) = a_c$$

Example

Figure 2-8 illustrates the window-level operation for an 8-bit, ND data type, monochrome image. The above and below clip values are 255 and 125, respectively. The window width is 200, and the window level is 150.

a
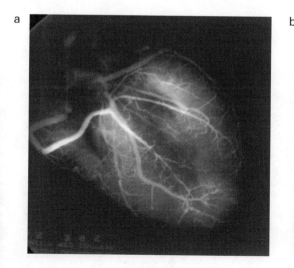
b
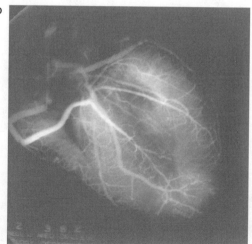

Figure 2-8.   Example of window-level operation: (a) source, "heart"; (b) destination, window level

2.2 Ensemble Operators

The following sections describe the PIKS ensemble operators. The ensemble operators perform arithmetic, extremal, and logical operations on a pair of images on an independent pixel-by-pixel basis.

2.2.1 *Alpha Blend, Constant*   InAlphaBlendConstant

The *alpha_blend_constant* operator performs alpha blending combination of a pair of images with a constant alpha blend factor.

Element input parameters

Description	Data type
First source image	ID
Second source image	ID
Destination image	ID
Alpha factor	RP

Object Restrictions

Source image structure	MON, COLR
Destination image structure	Same as source image structure
Source image data type	ND, SD
Destination image data type	Same as source image data type

Nomenclature

$S_1(x, y, 0, 0, b)$	$X \times Y \times 1 \times 1 \times B$ first source image
$S_2(x, y, 0, 0, b)$	$X \times Y \times 1 \times 1 \times B$ second source image
$D(x, y, 0, 0, b)$	$X \times Y \times 1 \times 1 \times B$ destination image
a	Alpha blend factor, $0 \leq a \leq 1$

Definition

For all x, y, b

$$D(x, y, 0, 0, b) = (a)[S_1(x, y, 0, 0, b)] + (1 - a)[S_2(x, y, 0, 0, b)]$$

Figure 2-9 illustrates the alpha blend operation for a pair of 8-bit, ND data type, monochrome images. The alpha blend factor is set at 0.5.

a

b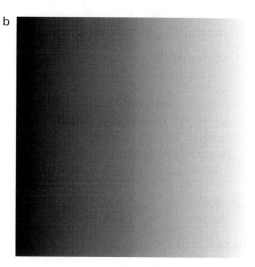

c

Figure 2-9. Example of alpha blend operation: (a) first source, "jet"; (b) second source, "ramp"; (c) destination, alpha blend, $a = 0.5$.

2.2.2 *Dyadic, Arithmetic*   `InDyadicArith`

The *dyadic_arithmetic* operator performs dyadic arithmetic combination of a pair of integer images.

Element input parameters

Description	Data type
First source image	ID
Second source image	ID
Destination image	ID

Description	Data type
Combination option	SP
absolute value difference	
addition	
addition, scaled	
arctangent ratio	
division	
maximum	
minimum	
multiplication	
subtraction	
subtraction, scaled	

Object Restrictions

Source image structure	MON, COLR
Destination image structure	Same as source image structure
Source image data type	ND, SD
Destination image data type	Same as source image data type

Remark

Result of division by zero is implementation dependent.

Nomenclature

$S_1(x, y, 0, 0, b)$ $X \times Y \times 1 \times 1 \times B$ first source image
$S_2(x, y, 0, 0, b)$ $X \times Y \times 1 \times 1 \times B$ second source image
$D(x, y, 0, 0, b)$ $X \times Y \times 1 \times 1 \times B$ destination image

Definition

For all x, y, b

Absolute value difference:

$$D(x, y, 0, 0, b) = S_1(x, y, 0, 0, b) - S_2(x, y, 0, 0, b) \quad \text{if } S_1(x, y, 0, 0, b) \geq S_2(x, y, 0, 0, b)$$

$$D(x, y, 0, 0, b) = S_2(x, y, 0, 0, b) - S_1(x, y, 0, 0, b) \quad \text{if } S_1(x, y, 0, 0, b) < S_2(x, y, 0, 0, b)$$

Addition:

$$D(x, y, 0, 0, b) = S_1(x, y, 0, 0, b) + S_2(x, y, 0, 0, b)$$

Addition, scaled:

$$D(x, y, 0, 0, b) = \frac{S_1(x, y, 0, 0, b) + S_2(x, y, 0, 0, b)}{2}$$

Arctangent ratio:

$$D(x, y, 0, 0, b) = \text{ATAN2}\{S_1(x, y, 0, 0, b), S_2(x, y, 0, 0, b)\}$$

where the arctangent function, ATAN2, is defined in Appendix A.

Division:

$$D(x, y, 0, 0, b) = \frac{S_1(x, y, 0, 0, b)}{S_2(x, y, 0, 0, b)}$$

Maximum:

$$D(x, y, 0, 0, b) = \text{MAX}\{S_1(x, y, 0, 0, b), S_2(x, y, 0, 0, b)\}$$

where the maxima function, MAX, is defined in Appendix A.

Minimum:

$$D(x, y, 0, 0, b) = \text{MIN}\{S_1(x, y, 0, 0, b), S_2(x, y, 0, 0, b)\}$$

where the minima function, MIN, is defined in Appendix A.

Multiplication:

$$D(x, y, 0, 0, b) = S_1(x, y, 0, 0, b) \times S_2(x, y, 0, 0, b)$$

Subtraction:

$$D(x, y, 0, 0, b) = S_1(x, y, 0, 0, b) - S_2(x, y, 0, 0, b)$$

Subtraction, scaled:

$$D(x, y, 0, 0, b) = \frac{S_1(x, y, 0, 0, b) + S_2(x, y, 0, 0, b)}{2}$$

Example

Figure 2-10 provides examples of the dyadic, arithmetic operator for a pair of 8-bit, ND data type, monochrome images.

2.2.3   *Dyadic, Logical*   `InDyadicLogical`

The *dyadic_logical* operator performs dyadic logical combination of a pair of Boolean or integer images.

Element input parameters

Description	Data type
First source image	ID
Second source image	ID
Destination image	ID

a
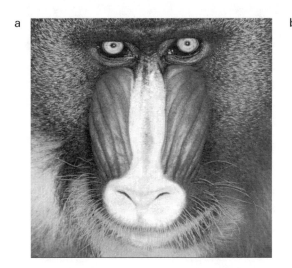

b
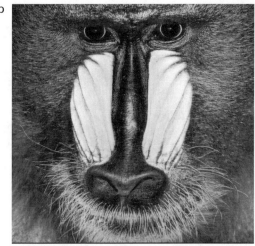

c

d
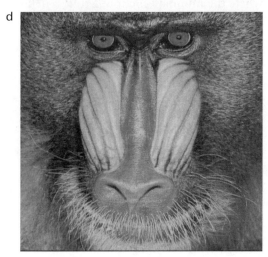

e
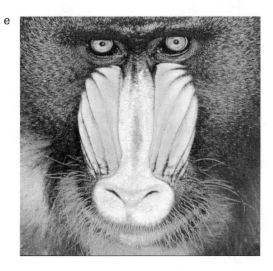

Figure 2-10 Examples of dyadic, arithmetic operation: (a) first source, "mandrill red band"; (b) second source, "mandrill blue band"; (c) destination, addition option; (d) destination, scaled addition option; (e) destination, maximum option

PIKS OPERATORS   CHAPTER 2

Description	Data type
Combination option	SP
bitwise AND	
bitwise NAND	
bitwise NOR	
bitwise OR	
bitwise XOR	
Boolean intersection	
Boolean union	

Object Restrictions

Source image structure	MON, COLR
Destination image structure	Same as source image structure
Source image data type	BD, ND, SD
Destination image data type	Same as source image data type

Remark

Bitwise operations apply to ND or SD data type images; Boolean operations apply to BD data type images.

Nomenclature

$S_1(x, y, 0, 0, b)$	$X \times Y \times 1 \times 1 \times B$ first source image
$S_2(x, y, 0, 0, b)$	$X \times Y \times 1 \times 1 \times B$ second source image
$D(x, y, 0, 0, b)$	$X \times Y \times 1 \times 1 \times B$ destination image
$S_1(p)$	pth bit of integer pixel of first source image
$S_2(p)$	pth bit of integer pixel of second source image
$d(p)$	pth bit of integer pixel of destination image

Definition

For all x, y, b, and, for integer operations, for all p

Integer bitwise AND:

$$d(p) = [s_1(p)] \oplus [s_2(p)]$$

where $\oplus$ denotes the AND operator defined in Appendix A.

Integer bitwise NAND:

$$d(p) = \overline{[s_1(p)] \oplus [s_2(p)]}$$

where the overbar denotes the complement operation defined in Appendix A.

Integer bitwise NOR:

$$d(p) = \overline{[s_1(p)] \ominus [s_2(p)]}$$

where $\ominus$ denotes the OR operator defined in Appendix A.

Integer bitwise OR:

$$d(p) = [s_1(p)] \ominus [s_2(p)]$$

Integer bitwise XOR:

$$d(p) = [s_1(p)] \otimes [s_2(p)]$$

where $\otimes$ denotes the exclusive-or, XOR, operator defined in Appendix A.

Boolean intersection:

$$D(x, y, 0, 0, b) = [S_1(x, y, 0, 0, b)] \cap [S_2(x, y, 0, 0, b)]$$

where denotes the intersection operator defined in Appendix A.

Boolean union:

$$D(x, y, 0, 0, b) = [S_1(x, y, 0, 0, b)] \cup [S_2(x, y, 0, 0, b)]$$

where $\cup$ denotes the union operator defined in Appendix A.

Example

Figure 2-11 shows examples of the dyadic, logical operator for the Boolean union and intersection opions on a pair of BD data type images.

2.2.4 *Dyadic Predicate*   InDyadicPredicate

The *dyadic_predicate* operator performs dyadic predicate combination of a pair of integer images.

Element input parameters

Description	Data type
First source image	ID
Second source image	ID
Destination image	ID

Predicate combination option
   greater than
   greater than or equal to
   less than
   less than or equal to
   equal to
   not equal to
	SP

Object Restrictions

Source image structure	MON, COLR
Destination image structure	Same as source image structure
Source image data type	ND, SD
Destination image data type	BD

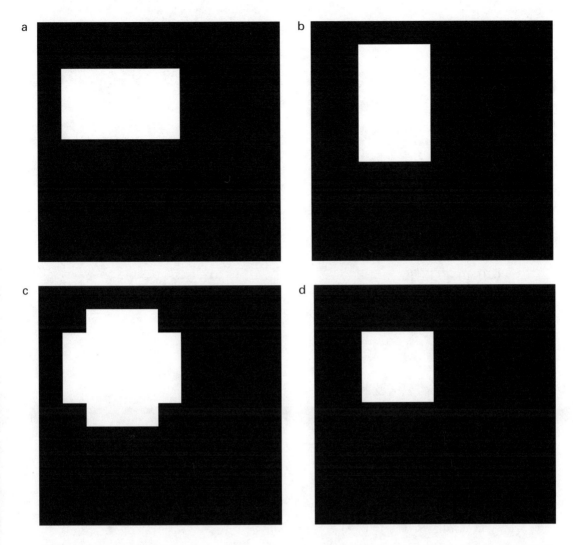

Figure 2-11. Examples of dyadic, logical operation: (a) first source, "horizontal rectangle"; (b) second source, "vertical rectangle"; (c) destination, Boolean union option; (d) destination, Boolean intersection option

Nomenclature

$S_1(x, y, 0, 0, b)$ $X \times Y \times 1 \times 1 \times B$ first source image
$S_2(x, y, 0, 0, b)$ $X \times Y \times 1 \times 1 \times B$ second source image
$D(x, y, 0, 0, b)$ $X \times Y \times 1 \times 1 \times B$ destination image

Definition

A destination image pixel is set to the TRUE state if the dyadic predicate condition is satisfied; otherwise it is set to the FALSE state.

For all x, y, b

Greater than option:

If
$\quad S_1(x, y, 0, 0, b) > S_2(x, y, 0, 0, b)$
then
$\quad D(x, y, 0, 0, b) = \text{TRUE}$
otherwise
$\quad D(x, y, 0, 0, b) = \text{FALSE}$

Greater than or equal to option:
If
$\quad S_1(x, y, 0, 0, b) \geq S_2(x, y, 0, 0, b)$
then
$\quad D(x, y, 0, 0, b) = \text{TRUE}$
otherwise
$\quad D(x, y, 0, 0, b) = \text{FALSE}$

Less than option:

$\quad$ If
$\quad\quad S_1(x, y, 0, 0, b) < S_2(x, y, 0, 0, b)$
$\quad$ then
$\quad\quad D(x, y, 0, 0, b) = \text{TRUE}$
$\quad$ otherwise
$\quad\quad D(x, y, 0, 0, b) = \text{FALSE}$

Less than or equal to option:

$\quad$ If
$\quad\quad S_1(x, y, 0, 0, b) \leq S_2(x, y, 0, 0, b)$
$\quad$ then
$\quad\quad D(x, y, 0, 0, b) = \text{TRUE}$
$\quad$ otherwise
$\quad\quad D(x, y, 0, 0, b) = \text{FALSE}$

Equal to option:

$\quad$ If
$\quad\quad S_1(x, y, 0, 0, b) = S_2(x, y, 0, 0, b)$
$\quad$ then
$\quad\quad D(x, y, 0, 0, b) = \text{TRUE}$
$\quad$ otherwise
$\quad\quad D(x, y, 0, 0, b) = \text{FALSE}$

Not equal to option:

$\quad$ If
$\quad\quad S_1(x, y, 0, 0, b) \neq S_2(x, y, 0, 0, b)$

Figure 2-12   Examples of dyadic predicate operation: (a) first source, "toys red band"; (b) second source, "toys blue band"; (c) Boolean destination, less than option; (d) Boolean destination, equal to option

then
$$D(x, y, 0, 0, b) = \text{TRUE}$$
otherwise
$$D(x, y, 0, 0, b) = \text{FALSE}$$

Example

Figure 2-12 presents examples of the dyadic, predicate operator for the less than and the equal to options on a pair of 8-bit, ND data type, monochrome images.

The *split_image* operator generates split image views of a pair of monochrome or colour images.

Element input parameters

Description	Data type
First source image	ID
Second source image	ID
Destination image	ID
Split position	SP
Split image option left 1-left 2 right 1-right 2 top 1-top 2 bottom 1-bottom 2 left 1-right 2 top 1-bottom 2	SP

Object restrictions

Source image structure	MON, COLR
Destination image structure	Same as source image structure
Source image data type	BD, ND, SD
Destination image data type	Same as source image data type

Nomenclature

$S_1(x, y, 0, 0, b)$ $X \times Y \times 1 \times 1 \times B$ first source image
$S_2(x, y, 0, 0, b)$ $X \times Y \times 1 \times 1 \times B$ second source image
$D(x, y, 0, 0, b)$ $X \times Y \times 1 \times 1 \times B$ destination image
x_c x index split position, $0 \leq x_c \leq X - 1$
y_c y index split position, $0 \leq y_c \leq Y - 1$

Definition

For all x, y, b

Left 1-left 2:

$$D(x, y, 0, 0, b) = S_1(x, y, 0, 0, b) \qquad 0 \leq x \leq x_c - 1$$
$$D(x, y, 0, 0, b) = S_2(x - x_c, y, 0, 0, b) \quad x_c \leq x \leq X - 1$$

Right 1-right 2:

$$D(x, y, 0, 0, b) = S_1(x + x_c, y, 0, 0, b) \quad 0 \leq x \leq x_c - 1$$
$$D(x, y, 0, 0, b) = S_2(x, y, 0, 0, b) \qquad x_c \leq x \leq X - 1$$

Top 1-top 2:

$$D(x, y, 0, 0, b) = S_1(x, y, 0, 0, b) \qquad 0 \leq y \leq y_c - 1$$
$$D(x, y, 0, 0, b) = S_2(x, y - y_c, 0, 0, b) \quad y_c \leq y \leq Y - 1$$

Bottom 1-bottom 2:

$$D(x, y, 0, 0, b) = S_1(x, y + y_c, 0, 0, b) \quad 0 \leq y \leq y_c - 1$$
$$D(x, y, 0, 0, b) = S_2(x, y, 0, 0, b) \qquad y_c \leq y \leq Y - 1$$

Left 1-right 2:

$$D(x, y, 0, 0, b) = S_1(x, y, 0, 0, b) \qquad 0 \leq x \leq x_c - 1$$
$$D(x, y, 0, 0, b) = S_2(x, y, 0, 0, b) \qquad x_c \leq x \leq X - 1$$

Top 1-bottom 2:

$$D(x, y, 0, 0, b) = S_1(x, y, 0, 0, b) \qquad 0 \leq y \leq y_c - 1$$
$$D(x, y, 0, 0, b) = S_2(x, y, 0, 0, b) \qquad y_c \leq y \leq Y - 1$$

Example

Figure 2-13 shows examples of the split image operator for several of its options for a pair of 8-bit, ND data type, monochrome images. Image 1 and image 2 are the source and destination images, respectively, of Figure 2-6.

2.3 Filtering and Morphological Operators

The following sections describe the filtering and morphological spatial operators. These operators form linear and nonlinear combinations of pixels within a neighbourhood of each source image pixel to generate a destination image pixel.

2.3.1 *Convolve, Two-dimensional*   `InConvolve2D`

The *convolve_2d* operator performs two-dimensional convolution with an impulse response function array for several image boundary conditions.

Element input parameters

Description	Data type
Source image	ID
Destination image	ID
Impulse response array	ID

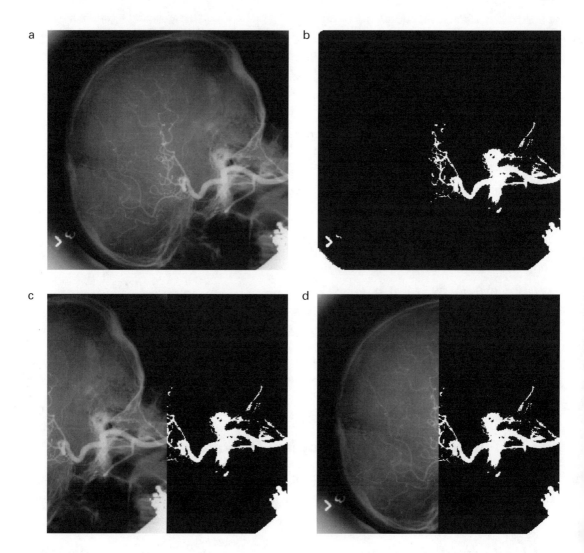

Figure 2-13 Example of split image operation: (a) first source, "brain" image; (b) second source, "threshold brain" image; (c) destination, right 1–right 2 split option; (d) destination, left 1–right 2 split option

Description	Data type

Convolution option
   upper left corner justified
   enclosed array
   key pixel, zero exterior
   key pixel, reflected exterior
	SP

Object Restrictions

Source image structure	MON, COLR
Destination image structure	Same as source image structure
Source image data type	ND, SD
Destination image data type	Same as source image data type
Array data type	SD

Nomenclature

$S(x, y, 0, 0, b)$ $X_S \times Y_S \times 1 \times 1 \times B_S$ source image
$D(x, y, 0, 0, b)$ $X_D \times Y_D \times 1 \times 1 \times B_D$ source image
$H(x, y)$ $X_H \times Y_H$ impulse function array
(x_k, y_k) Key pixel coordinate

The key pixel is referenced to the first row and column element of the impulse response function array. It is not restricted to be within the bounds of the impulse response function array.

Definition

Upper left corner justified mode:

The 2D impulse response function array is rotated 180 degrees and translated with respect to the x-y pixel plane of the source image. A destination pixel is computed for all spatial intersections of the array and the source image. The destination image x-y pixel plane is indexed from its upper left corner. The destination image x-y plane is larger than the source image x-y plane.

Figure 2-14a illustrates the spatial relationships between an image and a 3 × 3 impulse response array when the array is at its extremal positions as it is scanned across the image. Note that there is a one pixel overlap of the image and the array.

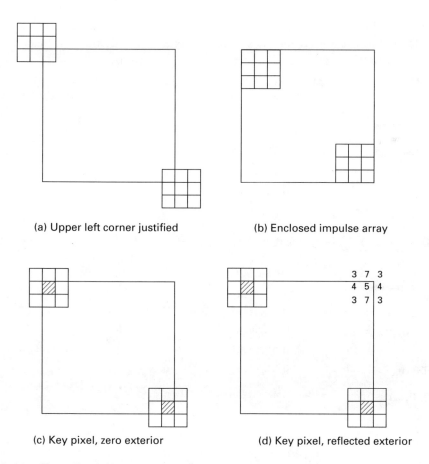

(a) Upper left corner justified   (b) Enclosed impulse array

(c) Key pixel, zero exterior   (d) Key pixel, reflected exterior

Figure 2-14   Two-dimensional convolution boundary conditions

For all x, y, b, and for

$$0 \leq x \leq X_D - 1$$
$$0 \leq y \leq Y_D - 1$$

$$D(x, y, 0, 0, b) = \sum_{x'} \sum_{y'} S(x', y', 0, 0, b) H(x - x', y - y')$$

The summation limits are

$$\text{MAX}\{0, x - X_H + 1\} \leq x' \leq \text{MIN}\{X_S - 1, x\}$$
$$\text{MAX}\{0, y - Y_H + 1\} \leq y' \leq \text{MIN}\{Y_S - 1, y\}$$

where the maxima function, MAX, and the minima function, MIN, are defined in Appendix A.

The pixel plane sizes are

$$X_D = X_S + X_H - 1$$
$$Y_D = Y_S + Y_H - 1$$
$$B_D = B_S = B$$

Enclosed impulse response array mode:

The 2D impulse response function array is rotated 180 degrees and translated with respect to the x-y pixel plane of the source image. A destination pixel is computed whenever all elements of the array lie within the bounds of the source image; all other destination pixels are set to zero. The destination image size is the same as the source image size.

Figure 2-14b shows the relationship between an image and a 3×3 impulse response array when the array is at its extremal positions. Note that the array never overlaps the image.

For all x, y, b, and for

$$
\begin{array}{ll}
x_c \leq x \leq X - 1 - x_c & \text{if } X_H \text{ is odd} \\
x_c - 1 \leq x \leq X - 1 - x_c & \text{if } X_H \text{ is even} \\
y_c \leq y \leq Y - 1 - y_c & \text{if } Y_H \text{ is odd} \\
y_c - 1 \leq y \leq Y - 1 - y_c & \text{if } Y_H \text{ is even}
\end{array}
$$

$$D(x, y, 0, 0, b) = \sum_{x'} \sum_{y'} S(x', y', 0, 0, b) H(x - x' + x_c, y - y' + y_c)$$

For all x, y, b, and for

$$
\begin{array}{lll}
x < x_c & \text{or } x > X - 1 - x_c & \text{if } X_H \text{ is odd} \\
x < x_c - 1 & \text{or } x > X - 1 - x_c & \text{if } X_H \text{ is even} \\
y < y_c & \text{or } y > Y - 1 - y_c & \text{if } Y_H \text{ is odd} \\
y < y_c - 1 & \text{or } y > Y - 1 - y_c & \text{if } Y_H \text{ is even}
\end{array}
$$

$$D(x, y, 0, 0, b) = 0$$

where

$$x_c = \frac{X_H - 1}{2} \qquad \text{if } X_H \text{ is odd}$$

$$x_c = \frac{X_H}{2} \qquad \text{if } X_H \text{ is even}$$

$$y_c = \frac{Y_H - 1}{2} \qquad \text{if } Y_H \text{ is odd}$$

$$y_c = \frac{Y_H}{2} \qquad \text{if } Y_H \text{ is even}$$

The summation limits are

$$\begin{array}{ll}
\text{MAX}\{0, x - x_c\} \leq x' \leq \text{MIN}\{X - 1, x + x_c\} & \text{if } X_H \text{ is odd} \\
\text{MAX}\{0, x - x_c + 1\} \leq x' \leq \text{MIN}\{X - 1, x + x_c\} & \text{if } X_H \text{ is even} \\
\text{MAX}\{0, y - y_c\} \leq y' \leq \text{MIN}\{Y - 1, y + y_c\} & \text{if } Y_H \text{ is odd} \\
\text{MAX}\{0, y - y_c + 1\} \leq y' \leq \text{MIN}\{Y - 1, y + y_c\} & \text{if } X_H \text{ is even}
\end{array}$$

The pixel plane sizes are

$$X_D = X_S = X$$
$$Y_D = Y_S = Y$$
$$B_D = B_S = B$$

Key pixel, zero exterior mode:

The 2D impulse response function array is rotated 180 degrees and translated with respect to the x-y pixel plane of the source image. A destination pixel is computed whenever the key pixel of the array is over a source pixel. The destination image size is the same as the source image size. Source pixels outside the x-y plane boundary are assumed to be zero valued.

Figure 2-14c illustrates the image and array relationship for the key pixel at the centre of the array. All pixels under the overlapped portions of the array are, conceptually, of zero value.

For all b, and for

$$\text{MAX}\{0, -x_k\} \leq x' \leq \text{MIN}\{X - 1, X - 1 + x_k\}$$
$$\text{MAX}\{0, -y_k\} \leq y' \leq \text{MIN}\{Y - 1, Y - 1 + y_k\}$$

$$D(x, y, 0, 0, b) = \sum_{x'} \sum_{y'} S(x', y', 0, 0, b) \, H(x - x' + x_k, y - y' + y_k)$$

For all b, and for

$$x < \text{MAX}\{0, -x_k\} \text{ or } x > \text{MIN}\{X - 1, X - 1 + x_k\}$$
$$y < \text{MAX}\{0, -y_k\} \text{ or } y > \text{MIN}\{Y - 1, Y - 1 + y_k\}$$

$$D(x, y, 0, 0, b) = 0$$

The summation limits are

$$\text{MAX}\{0, x - X_H + x_k + 1\} \leq x' \leq \text{MIN}\{X - 1, x + x_k\}$$
$$\text{MAX}\{0, y - Y_H + y_k + 1\} \leq y' \leq \text{MIN}\{Y - 1, y + y_k\}$$

The pixel plane sizes are

$$X_D = X_S = X$$
$$Y_D = Y_S = Y$$
$$B_D = B_S = B$$

Key pixel, reflected exterior mode:

The 2D impulse response function array is rotated 180 degrees and translated with respect to the x-y pixel plane of the source image. A destination pixel is computed whenever the key pixel of the array is over a source pixel. The destination image size is the same as the source image size. Source pixels outside the x-y plane boundary are assumed to be reflections of source pixels about each boundary, i.e., the source image is assumed to be reflected about its left, right, top, and bottom sides.

Figure 2-14d shows the image and array relationship for a centred key pixel. All pixels under the overlapped portions of the array are, conceptually, reflected values of pixels within the image, as shown in the upper right corner of the figure.

For all b, and for

$$0 \le x \le X - 1$$
$$0 \le y \le Y - 1$$

$$D(x, y, 0, 0, b) = \sum_{x'} \sum_{y'} S(x'', y'', 0, 0, b) \, H(x - x'' + x_k, y - y'' + y_k)$$

where

$x'' = 1 - x'$	$x' < 0$	$y'' = 1 - y'$	$y' < 0$
$x'' = x'$	$0 \le x' \le X - 1$	$y'' = y'$	$0 \le y' \le Y - 1$
$x'' = 2(x - 1) - x'$	$x' > X - 1$	$y'' = 2(Y - 1) - y'$	$y' > Y - 1$

The summation limits are

$$\text{MAX}\{0, x - X_H + x_k + 1\} \le x' \le \text{MIN}\{X - 1, x + x_k\}$$
$$\text{MAX}\{0, y - Y_H + y_k + 1\} \le y' \le \text{MIN}\{Y - 1, y + y_k\}$$

The pixel plane sizes are

$$X_D = X_S = X$$
$$Y_D = Y_S = Y$$
$$B_D = B_S = B$$

Example

Figure 2-15 presents two examples of two-dimensional convolution of an 8-bit, ND data type, monochrome image with a 3×3 high pass filter impulse response function array for the key pixel, reflected exterior boundary option. The high pass filter impulse response array is

$$H = \begin{bmatrix} 1 & -2 & 1 \\ -2 & 5 & -2 \\ 1 & -2 & 1 \end{bmatrix}$$

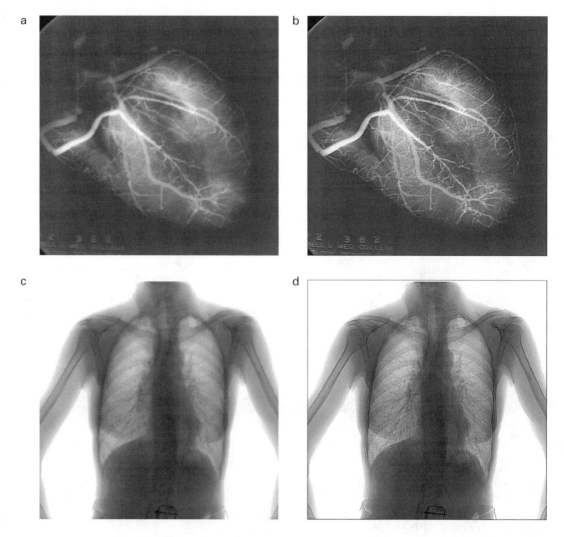

Figure 2-15 Examples of two-dimensional convolution operation: (a) source, "chest"; (b) destination, high pass convolution of "chest"; (c) source, "heart"; (d) destination, high pass convolution of "heart"

The following are printouts of the upper left corner of the source and destination image arrays for the four convolution boundary options. The source image is of constant value 252. The convolution is performed with the following 3×3 uniform amplitude low pass filter impulse response array.

$$H = \frac{1}{9} \begin{bmatrix} 1 & 1 & 1 \\ 1 & 1 & 1 \\ 1 & 1 & 1 \end{bmatrix}$$

Source image:

```
252 252 252 252 252 252 252 252
252 252 252 252 252 252 252 252
252 252 252 252 252 252 252 252
252 252 252 252 252 252 252 252
252 252 252 252 252 252 252 252
252 252 252 252 252 252 252 252
252 252 252 252 252 252 252 252
252 252 252 252 252 252 252 252
```

Destination image with upper left corner justified option:

```
 28  56  84  84  84  84  84  84
 56 112 168 168 168 168 168 168
 84 168 252 252 252 252 252 252
 84 168 252 252 252 252 252 252
 84 168 252 252 252 252 252 252
 84 168 252 252 252 252 252 252
 84 168 252 252 252 252 252 252
 84 168 252 252 252 252 252 252
```

Destination image with enclosed array option:

```
  0   0   0   0   0   0   0   0
  0 252 252 252 252 252 252 252
  0 252 252 252 252 252 252 252
  0 252 252 252 252 252 252 252
  0 252 252 252 252 252 252 252
  0 252 252 252 252 252 252 252
  0 252 252 252 252 252 252 252
  0 252 252 252 252 252 252 252
```

Destination image with key pixel, zero exterior option:

```
112 168 168 168 168 168 168 168
168 252 252 252 252 252 252 252
168 252 252 252 252 252 252 252
168 252 252 252 252 252 252 252
168 252 252 252 252 252 252 252
168 252 252 252 252 252 252 252
168 252 252 252 252 252 252 252
168 252 252 252 252 252 252 252
```

Destination image with key pixel, reflected exterior option:

```
252 252 252 252 252 252 252 252
252 252 252 252 252 252 252 252
252 252 252 252 252 252 252 252
252 252 252 252 252 252 252 252
252 252 252 252 252 252 252 252
252 252 252 252 252 252 252 252
252 252 252 252 252 252 252 252
252 252 252 252 252 252 252 252
```

The *morphic_processor* operator performs morphological processing on a Boolean image using a 3×3 hit or miss transformation with a specified transformation table.

Element input parameters

Description	Data type
Source image	ID
Destination image	ID
Hit or miss lookup table	ID
Number of iterations	SP

Element output parameters

Description	Data type
Number of cycles	NP

Object Restrictions

Source image structure	MON, COLR
Destination image structure	Same as source image structure
Source image data type	BD
Destination image data type	BD
Lookup table input data type	SD
Lookup table output data type	BD

Remark

If the iterations value is set to -1, the operation is performed until the destination image is unchanged after successive iterations. The parameter cycles is the number of iterations actually performed. If the parameter iterations is set to zero, the source image is copied into the destination image without modification.

Nomenclature

$S(x, y, 0, 0, b)$	$X \times Y \times 1 \times 1 \times B$ source image
$D(x, y, 0, 0, b)$	$X \times Y \times 1 \times 1 \times B$ destination image
$I(x, y, 0, 0, b)$	$X \times Y \times 1 \times 1 \times B$ intermediate image
P	Boolean state of centre pixel of 3×3 neighbourhood in x-y plane of S
P_0	Boolean state of east neighbour of P
P_1	Boolean state of northeast neighbour of P
P_2	Boolean state of north neighbour of P
P_3	Boolean state of northwest neighbour of P
P_4	Boolean state of west neighbour of P
P_5	Boolean state of southwest neighbour of P
P_6	Boolean state of south neighbour of P
P_7	Boolean state of southeast neighbour of P
Q	Boolean state of destination pixel spatially corresponding to P
id	Lookup table identifier

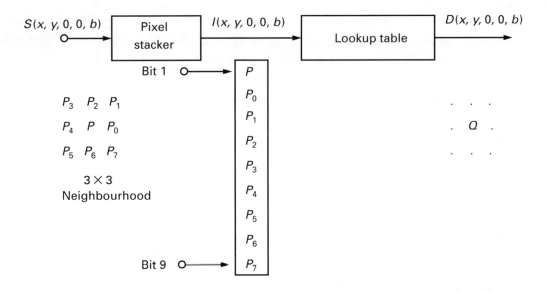

Figure 2-16   Morphic processor conceptual model

Definition

The morphic processor conceptual model is shown in Figure 2-16. For all b, at each pixel coordinate (x, y), the pixel stacker forms nine data bits in an intermediate pixel array $I(x, y, 0, 0, b)$. The intermediate pixel is a mapping of the Boolean states of the source image pixel and its eight nearest neighbours, whereby a Boolean TRUE state is mapped to a 1 state bit and a Boolean FALSE state is mapped to a 0 state bit. The intermediate pixel is passed through a 512 entry lookup table that generates a destination pixel whose Boolean state is Q.

For all x, y, b

$$D(x, y, 0, 0, b) = \text{LOOK}\{I(x, y, 0, 0, b), 0, 0, \text{id}\}$$

where the lookup table function, LOOK, is defined in Appendix A.

Example

Figure 2-17 provides examples of the morphic processor operator using dilation and erosion lookup tables and two iterations on a 64×64 pixel BD data type image. The source image consists of a rectangular ring of three pixel width enclosing a single pixel. The source and destination images have been zommed by a factor of eight for display.

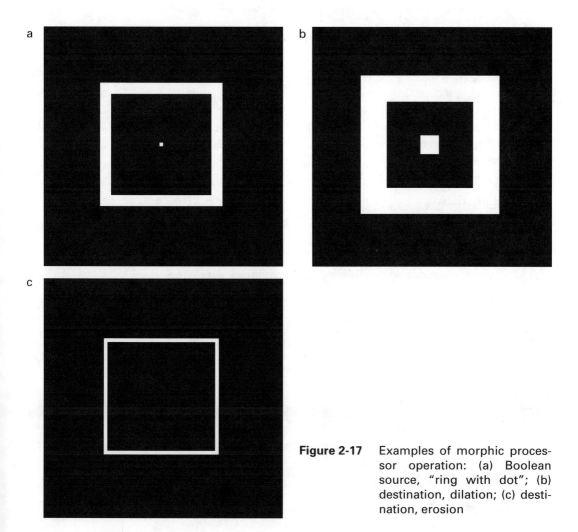

Figure 2-17 Examples of morphic processor operation: (a) Boolean
source, "ring with dot"; (b)
destination, dilation; (c) destination, erosion

2.4 Geometric Operators

The following sections describe the geometric operators. These operators modify the geometrical shape of an image.

2.4.1 *Flip, Spin, Transpose* `InFlipSpinTranspose`

The *flip_spin_transpose* operator performs flip, spin, or transpose manipulations on pixel
planes of an image.

Element input parameters

Description	Data type
Source image	ID
Destination image	ID

Description	Data type
Flip, spin, transpose option	SP
top-to-bottom flip	
left-to-right flip	
90 degrees counterclockwise spin	
180 degrees counterclockwise spin	
270 degrees counterclockwise spin	
transpose, upper left to lower right	
transpose, lower left to upper right	

Object Restrictions

Source image structure	MON, COLR
Destination image structure	Same as source image structure
Source image data type	BD, ND, SD
Destination image data type	Same as source image data type

Nomenclature

$S(x, y, 0, 0, b)$ $X_S \times Y_S \times 1 \times 1 \times B$ source image

$D(x, y, 0, 0, b)$ $X_D \times Y_D \times 1 \times 1 \times B$ destination image

Definition

As shown in Figure 2-18, for all x, y, b

Flip top-to-bottom:

$$D(x, y, 0, 0, b) = S(x, Y_S - 1 - y, 0, 0, b) \qquad 0 \le x \le X_S - 1 \text{ and } 0 \le y \le Y_S - 1$$

where $X_D = X_S$ and $Y_D = Y_S$

Flip left-to-right:

$$D(x, y, 0, 0, b) = S(X_S - 1 - x, y, 0, 0, b) \qquad 0 \le x \le X_S - 1 \text{ and } 0 \le y \le Y_S - 1$$

where $X_D = X_S$ and $Y_D = Y_S$

Spin 90 degrees counterclockwise:

$$D(x, y, 0, 0, b) = S(X_S - 1 - y, x, 0, 0, b) \qquad 0 \le x \le Y_S - 1 \text{ and } 0 \le y \le X_S - 1$$

where $X_D = Y_S$ and $Y_D = X_S$

Spin 180 degrees counterclockwise:

$$D(x, y, 0, 0, b) = S(X_S - 1 - x, Y_S - 1 - y, 0, 0, b) \qquad 0 \le x \le X_S - 1 \text{ and } 0 \le y \le Y_S - 1$$

where $X_D = X_S$ and $Y_D = Y_S$

Spin 270 degrees counterclockwise:

$$D(x, y, 0, 0, b) = S(y, Y_S - 1 - x, 0, 0, b) \qquad 0 \le x \le Y_S - 1 \text{ and } 0 \le y \le X_S - 1$$

where $X_D = Y_S$ and $Y_D = X_S$

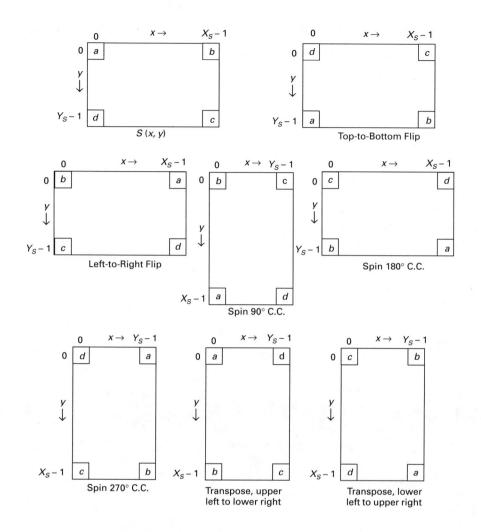

Figure 2-18   Flip, spin, transpose geometry

Transpose, upper left to lower right:

$D(x, y, 0, 0, b) = S(y, x, 0, 0, b)$ $0 \leq x \leq Y_S - 1$ and $0 \leq y \leq X_S - 1$

where $X_D = Y_S$ and $Y_D = X_S$

Transpose, lower left to upper right:

$D(x, y, 0, 0, b) = S(Y_S - 1 - y, X_S - 1 - x, 0, 0, b)$ $0 \leq x \leq Y_S - 1$ and $0 \leq y \leq X_S - 1$

where $X_D = Y_S$ and $Y_D = X_S$

2.4.2   *Flip, Spin, Transpose ROI*   `InFlipSpinTransposeROI`

The *flip_spin_transpose_roi* operator performs flip, spin, or transpose manipulations on a ROI.

Element input parameters

Description	Data type
Source ROI	ID
Destination ROI	ID

Flip, spin, transpose option
    top-to-bottom flip
    left-to-right flip
    90 degrees counterclockwise spin
    180 degrees counterclockwise spin
    270 degrees counterclockwise spin
    transpose, upper left to lower right
    transpose, lower left to upper right
	SP

Object Restrictions

Source ROI structure	ROI_RECT
Destination ROI structure	ROI_RECT
Source ROI data type	BD
Destination ROI data type	BD

Nomenclature

$R_S(x, y)$	$X_S \times Y_S$ source ROI virtual array
$R_D(x, y)$	$X_D \times Y_D$ destination ROI virtual array

Definition

For all x, y, b

Flip top-to-bottom:

$$R_D(x, y) = R_S(x, Y_S - 1 - y) \qquad 0 \le x \le X_S - 1 \text{ and } 0 \le y \le Y_S - 1$$

where $X_D = X_S$ and $Y_D = Y_S$

Flip left-to-right:

$$R_D(x, y) = R_S(X_S - 1 - x, y) \qquad 0 \le x \le X_S - 1 \text{ and } 0 \le y \le Y_S - 1$$

where $X_D = X_S$ and $Y_D = Y_S$

Spin 90 degrees counterclockwise:

$$R_D(x, y) = R_S(X_S - 1 - y, x) \qquad 0 \le x \le Y_S - 1 \text{ and } 0 \le y \le X_S - 1$$

where $X_D = Y_S$ and $Y_D = X_S$

Spin 180 degrees counterclockwise:

$$R_D(x, y) = R_S(X_S - 1 - x, Y_S - 1 - y) \qquad 0 \le x \le X_S - 1 \text{ and } 0 \le y \le Y_S - 1$$

where $X_D = X_S$ and $Y_D = Y_S$

Spin 270 degrees counterclockwise:

$$R_D(x, y) = R_S(y, Y_S - 1 - x) \qquad 0 \leq x \leq Y_S - 1 \text{ and } 0 \leq y \leq X_S - 1$$

where $X_D = Y_S$ and $Y_D = X_S$

Transpose, upper left to lower right:

$$R_D(x, y) = R_S(y, x) \qquad 0 \leq x \leq Y_S - 1 \text{ and } 0 \leq y \leq X_S - 1$$

where $X_D = Y_S$ and $Y_D = X_S$

Transpose, lower left to upper right:

$$R_D(x, y) = R_S(Y_S - 1 - y, X_S - 1 - x) \qquad 0 \leq x \leq Y_S - 1 \text{ and } 0 \leq y \leq X_S - 1$$

where $X_D = Y_S$ and $Y_D = X_S$

2.4.3 *Rescale* `InRescale`

The *rescale* operator performs size rescaling of a window of an image.

Element input parameters

Description	Data type
Source image	ID
Destination image	ID
Scale factor 5-tuple	ID
Upper value 5-tuple	ID
Lower value 5-tuple	ID

Object Restrictions

Source image structure	MON, COLR
Destination image structure	Same as source image structure
Source image data type	BD, ND, SD
Destination image data type	Same as source image data type

Remarks

1. For geometric operators, all image pixels are assumed to be of unit dimension. The geometric origin along a coordinate direction is at the centre of the pixel with index value zero. The geometric bounds of the origin pixel are −0.5 to 0.5.

2. The scale factor, upper value, and lower value 5-tuples contain parameters of the RD data type.

3. There is no rescaling along the band index of a colour image.

Nomenclature

$S(x, y, 0, 0, b)$	$X_S \times Y_S \times 1 \times 1 \times B$ source image
$D(x, y, 0, 0, b)$	$X_D \times Y_D \times 1 \times 1 \times B$ destination image
S_x	Horizontal index scale factor

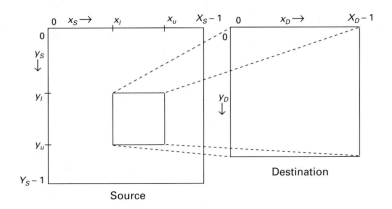

Figure 2-19   Two-dimensional rescaling

S_y	Vertical index scale factor
x_u	Horizontal index upper window coordinate
y_u	Vertical index upper window coordinate
x_l	Horizontal index lower window coordinate
y_l	Vertical index lower window coordinate

Definition

The *rescale* operator is based upon a two-stage algorithm. In the first stage, a reverse address calculation is made whereby $(x', y', 0, 0, b)$ source image coordinates are calculated for integer values of the destination image coordinates $(x, y, 0, 0, b)$. In general, the $(x', y', 0, 0, b)$ coordinates are not integer valued. The second stage of the algorithm entails two-dimensional resampling of each source image band to evaluate the destination image at integer coordinates. Nearest neighbour and bilinear interpolation resampling are supported in PIKS Foundation through the *set_globals* mechanism. The *rescale* operator is defined as follows:

As shown in Figure 2-19, for all x, y, b

$$D(x, y, 0, 0, b) = \mathrm{RES}_2\{S, x', y', 0, 0, b\}$$

where

$$x' = \frac{(x + 0.5)}{S_x} + x_l - 0.5$$

$$y' = \frac{(y + 0.5)}{S_y} + y_l - 0.5$$

and

$$X_D = \mathrm{NIV}\{(S_x)(x_u - x_l)\}$$

$$Y_D = \mathrm{NIV}\{(S_y)(y_u - y_l)\}$$

The function RES_2 denotes the two-dimensional resampling operation defined in Appendix A. The nearest integer value function, NIV, is also defined in Appendix A.

Tuple specifications

The scale factor 5-tuple has the following conceptual data structure:

5
RP
S_x
S_y
1.0
1.0
1.0

The upper value 5-tuple has the following conceptual data structure:

5
RP
x_u
y_u
0.0
0.0
0.0

The lower value 5-tuple has the following conceptual data structure:

5
RP
x_l
y_l
0.0
0.0
0.0

Example

Figure 2-20 presents an example of the rescaling of an 8-bit, ND data type, monochrome image. The destination image is generated from a window on the source image whose lower coordinate is (25, 25) and upper coordinate is (425, 425). The scale factor is computed to create a 512×512 pixel destination image. Nearest neighbour interpolation is used in the resampling.

2.4.4   *Rescale ROI*   InRescaleROI

The *rescale_roi* operator performs size rescaling of a window of a ROI.

Element input parameters

Description	Data type
Source ROI	ID
Destination ROI	ID
Scale factor 5-tuple	ID
Upper value 5-tuple	ID
Lower value 5-tuple	ID

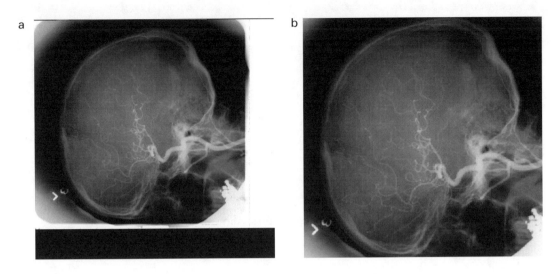

Figure 2-20 Example of rescaling operation: (a) source, "brainscan"; (b) destination of source window, $x_u = y_u = 425$, $x_l = y_l = 25$, $S_x = S_y = 1.28$

Object Restrictions

Source ROI structure	ROI_RECT
Destination ROI structure	ROI_RECT
Source ROI data type	BD
Destination ROI data type	BD

Remarks

1. For geometric operators, all ROI pixels are assumed to be of unit dimension. The geometric origin along a coordinate direction is at the centre of the pixel with index value zero. The geometric bounds of the origin pixel are –0.5 to 0.5.

2. The scale factor, upper value, and lower value 5-tuples contain parameters of the RD data type.

Nomenclature

$R_S(x, y)$	$X_S \times Y_S$ source ROI virtual array
$R_D(x, y)$	$X_D \times Y_D$ destination ROI virtual array
S_x	Horizontal index scale factor
S_y	Vertical index scale factor
x_u	Horizontal index upper window coordinate
y_u	Vertical index upper window coordinate
x_l	Horizontal index lower window coordinate
y_l	Vertical index lower window coordinate

Definition

The *rescale_roi* operator is based upon a two-stage algorithm. In the first stage, a reverse address calculation is made whereby (x', y') source ROI coordinates are calculated for integer values of the destination ROI coordinates (x, y). In general, the (x', y') coordinates are not integer valued. The second stage of the algorithm entails two-dimensional resampling of the ROI to evaluate the destination ROI at integer coordinates. Only nearest neighbour resampling is supported in PIKS Foundation. The *rescale_roi* operator is defined as follows.

For all x, y

$$R_D(x, y) = \text{RES}_2\{R_S, x', y'\}$$

where

$$x' = \frac{(x + 0.5)}{S_x} + x_l - 0.5$$

$$y' = \frac{(y + 0.5)}{S_y} + y_l - 0.5$$

and

$$X_D = \text{NIV}\{(S_x)(x_u - x_l)\}$$

$$Y_D = \text{NIV}\{(S_y)(y_u - y_l)\}$$

The function RES_2 denotes the two-dimensional resampling operation defined in Appendix A. The nearest integer value function, NIV, is also defined in Appendix A.

Tuple specifications

See Section 2.4.3.

2.4.5 Resize

InResize

The *resize* operator performs resizing of an image by reducing or enlarging its coordinate sizes.

Element input parameters

Description	Data type
Source image	ID
Destination image	ID
Destination size 5-tuple	ID

Object Restrictions

Source image structure	MON, COLR
Destination image structure	Same as source image structure
Source image data type	BD, ND, SD
Destination image data type	Same as source image data type

Remarks

1. For geometric operators, all image pixels are assumed to be of unit dimension. The geometric origin along a coordinate direction is at the centre of the pixel with index value zero. The geometric bounds of the origin pixel are –0.5 to 0.5.

2. The destination size 5-tuple contain parameters of the ND data type.

3. There is no resizing along the band index of a colour image.

Nomenclature

$S(x, y, 0, 0, b)$ $X_S \times Y_S \times 1 \times 1 \times B$ source image
$D(x, y, 0, 0, b)$ $X_D \times Y_D \times 1 \times 1 \times B$ destination image

Definition

The *resize* operator is based upon a two-stage algorithm. In the first stage, a reverse address calculation is made whereby $(x', y', 0, 0, b)$ source image coordinates are calculated for integer values of the destination image coordinates $(x, y, 0, 0, b)$. In general, the $(x', y', 0, 0, b)$ coordinates are not integer valued. The second stage of the algorithm entails two-dimensional resampling of each source image band to evaluate the destination image at integer coordinates. Nearest neighbour and bilinear interpolation resampling are supported in PIKS Foundation through the *set_globals* mechanism. The *resize* operator is defined as follows:

For all x, y, b

$$D(x, y, 0, 0, b) = \mathrm{RES}_2\{S, x', y', 0, 0, b\}$$

where

$$x' = \frac{X_S}{X_D}(x + 0.5) - 0.5$$

$$y' = \frac{Y_S}{Y_D}(y + 0.5) - 0.5$$

The function RES_2 denotes the two-dimensional resampling operation defined in Appendix A.

Tuple specification

The destination size 5-tuple has the following conceptual data structure:

5
ND
X_D
Y_D
1
1
B

Example

Figure 2-21 provides examples of the resizing operation on an 8-bit, ND data type, monochrome image for an increase in size of the source image by a factor of 3:2 along the x and y coordinates for nearest neighbor and bilinear interpolation. The destination images are 768×768 pixels.

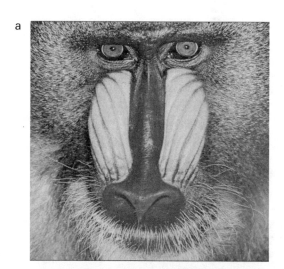

Figure 2-21a–b   Example of resizing operation: (a) source, "mandrill luminance"; (b) destination, 3:2 resize of source, nearest neighbour interpolation

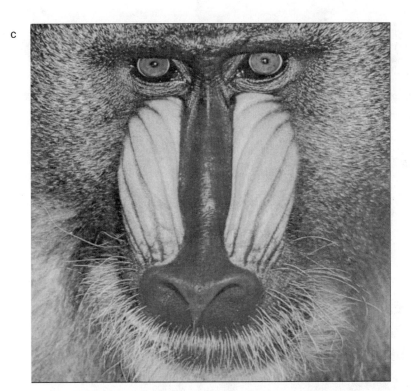

c

Figure 2-21c   Example of resizing operation (*Continued*): destination, 3:2 resize, bilinear interpolation

2.4.6   *Resize ROI*   InResizeROI

The *resize_roi* operator performs resizing of a ROI by reducing or enlarging its coordinate sizes.

Element input parameters

Description	Data type
Source ROI	ID
Destination ROI	ID
Destination size 5-tuple	ID

Object Restrictions

Source ROI structure	ROI_RECT
Destination ROI structure	ROI_RECT
Source ROI data type	BD
Destination ROI data type	BD

Remarks

1. For geometric operators, all ROI pixels are assumed to be of unit dimension. The geometric origin along a coordinate direction is at the centre of the pixel with index value zero. The geometric bounds of the origin pixel are –0.5 to 0.5.

2. The destination size 5-tuple contain parameters of the ND data type.

Nomenclature

$R_S(x, y)$ $X_S \times Y_S$ source ROI virtual array

$R_D(x, y)$ $X_D \times Y_D$ destination ROI virtual array

Definition

The *resize_roi* operator is based upon a two-stage algorithm. In the first stage, a reverse address calculation is made whereby (x', y') source ROI coordinates are calculated for integer values of the destination ROI coordinates (x, y). In general, the (x', y') coordinates are not integer valued. The second stage of the algorithm entails two-dimensional resampling of the ROI to evaluate the destination ROI at integer coordinates. Only nearest neighbour ROI resampling is supported in PIKS Foundation. The *resize_roi* operator is defined as follows:

For all x, y

$$R_D(x, y) = \text{RES}_2\{R_S, x', y'\}$$

where

$$x' = \frac{X_S}{X_D}(x + 0.5) - 0.5$$

$$y' = \frac{Y_S}{Y_D}(y + 0.5) - 0.5$$

The function RES_2 denotes the two-dimensional resampling operation defined in Appendix A.

Tuple specification

See Section 2.4.5.

2.4.7   *Rotate*   `InRotate`

The *rotate* operator performs two-dimensional rotation of an image about a point.

Element input parameters

Description	Data type
Source image	ID
Destination image	ID
First index rotation centre	RP
Second index rotation centre	RP
Third index rotation centre	RP, NULL
First plane rotation angle	RP
Second plane rotation angle	RP, NULL
Third plane rotation angle	RP, NULL
Rotation option 2D rotation	SP

Object Restrictions

Source image structure	MON, COLR
Destination image structure	Same as source image structure
Source image data type	BD, ND, SD
Destination image data type	Same as source image data type

Remarks

1. For geometric operators, all image pixels are assumed to be of unit dimension. The geometric origin along a coordinate direction is at the centre of the pixel with index value zero. The geometric bounds of the origin pixel are -0.5 to 0.5.

2. The rotation angle is positive for counterclockwise rotation about a vector emanating toward a viewer from the rotation centre of the x-y plane.

3. Rotation angles are measured in radians.

4. The rotation centre coordinates need not be integer valued.

5. Source image pixels outside its index range are assumed to be of zero value for ND and SD data type images, and are assumed to be of FALSE value for BD data type images.

Nomenclature

$S(x, y, 0, 0, b)$	$X_S \times Y_S \times 1 \times 1 \times B$ source image
$D(x, y, 0, 0, b)$	$X_D \times Y_D \times 1 \times 1 \times B$ destination image
x_c	First index rotation centre
y_c	Second index rotation centre
A	Rotation angle

Definition

The *rotate* operator is based upon a two-stage algorithm. In the first stage, a reverse address calculation is made whereby $(x', y', 0, 0, b)$ source image coordinates are calculated for integer values of the destination image coordinates $(x, y, 0, 0, b)$. In general, the $(x', y', 0, 0, b)$ coordinates are not integer valued. The second stage of the algorithm entails two-dimensional resampling of each source image band to evaluate the destination image at integer coordinates. Nearest neighbour and bilinear interpolation resampling are supported in PIKS Foundation through the *set_globals* mechanism. The *rotate* operator is defined as follows.

As shown in Figure 2-22, for all x, y, b

$$D(x, y, 0, 0, b) = \text{RES}_2\{S, x', y', 0, 0, b\}$$

where

$$x' = (x - x_c)\text{COS}\{A\} + (y - y_c)\text{SIN}\{A\} + x_c$$

$$y' = -(x - x_c)\text{SIN}\{A\} + (y - y_c)\text{COS}\{A\} + y_c$$

The function RES_2 denotes the two-dimensional resampling operation defined in Appendix A. The functions SIN and COS are the sine and cosine trigonometric functions.

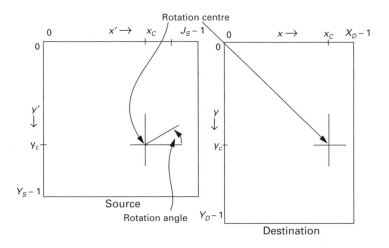

Figure 2-22   Two-dimensional rotation

Example

Figure 2-23 illustrates the rotation of an 8-bit, ND data type, monochrome image by an angle of 45 degrees about its centre. The destination image is of the same size as the source image, and therefore, there are some portions of the destination image that receive no data and remain zero valued. The corners of the source image have no destination image storage reservation, and consequently are spatially clipped.

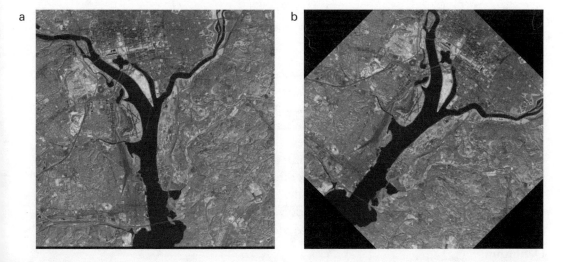

Figure 2-23   Example of rotation operation: (a) source, "washington infrared"; (b) destination, 45 degree rotation

The *subsample* operator performs spatial subsampling of an image. Pixels are extracted from a source window offset with respect to the source origin and placed in a destination image window offset with respect to the destination origin.

Element input parameters

Description	Data type
Source image	ID
Destination image	ID
Source first index subsampling factor	NP
Source second index subsampling factor	NP
Source first index offset	NP
Source second index offset	NP
Destination first index offset	NP
Destination second index offset	NP
Source first index window size	NP
Source second index window size	NP

Object Restrictions

Source image structure	MON, COLR
Destination image structure	Same as source image structure
Source image data type	BD, ND, SD
Destination image data type	Same as source image data type

Nomenclature

$S(x, y, 0, 0, b)$	$X_S \times Y_S \times 1 \times 1 \times B$ source image
$D(x, y, 0, 0, b)$	$X_D \times Y_D \times 1 \times 1 \times B$ destination image
S_x	Source first index subsampling factor
S_y	Source second index subsampling factor
x_s	Source first index offset
y_s	Source second index offset
x_d	Destination first index offset
y_d	Destination second index offset
x_w	Source first index window size
y_w	Source second index window size

Definition:

For all b and x_D and y_D in the range

$$x_d \leq x_D \leq \text{MIN}\{X_S - 1, X_M\}$$
$$y_d \leq y_D \leq \text{MIN}\{Y_S - 1, Y_M\}$$

$$D(x_D, y_D, 0, 0, b) = S(x_S, y_S, 0, 0, b)$$

where

$$x_S = (S_x)(x - x_d) + x_s$$
$$y_S = (S_y)(y - y_d) + y_s$$
$$X_M = \text{LIV}\{x_w / S_x\}$$
$$Y_M = \text{LIV}\{y_w / S_y\}$$

and $D(x, y, 0, 0, b)$ is unchanged otherwise.

The minima function, MIN, and the lowest integer value function, LIV, are defined in Appendix A.

Example:

Figure 2-24 shows an example of the subsampling of four 8-bit, ND data type, monochrome images. The red, green, and blue bands of the "toys colour" image and the "toys luminance" image generated as the example of Figure 2-29 have been subsampled by a factor of 2:1 along each axis. The destination offsets have been chosen to produce a composite destination image of the four source images.

2.4.9 *Translate* InTranslate

The *translate* operator performs a spatial translation of an image with respect to its origin.

Element input parameters:

Description	Data type
Source image	ID
Destination image	ID
Index offset 5-tuple	ID

Object Restrictions:

Source image structure	MON, COLR
Destination image structure	Same as source image structure
Source image data type	BD, ND, SD
Destination image data type	Same as source image data type

Figure 2-24 Example of subsample operation. destination, 2:1 subsampling of "toys red band," "toys green band," "toys blue band," and "toys luminance" source images

Remarks:

1. For geometric operators, all image pixels are assumed to be of unit dimension. The geometric origin along a coordinate direction is at the centre of the pixel with index value zero. The geometric bounds of the origin pixel are –0.5 to 0.5.

2. The offset coordinates need not be integer valued.

3. Positive offset values shift a source image pixel plane right and down with respect to its origin.

4. The index offset 5-tuple contains parameters of the RD data type.

5. There is no translation along the band index of a colour image.

Nomenclature:

$S(x, y, 0, 0, b)$	$X_S \times Y_S \times 1 \times 1 \times B$ source image
$D(x, y, 0, 0, b)$	$X_D \times Y_D \times 1 \times 1 \times B$ destination image
x_o	Horizontal index offset
y_o	Vertical index offset

Definition:

The *translate* operator is based upon a two-stage algorithm. In the first stage, a reverse address calculation is made whereby $(x', y', 0, 0, b)$ source image coordinates are calculated for integer values of the destination image coordinates $(x, y, 0, 0, b)$. In general, the $(x', y', 0, 0, b)$ coordinates are not integer valued. The second stage of the algorithm entails two-dimensional resampling of each source image band to evaluate the destination image at integer coordinates. Nearest neighbour and bilinear interpolation resampling are supported in PIKS Foundation through the *set_globals* mechanism. The *translate* operator is defined as follows:

For all b and for x and y in the range

$$\text{MAX}\{0, x_o\} \leq x \leq \text{MIN}\{X - 1, X - 1 + x_o\}$$
$$\text{MAX}\{0, y_o\} \leq y \leq \text{MIN}\{Y - 1, Y - 1 + y_o\}$$

$$D(x, y, 0, 0, b) = \text{RES}_2\{S, x - x_o, y - y_o, 0, 0, b\}$$

otherwise

$$D(x, y, 0, 0, b) = 0$$

The maxima function, MAX, and the minima function, MIN, are defined in Appendix A. The function RES_2, which denotes the two-dimensional resampling operation, is also defined in Appendix A.

Tuple specification:

The index offset 5-tuple has the following conceptual data structure:

5
RD
x_o
y_o
0.0
0.0
0.0

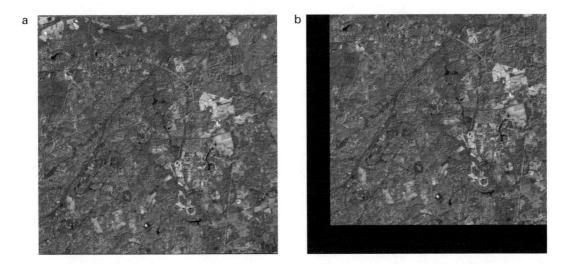

a   b

Figure 2-25   Example of translate operation: (a) source, "landsat infrared"; (b) destination, translation by (50.3, –60.5)

Example:

Figure 2-25 shows an example of the translation of an 8-bit, ND data type, monochrome image by an x axis offset of 50.3 pixels and a y axis offset of –60.5 pixels for bilinear interpolation resampling.

2.4.10   *Translate ROI*   `InTranslateROI`

The *translate_roi* operator performs a spatial translation of a ROI with respect to its origin.

Element input parameters:

Description	Data type
Source ROI	ID
Destination ROI	ID
Index offset 5-tuple	ID

Object Restrictions:

Source ROI structure	ROI_RECT
Destination ROI structure	ROI_RECT
Source ROI data type	BD
Destination ROI data type	BD

Remarks:

1. For geometric operators, all ROI pixels are assumed to be of unit dimension. The geometric origin along a coordinate direction is at the centre of the pixel with index value zero. The geometric bounds of the origin pixel are –0.5 to 0.5.

2. The offset coordinates need not be integer valued.

3. Positive offset values shift a source ROI pixel plane right and down with respect to its origin.

4. The parameter tuples contain parameters of the RD data type.

Nomenclature:

$R_S(x, y)$	$X_S \times Y_S$ source ROI virtual array
$R_D(x, y)$	$X_D \times Y_D$ destination ROI virtual array
x_o	Horizontal index offset
y_o	Vertical index offset

Definition:

The *translate_roi* operator is based upon a two-stage algorithm. In the first stage, a reverse address calculation is made whereby (x', y') source ROI coordinates are calculated for integer values of the destination ROI coordinates (x, y). In general, the (x', y') coordinates are not integer valued. The second stage of the algorithm entails two-dimensional resampling of the ROI to evaluate the destination ROI at integer coordinates. Only nearest neighbour ROI resampling is supported in PIKS Foundation. The *translate_roi* operator is defined as follows:

For all x and y in the range

$$\text{MAX}\{0, x_o\} \leq x \leq \text{MIN}\{X-1, X-1+x_o\}$$
$$\text{MAX}\{0, y_o\} \leq y \leq \text{MIN}\{Y-1, Y-1+y_o\}$$

$$R_D(x, y) = \text{RES}_2\{R_S, x-x_o, y-y_o\}$$

otherwise

$$R_D(x, y) = \text{FALSE}$$

The maxima function, MAX, and the minima function, MIN, are defined in Appendix A. The function RES_2, which denotes the two-dimensional resampling operation, is also defined in Appendix A.

Tuple specification:

See Section 2.4.9.

2.4.11 Zoom   InZoom

The *zoom* operator performs spatial zooming of an image by magnifying its pixel planes by integer scale factors.

Element input parameters:

Description	Data type
Source image	ID
Destination image	ID
Zoom factor 5-tuple	ID

Object Restrictions:

Source image structure	MON, COLR
Destination image structure	Same as source image structure
Source image data type	BD, ND, SD
Destination image data type	Same as source image data type

Remarks:

1. For geometric operators, all image pixels are assumed to be of unit dimension. The geometric origin along a coordinate direction is at the centre of the pixel with index value zero. The geometric bounds of the origin pixel are –0.5 to 0.5.

2. The zoom factor 5-tuple contains parameters of the ND data type.

3. There is no zooming along the band index of a colour image.

Nomenclature:

$S(x, y, 0, 0, b)$	$X_S \times Y_S \times 1 \times 1 \times B$ source image
$D(x, y, 0, 0, b)$	$X_D \times Y_D \times 1 \times 1 \times B$ destination image
S_x	Horizontal index scale factor
S_y	Vertical index scale factor

Definition:

For all b and for all x_D and y_D in the range

$$0 \leq x_D \leq (S_x)(X_D)$$
$$0 \leq y_D \leq (S_y)(Y_D)$$

$$D(x_D, y_D, 0, 0, b) = S(x_S, y_S, 0, 0, b)$$

where

$$x_S = \text{LIV}\left[\frac{x_D - \text{MOD}\{x_D, S_x\}}{S_x}\right]$$

$$y_S = \text{LIV}\left[\frac{y_D - \text{MOD}\{y_D, S_y\}}{S_y}\right]$$

The lowest integer value function, LIV, is defined in Appendix A.

Tuple specification:

The zoom scale factor 5-tuple has the following conceptual data structure:

5
ND
S_x
S_y
1
1
1

Example:

Figure 2-26 illustrates the zooming of an 8-bit, ND data type, monochrome by a a factor of 2:1 along the x axis and by a factor of 1:1 along the y axis.

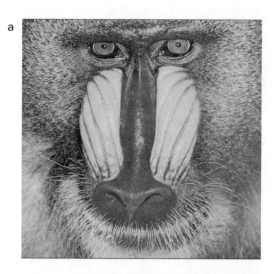

a

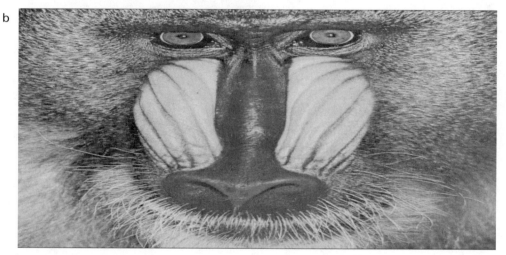

b

Figure 2-26 Example of zoom operation: (a) source, "mandrill luminance"; (b) destination, 2:1 horizontal and 1:1 vertical zoom

2.4.12 *Zoom ROI*   InZoomROI

The *zoom_roi* operator performs spatial zooming of a ROI by magnifying its pixel planes by integer scale factors.

Element input parameters:

Description	Data type
Source ROI	ID
Destination ROI	ID
Zoom factor 5-tuple	ID

Object Restrictions:

Source ROI structure	ROI_RECT
Destination ROI structure	ROI_RECT
Source ROI data type	BD
Destination ROI data type	BD

Remark:

1. For geometric operators, all ROI pixels are assumed to be of unit dimension. The geometric origin along a coordinate direction is at the centre of the pixel with index value zero. The geometric bounds of the origin pixel are −0.5 to 0.5.

2. The zoom factor 5-tuple contains parameters of the ND data type.

Nomenclature:

$R_S(x, y)$	$X_S \times Y_S$ source ROI virtual array
$R_D(x, y)$	$X_D \times Y_D$ destination ROI virtual array
S_x	Horizontal index scale factor
S_y	Vertical index scale factor

Definition:

For all x_D and y_D in the range

$$0 \leq x_D \leq (S_x)(X_D)$$
$$0 \leq y_D \leq (S_y)(Y_D)$$

$$R_D(x_D, y_D) = R_S(x_S, y_S)$$

where

$$x_S = \text{LIV} \left[\frac{x_D - \text{MOD}\{x_D, S_x\}}{S_x} \right]$$

$$y_S = \text{LIV} \left[\frac{y_D - \text{MOD}\{y_D, S_y\}}{S_y} \right]$$

The modulo function, MOD, and the lowest integer value function, LIV, are defined in Appendix A.

Tuple specification:

See Section 2.4.11.

2.5 Presentation Operators

This section describes the presentation operators. These operators manipulate an image to prepare it for display on a frame buffer.

2.5.1 Diffuse

The *diffuse* operator performs error diffusion halftoning on a source image to reduce the number of amplitude levels per pixel in a destination image.

Element input parameters:

Description	Data type
Source image	ID
Destination image	ID
Destination amplitude level *B*-tuple	ID

Object Restrictions:

Source image structure	MON, COLR
Destination image structure	MON
Source image data type	ND
Destination image data type	ND

Remark:

The amplitude level *B*-tuple contains parameters of the ND data type.

Nomenclature:

$S(x, y, 0, 0, b)$	$X \times Y \times 1 \times 1 \times B$ source image
$D(x, y, 0, 0, b)$	$X \times Y \times 1 \times 1 \times B$ destination image
$E(x, y, 0, 0, b)$	$X \times Y \times 1 \times 1 \times B$ diffusion image
R	Maximum value of implementation ND data type, $R \geq 1$
$V(b)$	Number of destination amplitude levels of bth pixel plane, $1 \leq V(b) \leq R$; $V(b)$ is the bth data element of the B-tuple
$Q(b)$	Source quantization scale factor of bth pixel plane, $0.0 \leq Q(b) \leq 1.0$
$C(b)$	Stride value of bth pixel plane

Definition:

The *diffuse* operator converts the integer range of pixels in the pixel planes corresponding to the bth index of a source image to a monochrome destination image with a virtual number, $V(b)$, of amplitude levels per pixel plane. This is accomplished by scaling source pixels and spatially distributing the roundoff error to neighbouring pixels based upon the Floyd-Steinberg error diffusion method.

The factor, $Q(b)$, quantizes the source image so that it only contains the requested number of quantization levels. The product of $Q(b)$ and $S(x, y, 0, 0, b)$ is truncated to its maximum quantization level. The value $C(b)$ denotes the stride increment in output value required to give the next higher value of the bth pixel plane.

If the source image has multiple pixel planes corresponding to the bth index, i.e., $B > 1$, the destination image must be passed through a B-dimensional pseudocolour lookup table for display presentation.

Let

$$C(0) = 1$$

and for $b > 0$

$$C(b) = [V(b-1)][V(b-2)] \dots [V(0)]$$

For all b

$$Q(b) = \frac{R}{V(b)}$$

For all $x, y, b,$

$$E(x, y, 0, 0, b) = \frac{7}{16} \text{MOD} \{ S(x-1, y, 0, 0, b), Q(b) \}$$

$$+ \frac{3}{16} \text{MOD} \{ S(x+1, y-1, 0, 0, b), Q(b) \}$$

$$+ \frac{5}{16} \text{MOD} \{ S(x, y-1, 0, 0, b), Q(b) \}$$

$$+ \frac{1}{16} \text{MOD} \{ S(x-1, y-1, 0, 0, b), Q(b) \}$$

then

$$D(x, y, 0, 0, 0) = \sum_{b=0}^{B-1} [C(b)] [\text{LIV} \{ (S(x, y, 0, 0, b)) / Q(b) \}]$$

$$+ \text{LIV} \{ [2] [E(x, y, 0, 0, b) / Q(b)] \}$$

The modulo function, MOD, and the lowest integer value function, LIV, are defined in Appendix A.

Tuple specification:

The destination amplitude level B-tuple has the following conceptual data structure:

B
ND
Value 1
Value 2
.
.
Value B

2.5.2   *Dither*

The *dither* operator performs ordered dither halftoning on a source image to reduce the number of amplitude levels per pixel in a destination image.

Element input parameters:

Description	Data type
Source image	ID
Destination image	ID
Dither Neighbourhood array	ID
Destination amplitude level *B*-tuple	ID

Object Restrictions:

Source image structure	MON, COLR
Destination image structure	MON
Array structure	NBHOOD_ARRAY
Source image data type	ND
Destination image data type	ND
Array data type	RD

Remarks:

1. The data object repository contains the following dither arrays:
DITHER_2x2	2×2 dither array
DITHER_4x4	4×4 dither array
DITHER_8x8	8×8 dither array
DITHER_16x16	16×16 dither array

2. The amplitude level *B*-tuple contains parameters of the ND data type.

Nomenclature:

$S(x, y, 0, 0, b)$	$X \times Y \times 1 \times 1 \times B$ source image
$D(x, y, 0, 0, b)$	$X \times Y \times 1 \times 1 \times B$ destination image
$A(c, r)$	$W \times W$ dither array, $0.0 \leq A(c, r) \leq 1.0$
W	Dither array size
R	Maximum value of implementation ND data type, $R \geq 1$
$V(b)$	Number of destination amplitude levels of *b*th pixel plane, $1 \leq V(b) \leq R$; $V(b)$ is the *b*th data element of the *B*-tuple.
$Q(b)$	Source quantization scale factor of *b*th pixel plane, $0.0 \leq Q(b) \leq 1.0$
$C(b)$	Stride value of *b*th pixel plane

Definition:

The *dither* operator converts the integer range of pixels in the band pixel planes corresponding to the *b*th index of a source image to a monochrome destination image with a virtual number, $V(b)$, of amplitude levels per pixel plane. This is accomplished by scaling source pixels and spatially distributing the roundoff error to neighbouring pixels based upon a dither array, $A(c, r)$.

The factor, $Q(b)$, quantizes the source image so that it only contains the requested number of quantization levels. The product of $Q(b)$ and $S(x, y, 0, 0, b)$ is truncated to its maximum quantization level. The value $C(b)$ denotes the stride increment in output value required to give the next higher value of the bth pixel plane.

If the source image has multiple pixel planes corresponding to the bth index, i.e., $B > 1$, the destination image must be passed through an B-dimensional pseudocolour lookup table for display presentation.

For all x, y set

$$D(x, y, 0, 0, 0) = 0$$

For all x, y, b, if

$$MOD\{S(x, y, 0, 0, b), Q(b)\} > [Q(b)][A(MOD\{x, W\}, MOD\{y, W\})]$$

then

$$D(x, y, 0, 0, 0) = D(x, y, 0, 0, 0) + [C(b)][1 + LIV\{[S(x, y, 0, 0, b)][Q(b)]\}]$$

else

$$D(x, y, 0, 0, 0) = D(x, y, 0, 0, 0) + [C(b)][LIV\{S(x, y, 0, 0, b)\}/[Q(b)\}]$$

where

$$Q(b) = \frac{R}{V(b)}$$

$$C(b) = [V(b-1)][V(b-2)]...[V(0)]$$

with

$$C(0) = 1$$

The modulo function, MOD, and the lowest integer value function, LIV, are defined in Appendix A.

Tuple specification:

See Section 2.3.1.

2.6   Colour Operators

This section describes the PIKS colour operators. These operators convert a colour image from one colour space to another and generate the luminance component of a colour image.

2.6.1   *Colour Conversion, Linear*   InColourConvLin

The *colour_conversion_linear* operator performs linear interband colour conversion of a trichromatic colour image between colour spaces.

Element input parameters:

Description	Data type
Source image	ID
Destination image	ID
Colour transformation matrix	ID, NULL

Object Restrictions:

Source image structure	COLR
Destination image structure	COLR
Matrix structure	MATRIX
Source image data type	SD
Destination image data type	Same as source image data type
Matrix data type	SD, RD

Remarks:

1. The red, green, and blue colour components are assumed to be stored in bands 0, 1, and 2, respectively, of a RGB colour image.

2. Colour conversions within "video" colour spaces, e.g., RGB to and from YIQ, assume gamma corrected (point nonlinear) RGB components.

3. Colour conversions within "colourimetry" colour spaces and between video and colourimetry colour spaces, e.g., RGB to and from XYZ, assume point linear RGB colour components.

4. The *colour_conversion_linear* operator does not perform point transformations that gamma correct linear components or that linearize gamma corrected components.

5. The PIKS data object repository contains a collection of 3×3 colour transformation matrices for conversion between commonly used colour space. These are listed in the following tables by their repository indices.

6. If the matrix identifier is NULL, the appropriate transformation matrix in the data object repository is used in the colour conversion based upon the source and destination image colour space codes.

Nomenclature:

$S(x, y, 0, 0, b)$	$X \times Y \times 1 \times 1 \times B$ source image
$D(x, y, 0, 0, b)$	$X \times Y \times 1 \times 1 \times B$ destination image
$M(r, c)$	General term of 3×3 colour conversion matrix

Definition:

For all x, y

$$\begin{bmatrix} D(x, y, 0, 0, 0) \\ D(x, y, 0, 0, 1) \\ D(x, y, 0, 0, 2) \end{bmatrix} = \begin{bmatrix} M(1, 1) & M(1, 2) & M(1, 3) \\ M(2, 1) & M(2, 2) & M(2, 3) \\ M(3, 1) & M(3, 2) & M(3, 3) \end{bmatrix} \begin{bmatrix} S(x, y, 0, 0, 0) \\ S(x, y, 0, 0, 1) \\ S(x, y, 0, 0, 2) \end{bmatrix}$$

Example:

Colour image Plate 1 shows the result of the conversion of an 8-bit per band, ND data type, colour image from NTSC illuminant C colour space to NTSC illuminant D65 Colour space. The source image has been converted to SD data types, then colour converted, and the resultant SD data type image has been converted to ND data type.

2.6.2 Colour Conversion, Subtractive InColourConvSubtractive

The *colour_conversion_subtractive* operator performs a conversion of a colour image between additive uncalibrated RGB and subtractive uncalibrated CMY or CMYK colour spaces.

Element input parameters:

Description	Data type
Source image	ID
Destination image	ID
Blackness factor	RP, NULL
Maximum integer size	NP, NULL
Method information	IP, NULL

Conversion option
  RGB to CMY
  RGB to CMYK
  CMY to RGB
  CMYK to RGB
	SP

Method option
  simple
  implementation-dependent
	SP

Object Restrictions:

Source image structure	COLR
Destination image structure	COLR
Source image data type	ND, SD
Destination image data type	Same as source image data type

Remarks:

1. The red, green, and blue colour components are assumed to be stored in bands 0, 1, and 2, respectively, of a RGB colour image.

2. The cyan, magenta, yellow, and black colour components are assumed to be stored in bands 0, 1, 2, and 3, respectively, of a CMYK colour image.

3. The appropriate colour space image attribute information is entered in the image attribute list of the destination image if the entry is NULL.

4. This operator provides a simple conversion method or access to a nonstandardized, implementation-dependent conversion method.

Nomenclature:

$S(x, y, 0, 0, b)$	$X \times Y \times 1 \times 1 \times B$ source image, $S \geq 0$
$D(x, y, 0, 0, b)$	$X \times Y \times 1 \times 1 \times B$ destination image, $D \geq 0$
f	Blackness factor, $0 \leq f \leq 1.0$
I	Maximum integer positive amplitude value

Definition:

Simple conversion method:

For all x, y

RGB to CMY conversion:

$D(x, y, 0, 0, 0) = I - S(x, y, 0, 0, 0)$
$D(x, y, 0, 0, 1) = I - S(x, y, 0, 0, 1)$
$D(x, y, 0, 0, 2) = I - S(x, y, 0, 0, 2)$

RGB to CMYK conversion:

$D(x, y, 0, 0, 3) = (f) \text{MIN}\{I - S(x, y, 0, 0, 0), I - S(x, y, 0, 0, 1), I - S(x, y, 0, 0, 2)\}$
$D(x, y, 0, 0, 0) = I - S(x, y, 0, 0, 0) - D(x, y, 0, 0, 3)$
$D(x, y, 0, 0, 1) = I - S(x, y, 0, 0, 1) - D(x, y, 0, 0, 3)$
$D(x, y, 0, 0, 2) = I - S(x, y, 0, 0, 2) - D(x, y, 0, 0, 3)$

CMY to RGB conversion:

$D(x, y, 0, 0, 0) = I - S(x, y, 0, 0, 0)$
$D(x, y, 0, 0, 1) = I - S(x, y, 0, 0, 1)$
$D(x, y, 0, 0, 2) = I - S(x, y, 0, 0, 2)$

CMYK to RGB conversion:

$D(x, y, 0, 0, 0) = I - S(x, y, 0, 0, 0) - S(x, y, 0, 0, 3)$
$D(x, y, 0, 0, 1) = I - S(x, y, 0, 0, 1) - S(x, y, 0, 0, 3)$
$D(x, y, 0, 0, 2) = I - S(x, y, 0, 0, 2) - S(x, y, 0, 0, 3)$

The minima function, MIN, is defined in Appendix A.

Implementation-dependent method:

The method information identifier provides access to all parameters required for the implementation-dependent method.

Example:

Figure 2-27 shows the ND data type red, green, and blue bands of the "toys colour" image of Plate 1 and the cyan, magenta, and yellow monochrome component images after the colour conversion, subtractive operation.

2.6.3   *Luminance Generation*   InLumGeneration

The *luminance_generation* operator generates a luminance image from a trichromatic colour image.

Element input parameters:

Description	Data type
Source image	ID
Destination image	ID

Figure 2-27 Example of colour conversion, subtractive operation: (a) source red component, "toys red band"; (b) source green component, "toys green band"; (c) source blue component, "toys blue band"; (d) destination, *C* component; (e) destination, *M* component; (f) destination, *Y* component

Description	Data type
RGB Colour option	SP
linear CCIR illuminant D65 RGB	
linear CIE illuminant E RGB	
linear EBU illuminant C RGB	
linear EBU illuminant D65 RGB	
linear NTSC illuminant C RGB	
linear NTSC illuminant D65 RGB	
linear SMPTE illuminant D65 RGB	
gamma EBU illuminant C RGB	
gamma EBU illuminant D65 RGB	
gamma NTSC illuminant C RGB	
gamma NTSC illuminant D65 RGB	
gamma SMPTE illuminant D65 RGB	

Object Restrictions:

Source image structure	COLR
Destination image structure	MON
Source image data type	ND, SD
Destination image data type	Same as source image data type

Remark:

The red, green, and blue components are assumed to be stored in bands 0, 1, and 2, respectively, of the RGB colour image.

Nomenclature:

$S(x, y, 0, 0, b)$	$X \times Y \times 1 \times 1 \times B$ source image
$D(x, y, 0, 0, b)$	$X \times Y \times 1 \times 1 \times B$ destination image
c_0	Band zero weighting factor
c_1	Band one weighting factor
c_2	Band two weighting factor

Definition:

For all x, y

$$D(x, y, 0, 0, 0) = (c_0)[S(x, y, 0, 0, 0)] + (c_1)[S(x, y, 0, 0, 1)] + (c_2)[S(x, y, 0, 0, 2)]$$

where the conversion factors are listed in the following table.

RGB to luminance conversion factors

Option	Weighting factors		
	c_0	c_1	c_2
ILUM_LIN_CCIR_D65_RGB	0.21261719	0.71520276	0.07218005
ILUMR_LIN_CIE_E_RGB	0.17701522	0.81232418	0.01066060
ILUM_LIN_EBU_C_RGB	0.23272304	0.68867804	0.07859892
ILUM_LIN_EBU_D65_RGB	0.22198294	0.70668844	0.07132862
ILUM_LIN_NTSC_C_RGB	0.29889531	0.58662247	0.11448223
ILUM_LIN_NTSC_D65_RGB	0.28964261	0.60567484	0.10468256
ILUM_LIN_SMPTE_D65_RGB	0.21235295	0.70109788	0.08654917
ILUM_GAMMA_EBU C_RGB	0.29900000	0.58700000	0.11400000
ILUM_GAMMA_EBU_65_RGB	0.29900000	0.58700000	0.11400000
ILUM_GAMMA_NTSC_C_RGB	0.29889531	0.58662247	0.11448223
ILUM_GAMMA_NTSC_D65_RGB	0.29889531	0.58662247	0.11448223
ILUM_GAMMA_SMPTE_D65_RGB	0.29900000	0.58700000	0.11400000

Example:

Figure 2-28 shows the luminance representation of the 8-bit per band, ND data type, "toys colour" image of Plate 1.

Figure 2-28 Example of luminance conversion operation. Destination, NTSC Illuminant C luminance image of "toys colour"

2.7 Pixel Modification Operator

This section describes the pixel modification operator.

2.7.1 Draw Pixels

InDrawPixels

The *draw_pixels* operator inserts pixels specified by an external array into an image.

Element input parameters:

Description	Data type
Pixel collection	IP
Destination image	ID
Number of array entries	NP

Object Restrictions:

Pixel collection structure	EXT
Destination image structure	MON, COLR
Pixel collection data type	See Remarks
Destination image data type	BD, ND, SD

Remarks:

1. If a pixel coordinate is repeated in the collection, the previous pixel value is overwritten by the later pixel value.

2. The collection data type is ND for pixel coordinates and the same as the destination image for pixel values.

Nomenclature:

$S(x, y, 0, 0, b)$	$X \times Y \times 1 \times 1 \times B$ source image
E	Number of entries in external array
$p_v(e)$	eth pixel value, $0 \le e \le E - 1$
$x_v(e)$	eth x index value, $0 \le e \le E - 1$
$y_v(e)$	eth y index value, $0 \le e \le E - 1$
$b_v(e)$	eth b index value, $0 \le e \le E - 1$

Definition:

Each pixel value in the collection is recorded in the destination image at the corresponding value of its coordinates with respect to the destination image origin.

For all $0 \le e \le E - 1$

$$D[x_v(e), y_v(e), 0, 0, b_v(e)] = p_v(e)$$

and $D(x, y, 0, 0, b)$ is unchanged otherwise.

The external collection is defined as follows:

$x_v(0)$	$y_v(0)$	0	0	$b_v(0)$
.	.	.	.	.
.	.	.	.	.
.	.	.	.	.
$x_v(e)$	$y_v(e)$	0	0	$b_v(e)$
.	.	.	.	.
.	.	.	.	.
.	.	.	.	.
$x_v(E-1)$	$y_v(E-1)$	0	0	$b_v(E-1)$

2.8 Analysis Operators

This section describes the analysis operators. These operators extract information from an image.

2.8.1 Accumulator   `ItraAccumulator`

The *accumulator* operator accumulates amplitudes of pixels of an image.

Element input parameters:

Description	Data type
Source image	ID
Accumulation mode	SP
zero	
one	
two	
three	
four	

Element output parameters:

Description	Data type
Sum of pixels external array	IP

Object Restrictions:

Source image structure	MON, COLR
Array structure	EXT
Source image data type	ND, SD
Array data type	RP

Nomenclature:

$S(x, y, 0, 0, b)$	$X \times Y \times 1 \times 1 \times B$ source image
a	Sum of pixels in image
$a(b)$	Sum of pixels in bth band
$a(y, b)$	Sum of pixels in yth row and bth band

Definition:

Accumulation mode zero – sum of pixels in image:

$$a = \sum_{x=0}^{X-1} \sum_{y=0}^{Y-1} \sum_{b=0}^{B-1} S(x, y, 0, 0, b)$$

Accumulation modes one, two, and three – sum of pixels in each band:

$$a(b) = \sum_{x=0}^{X-1} \sum_{y=0}^{Y-1} S(x, y, 0, 0, b)$$

Accumulation mode four – sum of pixels in each image row:

$$a(y, b) = \sum_{x=0}^{X-1} S(x, y, 0, 0, b)$$

Example:

The following are the accumulation results for the "toys colour" image.

Mode zero:

$a = 88, 917, 714$

Mode one:

$a(0) = 28, 400, 748$
$a(1) = 29, 701, 148$
$a(2) = 30, 815, 818$

2.8.2 *Extrema*   IvExtrema

The *extrema* operator detects the smallest and largest pixels of an image and records their values in an external array.

Element input parameters:

Description	Data type
Source image	ID
Extrema mode option	SP
zero	
one	
two	
three	
four	

Element output parameters:

Description	Data type
Minima external array	IP
Maxima external array	IP

Object Restrictions:

Source image structure	MON, COLR
Minima array structure	EXT
Maxima array structure	EXT
Source image data type	ND, SD
Minima array data type	RP
Maxima array data type	RP

Nomenclature:

$S(x, y, 0, 0, b)$	$X \times Y \times 1 \times 1 \times B$ source image
x_n	x index value of smallest pixel
y_n	y index value of smallest pixel
b_n	b index value of smallest pixel
x_m	x index value of largest pixel
y_m	y index value of largest pixel
b_m	b index value of largest pixel

Definition:

For all x, y, b, the source image is searched for the smallest and largest pixels, and the following maxima and minima arrays are created.

Extrema mode zero – extrema of image:

$$S(x_n, y_n, 0, 0, b_n) \qquad\qquad S(x_m, y_m, 0, 0, b_m)$$

Extrema modes one, two, three – extrema along each image band:

$$S(x_n, y_n, 0, 0, 0) \qquad\qquad S(x_m, y_m, 0, 0, 0)$$
$$\cdot \qquad\qquad\qquad\qquad \cdot$$
$$\cdot \qquad\qquad\qquad\qquad \cdot$$
$$\cdot \qquad\qquad\qquad\qquad \cdot$$
$$S(x_n, y_n, 0, 0, B-1) \qquad\qquad S(x_m, y_m, 0, 0, B-1)$$

Extrema mode four – extrema along each image row:

$$S(x_n, 0, 0, 0, 0) \qquad\qquad S(x_m, 0, 0, 0, 0)$$
$$\cdot \qquad\qquad\qquad\qquad \cdot$$
$$\cdot \qquad\qquad\qquad\qquad \cdot$$
$$\cdot \qquad\qquad\qquad\qquad \cdot$$
$$S(x_n, Y-1, 0, 0, B-1) \qquad\qquad S(x_m, Y-1, 0, 0, B-1)$$

Example:

The following are the extrema values of the "toys colour" image.

Component	Min	Max
Red	0	251
Green	0	255
Blue	0	251

2.8.3   *Histogram, One-dimensional*   InHist1D

The *histogram_1d* operator generates a one-dimensional histogram of an image.

Element input parameters:

Description	Data type
Source image	ID
Histogram	ID
Number of histogram bins	NP
Lower amplitude bound	RP, NULL
Upper amplitude bound	RP, NULL
Histogram computation option specified limits image extrema limits	SP

Object Restrictions:

Source image structure	MON, COLR
Histogram structure	HIST
Source image data type	ND, SD
Histogram data type	ND

Nomenclature:

$S(x, y, 0, 0, b)$	$X \times Y \times 1 \times 1 \times B$ source image
E	Number of histogram amplitude bins
$H(e)$	Histogram array, $0 \le e \le E - 1$
L	Lower amplitude bound
U	Upper amplitude bound

Definition:

The histogram array contains the counts of the number of pixels that have certain quantized amplitude values. The histogram algorithm is as follows:

Step 1: Initialize histogram to zero.

For $0 \le e \le E - 1$

$H(e) = 0$

Step 2: Compute histogram.

For all x, y, b, and for $0 \leq e \leq E - 1$, if a pixel lies within the eth quantization levels

$$q(e) \leq S(x, y, 0, 0, b) < q(e + 1)$$

then increment the histogram array by one

$$H(e) = H(e) + 1$$

where for specified histogram amplitude bounds

$$q(e) = \frac{e[U - L]}{E} + L$$

and for image extrema amplitude limits, with $0 < x < X - 1$ and $0 < y < Y - 1$

$$q(e) = \frac{e[\text{MAX}\{S(x, y, 0, 0, b)\} - \text{MIN}\{S(x, y, 0, 0, b)\}]}{E} + \text{MIN}\{S(x, y, 0, 0, b)\}$$

where the maxima function, MAX, and the minima function, MIN, are defined in Appendix A.

Example:

The following is a list of the histogram values of the "brainscan" image for 16 amplitude bins.

bin 0:	81, 543
bin 1:	18, 725
bin 2:	19, 885
bin 3:	22, 492
bin 4:	22, 303
bin 5:	22, 774
bin 6:	17, 293
bin 7:	7, 903
bin 8:	4, 690
bin 9:	3, 398
bin 10:	2, 554
bin 11:	1, 888
bin 12:	1, 203
bin 13:	1, 597
bin 14:	3, 617
bin 15:	30, 279

2.8.4 Moments

IvMoments

The *moments* operator computes the mean and standard deviation moments of an image.

Element input parameters:

Description	Data type
Source image	ID

Element output parameters:

Description	Data type
Mean value	RP
Standard deviation value	RP

Object Restrictions:

Source image structure	MON, COLR
Source image data type	ND, SD

Nomenclature:

$S(x, y, 0, 0, b)$	$X \times Y \times 1 \times 1 \times B$ source image
m	Image mean
s	Image standard deviation

Definition:

For all x, y, b

$$m = \frac{1}{XYB} \sum_{x=0}^{X-1} \sum_{y=0}^{Y-1} \sum_{b=0}^{B-1} S(x, y, 0, 0, b)$$

$$s = \left[\frac{1}{XYB} \sum_{x=0}^{X-1} \sum_{y=0}^{Y-1} \sum_{b=0}^{B-1} [S(x, y, 0, 0, b) - m]^2 \right]^{1/2}$$

Example:

The following are the mean and standard deviation values of the "brainscan" image.

Mean = 74.68
Deviation = 82.59

3

PIKS Tools

This chapter describes the functionality of PIKS tools that create images, ROIs, and other nonimage data objects.

3.1   Image and ROI Generation Tools

This section describes tools that generate images and ROIs.

3.1.1   *Image Constant* `InImageConstant`

The *image_constant* tool creates an image whose pixels have the same constant value.

Element input parameters:

Description	Data type
Destination image	ID
Image size 5-tuple	ID
Value of constant	BP, NP, SP
Destination data type option BD ND SD	SP

Object restrictions:

Destination image structure	MON, COLR
Destination image data type	BD, ND, SD

Remark:

The image size 5-tuple contains parameters of the ND data type.

Nomenclature:

$D(x, y, 0, 0, b)$	$X \times Y \times 1 \times 1 \times B$ destination image
c	Value of constant

Definition:

For all x, y, b

$$D(x, y, 0, 0, b) = c$$

Tuple Specification:

The image size 5-tuple has the following conceptual data structure:

5
ND
X
Y
1
1
B

3.1.2   *ROI Rectangular*   `InROIRectangular`

The *roi_rectangular* tool generates a rectangular-shaped ROI object.

Element input parameters:

Description	Data type
Destination ROI	ID
ROI size 5-tuple	ID
Start position 5-tuple	ID
End position 5-tuple	ID
Index manipulation 5-tuple	ID

Rectangle dimension option
    1D
    2D
	SP

Polarity option
    set TRUE
    set FALSE
	EP

Object restrictions:

Destination ROI structure	ROI_RECT
Destination ROI data type	BD

Remarks:

1. The ROI size, start position, and end position 5-tuples contain parameters of the ND data type.

2. The index manipulation 5-tuple for PIKS Foundation is a NULL identifier.

Nomenclature:

$R(x, y)$	$X \times Y$ destination ROI virtual array
x_s	Horizontal index start position
y_s	Vertical index start position
x_e	Horizontal index end position
y_e	Vertical index end position

Definition:

For all x, y

1D mode:

If $x_s \leq x \leq x_e$, then

$R(x, y)$ = TRUE   if polarity is set TRUE
$R(x, y)$ = FALSE   if polarity is set FALSE

otherwise

$R(x, y)$ = FALSE   if polarity is set TRUE
$R(x, y)$ = TRUE   if polarity is set FALSE

2D mode:

If $x_s \leq x \leq x_e$ and $y_s \leq y \leq y_e$, then

$R(x, y)$ = TRUE   if polarity is set TRUE
$R(x, y)$ = FALSE   if polarity is set FALSE

otherwise

$R(x, y)$ = FALSE   if polarity is set TRUE
$R(x, y)$ = TRUE   if polarity is set FALSE

Tuple Specifications:

The ROI size 5-tuple has the following conceptual data structure:

5
ND
X
Y
1
1
1

The ROI start position 5-tuple has the following conceptual data structure:

5
ND
x_s
y_s
0
0
0

The ROI end position 5-tuple has the following conceptual data structure:

5
ND
x_e
y_e
0
0
0

3.2 Nonimage Object Generation Tools

This section describes tools that generate nonimage data objects other than ROIs.

3.2.1 *Array to Lookup Table* InArrayToLUT

The *array_to_lut* tool inserts an external array of values into a lookup table at a specified index offset.

Element input parameters:

Description	Data type
Destination lookup table	ID
Source external array	IP
Lookup table entry offset	NP
Lookup table band offset	NP
Number of array columns	NP
Number of array rows	NP

Object restrictions:

Source array structure	EXT
Destination lookup table structure	LUT
Source external array data type	BP, NP, SP
Destination lookup table data type	BD, ND, SD

Remark:

The array data type must be of the same class as the lookup table data type.

Nomenclature:

$T(b, e)$	Lookup table array, $0 \le b \le B - 1$, $0 \le e \le E - 1$
e_o	Lookup table entry offset, $0 \le e_o \le E - 1$
b_o	Lookup table band offset, $0 \le b_o \le B - 1$
$A(c, r)$	External array, $0 \le c \le C - 1$, $0 \le r \le R - 1$
C	Number of array columns
R	Number of array rows

Definition:

For $0 \leq c \leq C - 1$, $0 \leq b \leq B - 1$

$$T(b_o + c, e_o + r) = A(c, r)$$

The external array has the following conceptual data structure:

$$
\begin{array}{ccccccc}
A(0, 0) & \cdots & A(c, 0) & \cdots & A(C - 1, 0) \\
\cdot & \cdot & & & \\
A(0, r) & \cdots & A(c, r) & \cdots & A(C - 1, r) \\
\cdot & \cdot & & & \\
A(0, R-1) & \cdots & A(c, R-1) & \cdots & A(C - 1, R - 1)
\end{array}
$$

3.2.2   *Colour Conversion Matrix*   `IvColourConvMatrix`

The *colour_conversion_matrix* tool generates 3×3 colour conversion matrices for conversion between XYZ and RGB colour spaces.

Element input parameters:

Description	Data type
Destination XYZ to RGB matrix	ID
Destination RGB to XYZ matrix	ID
Red primary x chromaticity coordinate	RP
Red primary y chromaticity coordinate	RP
Green primary x chromaticity coordinate	RP
Green primary y chromaticity coordinate	RP
Blue primary x chromaticity coordinate	RP
Blue primary y chromaticity coordinate	RP
White x chromaticity coordinate	RP
White y chromaticity coordinate	RP

Object restrictions:

Destination XYZ to RGB matrix structure	MATRIX
Destination RGB to XYZ matrix structure	MATRIX
Destination XYZ to RGB matrix data type	RD
Destination RGB to XYZ matrix data type	RD

Nomenclature:

x_R	Red primary x chromaticity coordinate
y_R	Red primary y chromaticity coordinate
z_R	Red primary z chromaticity coordinate
x_G	Green primary x chromaticity coordinate
y_G	Green primary y chromaticity coordinate
z_G	Green primary z chromaticity coordinate
x_B	Blue primary x chromaticity coordinate

y_B	Blue primary y chromaticity coordinate
z_B	Blue primary z chromaticity coordinate
x_W	White reference x chromaticity coordinate
y_W	White reference y chromaticity coordinate
z_W	White reference z chromaticity coordinate
$M(p, q)$	RGB to XYZ conversion matrix, $p, q = 1, 2, 3$
$N(p, q)$	XYZ to RGB conversion matrix, $p, q = 1, 2, 3$

Definition:

The following is a procedure for computing the colour conversion matrices.

Step 1:

Compute the colourimetric weighting coefficients, $a(i)$, for $i = 1, 2, 3$.

$$
\begin{bmatrix} a(1) \\ a(2) \\ a(3) \end{bmatrix} = \begin{bmatrix} x_R & x_G & x_B \\ y_R & y_G & v_B \\ z_R & z_G & z_B \end{bmatrix}^{-1} \begin{bmatrix} x_W/y_W \\ 1 \\ z_W/y_W \end{bmatrix}
$$

where

$$z_R = 1 - x_R - y_R$$
$$z_G = 1 - x_G - y_G$$
$$z_B = 1 - x_B - y_B$$
$$z_W = 1 - x_W - y_W$$

Step 2:

Compute the RGB to XYZ conversion matrix.

$$
\begin{bmatrix} M(1,1) & M(1,2) & M(1,3) \\ M(2,1) & M(2,2) & M(2,3) \\ M(3,1) & M(3,2) & M(3,3) \end{bmatrix} = \begin{bmatrix} x_R & x_G & x_B \\ y_R & y_G & y_B \\ z_R & z_G & z_B \end{bmatrix} \begin{bmatrix} a(1) & 0 & 0 \\ 0 & a(2) & 0 \\ 0 & 0 & a(3) \end{bmatrix}
$$

Step 3:

Compute the XYZ to RGB conversion matrix.

$$
\begin{bmatrix} N(1,1) & N(1,2) & N(1,3) \\ N(2,1) & N(2,2) & N(2,3) \\ N(3,1) & N(3,2) & N(3,3) \end{bmatrix} = \begin{bmatrix} M(1,1) & M(1,2) & M(1,3) \\ M(2,1) & M(2,2) & M(2,3) \\ M(3,1) & M(3,2) & M(3,3) \end{bmatrix}^{-1}
$$

Example:

The following chromaticity coordinates yield colour conversion matrices between the NTSC Illuminant C RGB and XYZ colour spaces.

$$
\begin{aligned}
x_R &= 0.670 & y_R &= 0.330 \\
x_G &= 0.210 & y_G &= 0.710 \\
x_B &= 0.140 & y_B &= 0.080 \\
x_W &= 0.310 & y_W &= 0.316
\end{aligned}
$$

RGB to XYZ:

$$
\begin{bmatrix}
0.606993 & 0.173449 & 0.200571 \\
0.298967 & 0.586421 & 0.114612 \\
0.000000 & 0.066076 & 1.117469
\end{bmatrix}
$$

XYZ to RGB:

$$
\begin{bmatrix}
1.909675 & -0.532365 & -0.288161 \\
-0.984965 & 1.999776 & -0.028316 \\
0.058241 & -0.118246 & 0.896554
\end{bmatrix}
$$

3.2.3 *Impulse Rectangular*   `InImpulseRectangular`

The *impulse_rectangular* tool generates a uniform amplitude rectangular-shaped two-dimensional impulse response function neighbourhood array object.

Element input parameters:

Description	Data type
Destination impulse response array	ID
Array size 5-tuple	ID
Key pixel 5-tuple	ID

Object restrictions:

Destination impulse array structure	NBHOOD_ARRAY
Destination impulse array data type	SD

Remarks:

1. The key pixel associated with the neighbourhood array is used by some operators as a reference point of the impulse response function array.

2. The array size 5-tuple contains parameters of the ND data type.

3. The key pixel 5-tuple contains parameters of the SD data type.

Nomenclature:

$A(c, r)$	$C \times R$ impulse response array
C	Number of array columns
R	Number of array rows
c_k	Column key pixel coordinate
r_k	Row key pixel coordinate

Definition:

For all c and r

$$A(c, r) = \frac{1}{RC}$$

Tuple specifications:

The array size 5-tuple has the following conceptual data structure:

5
ND
C
R
1
1
1

The key pixel 5-tuple has the following conceptual data structure:

5
SD
c_k
r_k
0
0
0

4

PIKS Mechanisms

This chapter describes the functionality of PIKS mechanisms that perform system control, allocate and deallocate data objects, inquire about the state of PIKS and its objects, and perform error reporting.

4.1   Control Mechanisms

This section describes the PIKS control mechanisms that open and close PIKS sessions.

4.1.1   Close PIKS   `IvClosePIKS`

The *close_piks* mechanism performs normal closure of a PIKS session.

Element parameters:

None

Definition:

This control mechanism deallocates all previously allocated PIKS data objects, terminates all PIKS functionality, and returns control to the application.

4.1.2   Close PIKS Emergency   `IvClosePIKSEmergency`

The *close_piks_emergency* mechanism performs an emergency closure of a PIKS session.

Element parameters:

None

Definition:

When a fatal error occurs, this control mechanism deallocates all previously allocated PIKS data objects, terminates all PIKS functionality, and returns control to the application if possible.

4.1.3   Open PIKS   `IvOpenPIKS`

The *open_piks* mechanism opens a PIKS session.

Element input parameters:

Description	Data type
Error file identifier	IP

Definition:

This control mechanism initiates a PIKS session. It initializes the PIKS state tables, establishes default global element control modes, and sets the PIKS state to *PIKS_OPEN*.

The following are the PIKS Foundation default global control settings:

State	Default
ROI control	ROI control disengaged
Image resampling selection	Support 1 constant (nearest neighbour)
ROI resampling selection	Support 1 constant (nearest neighbour)

The application is responsible for allocating the error file.

4.2   Allocation and Deallocation Mechanisms

This section describes the PIKS data object allocation and deallocation mechanisms. All PIKS data objects must be allocated prior to their usage. When a data object is allocated, certain object attributes, e.g., image size, may be left unspecified. These unspecified attributes will be given values by PIKS elements using the data objects upon invocation of the element according to parameter specifications of the element. For example, the size of a destination image for the *zoom* operator may be left unspecified upon its allocation. When the *zoom* operator is invoked, the destination image size will be set by the *zoom* operator based upon knowledge of the source image size and the zoom parameters. If PIKS element parameter specifications do not match specified data object attributes, an error indication will be issued.

4.2.1   *Allocate Histogram*   `InAllocateHist`

The *allocate_histogram* mechanism allocates a reference to a histogram object and creates its attributes.

Element input parameters:

Description	Data type
histogram size	NP, NULL
Lower amplitude bound	RP, NULL
Upper amplitude bound	RP, NULL

Element output parameters:

Description	Data type
Histogram identifier	ID

Object restrictions:

Object structure   HIST
Object data type   ND

Definition:

This mechanism returns a histogram object identifier to the application and creates the object attributes if this information is specified as input parameters.

Upon allocation, the histogram object attributes collection has the following conceptual data structure:

NULL or histogram size value
NULL or lower amplitude bound value
NULL or upper amplitude band value

4.2.2 *Allocate Image*   `InAllocateImage`

The *allocate_image* mechanism allocates a reference to an image object and creates representation, channel, and colour descriptor attributes.

Element input parameters:

Description	Data type
Image size 5-tuple	ID, NULL
Band data type *B*-tuple	ID, NULL
Band precision *B*-tuple	ID, NULL
X tristimulus value white point	RP, NULL
Y tristimulus value white point	RP, NULL
Z tristimulus value white point	RP, NULL
Image structure option MON COLR	SP, NULL
Colour space option unspecified nonstandard RGB linear CCIR illuminant D65 RGB linear CIE illuminant E RGB linear EBU illuminant C RGB linear EBU illuminant D65 RGB linear NTSC illuminant C RGB linear NTSC illuminant D65 RGB linear SMPTE illuminant D65 RGB	SP, NULL

Description	Data type
gamma CCIR illuminant C RGB	
gamma EBU illuminant C RGB	
gamma EBU illuminant D65 RGB	
gamma NTSC illuminant C RGB	
gamma NTSC illuminant D65 RGB	
gamma SMPTE illuminant D65 RGB	
luminance/chrominance EBU illuminant C YUV	
luminance/chrominance EBU illuminant D65 YUV	
luminance/chrominance NTSC illuminant C YIQ	
luminance/chrominance NTSC illuminant D65 YIQ	
luminance/chrominance SMPTE illuminant D65 YCbCr	
CIE XYZ	
CIE UVW	
CIE Yxy	
CIE Yuv	
CIE L*a*b*	
CIE L*u*v*	
IHS	
CMY	
CMYK	

Element output parameters:

Description	Data type
Image identifier	ID

Object restrictions:

Image structure	As specified
Image data type	As specified

Remarks:

1. Each image attribute may be specified as NULL. In each instance, the attribute will be set when the image data is created by a PIKS element.

2. The band precision tuple of the channel descriptor may be set as a request for a certain storage precision for arithmetic data types. PIKS implementations are not required to grant such requests.

3. The *bind_roi* mechanism provides identifiers to a ROI object and a ROI offset tuple, which override the NULL default states for these items.

Nomenclature:

X Horizontal index image size
Y Vertical index image size
B Band index image size

Definition:

This mechanism performs the following functions:

- Returns an object identifier to the application;

- Binds the image size, band data type, and band precision tuples to the image if their identifiers are supplied as input parameters;
- Creates the white point, image structure, and colour space attributes if this information is supplied as input parameters;
- Creates ROI default states.

The ROI default states are:

State	Default
ROI identifier	ROI control object TRUE for all pixels
ROI offset	Zero value index offsets

Upon allocation, the image object attributes collection has the following conceptual data structure:

NULL or image size 5-tuple identifier
NULL or band data type B-tuple identifier
NULL or band precision B-tuple identifier
NULL or X tristimulus white point value
NULL or Y tristimulus white point value
NULL or Z tristimulus white point value
NULL or image structure code
NULL or colour space code

Tuple Specifications:

The image size 5-tuple has the following conceptual data structure:

5
ND
X
Y
1
1
B

The band data type tuple has the following conceptual data structure:

B
ND
CHOICE{BD, ND, SD}
CHOICE{BD, ND, SD}
.
.
.
.
CHOICE{BD, ND, SD}

where the band data type choice must be the same for each band in the PIKS Foundation profile.

The band precision tuple has the following conceptual data structure:

B
ND
Band 1 value
Band 2 value

.
.

Band *B* value

where the band precision value must be the same for each band in the PIKS Foundation profile.

4.2.3 *Allocate Lookup Table* InAllocateLUT

The *allocate_lookup_table* mechanism allocates a reference to a lookup table object and creates its attributes.

Element input parameters:

Description	Data type
Lookup table entries	NP, NULL
Lookup table bands	NP, NULL

Lookup table input data type option
    ND
    SD
	SP, NULL

Lookup table output data type option
    BD
    ND
    SD
	SP, NULL

Element output parameters:

Description	Data type
Lookup table identifier	ID

Object restrictions:

Object structure	LUT
Object input data type	As specified
Object output data type	As specified

Definition:

This mechanism returns a lookup table object identifier to the application and creates the object attributes if this information is specified as input parameters.

Upon allocation, the lookup table object attributes collection has the following conceptual data structure:

NULL or lookup table entries value
NULL or lookup table bands value
NULL or lookup table input data type code
NULL or lookup table output data type code

The *allocate_matrix* mechanism allocates a reference to a matrix array object and creates its attributes.

Element input parameters:

Description	Data type
Matrix column size	NP, NULL
Matrix row size	NP, NULL
Matrix data type option ND SD RD	SP, NULL

Element output parameters:

Description	Data type
Matrix identifier	ID

Object restrictions:

Object structure	MATRIX
Object data type	As specified

Definition:

This mechanism returns a matrix object identifier to the application and creates the object attributes if this information is specified as input parameters.

Upon allocation, the matrix object attributes collection has the following conceptual data structure:

NULL or matrix column size value
NULL or matrix row size value
NULL or matrix data type code

4.2.5   *Allocate Neighbourhood Array*   `InAllocateNbhoodArray`

The *allocate_neighbourhood_array* mechanism allocates a reference to a neighbourhood array object and creates its attributes.

Element input parameters:

Description	Data type
Array size 5-tuple	ID, NULL
Key pixel 5-tuple	ID, NULL
Scale factor	SP, NULL

Description	Data type
Semantic label option	SP, NULL
generic	
dither	
impulse response	
mask	
structuring element	
Array data type option	SP, NULL
BD	
ND	
SD	
RD	

Element output parameters:

Description	Data type
Array identifier	ID

Object restrictions:

Object structure	NBHOOD_ARRAY
Object data type	As specified

Nomenclature:

X Horizontal index array size
Y Vertical index array size
x_k Horizontal index key pixel
y_k Vertical index key pixel

Definition:

This mechanism returns a neighbourhood array object identifier to the application and creates the object attributes if this information is specified as input parameters.

Upon allocation, the neighbourhood array object attributes collection has the following conceptual data structure:

NULL or array size 5-tuple identifier
NULL or key pixel 5-tuple identifier
NULL or scale factor value
NULL or semantic label code
NULL or array data type code

Tuple Specifications:

The array size 5-tuple has the following conceptual data structure:

5
ND
X
Y
1
1
1

The array key pixel 5-tuple has the following conceptual data structure:

5
SD
x_k
y_k
0
0
0

4.2.6   *Allocate Region-of-Interest*   `InAllocateROI`

The *allocate_roi* mechanism allocates a reference to a ROI object and creates its attributes.

Element input parameters:

Description	Data type
Virtual array size 5-tuple	ID, NULL
ROI option ROI rectangular	SP, NULL
Polarity option set TRUE set FALSE	EP, NULL

Element output parameters:

Description	Data type
ROI identifier	ID

Object restrictions:

Object structure	ROI_RECT
Object data type	BD

Nomenclature:

X   Horizontal index ROI virtual array size
Y   Vertical index ROI virtual array size

Definition:

This mechanism returns a region-of-interest object identifier to the application and creates the object attributes if this information is specified as input parameters.

Upon allocation, the ROI object attributes collection has the following conceptual data structure:

NULL or virtual array size 5-tuple identifier
NULL or ROI structure code
NULL or polarity code

Tuple Specifications:

The ROI array size 5-tuple has the following conceptual data structure:

5
ND
X
Y
1
1
1

4.2.7 *Allocate Tuple*   `InAllocateTuple`

The *allocate_tuple* mechanism allocates a reference to a tuple object and creates its attributes.

Element input parameters:

Description	Data type
Number of tuple entries	NP, NULL
Tuple data type option	SP, NULL
BD	
ND	
SD	
RD	
CS	

Element output parameters:

Description	Data type
Tuple identifier	ID

Object restrictions:

Object structure   TUPLE
Object data type   As specified

Nomenclature:

E Number of tuple entries

Definition:

This mechanism returns a tuple object identifier to an application and creates the tuple attributes if this information is specified as input parameters.

Upon allocation, the tuple object attributes collection has the following conceptual data structure:

NULL or *E*
NULL or tuple data type code

4.2.8   *Deallocate Data Object*   IvDeallocateDataObject

The *deallocate_data_object* mechanism deallocates physical storage associated with an image or nonimage data object and destroys its attributes.

Element input parameters:

Description	Data type
Data object	ID

Object restrictions:

Object structure	As specified
Object data type	As specified

Definition:

This mechanism removes reservation of physical memory for the referenced data object and destroys it associated attributes.

4.3   Inquiry Mechanisms

This section describes the PIKS inquiry mechanisms.

4.3.1   *Inquire Elements*   IvInquireElements

The *inquire_elements* mechanism returns an array of information to an application regarding an implementation's support of elements.

Element input parameters:

Description	Data type
Element registration numbers array	IP
Array size	NP

Element output parameters:

Description	Data type
Element registration responses array	IP
Private label information	CS
Data validity indicator AVAILABLE NOT-AVAILABLE	EP

Object restrictions:

Numbers array structure	EXT
Responses array structure	EXT
Numbers array data type	SP
Responses array data type	BP

Definition:

Let $s(e)$ and $d(e)$ denote the e-th entry of the registration numbers array and the registration responses array, respectively. If a PIKS implementation supports the inquired registration number, $s(e)$, the corresponding entry, $d(e)$, of the registration responses array is set to TRUE; otherwise, $d(e)$, is set to FALSE.

4.3.2   Inquire Image   IvInquireImage

The *inquire_image* mechanism returns image attribute information to an application.

Element input parameters:

Description	Data type
Source image	ID

Element output parameters:

Description	Data type
Image size 5-tuple	ID
Band data type B-tuple	ID
Band precision B-tuple	ID
Match point 5-tuple	NULL
ROI identifier	ID
ROI offset 5-tuple	ID
X tristimulus value white point	RP
Y tristimulus value white point	RP
Z tristimulus value white point	RP
Image structure code MON COLR	SP

Description	Data type
Color space code	SP
unspecified	
nonstandard RGB	
linear CCIR illuminant D65 RGB	
linear CIE illuminant E RGB	
linear EBU illuminant C RGB	
linear EBU illuminant D65 RGB	
linear NTSC illuminant C RGB	
linear NTSC illuminant D65 RGB	
linear SMPTE illuminant D65 RGB	
gamma CCIR illuminant C RGB	
gamma EBU illuminant C RGB	
gamma EBU illuminant D65 RGB	
gamma NTSC illuminant C RGB	
gamma NTSC illuminant D65 RGB	
gamma SMPTE illuminant D65 RGB	
luminance/chrominance EBU illuminant C YUV	
luminance/chrominance EBU illuminant D65 YUV	
luminance/chrominance NTSC illuminant C YIQ	
luminance/chrominance NTSC illuminant D65 YIQ	
luminance/chrominance SMPTE illuminant D65 YCbCr	
CIE XYZ	
CIE UVW	
CIE Yxy CIE Yuv	
CIE L*a*b*	
CIE L*u*v*	
IHS	
CMY	
CMY	
Data validity indicator	EP
AVAILABLE	
NOT-AVAILABLE	

Object restrictions:

Source image structure	MON, COLR
Source image data type	BD, ND, SD

Remarks:

1. The *inquire_image* utility returns identifiers to the PIKS internal image attribute data structures. These identifiers can be used to export the image attribute information to an application.

2. The data validity indicator is NOT-AVAILABLE if and only if PIKS is not currently open when this utility is invoked.

3. The image size 5-tuple and band precision *B*-tuple contain parameters of the ND data type.

4. The band data type *B*-tuple and ROI offset *B*-tuple contain parameters of the SD data type.

5. Match point functionality is not supported in PIKS Foundation. The inquiry return is NULL.

Definition:

This utility indirectly returns image attribute information to an application.

The image object attributes collection has the following conceptual data structure:

> NULL or image size 5-tuple identifier
> NULL or band data type *B*-tuple identifier
> NULL or band precision *B*-tuple identifier
> NULL
> NULL or ROI identifier
> NULL or ROI offset 5-tuple identifier
> NULL or *X* tristimulus white point value
> NULL or *Y* tristimulus white point value
> NULL or *Z* tristimulus white point value
> NULL or image structure code
> NULL or colour space code

4.3.3   *Inquire Nonimage Object*   `IvInquireNonImageObject`

The *inquire_non_image_object* mechanism returns nonimage data object attribute information to an application.

Element input parameters:

Description	Data type
Object	ID

Object type option
    histogram
    lookup table
    matrix
    neighbourhood array
    ROI rectangular
    tuple
	SP

Element output parameters:

Description	Data type
Information identifier	IP

Data validity indicator
    AVAILABLE
    NOT-AVAILABLE
	EP

Object restrictions:

Object structure	HIST, LUT, MATRIX, NBHOOD, ROI, TUPLE
Object data type	As specified

Definition:

This utility indirectly returns nonimage data object attribute information to an application. The following information is returned to the application for each nonimage data object.

Histogram:

Array size	NP
Lower amplitude bound	RP
Upper amplitude bound	RP

Lookup table:

Table entries	NP
Table bands	NP
Table input data type code	SP
ND	
SD	
Table output data type code	SP
BD	
ND	
SD	

Matrix:

Matrix column size	NP
Matrix row size	NP
Matrix data type code	SP
ND	
SD	
RD	

Neighbourhood array:

Array size 5-tuple	ID
Key pixel 5-tuple	ID
Scale factor	SP
Semantic label code	SP
generic	
dither	
impulse response	
mask	
structuring element	
Array data type code	SP
BD	
ND	
SD	
RD	

ROI rectangular:

Virtual array size 5-tuple	ID
Start position 5-tuple	ID
End position 5-tuple	ID
Index manipulate 5-tuple	ID
Rectangle dimension code	EP
1D	
2D	

Polarity code	EP
TRUE	
FALSE	

Tuple:

Tuple size	NP
Tuple data type code	SP
BD	
ND	
SD	
RD	
CS	

4.3.4 *Inquire PIKS Implementation*   `IvInquirePIKSImpl`

The *inquire_piks_implementation* mechanism returns information about a PIKS implementation.

Element output parameters:

Description	Data type
Conformance profile	CS
Image size limit 5-tuple	ID
ND data type precision	SP
SD data type precision	SP
RD data type precision	NULL
RD implementation	NULL
Implementation notes	ID
Asynchronous support code	EP
yes	
no	
Data validity indicator	EP
AVAILABLE	
NOT-AVAILABLE	

Definition:

This control mechanism returns information about a PIKS implementation. A more detailed explanation of the information returned is provided below.

Profile   Specifies the profile of PIKS conformance. The only valid profile is:

        FOUNDATION   PIKS Foundation

Size limit   Defines the maximum extent of an image object along a particular dimension supported by an implementation. The five dimensions include x, y, z, t, b. Note that, based upon the profile conformance level, the implementation may not support the full complement of five dimensional objects. If this is the case, the size limit will be zero for that dimension, as shown below.

−1   No limit established

  0   Objects have no extent along the dimension

>0   Limit value

Note also that the maximum extent of the dimensions supported should not be construed as a guaranty that an image object of maximum extent along all dimensions can be created at any point in time because of memory management limitations.

ND precision   Number of bits of storage for ND data type.

SD precision   Number of bits of storage for SD data type.

RD precision   Number of bits of storage for RD data type.

RD implementation   Implementation technique for RD data type.

           TI   Fixed point integer

           Rf   Real floating point number

Implementation   Pointer to implememtation specific character string which may be used to communicate implementation private information.

4.3.5   *Inquire PIKS Status*   `IvInquirePIKSStatus`

The *inquire_piks_status* mechanism returns information about PIKS state and global control mode status.

Element output parameters:

Description	Data type

PIKS operational state code
  PIKS_CLOSED
  PIKS_OPEN
	EP

PIKS chain state code
  BUILD_CHAIN
  EXECUTE_CHAIN
  NOT_CHAIN
	EP

PIKS error state code
  ERROR_SUBSTATE
  NO_ERROR
	EP

ROI control mode code
  ROI_CONTROL_ON
  ROI_CONTROL_OFF
	EP

ROI processing mode code
  ROI_PROCESS_ON
  ROI_PROCESS_OFF
	EP

Match point control mode
  MP_ON
  MP_OFF
	EP

Description	Data type

Index assignment mode code
    INDEX_ASSIGN_ON
    INDEX_ASSIGN_OFF
	EP

Synchronicity mode code
    SYNCH_ON
    ASYNCH_ON
	EP

Error reporting mode code
    ERROR_REPORT_ON
    ERROR_REPORT_OFF
	EP

Image resampling mode
    support 1 constant
    support 2 linear
	SP

ROI resampling mode code support 1 constant	SP

Data validity indicator code
    AVAILABLE
    NOT-AVAILABLE
	EP

Remark:

The element output parameters list only contains the SP code returns supported by PIKS Foundation.

Definition:

This mechanism returns information about the status of the PIKS state and global control to an application.

4.3.6   *Inquire Repository*   IvInquireRepository

The *inquire_repository* mechanism returns an array of information regarding an implementation's support of data object repository entries.

Element input parameters:

Description	Data type
Element registration numbers array	IP
Array size	NP

Repository class option
    impulse response array
    dither array
    colour conversion matrix
	SP

Element output parameters:

Description	Data type
Element registration responses array	IP
Private label information	CS
Data validity indicator AVAILABLE NOT-AVAILABLE	EP

Object restrictions:

Numbers array structure	EXT
Responses array structure	EXT
Numbers array data type	SP
Responses array data type	BP

Definition:

Let $s(e)$ and $d(e)$ denote the eth entry of the registration numbers array and the registration responses array, respectively. If a PIKS implementation supports the inquired registration number, $s(e)$, for a specified repository class, the corresponding entry, $d(e)$, of the registration responses array is set to TRUE; otherwise, $d(e)$, is set to FALSE.

4.3.7 *Inquire Resampling* `IvInquireResampling`

The *inquire_resampling* mechanism returns an array of information to an application regarding an implemention's support of resampling options.

Element input parameters:

Description	Data type
Element registration numbers array	IP
Array size	NP

Element output parameters:

Description	Data type
Element registration responses array	IP
Private label information	CS
Data validity indicator AVAILABLE NOT-AVAILABLE	EP

Object restrictions:

Numbers array structure	EXT
Responses array structure	EXT
Numbers array data type	SP
Responses array data type	BP

Definition:

Let $s(e)$ and $d(e)$ denote the e-th entry of the registration numbers array and the registration responses array, respectively. If a PIKS implementation supports the inquired registration number, $s(e)$, for a specified repository class, the corresponding entry, $d(e)$, of the registration responses array is set to TRUE; otherwise, $d(e)$, is set to FALSE.

4.4 Management Mechanisms

This section describes the PIKS system management mechanisms.

4.4.1 Bind ROI   InBindROI

The *bind_roi* mechanism binds a ROI object and a ROI offset tuple to an image.

Element input parameters:

Description	Data type
Source image	ID
ROI	ID, NULL
ROI offset 5-tuple	ID, NULL

Object restrictions:

Source image structure	MON, COLR
ROI structure	ROI_RECT
Source image data type	BD, ND, SD
ROI data type	BD

Remark:

The ROI offset 5-tuple contains parameters of the SD data type.

Nomenclature:

x_o Horizontal index offset value
y_o Vertical index offset alue

Definition:

The ROI binding mechanism relates the ROI object identifier in the source image attribute list to the identifier of the ROI in the parameter list, and relates the ROI offset identifier in the source image attribute list to the ROI offset identifier in the parameter list. The physical or logical mapping of the ROI data object to the virtual ROI control object within the PIKS operator model is implementation dependent and hidden from an application.

If the *bind_roi* mechanism is invoked on an image that has an ROI presently bound to it, the present ROI is replaced by the new ROI object.

If the ROI offset parameter is NULL, the ROI offset is set to zero along each coordinate index.

If the ROI identifier is NULL and the source image has an ROI presently bound to it, the present ROI is rebound to the image at the specified ROI offset.

Tuple Specifications:

The ROI offset 5-tuple has the following conceptual data structure:

5
SD
x_o
y_o
0
0
0

4.4.2   *Define Sub Image*   `InDefineSubImage`

The *define_sub_image* mechanism creates a reference to a sub-image.

Element input parameters:

Description	Data type
Source image	ID
Destination image	ID
Source image index offset 5-tuple	ID
Sub-image size 5-tuple	ID

Object restrictions:

Source image structure	MON, COLR
Destination image structure	MON, COLR
Source image data type	BD, ND, SD
Destination image data type	Same as source image data type

Nomenclature:

x_o Horizontal index offset
y_o Vertical index offset
b_o Band index offset
X_w Horizontal index sub-image size
Y_w Vertical index sub-image size

Definition:

This mechanism creates an identifier to a sub-image of a source image. This sub-image can be used as a source or destination image to other PIKS elements that utilize source and destination images. Any modification to pixels of a sub-image results in the same modification to the corresponding pixels of the source image from which the sub-image was derived.

Monochrome source and destination images:

$$D(x, y, 0, 0, 0) = S(x - x_o, y - y_o, 0, 0, 0)$$

for

$$x_o \le x \le x_o + X_w$$
$$y_o \le y \le y_o + Y_w$$

Colour source and destination images:

$$D(x, y, 0, 0, b) = S(x - x_o, y - y_o, 0, 0, b)$$

for

$$x_o \le x \le x_o + X_w$$
$$y_o \le y \le y_o + Y_w$$
$$0 \le b \le B - 1$$

Colour source and monochrome destination images:

$$D(x, y, 0, 0, 0) = S(x - x_o, y - y_o, 0, 0, b_o)$$

for

$$x_o \le x \le x_o + X_w$$
$$y_o \le y \le y_o + Y_w$$
$$0 \le b_o \le B - 1$$

An error is reported if

$$x_o + X_w > X$$
$$y_o + Y_w > Y$$

Tuple Specifications:

The source index offset 5-tuple has the following conceptual data structure:

5
ND
x_o
y_o
0
0
b_o

The sub-image size 5-tuple has the following conceptual data structure:

5
ND
X_w
Y_w
1
1
B

4.4.3 Return Repository Identifier InReturnRepositoryId

The *return_repository_id* mechanism returns an identifier of a data object repository entry to an application.

Element input parameters:

Description	Data type
Repository index	SP

Repository class option
    impulse response array
    dither array
    colour conversion matrix
	SP

Element output parameters:

Description	Data type
Repository identifier	ID

Definition:

An identifier associated with a data object repository entry index and class is returned to the application.

4.4.4 Set Globals IvSetGlobals

The *set_globals* mechanism sets the PIKS global modes.

Element input parameters:

Description	Data type

ROI control mode option
    ROI control engaged
    ROI control disengaged
	EP

ROI processing mode option
    ROI source processing engaged
    ROI source processing disengaged
	EP

Match point control mode option
    match point control engaged
    match point control disengaged
	EP

Index assignment mode option
    index assignment engaged
    index assignment disengaged
	EP

Synchronicity mode option
    synchronous
    asynchronous
	EP

Error reporting mode option
    errors reported
    errors not reported
	EP

Description	Data type

Image resampling mode option
    support 1 constant
    support 2 linear
	SP

ROI resampling mode option support 1 constant	SP

Remark:

The element input parameters list only contains the SP input options supported by PIKS Foundation.

Definition:

This control mechanism sets the PIKS Foundation global modes:

4.4.5   *Set Image Attribuutes*   `InSetImageAttrs`

The *set_image_attributes* mechanism sets image attributes of a previously allocated image.

Element input parameters:

Description	Data type
Destination image	ID
Image size 5-tuple	ID, NULL
Band data type *B*-tuple	ID, NULL
Band precision *B*-tuple	ID, NULL
X tristimulus value white point	RP, NULL
Y tristimulus value white point	RP, NULL
Z tristimulus value white point	RP, NULL

Image structure option
    MON
    COLR
	SP, NULL

Colour space option
    unspecified
    nonstandard RGB
    linear CCIR illuminant D65 RGB
    linear CIE illuminant E RGB
    linear EBU illuminant C RGB
    linear EBU illuminant D65 RGB
    linear NTSC illuminant C RGB
    linear NTSC illuminant D65 RGB
    linear SMPTE illuminant D65 RGB
    gamma CCIR illuminant C RGB
    gamma EBU illuminant C RGB
    gamma EBU illuminant D65 RGB
    gamma NTSC illuminant C RGB
    gamma NTSC illuminant D65 RGB
    gamma SMPTE illuminant D65 RGB
	SP, NULL

Description	Data type
luminance/chrominance EBU illuminant C YUV	
luminance/chrominance EBU illuminant D65 YUV	
luminance/chrominance NTSC illuminant C YIQ	
luminance/chrominance NTSC illuminant D65 YIQ	
luminance/chrominance SMPTE illuminant D65 YCbCr	
CIE XYZ	
CIE UVW	
CIE Yxy	
CIE Yuv	
CIE L*a*b*	
CIE L*u*v*	
IHS	
CMY	
CMYK	

Object restrictions:

Destination image structure	As specified
Destination image data type	As specified

Remarks:

1. Each image attribute may be specified as NULL. In each instance, the attribute will be set when the image data is created by a PIKS element.

2. The band precision B-tuple may be set as a request for a certain precision for arithmetic data types. PIKS implementations are not required to grant such requests.

3. The image size 5-tuple and band precision B-tuple contain parameters of the ND data type.

4. The band data type B-tuple contains parameters of the SD data type.

Definition:

This mechanism performs the following functions:

- Replaces image size, band data type, and band precision tuples in the image attributes collection;

- Replaces image structure and colour space information in the image attributes collection.

Tuple specifications:

See Section 4.2.2 for specification of the tuples.

4.5   Error Mechanisms

The following subsections describe the PIKS error reporting mechanisms.

4.5.1   *Error Handler*   IvErrorHandler

The *error_handler* mechanism handles error conditions detected by a PIKS element during execution.

Element input parameters:

Description	Data type
Error identifier code	SP
Element detecting error	SP
Error file identifier	IP

Synchronicity state option
    synchronous
    asynchronous
	EP

Remark:

See the *open_piks* mechanism for a description of the error file.

Definition:

This mechanism handles all errors detected by PIKS elements. Upon invocation, it sets the PIKS Error Substate. This action prohibits the execution of all image related elements until the Error Substate has been reset by completion of this mechanism.

PIKS Error Substate prohibits modification of any PIKS State Table value. In PIKS Error Substate, only the following PIKS mechanisms may be invoked:

an inquiry mechanism
error_logger
close_piks_emergency

The *error_handler* mechanism:

■ Calls the *error_logger* mechanism to provide information about the error condition, and then returns to the *error_handler* mechanism. The same parameter values input to the *error_handler* mechanism are passed through to the *error_logger* mechanism.

■ Resets the PIKS Error Substate.

■ Performs a predetermined action, which depends upon the severity of the particular error condition.

The predetermined actions, chosen by the error number, are:

■ Set error file identifier to NULL.

■ Return to the calling PIKS element to resume execution as if no error had occurred (error file parameter set to 0).

■ Enter *error_handler* mechanism to perform designated error reaction (such as cleaning up in-process and incomplete operations of the element detecting the error) if it is capable of doing so, before returning to the application.

■ Abort operation, invoke *close_piks_emergency*, and terminate the application (without returning to the calling element).

An application may elect to replace the PIKS *error_handler* mechanism with its own special error handler. However, it must support the defined error handling concepts to maintain conformance with the standard.

4.5.2 Error Logger

The *error_logger* mechanism logs detected error conditions.

Element input parameters:

Description	Data type
Error identifier code	SP
Element detecting error	SP
Error file identifier	IP
Synchronicity state option synchronous asynchronous	EP

Remark:

See the *open_piks* mechanism for a description of the error file.

Definition:

This mechanism logs all errors detected by PIKS elements. It is called by the *error_handler* mechanism in the Error Substate.

The PIKS *error_logger* mechanism:

■ Logs the appropriate error message (chosen by the error number) on the designated error logging device.

■ Returns to the calling element to complete the error handling.

An application may elect to replace the PIKS *error_logger* mechanism with its own special error logger, however it must support the defined error handling concepts to maintain conformance with the standard. The application's error logger may use any inquiry function to obtain information about the nature of the error or PIKS status for presentation to the application.

4.5.3 Error Test
IbErrorTest

The *error_test* mechanism tests for any occurence of a detected error since the last *error_test* mechanism was invoked.

Element output parameters:

Description	Data type
Error flag	BP

Definition:

This mechanism tests an error flag, which is set by the *error_handler* mechanism when any error is detected by a PIKS element. This mechanism always returns to the calling element with the previous value of the error flag after resetting it to the 'no error' state.

The error flag is set FALSE if there is no error. The error flag is set TRUE if there is an error.

4.5.4   *Set Error Handler*   `ItfSetErrorHandler`

The *set_error_handler* mechanism replaces an error handler.

Element input parameter:

Description	Data type
Error handler	ID

Definition:

This mechanism replaces the presently installed error handler with a newly specified error handler.

5

PIKS Utilities

Chapter 5 describes the functionality of PIKS utilities that perform internal mechanical manipulations on data objects and that import and export data objects.

5.1 Internal Utilities

This section describes the PIKS internal utilities, which perform basic manipulations of data objects.

5.1.1 *Convert Array to Image*   `InConvertArrayToImage`

The *convert_array_to_image* utility converts a matrix or a two-dimensional neighbourhood array object to a monochrome image.

Element input parameters:

Description	Data type
Destination image	ID
Source array	ID

Object restrictions:

Destination image structure	MON
Source array structure	MATRIX, NBHOOD
Destination image data type	Same as source array data type
Source array data type	BD, ND, SD

Nomenclature:

$D(x, y, 0, 0, 0)$	$X \times Y \times 1 \times 1 \times 1$ destination image
$A(x, y)$	$X \times Y$ array

Definition:

For all x, y

$$D(x, y, 0, 0, 0) = A(x, y)$$

5.1.2 *Convert Image Data Type* InConvertImageDatatype

The *convert_image_datatype* utility converts a PIKS image from one arithmetic data type to another.

Element input parameters:

Description	Data type
Source image	ID
Destination image	ID

Object restrictions:

Source image structure	MON, COLR
Destination image structure	Same as source image structure
Source image data type	BD, ND, SD
Destination image data type	BD, ND, SD

Remarks:

1. The image data types are specified by the band data type tuples, which are bound to the source and destination images upon their allocation or by the *set_image_attributes* mechanism.

2. The *convert_image_datatype* utility provides an optional, implementation-dependent means for converting between the same data type, but different internal precisions or different internal representations.

3. PIKS implementations may use the pixel precision image attribute as a hint of the pixel precision desired by an application.

4. The conversion process is implementation dependent.

Nomenclature:

$S(x, y, 0, 0, b)$ $X \times Y \times 1 \times 1 \times B$ source image
$D(x, y, 0, 0, b)$ $X \times Y \times 1 \times 1 \times B$ destination image

Definition:

For all x, y, b

$$D(x, y, 0, 0, b) = S(x, y, 0, 0, b)$$

where the conversion is according to the PIKS definition of data types, but is implementation dependent.

Common practice in converting from ND to SD is to copy the source pixel bits to the destination pixel bits with the least significant bits aligned. If the source pixel contains more bits than the destination pixel, the remaining most significant bits of the source pixel are discarded. If the source pixel contains fewer bits than the destination pixel, the remaining destination pixel bits are set to zero. In the case of SD to ND conversion, negative value pixels are sign inverted before the previously described conversion process is performed.

Common practice in converting between BD and ND data types is to consider the TRUE state pixel to be of unsigned integer value one and the FALSE state pixel to be of unsigned integer value zero.

Plate 1   Example of colour conversion, linear operation: (a) source, "toys colour";
(b) destination NTSC illuminant C to NTSC illuminant D65 conversion

Plate 2   Example of unsharp masking: (Plate 1a) source "toys colour"; (a) blurred source
image; (b) destination, unsharp masking

5.1.3 Convert Image to Array   IsnConvertImageToArray

The *convert_image_to_array* utility converts a monochrome image to a matrix or a two-dimensional neighbourhood array object.

Element input parameters:

Description	Data type
Source image	ID
Destination array	ID

Object restrictions:

Source image structure	MON
Destination array structure	MATRIX, NBHOOD
Source image data type	BD, ND, SD
Destination array data type	Same as source image data type

Nomenclature:

$S(x, y, 0, 0, 0)$	$X \times Y \times 1 \times 1 \times 1$ source image
$A(x, y)$	$X \times Y$ array

Definition:

For all x, y

$$A(x, y) = S(x, y, 0, 0, 0)$$

5.1.4 Convert ROI to Image   InConvertROIToImage

The *convert_roi_to_image* utility converts a two-dimensional region-of-interest object to a monochrome image.

Element input parameters:

Description	Data type
Destination image	ID
Source ROI	ID

Object restrictions:

Destination image structure	MON
Source ROI structure	ROI_RECT
Destination image data type	BD
Source array data type	BD

Nomenclature:

$D(x, y, 0, 0, 0)$	$X \times Y \times 1 \times 1 \times 1$ destination image
$R(x, y)$	$X \times Y$ source ROI virtual array

Definition:

For all x, y

$$D(x, y, 0, 0, 0) = R(x, y)$$

5.1.5 Copy Window

The *copy_window* utility copies a rectangular-shaped window from a source image into a destination image.

Element input parameters:

Description	Data type
Source image	ID
Destination image	ID
Source index offset 5-tuple	ID
Destination index offset 5-tuple	ID
Window size 5-tuple	ID

Object restrictions:

Source image structure	MON, COLR
Destination image structure	Same as source image structure
Source image data type	BD, ND, SD
Destination image data type	Same as source image data type

Remarks:

1. The source index offset and destination index offset 5-tuples contain parameters of the SD data type.

2. The window size 5-tuple contains parameters of the ND data type.

Nomenclature:

$S(x, y, 0, 0, b)$	$X_S \times Y_S \times 1 \times 1 \times B$ source image
$D(x, y, 0, 0, b)$	$X_D \times Y_D \times 1 \times 1 \times B$ destination image
x_{so}	Horizontal index source offset
y_{so}	Vertical index source offset
x_{do}	Horizontal index destination offset
y_{do}	Vertical index destination offset
x_w	Horizontal index window size
y_w	Vertical index window size

Definition:

For

$$x_{do} \leq x_D \leq \text{MIN}\{X_D - 1, x_D + x_w - 1\}$$
$$y_{do} \leq y_D \leq \text{MIN}\{Y_D - 1, y_D + x_w - 1\}$$
$$0 \leq b \leq B - 1$$

then

$$D(x_D, y_D, 0, 0, b) = S(x_S, y_S, 0, 0, b)$$

where

$$x_S = x_D + x_{so} - x_{do}$$
$$y_S = y_D + y_{so} - y_{do}$$

and $D(x_D, y_D, 0, 0, b)$ is unchanged otherwise.

Tuple Specifications:

The source index offset 5-tuple has the following conceptual data structure:

5
SD
x_{so}
y_{so}
0
0
0

The destination index offset 5-tuple has the following conceptual data structure:

5
SD
x_{do}
y_{do}
0
0
0

The destination window size 5-tuple has the following conceptual data structure:

5
ND
x_w
y_w
1
1
1

5.1.6   *Create Tuple*   `InCreateTuple`

The *create_tuple* utility creates a tuple data object.

Element input parameters:

Description	Data type
Tuple	ID
Tuple size	NP
First data value	BP, NP, SP, RP, CS

Description	Data type
Second data value	BP, NP, SP, RP, CS
.	.
.	.
.	.
Last data value	BP, NP, SP, RP, CS
Tuple data type option	SP
BD	
ND	
SD	
RD	
CS	

Object restrictions:

Object structure	TUPLE
Object data type	BD, ND, SD, RD, CS

Remark:

The data type of each tuple data value must be the same class as the data type option, e.g., if the tuple data type is ND, all data values must be NP.

Nomenclature:

E Number of tuple entries

Definition:

The tuple has the following conceptual data structure.

E
CHOICE{BD, ND, SD, RD, CS}
Value 1
Value 2
.
.
.
Value E

5.1.7   *Extract Pixel Plane*   `InExtractPixelPlane`

The *extract_pixel_plane* utility extracts a monochrome image from a colour image.

Element input parameters:

Description	Data type
Source image	ID
Destination image	ID
Depth index value	NP
Temporal index value	NP
Band index value	NP

Object restrictions:

Source image structure	COLR
Destination image structure	MON
Source image data type	BD, ND, SD
Destination image data type	Same as source image data type

Nomenclature:

$S(x, y, 0, 0, b)$	$X \times Y \times 1 \times 1 \times B$ source image
$D(x, y, 0, 0, 0)$	$X \times Y \times 1 \times 1 \times 1$ destination image
b_v	Band index value

Definition:

For all x, y

$$D(x, y, 0, 0, 0) = S(x, y, 0, 0, b_v)$$

5.1.8   *Insert Pixel Plane*   `InInsertPixelPlane`

The *insert_pixel_plane* utility inserts a monochrome image into a colour image.

Element input parameters:

Description	Data type
Source image	ID
Destination image	ID
Depth index value	NP
Temporal index value	NP
Band index value	NP

Object restrictions:

Source image structure	MON
Destination image structure	COLR
Source image data type	BD, ND, SD
Destination image data type	Same as source image data type

Nomenclature:

$S(x, y, 0, 0, 0)$	$X \times Y \times 1 \times 1 \times 1$ source image
$D(x, y, 0, 0, b)$	$X \times Y \times 1 \times 1 \times B$ destination image
b_v	Band index value

Definition:

For all x, y

$$D(x, y, 0, 0, b_v) = S(x, y, 0, 0, 0)$$

5.2   Import Utilities

This section describes the PIKS import utilities, which transport data objects from an application to PIKS.

5.2.1   *Import Histogram*   `InImportHist`

The *import_histogram* utility imports an external array of data values from an application and puts it into a histogram object.

Element input parameters:

Description	Data type
Source array	IP
Destination histogram	ID
Array size	NP, NULL
Lower amplitude bound	RP, NULL
Upper amplitude bound	RP, NULL

Object restrictions:

Source array structure	EXT
Destination histogram structure	HIST
Source array data type	NP
Destination histogram data type	ND

Nomenclature:

E array size
l_b lower amplitude bound
u_b upper amplitude bound
id   histogram array private identifier

Definition:

The histogram object created from an external array has the following conceptual data structure:

E
l_b
u_b
id

The external array has the following conceptual data structure:

Histogram value 1
Histogram value 2
.
.
.
Histogram value E

The *import_image* utility imports an image from an application and converts it to the internal PIKS data type.

Element input parameters:

Description	Data type
Source image array	IP
Destination image	ID
Number of source bits per pixel	NP

Source data type option
   BI
   NI
   SI
   TI
	SP

Object restrictions:

Source image structure	EXT
Destination image structure	MON, COLR
Source image data type	BI, NI, SI, TI
Destination image data type	BD, ND, SD

Remarks:

1. Import is allowed only to an allocated destination image whose data type is specified.

2. The external image must have homogeneous bands.

3. The data type conversion is implementation dependent.

4. The following are valid data type conversions upon import:

Source	Destination
BI	BD
NI	ND, SD
SI	SD
TI	SD

Nomenclature:

$A(x, y, 0, 0, b)$	External image array
$D(x, y, 0, 0, b)$	$X \times Y \times 1 \times 1 \times B$ destination image

Definition:

For all x, y, b

$$D(x, y, 0, 0, b) = A(x, y, 0, 0, b)$$

5.2.3   *Import Lookup Table*

InImportLUT

The *import_lut* utility imports an external array of data values from an application and puts it into a lookup table object.

Element input parameters:

Description	Data type
Source array	IP
Destination lookup table	ID
Table entries	NP
Table bands	NP

Lookup table data type input option
    ND
    SD
	SP

Lookup table data type output option
    BD
    ND
    SD
	SP

Object restrictions:

Source array structure	EXT
Destination lookup table structure	LUT
Source array data type	BP, NP, SP
Destination lookup table input data type	ND, SD
Destination lookup table output data type	BD, ND, SD

Remark:

The data type of each external data value must be of the same class as the data type option.

Nomenclature:

E Table entries
B Band entries
id   Lookup table array private identifier

Definition:

The lookup table object created from an external array has the following conceptual data structure:

E
B
CHOICE{BD, ND, SD}
id

The external array has the following conceptual data structure:

    LUT value 1, 1
    LUT value 2, 1
    .

    .

    .

    LUT value *E*, 1
    LUT value 1, 2
    .

    .

    .

    LUT value *E*, *B*

5.2.4   *Import Matrix*   `InImportMatrix`

The *import_matrix* utility imports an external array of data values from an application and puts it into a matrix object.

Element input parameters:

Description	Data type
Source array	IP
Destination matrix	ID
Matrix column size	NP
Matrix row size	NP
Matrix data type option ND SD RD	SP

Object restrictions:

Source array structure	EXT
Destination matrix structure	MATRIX
Source array data type	NP, SP, RP
Destination matrix data type option	ND, SD, RD

Remark:

The data type of each external data value must be of the same class as the data type option.

Nomenclature:

- *C*   Number of array columns
- *R*   Number of matrix rows
- id   Matrix array private identifier

Definition:

The matrix object created from an external array has the following conceptual data structure:

    C
    R
    CHOICE{ND, SD, RD}
    id

The external array has the following conceptual data structure:

Matrix value 1, 1
matrix value 2, 1

.
.
.

Matrix value C, 1
Matrix value 1, 2

.
.
.

Matrix value C, R

5.2.5   *Import Neighbourhood Array*   InImportNbhoodArray

The *import_neighbourhood_array* utility imports an external array of data values from an application and puts it into a neighbourhood array object.

Element input parameters:

Description	Data type
Source array	IP
Destination neighbourhood array	ID
Array size 5-tuple	ID
Key pixel 5-tuple	ID
Scale factor	SP, NULL

Semantic label option
  generic
  dither
  impulse Response
  mask
  structuring element
	SP

Neighbourhood data type option
  BD
  ND
  SD
  RD
	SP

Object restrictions:

Source array structure	EXT
Destination neighbourhood structure	NBHOOD
Source array data type	BP, NP, SP, RP
Destination neighbourhood data type	BD, ND, SD, RD

Remarks:

1. The data type of each external data value must be of the same class as the data type option.
2. The array size 5-tuple contains parameters of the ND data type.
3. The key pixel 5-tuple contains parameters of the SD data type.
4. The scale factor must be unity for the BD, ND, and RD neighbourhood array data types.

Nomenclature:

C number of array columns
R number of array rows
c_k column index key pixel
r_k row index key pixel
id   neighbourhood array private identifier

Definition:

The neighbourhood array object created from an external array has the following conceptual data structure:

CHOICE{GL, DL, IL, ML, SL}
CHOICE{BD, ND, SD, RD}
Neighbourhood size 5-tuple identifier
Key pixel 5-tuple identifier
Scale factor value
id

The external array has the following conceptual data structure:

Array value 1, 1
Array value 2, 1

.

.

Array value C, 1
Array value 1, 2

.

.

Array value C, R

Tuple Specifications:

The neighbourhood array size 5-tuple has the following conceptual data structure:

5
ND
C
R
1
1
1

The neighbourhood array key pixel 5-tuple has the following conceptual data structure:

5
SD
c_k
r_k
0
0
0

5.2.6 *Import Tuple*

The *import_tuple* utility imports an external array of data values from an application and puts it into a tuple object.

Element input parameters:

Description	Data type
Source array	IP
Destination tuple	ID
Tuple size	NP
Table data type option	SP
BD	
ND	
SD	
RD	
CS	

Object restrictions:

Source array structure	EXT
Destination tuple structure	TUPLE
Source array data type	BP, NP, SP, RP, CS
Destination tuple data type	BD, ND. SD, RD, CS

Remark:

The data type of each external data value must be of the same class as the data type option.

Nomenclature:

E   Tuple size
id   Tuple array private identifier

Definition:

The tuple object created from an external array has the following conceptual data structure:

E
CHOICE{BD, ND, SD, RD, CS}
id

The external array has the following conceptual data structure:

Value 1
Value 2
.
.
.
Value E

The *put_colour_pixel* utility inserts a colour pixel from an application into a colour image.

Element input parameters:

Description	Data type
Destination image	ID
Band 0 pixel value	BP, NP, SP
Band 1 pixel value	BP, NP, SP
Band 2 pixel value	BP, NP, SP
Band 3 pixel value	BP, NP, SP, NULL
Horizontal index value	NP
Vertical index value	NP
Depth index value	NP
Temporal index value	NP
Band index value	NP

Object restrictions:

Destination image structure	COLR
Destination image data type	BD, ND, SD

Remark:

The data parameters must be of the same data type class as the destination image data type.

Nomenclature:

$D(x, y, 0, 0, b)$	$X \times Y \times 1 \times 1 \times B$ destination image
p_{v0}	Band 0 pixel value
p_{v1}	Band 1 pixel value
p_{v2}	Band 2 pixel value
p_{v3}	Band 3 pixel value
x_v	Horizontal index value
y_v	Vertical index value
b_v	Band index value

Definition:

Three-band colour image:

$$D(x_v, y_v, 0, 0, 0) = p_{v0}$$
$$D(x_v, y_v, 0, 0, 1) = p_{v1}$$
$$D(x_v, y_v, 0, 0, 2) = p_{v2}$$

Four-band colour image:

$$D(x_v, y_v, 0, 0, 0) = p_{v0}$$
$$D(x_v, y_v, 0, 0, 1) = p_{v1}$$

$$D(x_v, y_v, 0, 0, 2) = p_{v2}$$
$$D(x_v, y_v, 0, 0, 3) = p_{v3}$$

5.2.8 *Put Pixel*   `InPutPixel`

The *put_pixel* utility inserts a pixel from an application into an image.

Element input parameters:

Description	Data type
Destination image	ID
Pixel value	BP, NP, SP
Horizontal index value	NP
Vertical index value	NP
Depth index value	NP
Temporal index value	NP
Band index value	NP

Object restrictions:

Destination image structure	MON, COLR
Destination image data type	BD, ND, SD

Remark:

The data parameter must be of the same data type class as the destination image data type.

Nomenclature:

$D(x, y, 0, 0, b)$	$X \times Y \times 1 \times 1 \times B$ destination image
p_v	Pixel value
x_v	Horizontal index value
y_v	Vertical index value
b_v	Band index value

Definition:

$$D(x_v, y_v, 0, 0, b_v) = p_v$$

5.2.9 *Put Pixel Array*   `InPutPixelArray`

The *put_pixel_array* utility inserts an array of pixels from an application into an image.

Element input parameters:

Description	Data type
Destination image	ID
Source array	ID
Horizontal index offset	NP
Vertical index offset	NP

Description	Data type
Depth index value	NP
Temporal index value	NP
Band index value	NP
Number of array columns	NP
Number of array rows	NP

Object restrictions:

Destination image structure	MON, COLR
Source array structure	EXT
Destination image data type	BD, ND, SD
Source array data type	BP, NP, SP

Nomenclature:

$D(x, y, 0, 0, b)$	$X \times Y \times 1 \times 1 \times B$
x_o	Horizontal index offset
y_o	Vertical index offset
b_v	Band index value
$A(c, r)$	$C \times R$ array
C	Number of array columns
R	Number of array rows

Definition:

For

$$x_o \leq x \leq X - 1$$
$$y_o \leq y \leq Y - 1$$
$$0 \leq r \leq R - 1$$
$$0 \leq c \leq C - 1$$

then

$$D(c + x_o, r + y_o, 0, 0, b_v) = A(c, r)$$

and

$D(x, y, 0, 0, b)$ is unchanged otherwise.

5.3   Export Utilities

This section describes the PIKS export utilities, which transport data objects from PIKS to an application.

5.3.1   *Export Histogram*   `ItuaExportHist`

The *export_histogram* utility exports the array data of a histogram object to an application.

Element input parameters:

Description	Data type
Source histogram	ID
Destination array	IP

Object restrictions:

Source histogram structure	HIST
Destination array structure	EXT
Source histogram data type	ND
Destination array data type	NP

Nomenclature:

 E   Array size

Definition:

The external array has the following conceptual data structure:

Histogram value 1
Histogram value 2
.
.
.
Histogram value *E*

5.3.2   *Export Image*   `IstExportImage`

The *export_image* utility exports a PIKS image to an application and converts the image to the external data type.

Element input parameters:

Description	Data type
Source image	ID
Destination array	IP
Number of destination bits per pixel	NP

Destination data type option
    BI
    NI
    SI
    TI
	SP

Object restrictions:

Source image structure	MON, COLR
Destination array structure	EXT
Source image data type	BD, ND, SD
Destination array data type	BI, NI, SI, TI

Remarks:

1. The image attribute collection associated with the source image contains the image size specification and source bits per pixel specification.

2. All bands of the external source image must be of the same data type.

3. The data type conversion is implementation dependent.

4. The following are valid data type conversions upon export.

Source	Destination
BD	BI
ND	NI, SI, TI
SD	SD, SI, TI

Nomenclature:

$S(x, y, 0, 0, b)$ $X \times Y \times 1 \times 1 \times B$ source image
$A(x, y, 0, 0, b)$ External image array

Definition:

For all x, y, b

$$A(x, y, 0, 0, b) = D(x, y, 0, 0, b)$$

5.3.3   *Export Lookup Table*   `IstExportLUT`

The *export_lut* utility exports the array data of a lookup table object to an application.

Element input parameters:

Description	Data type
Source lookup table	ID
Destination array	IP

Object restrictions:

Source lookup table structure	LUT
Destination array structure	EXT
Source lookup table output data type	BD, ND, SD
Destination array data type	BP, NP, SP

Remark:

The data type of each external data value must be of the same class as the lookup table output data type.

Nomenclature:

E Table entries
B Band entries

Definition:

The external array has the following conceptual data structure:

LUT value 1, 1
LUT value 2, 1
.

.
LUT value E, 1
LUT value 1, 2
.

.
LUT value E, B

5.3.4 *Export Matrix* `IstExportMatrix`

The *export_matrix* utility exports the array data of a matrix object to an application.

Element input parameters:

Description	Data type
Source matrix	ID
Destination array	IP

Object restrictions:

Source matrix structure	MATRIX
Destination array structure	EXT
Source matrix data type	ND, SD, RD
Destination array data type option	NP, SP, RP

Remark:

The data type of each external data value must be of the same class as the matrix data type.

Nomenclature:

C Number of array columns
R Number of matrix rows

Definition:

The external array has the following conceptual data structure:

Matrix value 1, 1
Matrix value 2, 1
.

.
Matrix value C, 1
Matrix value 1, 2
.

.
Matrix value C, R

5.3.5 *Export neighbourhood Array*   `IstExportNbhoodArray`

The *export_neighbourhood_array* utility exports the array data of a neighbourhood array object to an application.

Element input parameters:

Description	Data type
Source neighbourhood array	ID
Destination array	IP
Scale factor	SP

Object restrictions:

Source neighbourhood array structure	NBHOOD_ARRAY
Destination array structure	EXT
Source neighbourhood array data type	BD, ND, SD, RD
Destination array data type	BP, NP, SP, RP

Remarks:

1. The data type of each external data value must be the same class as the neighbourhood array.
2. The scale factors for the BD, ND, and RD data types must be unity.

Nomenclature:

- C Number of array columns
- R Number of matrix rows

Definition:

The external array has the following conceptual data structure:

Array value 1, 1
Array value 2, 1
.
.
.
Array value C, 1
Array value 1, 2
.
.
.
Array value C, R

5.3.6 *Export Tuple*   `IstExportTuple`

The *export_tuple* utility exports the array data of a tuple object to an application.

Element input parameters:

Description	Data type
Source tuple	ID
Destination array	IP

Object restrictions:

Source tuple structure	TUPLE
Destination array structure	EXT
Source tuple data type	BD, ND, SD, RD, CS
Destination array data type	BP, NP, SP, RP, CS

Remark:

The data type of each external data value must be the same class as the tuple data type.

Nomenclature:

E Tuple size

Definition:

The external array has the following conceptual data structure:

Value 1
Value 2
.
.
.
Value E

5.3.7   *Get Colour Pixel*   `IvGetColourPixel`

The *get_colour_pixel* utility returns the value of a colour image pixel to an application.

Element input parameters:

Description	Data type
Source image	ID
Horizontal index value	NP
Vertical index value	NP
Depth index value	NP
Temporal index value	NP

Element output parameters:

Description	Data type
Band 0 pixel value	BP, NP, SP
Band 1 pixel value	BP, NP, SP
Band 2 pixel value	BP, NP, SP
Band 3 pixel value	BP, NP, SP, NULL

Object restrictions:

Source image structure	COLR
Source image data type	BD, ND, SD

Nomenclature:

$S(x, y, 0, 0, b)$ $X \times Y \times 1 \times 1 \times B$ source image
p_{v0} Band 0 pixel value
p_{v1} Band 1 pixel value
p_{v2} Band 2 pixel value
p_{v3} Band 3 pixel value
x_v Horizontal index value
y_v Vertical index value

Definition:

Three-band colour image:

$$p_{v0} = S(x_v, y_v, 0, 0, 0)$$
$$p_{v1} = S(x_v, y_v, 0, 0, 1)$$
$$p_{v2} = S(x_v, y_v, 0, 0, 2)$$

Four-band colour image:

$$p_{v0} = S(x_v, y_v, 0, 0, 0)$$
$$p_{v1} = S(x_v, y_v, 0, 0, 1)$$
$$p_{v2} = S(x_v, y_v, 0, 0, 2)$$
$$p_{v3} = S(x_v, y_v, 0, 0, 3)$$

5.3.8   *Get Pixel*   `IstGetPixel`

The *get_pixel* utility returns the value of a single image pixel to an application.

Element input parameters:

Description	Data type
Source image	ID
Pixel value	BP, NP, SP
Horizontal index value	NP
Vertical index value	NP
Depth index value	NP
Temporal index value	NP
Band index value	NP

Element output parameters:

Description	Data type
Pixel value	BP, NP, SP

Object restrictions:

Source image structure	MON, COLR
Source image data type	BD, ND, SD

Remark:

The data type of the returned pixel value is of the same data class as the pixel value extracted from the source image.

Nomenclature:

$S(x, y, 0, 0, b)$	$X \times Y \times 1 \times 1 \times B$ source image
p_v	Pixel value
x_v	Horizontal index value
y_v	Vertical index value
b_v	Band index value

Definition:

$$p_v = S(x_v, y_v, 0, 0, b_v)$$

5.3.9 *Get Pixel ROI*   `IbGetPixelROI`

The *get_pixel_roi* utility returns the value of a single ROI pixel to an application.

Element input parameters:

Description	Data type
Source ROI	ID
Horizontal index value	NP
Vertical index value	NP
Depth index value	NP
Temporal index value	NP
Band index value	NP

Element output parameters:

Description	Data type
Pixel value	BP

Object restrictions:

Source ROI structure	ROI_RECT
Source ROI data type	BD

Nomenclature:

$R(x, y)$	$X \times Y$ source ROI virtual array
p_v	Pixel value
x_v	Horizontal index value
y_v	Vertical index value

Definition:

$$p_v = R(x_v, y_v)$$

5.3.10 *Get Pixel Array* IstGetPixelArray

The *get_pixel_array* utility returns a rectangular array of image pixels to an application.

Element input parameters:

Description	Data type
Source image	ID
Destination array	ID
Number of array columns	ID
Number of array rows	ID
Horizontal index offset	NP
Vertical index offset	NP
Depth index value	NP
Temporal index value	NP
Band index value	NP

Object restrictions:

Source image structure	MON, COLR
Destination array structure	EXT
Source image data type	BD, ND, SD
Destination array data type	BP, NP, SP

Remark:

The data type of the returned pixel values is of the same data class as the pixel values extracted from the source image.

Nomenclature:

$S(x, y, 0, 0, b)$	$X \times Y \times 1 \times 1 \times B$ source image
x_o	Horizontal index offset
y_o	Vertical index offset
b_v	Band index value
$A(c, r)$	$C \times R$ array
C	Number of array columns
R	Number of array rows

Definition:

For

$$0 \le r \le R - 1$$
$$0 \le c \le C - 1$$

then

$$A(c, r) = S(c + x_o, r + y_o, 0, 0, b_v)$$

5.3.11 *Get Pixel Array ROI*

The *get_pixel_array_roi* utility returns a rectangular array of ROI pixels to an application.

Element input parameters:

Description	Data type
Source ROI	ID
Destination array	ID
Number of array columns	ID
Number of array rows	ID
Horizontal index offset	NP
Vertical index offset	NP
Depth index value	NP
Temporal index value	NP
Band index value	NP

Object restrictions:

Source ROI structure	ROI_RECT
Destination array structure	EXT
Source ROI data type	BD
Destination array data type	BP

Nomenclature:

$R(x, y)$	$X \times Y$ source ROI virtual array
x_o	Horizontal index offset
y_o	Vertical index offset
$A(c, r)$	$C \times R$ array
C	Number of array columns
R	Number of array rows

Definition:

For

$$0 \le r \le R - 1$$
$$0 \le c \le C - 1$$

then

$$A(c, r) = R(c + x_o, r + y_o)$$

PART 3

Syntactical Description of PIKS Elements

Chapters 6 to 8 provide syntactical descriptions of the usage of PIKS elements. Chapter 6 defines the notation and structure of the PIKS C language binding. This chapter also contains three complete PIKS programs with annotations describing the workings of each code segment. Chapter 7 is an alphabetical listing of all 96 of the PIKS Foundation element prototypes according to their C binding names. Definitions of the convenience functions and the PixelSoft, Inc. program utilities are presented in Chapter 8.

Chapters 7 and 8 have been written in a reference book style. Each prototype function is described in a manner akin to a Unix "manpage." A PIKS manpage begins with a specification of the prototype—the calling sequence that will appear in a PIKS program. This is followed, if applicable, by the specifications of any enumerated type, data type union, or structure type definitions. If applicable, there next appears the specifications of #define macro definitions. Then, a code snippet illustrating the usage of the pertinent prototype function is presented.

Upon first encounter of Part 3, the reader is advised to thoroughly read Chapter 6 and to skim through Chapters 7 and 8 to obtain a feeling of their style and content.

In order to write PIKS programs, the programmer must understand both the semantic functionality of each PIKS element and the syntactical rules for its usage. This means that a programmer must, at least in the beginning learning phase, shuffle between the functional specification material of Chapters 2 to 5 and the C binding manpages of Chapter 7. To make this task somewhat easier, the functional specification section number of the applicable element is printed on each element manpage.

6

PIKS C Language Binding

The four previous chapters have described the semantic usage of PIKS (how it functions). This chapter and the next chapter describe the syntactic usage of PIKS for the C programming language (how to use it).

6.1 Binding Notation

The PIKS C language binding has adopted the so called "Hungarian" notation based upon the prototype naming convention developed by Charles Simonyi. This notation explicitly specifies the data types of all entities by prefix codes. Strict adherence to this notation in application programs helps to avoid data typing errors. The penalty paid for this feature is that entity names are longer because of the prefixes. Readers unfamiliar with this notation will likely be opposed to it on first encounter (this author was). However, the notational style is easily learned, and the benefits of better code readability and visual data type checking are worth the extra key strokes.

Table 6-1 lists the PIKS Foundation prefix codes for type names.

Table 6-1 Data type prefix codes

Prefix	Definition
a	array
b	Boolean
c	character
d	internal data type
e	enumerated data type
f	function
i	integer
m	external image data type
n	identifier
p	parameter type
r	real
s	structure

Table 6-1 *(Continued)*   Data type prefix codes

Prefix	Definition
t	pointer
u	unsigned integer
v	void
z	zero terminated string

The following is the general structure of the C language binding of PIKS element prototypes.

```
void IvElementName
```

or

```
I(prefix1)returnname I(compoundprefix)ElementName
```

or

```
I(prefix1)(prefix2)returnname I(compoundprefix)ElementName
```

or

```
I(prefix1)(prefix2)(prefix3)returnname I(compoundprefix)ElementName
```

where

```
prefix1:
```
d	Internal data type or parameter type
p	External parameter type
m	External image data type

```
prefix2:
```
e	Enumerated data type
s	Structure, including union
t	Pointer

```
prefix3:
```
f	Function

```
compoundprefix:
```
b	Boolean data type
n	Identifier
st	Structure or union pointer
tba	Pointer to Boolean array
tf	Pointer to function
tra	Pointer to real array
tua	Pointer to unsigned integer array

The return name indicates the data type, data object, data type union, enumerated type, or structure as the return value. Table 6-2 lists the return designaters in PIKS Foundation. The PIKS Foundation C binding element names and associated Functional Specification names are listed in Table 6-3.

Table 6-2 Relationship of C Binding designaters to Functional Specification data types and data object.

Binding	Functional	Description
Imbool	BI	External Boolean data type
Imuint	NI	External nonnegative integer data type
Imint	SI	External signed integer data type
Imfixed	TI	External fixed point integer data type
Ipbool	BP	Parameter Boolean data type
Ipint	SP	Parameter signed integer data type
Ipuint	NP	Parameter nonnegative (unsigned) integer data type
Ipfloat	RP	Parameter real arithmetic data type
Idnchain	CHAIN	Chain data object
Idnhist	HIST	Histogram data object
Idnimage	SRC, DST	Image data object
Idnlut	LUT	Lookup table data object
Idnmatrix	MATRIX	Matrix data object
Idndbhood	NBHOOD_ARRAY	Neighbourhood array data object
Idnroi	ROI_RECT	Rectangular ROI data object
Idntuple	TUPLE	Tuple data object
Ipsarray_id	ID	Matrix, nbhood array identifier union
Idnrepository	IP	External repository identifier
Ipnerror	IP	External error file identifier
Ipsparameter_basic	IP	External tuple data array pointer union
Ipsparameter_numeric	IP	External matrix data array pointer union
Ipsparameter_pixel	IP	External LUT, nbhood, pixel data array pointer union
Ipspiks_pixel_types	IP	External image data array pointer union
Iptferror_function	IP	External handler function pointer

Table 6-3   Relationship of C Binding element names to
Functional Specification element names

Binding	Functional
IbErrorTest	*error_test*
IbGetPixelROI	*get_pixel_roi*
InAllocateHist	*allocate_histogram*
InAllocateImage	*allocate_image*
InAllocateLUT	*allocate_lut*
InAllocateMatrix	*allocate_matrix*
InAllocateNbhoodArray	*allocate_neighbourhood_array*
InAllocateROI	*allocate_roi*
InAllocateTuple	*allocate_tuple*
InAlphaBlendConstant	*alpha_blend_constant*
InArrayToLUT	*array_to_lut*
InBindROI	*bind_roi*
InBitShift	*bit_shift*
InColourConvLin	*colour_conversion_linear*
InColourConvSubtractive	*colour_conversion_subtractive*
InComplement	*complement*
InConvertArrayToImage	*convert_array_to_image*
InConvertImageDatatype	*convert_image_data_type*
InConvertROIToImage	*convert_roi_to_image*
InConvolve2D	*convolve_2d*
InCopyWindow	*copy_window*
InCreateTuple	*create_tuple*
InDefineSubImage	*define_sub_image*
InDiffuse	*diffuse*
InDither	*dither*
InDrawPixels	*draw_pixels*
InDyadicArith	*dyadic_arithmetic*
InDyadicLogical	*dyadic_logical*
InDyadicPredicate	*dyadic_predicate*
InExtractPixelPlane	*extract_pixel_plane*
InFlipSpinTranspose	*flip_spin_transpose*
InFlipSpinTransposeROI	*flip_spin_transpose_roi*
InHist1D	*histogram_1d*
InImageConstant	*image_constant*
InImportHist	*import_histogram*

Table 6-3 *(Continued)* Relationship of C Binding element names to Functional Specification element names

Binding	Functional
InImportImage	*import_image*
InImportLUT	*import_lut*
InImportMatrix	*import_matrix*
InImportNbhoodArray	*import_neighbourhood_array*
InImportTuple	*import_tuple*
InImpulseRectangular	*impulse_rectangular*
InInsertPixelPlane	*insert_pixel_plane*
InLookup	*lookup*
InLumGeneration	*luminance_generation*
InMonadicArith	*monadic_arithmetic*
InMonadicLogical	*monadic_logical*
InMorphicProcessor	*morphic_processor*
InPutColourPixel	*put_colour_pixel*
InPutPixel	*put_pixel*
InPutPixelArray	*put_pixel_array*
InRescale	*rescale*
InRescaleROI	*rescale_roi*
InResize	*resize*
InResizeROI	*resize_roi*
InReturnRepositoryId	*return_repository_id*
InROIRectangular	*roi_rectangular*
InRotate	*rotate*
InSetImageAttrs	*set_image_attributes*
InSplitImage	*split_image*
InSubsample	*subsample*
InThreshold	*threshold*
InTranslate	*translate*
InTranslateROI	*translate_roi*
InUnaryInteger	*unary_integer*
InWindowLevel	*window_level*
InZoom	*zoom*
InZoomROI	*zoom_roi*
IsnConvertImageToArray	*convert_image_to_array*
IstExportImage	*export_image*
IstExportLUT	*export_lut*

Table 6-3 *(Continued)*   Relationship of C Binding element names
to Functional Specification element names

Binding	Functional
IstExportMatrix	*export_matrix*
IstExportNbhoodArray	*export_neighbourhood_array*
IstExportTuple	*export_tuple*
IstGetPixel	*get_pixel*
IstGetPixelArray	*get_pixel_array*
ItbaGetPixelArrayROI	*get_pixel_array_roi*
ItfSetErrorHandler	*set_error_handler*
ItraAccumulator	*accumulator*
ItuaExportHist	*export_histogram*
IvClosePIKS	*close_piks*
IvClosePIKSEmergency	*close_piks_emergency*
IvColourConvMatrix	*colour_conversion_matrix*
IvDeallocateDataObject	*deallocate_data_object*
IvErrorHandler	*error_handler*
IvErrorLogger	*error_logger*
IvExtrema	*extrema*
IvGetColourPixel	*get_colour_pixel*
IvInquireElements	*inquire_elements*
IvInquireImage	*inquire_image*
IvInquireNonImageObject	*inquire_non_image_object*
IvInquirePIKSImpl	*inquire_piks_implementation*
IvInquirePIKSStatus	*inquire_piks_status*
IvInquireRepository	*inquire_repository*
IvInquireResampling	*inquire_resampling*
IvMoments	*moments*
IvOpenPIKS	*open_piks*
IvSetGlobals	*set_globals*

The following is an example of an element C binding prototype.

```
Idnimage InConvolve2D(                       /* OUT destination image identifier      */
   Idnimage            nSourceImage,         /* source image identifier               */
   Idnimage            nDestImage,           /* destination image identifier          */
   Idnnbhood           nImpulse,             /* impulse response array identifier     */
   Ipint               iOption               /* convolution 2D option                 */
);
```

This example is the prototype for the two-dimensional convolution operator. The first two components are the identifiers of the source and destination images, respectively. Next, is the identifier of the impulse response neighbourhood array. The last component is the integer option parameter for the convolution boundary options.

Elements that create a single destination image or nonimage object, return the object identifier even if the identifier is specified as an input to an element parameter list. This methodology also applies to elements that create data values. The purpose of this design methodology is to permit the nesting of element calls. To avoid ambiguity, no identifier or value is returned for elements that create more than one output. Return values are void for elements that do not create destination objects or values. Elements that set flags return Boolean state values.

As an example, let nSrc, nDst, and nImpulse denote the identifiers assigned to a source image, a destination image, and an impulse response neighbourhood array upon the allocation of the data objects. Then, the two-dimensional convolution element can be invoked in a program by

```
InConvolve2D(nSrc, nDst, nImpulse, ICONVOLVE_ENCLOSED);
```

or by

```
nDst = InConvolve2D(nSrc, nDst, nImpulse, ICONVOLVE_ENCLOSED);
```

where ICONVOLVE_ENCLOSED is the #define macro name that specifies the convolution border option.

6.2   Header Information

PIKS implementations supply a header file that defines the PIKS data types and structures. This header file should be included in the compilation of an application program that utilizes PIKS. The header file contains definitions of the following:

External physical image data types
Parameter data types
Data object identifiers
Enumerated type definitions
Data type union definitions
Structure type definitions
Macro definitions
Element designaters
Convenience function designaters
Impulse response array repository entry designaters
Dither array repository entry designaters
Colour conversion matrix repository entry designaters
Error code designaters

Appendix B contains a listing of the data types and structures to be found in a PIKS header file. It should be noted that the information presented in Appendix B is arranged for human access and understanding. In an actual header file, these items will be ordered differently.

A PIKS header file may also contain implementation-dependent items, for example, image display utilities, which are not part of the PIKS standard.

6.3   Memory Management

PIKS requires the allocation of internal memory space to store its image and nonimage objects. Such objects are denoted as `Idnxxx` in Table 6-2, where xxx is the return type. In PIKS, the application has no control over the memory allocated to individual PIKS internal d-type data objects.

PIKS also requires external memory space for data structures denoted as `Ipsxxx` in Table 6-2, where xxx is the return type. Such structures are the means by which PIKS receives input data parameters from an application or returns output data values to an application. It is the responsibility of the application to allocate sufficient memory space for p-type data structures.

Many of the import and export utilities have the potential to accept a large amount of data from an application or to deliver a large amount of data to an application. Also, some elements, e.g., extrema, can generate an unpredictable amount of data. For sensible memory management, for both cases, the PIKS C binding specifies a fixed length data buffering method for data transfer between PIKS and the application. Under this method, the application can specify a fixed length one-dimensional data buffer array, which provides and accepts data in a piecewise manner. PIKS elements that support data buffering require the specification of the following parameters.

- `iApplBufferSize`   This is an integer input parameter of type `Ipint`, which specifies the size of the application data buffer. It is dimensioned as the number of datum of the data type listed elsewhere in the parameter list for input or output. Setting the value of `iAppl-BufferSize` to -1, results in the transfer of data in one transaction. Setting the value to 0, provides a means to determine the internal data size through the entity, `tuDataSize`, as defined below. The data buffer size may be larger than the data length of data to be transferred into it.

- `uStartPoint`   This is an unsigned integer input parameter of type `Ipuint`. It is the data buffer index offset of the implementation's internal data structure data space, which is conceptually ordered as a one-dimensional array for data transfer. Setting `uStartPoint` to 0, references the first datum in the application's data buffer and the implementation's virtual data array. The transfer of data proceeds by repeated invocation of the PIKS data buffering element with `uStartPoint` indexed in strides of the application buffer size, `iApplBuffer-Size`, until there is no more data to transfer.

- `tuDataSize`   This is an unsigned integer output pointer of type `Ipuint`. Upon invocation of an element using data buffering, the element returns a value, which is the size of the data remaining beyond the specified `uStartPoint`, less the amount of data transferred by the element. In other words, `tuDataSize` tells the application how much data remains to be transferred after the execution of the element. This parameter may be specified as `NULL` if a return value is not desired.

Example:

An 8-bit, unsigned integer image of size 200x300 pixels is to be imported from an application with a data buffer size of 1024 bytes. The following steps are taken:

(a) Invoke `InImportImage` with `iApplBufferSize` set to 0 and `uStartPoint` set to 0. The return value referenced by `tuDataSize` of 60,000 is the number of bytes in the PIKS image array.

(b) In a loop of 59 cycles, while `uDataSize` remains nonzero, invoke `InImportImage` with `iApplBufferSize` set to 1024. The final data transfer will contain 608 valid pixels and 416 unfilled pixels. ($59 \times 1024 - 60,000 = 416$).

6.4 Convenience Functions

The PIKS C Binding has defined several standardized convenience functions, which are built upon other PIKS elements. The purpose of these convenience functions is to simplify programming for the common, but special cases often encountered in application programs. For example, usage of the `InPrepareMonochormeImage` convenience function avoids the need to explicitly create the image size, band data type, and band precision tuples.

Chapter 8 defines the following convenience functions:

Generate ND 1-tuple
Generate ND 3-tuple
Generate ND 4-tuple
Generate ND 5-tuple
Generate RD 5-tuple
Generate SD 1-tuple
Generate SD 3-tuple
Generate SD 4-tuple
Generate SD 5-tuple
Generate 2D ROI rectangular
Prepare colour image
Prepare monochrome image
Prepare 2D ROI rectangular

6.5 Implementation-specific Utilities

The PIKS standard does not specify any file, window, and display utilities because such functionality tends to be implementation specific. However, it is expected that PIKS vendors will provide file, window, and image display utilities as part of their products. As an example of such functionality, the following sections describe the file, window, and display utilities provided in the PixelSoft, Inc. implementation of PIKS Foundation.

6.5.1 File Reading and Writing

In many application programs, a source image is read from a disk file into the application's memory space prior to import to PIKS. Likewise, a destination image exported from PIKS will be written to a file. PIKS does not provide any standardized means of file reading and writing. The program examples provide a simple example of file reading under the Unix operating system.

Chapter 8 defines the following nonstandard PixelSoft, Inc. file manipulation utilities.

```
IstGetFile
IvPutFile
```

These file utilities utilize a simple file format. The file name is a pointer to a header file `name.header`, which defines the image width, height, bit precision, and number of bands in that order. The second line of the header references the image data file called `name.data`. For example, the image file named `toys` has the following header

```
512 512 8 3
toys.data
```

This header file specifies that the image has 512 columns, 512 rows, 8 bit per pixel precision, and 3 bands.

6.5.2   Window Manipulation

The following program examples utilize the SunSoft, Inc. OpenLook X window system for image display. The basic paradigm for its usage for image display is:

Open an X window of specified size;

Display an image by copying from an internal PIKS image to the frame buffer associated with the window;

Close the window.

It is possible to open and use multiple windows if they are uniquely opened, copied to, and closed. Also, it is possible to use a single window to sequentially display multiple images of the same size.

In the X window system, low amplitude integer image pixel values are reserved for pseudo-coloring of the screen background and window frames. In order to avoid unwanted colouring in an image display window, the displayed images are amplitude rescaled prior to display. This is automatically performed by the image display utilities.

Chapter 8 defines the following nonstandard PixelSoft, Inc. X window display functions.

```
IvCloseWindow
ItOpenWindow
IvKeyDelay
```

6.5.3   Image Display

Chapter 8 defines the following simple, nonstandard PixelSoft, Inc. image display utilities.

```
InBooleanDisplay
InColourDisplay
InMonochromeDisplay
InPseudocolourDisplay
```

The last three utilities are used for displaying colour, monochrome, and pseudocolour, unsigned integer data type images. These utilities automatically convert from the internal precision of the source image to be displayed to the bit depth of an unsigned integer display buffer. The source image must be of the same dimension as the display window. The Boolean display utility displays a Boolean image by mapping TRUE state pixels to the maximum integer display amplitude, and by mapping FALSE state pixels to a zero integer amplitude display value.

6.6   Program Structure

The PIKS standard does not dictate any particular program structure or style. The program structure that has been utilized in the program examples of the following sections is as follows.

Preamble

Program name
Operational steps
Creation history

Includes

Header file designations

Defines

Program define designations

Main routine

Main program declaration

Local entities

Specification of program entities that are not PIKS-specific, e.g., window display variables, input and output variables, and elementary routine variables, such as integer index variables

PIKS entities

Specification of program entities that are PIKS-specific, e.g., image and tuple identifiers

Open PIKS session

Open error file
Open PIKS

Allocation

Allocate source, destination, and work images allocate nonimage objects, e.g., lookup table, histogram, neighbourhood array

Import

Read source image files
Import source images
Import nonimage objects

Source display

Open display window
Display source images
Close display window

Processing

Sequence of image processing operations, e.g., convolve, histogram

Destination display

Open display window
Display destination images
Close display window

Export

    Export destination images
    Export destination nonimage objects
    Write destination image files

Close PIKS session

    Close PIKS

6.7   ROI Complement Example

This section presents a program example of the complement of a monochrome image under source ROI control. The example has been developed for a Unix computing environment using the SunSoft, Inc. Solaris operating system. The implementation-specific segments of the example utilizes the PixelSoft, Inc. file, window, and display utilities defined in Chapter 8.

Appendix C contains the listing of the program `roi_complement.c`. The following is a segment-by-segment description of the program.

```
/*** Program:
***
***        roi_complement.c
***
***
*** Function:
***
***        Image complement under source ROI control
***
***
*** Operational steps:
***
***        Allocate monochrome source and destination images
***        Generate source image ROI
***        Read source image from file to buffer
***        Import source image from buffer
***        Copy source image into destination image
***        Display destination image
***        Enable ROI control
***        Bind source ROI to source image
***        Complement source image into destination image
***        Display destination image
***        Export destination image to buffer
***        Write destination image in buffer to file
***
***
*** History:
***
***        Created             28 September 1994      W. K. Pratt
***
***/
```

These comments are obviously not required for program execution. However, it is good programming practice to include such information.

```
/* Includes                                                      */

    #include <stdio.h>
    #include <stdlib.h>
    #include <sys/types.h>
    #include <sys/stat.h>
    #include <fcntl.h>
    #include <piks.h>
```

The first five includes are standard Unix header files. The last is the *piks.h* header file that is provided with a PIKS implementation. It contains the header information of Appendix B plus vendor-specific information.

```
/* Defines                                                                    */

    #define HEIGHT 512
    #define WIDTH 512
    #define BANDS 1
    #define ND_PRECISION 8
```

These entities are local program definitions of the image size, and pixel storage precision.

```
/* Main                                                                       */

main(int argc, char **argv)
{
```

The arguments are used in the file reading routine.

```
/* Local entities                                                             */

    char                    err_name[] ="piks_errors";

    void                    *tDisplay;
```

The first entry specifies the PIKS error file name. The second entry is the image display reference.

```
/* PIKS entities                                                              */

    Idnimage                nSrcND, nDstND;

    Idnroi                  nSrcROI;

    Idntuple                nROIOffset;

    Idntuple                nSrcOff, nDstOff, nSrcWin;

    Ipnerror                nErrorFile;

    Ipspiks_pixel_types     stExtImageArray;

    Ipspiks_modes           sModes, *tsModes = &sModes;

    Ipevalidity             eValid, *teValid = &eValid;

    Ipint                   iApplBufferSize;

    Ipuint                  uDataSize, *tuDataSize = &uDataSize;
```

These are the declarations of the PIKS data objects and associated data structures, which will be subsequently used in the program. The first entry gives the names of the source and destination images, nSrcND and nDstND. Note the prefix n, which designates these as identifiers. Next, the ROI to be associated with the source image is declared.

The ROI offset tuple and the tuples used by the *copy_window* utility are declared.

The Ipnerror identifier provides a pointer to the error file. An empty error file with this name must be created prior to program execution.

Ipspiks_pixel_types is a union that specifies the data type of the pixels of the external image to be imported to PIKS.

Ipspiks_modes is a struct that specifies the PIKS operational modes. Ipevalidity is an enum that indicates the availability or nonavailability of data upon an inquiry.

Finally, the application buffer size and data transfer size are specified as integer and unsigned integer, respectively. These entries are associated with the import and export utilities.

```
/* Open PIKS session                                                          */

    if((nErrorFile = (Ipnerror)fopen(err_name, "w")) == NULL)
            exit(1);

    InOpenPIKS(nErrorFile);
```

The error file to be used in the session is identified and PIKS is opened.

```
/* Allocate monochrome images                                           */

    nSrcND = InPrepareMonochromeImage(WIDTH, HEIGHT, IDATA_TYPE_INTERNAL_ND,
            ND_PRECISION);

    nDstND = InPrepareMonochromeImage(WIDTH, HEIGHT, IDATA_TYPE_INTERNAL_ND,
            ND_PRECISION);
```

This form of allocation of the source and destination images uses the prepare monochrome image convenience function defined in Chapter 8. This convenience function creates the image attributes in a single step, thereby reducing programming labour. The *allocate_image* manual page in the next chapter illustrates the long form for image allocation. Usage of the prepare image convenience function is possible in PIKS Foundation because of the restriction that image bands must be homogeneous.

```
/* Create rectangular ROI                                               */

    nROIOffset = InGenerateSD5Tuple(0, 0, 0, 0, 0);

    nSrcROI = InGenerate2DROIRectangular(WIDTH, HEIGHT, 50, 100, 300, 250,
            IPOLARITY_TRUE);
```

In this segment, a tuple generation convenience function is used to specify the ROI offset tuple. The generate two-dimensional rectangular ROI convenience function is used to create the ROI. The ROI is of the same dimension as the source and destination images. It is set logically TRUE in the rectangle whose upper left corner is at coordinate (50, 100) and lower right corner is at coordinate (300, 250).

```
/* Read source image file into buffer                                   */

    stExtImageArray.tuPixel = IstGetFile("brainscan").tuPixel;
```

This program segment is a nonstandardized method of opening an image file, reading it, and transferring its content to an internal data buffer. The name of the image is brainscan. The extension ".tuPixel" specifies that the image data type is unsigned integer. The IstGet-File utility reads the image size (width, height, bands) from the brainscan.header file, and dimensions the internal data buffer accordingly.

```
/* Import source image from buffer                                      */

    iApplBufferSize = WIDTH * HEIGHT;

    InImportImage(stExtImageArray, nSrcND, ND_PRECISION, IPIXEL_NI_PLANAR,
            iApplBufferSize, 0, tuDataSize);
```

The application buffer size is set at the image array size of 262, 144 bytes. The import image utility is then invoked.

```
/* Copy source image into destination image                            */

    nSrcOff = InGenerateSD5Tuple(0, 0, 0, 0, 0);

    nDstOff = InGenerateSD5Tuple(0, 0, 0, 0, 0);

    nSrcWin = InGenerateND5Tuple(WIDTH, HEIGHT, 1, 1, 1);

    InCopyWindow(nSrcND, nDstND, nSrcOff, nDstOff, nSrcWin);
```

This segment creates *copy_window* tuples that specify the source and destination window offsets (none) and a tuple that specifies the window size (the entire source image). The source image is then copied into the destination image. Alternatively, the copy image functionality could have been achieved in one step by invoking the *monadic_arithmentic* element with an addition of a constant of value zero.

```
/* Open X display window and display destination image                     */

    tDisplay = ItOpenWindow(WIDTH, HEIGHT, BANDS);

    InMonochromeDisplay(nDstND, tDisplay);

    printf("Destination image: copied source image \n");
    printf("             Press any key in window to continue \n");

    IvKeyDelay(tDisplay);
```

An empty X display window is generated by this program segment. An observer will see the window frame with the screen background showing through the frame until the following source display segment is executed.

The entry `InMonochromeDisplay` causes the destination image to be displayed in the display window. This function is not a PIKS element. If the cursor is not within the window, some pseudocolouring of the image may be visible. This can be eliminated by moving the cursor inside of the window. The image is displayed until a key is pressed.

```
/* Enable ROI processing                                                   */

    IvInquirePIKSStatus(NULL, tsModes, teValid);

    if(eValid == IVALIDITY_VALID) {
        sModes.eROIControlMode = IROI_CONTROL_ON;
        IvSetGlobals(sModes);
    }
    else
        printf ("Error: PIKS reports not open\n");
```

The ROI control mode is engaged.

```
/* Bind source ROI to source image                                         */

    InBindROI(nSrcND, nSrcROI, nROIOffset);
```

The source ROI is bound to the source image.

```
/* Complement source image into destination image                          */

    InComplement(nSrcND, nDstND);
```

The source image is complemented. Each bit of each unsigned integer source pixel, which lies in the rectangular ROI logical TRUE region, is reversed in state and recorded in the destination image. Destination image pixels corresponding, spatially, to the source ROI FALSE state remain unchanged.

```
/* Display destination image and close window                              */

    InMonochromeDisplay(nDst, tDisplay);

    printf("Destination image; complemented source window inlay \n");
    printf("             Press any key in window to continue \n");

    IvKeyDelay(tDisplay);

    IvCloseWindow(tDisplay);
```

The destination image is displayed in the previously opened window, overwriting the previously displayed destination image. The display window is closed.

```
/* Export destination image to buffer                                      */

    IstExportImage(nDstND, stExtImageArray, ND_PRECISION, IPIXEL_NI_PLANAR,
        iApplBufferSize, 0, tuDataSize);
```

6.7 ROI COMPLEMENT EXAMPLE   187

The destination image is exported to the previously created application buffer.

```
/* Write buffer to image file                                         */

    IvPutFile(stExtImageArray, "roi_inlay", WIDTH, HEIGHT, ND_PRECISION, BANDS);
```

The destination image in the application buffer is written to a file named `roi_inlay` by the nonstandard utility `IvPutFile`.

```
/* Check for errors                                                    */

    fclose(nErrorFile);

    if(IbErrorTest())
        printf("Error exists, check log\n");
```

The error file is closed and a check is made to determine if any errors were generated during program execution.

```
/* Close PIKS session                                                  */

    IvClosePIKS();

    free(stExtImageArray.tuPixel);
}
```

The PIKS session is then terminated and the application buffer storage is freed.

The following occurs when the `roi_complement` program is executed.

An X window frame is displayed, followed quickly by the display of the destination image, which is a copy of the source image. This will likely appear as a single step. Then the following text is displayed on the screen.

```
Destination image: copied source image
    Press any key in window to continue
```

After striking a key, the second destination image is displayed and the following text is displayed on the screen.

```
Destination image: complemented source image inlay
    Press any key in window to continue
```

Figure 6-1 presents the destination images generated by the `roi_complement` program.

a 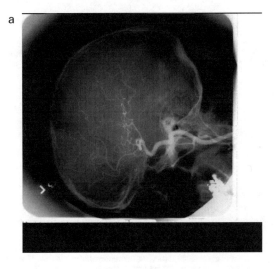 b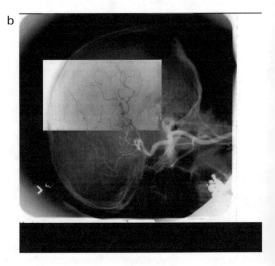

Figure 6-1   Example of ROI complement: (a) source, "brainscan"; (b) destination, ROI complement inlay

6.8 Image Histogram Example

This program is an example of the computation of the histogram of the green band of a colour image. Appendix C contains the listing of the program `histogram.c`. The following is an abbreviated explanation of the program segments. Only differences from the previous example are described.

```
/*** Program:
 ***
 *** histogram.c
 ***
 *** Operational steps:
 ***
 *** Allocate colour source image and monochrome green band sub-image
 *** Import source image from file
 *** Display source image
 *** Define green band sub-image
 *** Display green band sub-image
 *** Compute histogram of green band
 *** Export histogram
 *** Print histogram
 ***
 ***
 *** History:
 ***
 *** Created        28 September 1994       W. K. Pratt
 ***
 ***/


/* Includes                                                          */

#include <stdio.h>
#include <stdlib.h>
#include <sys/types.h>
#include <sys/stat.h>
#include <fcntl.h>
#include <piks.h>


/* Defines                                                           */

#define HEIGHT 512
#define WIDTH 512
#define COLOUR_BANDS 3
#define MON_BANDS 1
#define ND_PRECISION 8


/* Main                                                              */

main(int argc, char **argv)
{

/* Local entities                                                    */

    char            err_name[] ="piks_errors";

    int             i, sum;

    void            *tDisplay;
```

The int entries are used to print the histogram values and the histogram sum.

```
/* PIKS entities                                                     */

    Idnimage        nSrc, nSubSrc;

    Idnhist         nHist;

    Idntuple        nOffset, nSubSize;
```

```
Ipnerror              nErrorFile;

Ipspiks_pixel_types   stExtImageArray;

Ipsattrs_hist         sAttrsHist;

Ipuint                uaExtHistArray[16], *tuaExtHistArray = &uaExtHistArray[0];

Ipuint                uBins;

Ipfloat               rLower, rUpper

Ipint                 iApplBufferSize;

Ipuint                uDataSize, *tuDataSize = &uDataSize;
```

The entry for uaExtHistArray is the storage for the histogram data to be exported to the application. The next two entries declare the number of histogram bins and the upper and lower amplitude values over which the histogram is to be computed.

```
/* Open PIKS session                                                           */

    if((nErrorFile = (Ipnerror)fopen(err_name, "w")) == NULL)
                    exit(1);

    InOpenPIKS(nErrorFile);


/* Allocate images                                                             */

    nSrc = InPrepareColourImage(WIDTH, HEIGHT, COLOUR_BANDS, IDATA_TYPE_INTERNAL_ND,
            ND_PRECISION, 1.0, 1.0, 1.0, ICOLOUR_NON_STANDARD_RGB);

    nSubSrc = InPrepareMonochromeImage(WIDTH, HEIGHT, IDATA_TYPE_INTERNAL_ND,
            ND_PRECISION);
```

Allocation is performed using the colour and monochrome image prepare convenience functions.

```
/* Allocate histogram                                                          */

    sAttrsHist.uHistSize = 16;

    sAttrsHist.rLowerBound = 0.0;

    sAttrsHist.rUpperBound = 255.0;

    nHist = InAllocateHist(sAttrsHist);
```

The histogram is specified to have 16 amplitude bins and to be computed over the image amplitude range of 0 to 255.

```
/* Read image file into buffer and import image from buffer                    */

    stExtImageArray.tuPixel = IstGetFile("toys").tuPixel;

    iApplBufferSize = WIDTH * HEIGHT * COLOUR_BANDS;

    InImportImage(stExtImageArray, nSrc, PRECISION, IPIXEL_NI_PLANAR,
        iApplBufferSize, 0, tuDataSize);
```

The "toys" colour image is imported with a buffer size of 786,432 bytes.

```
/* Open X display window                                                       */

    tDisplay = ItOpenWindow(WIDTH, HEIGHT, COLOUR_BANDS);


/* Display source colour image                                                 */

    printf("Source colour image \n");
    printf("            Press any key in window to continue \n");
```

```
        InColourDisplay(nSrc, tDisplay);

        IvKeyDelay(tDisplay);
```

The nonstandard colour image display function is invoked. This function performs dithering of the unsigned integer, 8-bit per component colour image to an 8-bit per pixel display frame buffer using a pseudocolour colour mapping.

```
    /* Close X display window                                              */
        IvCloseWindow(tDisplay);


    /* Define green band sub-image                                         */
        nOffset = InGenerateND5Tuple(0, 0, 0, 0, 1);

        nSubSize = InGenerateND5Tuple(WIDTH, HEIGHT, 1, 1, MON_BANDS);

        InDefineSubImage(nSrc, nSubSrc, nOffset, nSubSize);
```

The nOffset tuple specifies the green band. An alternative to the use of the *define_sub_image* element for subsequent histogram computation would have been to extract the green band and copy it to a monochrome image using the *extract_pixel_plane* utility. The approach taken here is more efficient because it avoids the copying and storage of the data associated with the green band.

```
    /* Open X display window                                               */
        tDisplay = ItOpenWindow(WIDTH, HEIGHT, MON_BANDS);


    /* Display source green band monochrome sub-image                      */
        printf("Source green band sub-image \n");

        InMonochromeDisplay(nSubSrc, tDisplay);

        printf("          Press any key in window to continue \n");

        IvKeyDelay(tDisplay);
```

The green band is displayed as a monochrome image.

```
    /* Close X display window                                              */
        IvCloseWindow(tDisplay);


    /* Compute histogram for 0 to 255 amplitude limits                     */
        uBins = 16;

        rLower = 0.0;

        rUpper = 255.0;

        InHist1D(nSubSrc, nHist, uBins, rLower, rUpper, IHIST_LIMIT_SPECIFIED);
```

The histogram is computed for the specified limits option.

```
    /* Export histogram and print results                                  */
        ItuaExportHist(nHist, tuaExtHistArray);

        printf("Histogram printout\n");

        sum = 0;
        for(i = 0; i < uBins; i++) {
                sum += tuaExtHistArray[i];
                printf("h[%d] = %u\n", i, tuaExtHistArray[i]);
```

```
        }
        printf("sum = %d\n", sum);
```

The histogram results are exported and displayed. The sum is printed as a check. It should equal the number of pixels in the monochrome green band image, $512 \times 512 = 262,144$.

```
/* Check for errors                                               */

    fclose(nErrorFile);

    if(IbErrorTest())
            printf("Error exists, check log\n");

/* Close PIKS session                                             */

    IvClosePIKS();

    free(stExtImageArray.tuPixel);
}
```

Execution of this program produces a dithered colour image display. Then, the green band image is displayed as a monochrome image. Finally, the following histogram result is printed:

```
Histogram printout

h[0]  = 47611
h[1]  = 9464
h[2]  = 15116
h[3]  = 15301
h[4]  = 12504
h[5]  = 10754
h[6]  = 9816
h[7]  = 11517
h[8]  = 11358
h[9]  = 15625
h[10] = 19813
h[11] = 29108
h[12] = 38923
h[13] = 9749
h[14] = 5435
h[15] = 50

sum = 262144
```

6.9   Unsharp Mask Example

The program example in this section illustrates the generation of a PIKS Technical profile operator by calls to PIKS Foundation operators. Appendix C contains the listing of the program unsharp_mask.c. The following is an abbreviated explanation of the program segments. One of the purposes of this program is to illustrate the processing of an SD data type image. There are simpler programs for the computation of the unsharp mask function.

```
/*** Program:
 ***
 ***  unsharp_mask.c
 ***
 *** Function:
 ***
 ***  Unsharp masking.
 ***
 ***
 *** Operational steps:
 ***
 ***  Allocate colour source and destination images
 ***  Generate 5x5 uniform amplitude impulse response array
 ***  Import source image
 ***  Display source image
```

```
    ***   Convolve source image with impulse response array to create blurred image
    ***   Display blurred image
    ***   Weight source and blurred image
    ***   Add weighted images to obtain unsharp masked destination image
    ***   Display destination image
    ***
    ***
    ***   History:
    ***
    ***   Created          28 September 1994          W. K. Pratt
    ***
    ***/


    /*Includes                                                              */

    #include <stdio.h>
    #include <stdlib.h>
    #include <sys/types.h>
    #include <sys/stat.h>
    #include <fcntl.h>
    #include <piks.h>


    /*                    Defines                                           */

    #define HEIGHT 512
    #define WIDTH 512
    #define BANDS 3
    #define ND_PRECISION 8
    #define SD_PRECISION 16


    /* Main                                                                 */

    main(int argc, char **argv)
    {
    /* Local entities                                                       */

        char                        err_name[] ="piks_errors";

        void                        *tDisplay1, *tDisplay2, *tDisplay3;

        float                       p;
```

Three display windows are declared. The float entity, p, is used as a weighting factor.

```
    /* PIKS entities                                                        */

        Idnimage                    nSrcND, nDstND, nWrkND;

        Idnimage                    nSrcSD, nDstSD, nWrk1SD, nWrk2SD;

        Idnnbhood                   nImpulse;

        Idntuple                    nImpulseSize, nKeyPixel;

        Ipnerror                    nErrorFile;

        Ipspiks_pixel_types         stExtImageArray;

        Ipsattrs_nbhood             sAttrsNbhood;

        Ipsparameter_arith          stw1_numerator, stw2_numerator, stw_denominator;

        Ipsparameter_arith          stAbove, stBelow, stWidth, stLevel;

        Ipint                       iw1_numerator, iw2_numerator, iw_denominator;

        Ipuint                      uAbove, uBelow, uWidth, uLevel;

        Ipint                       iApplBufferSize;

        Ipuint                      uDataSize, *tuDataSize = &uDataSize;
```

The first two entries decare the ND and SD data type versions of the source, destination, and work images. The impulse response array is declared by the next entry.

```
/* Open PIKS session                                                     */

    if((nErrorFile = (Ipnerror)fopen(err_name, "w")) == NULL)
        exit(1);

    InOpenPIKS(nErrorFile);


/* Allocate colour images                                                 */

    nSrcND = InPrepareColourImage(WIDTH, HEIGHT, BANDS, IDATA_TYPE_INTERNAL_ND,
        ND_PRECISION, 1.0, 1.0, 1.0, ICOLOUR_NON_STANDARD_RGB);

    nDstND = InPrepareColourImage(WIDTH, HEIGHT, BANDS, IDATA_TYPE_INTERNAL_ND,
        ND_PRECISION, 1.0, 1.0, 1.0, ICOLOUR_NON_STANDARD_RGB);

    nWrkND = InPrepareColourImage(WIDTH, HEIGHT, BANDS, IDATA_TYPE_INTERNAL_ND,
        ND_PRECISION, 1.0, 1.0, 1.0, ICOLOUR_NON_STANDARD_RGB);

    nSrcSD = InPrepareColourImage(WIDTH, HEIGHT, BANDS, IDATA_TYPE_INTERNAL_SD,
        SD_PRECISION, 1.0, 1.0, 1.0, ICOLOUR_NON_STANDARD_RGB);

    nDstSD = InPrepareColourImage(WIDTH, HEIGHT, BANDS, IDATA_TYPE_INTERNAL_SD,
        SD_PRECISION, 1.0, 1.0, 1.0, ICOLOUR_NON_STANDARD_RGB);

    nWrk1SD = InPrepareColourImage(WIDTH, HEIGHT, BANDS, IDATA_TYPE_INTERNAL_SD,
        SD_PRECISION, 1.0, 1.0, 1.0, ICOLOUR_NON_STANDARD_RGB);

    nWrk2SD = InPrepareColourImage(WIDTH, HEIGHT, BANDS, IDATA_TYPE_INTERNAL_SD,
        SD_PRECISION, 1.0, 1.0, 1.0, ICOLOUR_NON_STANDARD_RGB);
```

The ND data type source image will be converted to SD data type for computation in order to prevent overflow and underflow in the subsequent computation steps.

```
/* Allocate and create 5x5 impulse response neighbourhood array           */

    nImpulseSize = InGenerateND5Tuple(5, 5, 1, 1, 1);

    nKeyPixel = InGenerateSD5Tuple(2, 2, 0, 0, 0);

    sAttrsNbhood.iLabelOption = INBHOOD_LABEL_IMPULSE;

    sAttrsNbhood.iTypeOption = IDATA_TYPE_INTERNAL_SD;

    sAttrsNbhood.nArraySize = nImpulseSize;

    sAttrsNbhood.nKeyPixel = nKeyPixel;

    sAttrsNbhood.iScaleFactor = 1;

    nImpulse = InAllocateNbhoodArray(sAttrsNbhood);

    InImpulseRectangular(nImpulse, nImpulseSize, nKeyPixel);
```

A 5×5 pixel, SD data type, uniform amplitude, impulse response array is created. Each element of the array has a value of 1/25. The key pixel is at the center of the array.

```
/* Read image file into buffer and import image from buffer               */

    stExtImageArray.tuPixel = IstGetFile("toys").tuPixel;

    iApplBufferSize = WIDTH * HEIGHT * BANDS;

    InImportImage(stExtImageArray, nSrcND, ND_PRECISION, IPIXEL_NI_PLANAR,
        iApplBufferSize, 0, tuDataSize);
```

The source image "toys" is read from a file and imported to PIKS.

```
/* Open X display window and display source image                              */

    tDisplay1 = ItOpenWindow(WIDTH, HEIGHT, BANDS);

    InColourDisplay(nSrcND, tDisplay1);

    printf("Source image \n");
    printf("            Press any key in window to continue \n");

    IvKeyDelay(tDisplay1);

/* Convert ND source image to SD data type                                     */

    InConvertImageDatatype(nSrcND, nSrcSD);
```

The source ND data type image is converted to SD data type for subsequent computation.

```
/* Blur source image                                                           */

    InConvolve2D(nSrcSD, nWrk2SD, nImpulse, ICONVOLVE_ENCLOSED);

/* Convert SD blurred image to ND data type and display it                     */

    InConvertImageDatatype(nWrk2SD, nWrkND);

    tDisplay2 = ItOpenWindow(WIDTH, HEIGHT, BANDS);

    InColourDisplay(nWrkND, tDisplay2);

    printf("Work image: blurred source image \n");
    printf("            Press any key in window to continue \n");

    IvKeyDelay(tDisplay2);

/* Weight source image                                                         */

    p = 0.6;

    iw1_numerator = 100.0 * p;

    iw_denominator = 100.0 * (2.0 * p - 1.0);

    stw1_numerator.tiArith = &iw1_numerator;

    stw_denominator.tiArith = &iw_denominator;

    InMonadicArith(nSrcSD, nWrk1SD, stw1_numerator, IMONADIC_MULTIPLICATION);

    InMonadicArith(nWrk1SD, nWrk1SD, stw_denominator, IMONADIC_DIVISION_BY);
```

This segment performs a weighted sum of the source image.

```
/* Weight blurred image                                                        */

    iw2_numerator = 100.0 * (1.0 - p);

    stw2_numerator.tiArith = &iw2_numerator;

    InMonadicArith(nWrk2SD, nWrk2SD, stw2_numerator, IMONADIC_MULTIPLICATION);

    InMonadicArith(nWrk2SD, nWrk2SD, stw_denominator, IMONADIC_DIVISION_BY);
```

This segment performs a weighted sum of the blurred image.

```
/* Subtract weighted blurred image from weighted source image                  */

    InDyadicArith(nWrk1SD, nWrk2SD, nDstSD, IDYADIC_SUBTRACTION);
```

This segment performs a subtraction of the weighted blurred source image from the source image.

```
    /* Clip unsharp mask image                                               */

        uAbove = 255;

        uBelow = 0;

        uWidth = 256;

        uLevel = 127;

        stAbove.tuArith = &uAbove;

        stBelow.tuArith = &uBelow;

        stWidth.tuArith = &uWidth;

        stLevel.tuArith = &uLevel;

        InWindowLevel(nDstSD, nDstSD, stAbove, stBelow, stWidth, stLevel);
```

The difference image between the weighted source image and the blurred source image usually will exhibit overshoots and undershoots of the dynamic range of the source image, in this example, 0 to 255. This segment forms a linear amplitude clip over the range of 0 to 255.

```
    /* Convert SD unsharp mask image to ND data type and display it           */

        InConvertImageDatatype(nDstSD, nDstND);


    /* Display unsharp mask image                                             */

        tDisplay3 = ItOpenWindow(WIDTH, HEIGHT, BANDS);

        InColourDisplay(nDstND, tDisplay3);

        printf("Work image: unsharp mask image \n");
        printf("            Press any key in window to continue \n");

        IvKeyDelay(tDisplay3);


    /* Close windows                                                          */

        IvCloseWindow(tDisplay1);
        IvCloseWindow(tDisplay2);
        IvCloseWindow(tDisplay3);


    /* Check for errors                                                       */

        fclose(nErrorFile);

        if (IbErrorTest())
                printf("Error exists, check log\n");


    /* Close PIKS session                                                     */

        IvClosePIKS();

        free(stExtImageArray.tuPixel);
    }
```

The following occurs when the unsharp_mask program is executed.

The original source image is displayed. Next, a blurred version of the source image is displayed in a second window. The second window may overlap the first window, dependent upon the location of the cursor when the second window display is invoked. Then, the unsharp mask image is displayed in the third window.

Colour Plate 2 shows the blurred and unsharp mask images.

7

PIKS C Element Prototypes

The following pages of this chapter contain the syntactical C language binding definitions of each element in PIKS Foundation. This chapter is organized alphabetically by the functional specification name of each PIKS element. The structure of each manual page is as follows:

- Syntactical definition of PIKS element
- Syntactical definitions of enums, unions, structs, and #defines associated with PIKS element
- Code snippets of the usage of PIKS element

accumulator
See Section 2.8.1

The accumulator operator accumulates amplitudes of pixels of an image. Its API is:

```
Ipfloat *ItraAccumulator(              /* OUT sum of pixels data pointer     */
    Idnimage        nSourceImage,      /* source image identifier            */
    Ipfloat         *traSum,           /* sum of pixels data pointer         */
    Ipeprocess      eMode,             /* processing mode option             */
    Ipint           iApplBufferSize,   /* data transfer buffer size or option */
    Ipuint          uStartPoint,       /* index offset within internal data  */
    Ipuint          *tuDataSize        /* OUT post transfer data size pointer */
);
```

where Ipeprocess is the name of the following *piks.h* enum that specifies the processing mode option:

```
IPROCESS_MODE_0                        /* processing mode zero               */
IPROCESS_MODE_1                        /* processing mode one                */
IPROCESS_MODE_2                        /* processing mode two                */
IPROCESS_MODE_3                        /* processing mode three              */
IPROCESS_MODE_4                        /* processing mode four               */
```

Note: Processing modes one, two, and three give the same results in PIKS Foundation.

■**Example 1:** Accumulation of pixels in a colour image.

```
Idnimage        nSrc;                  /* Source image identifier            */

Ipfloat         rSum, *trSum = &rSum;  /* Sum of pixels data structure pointer */

unsigned int    uSum;                  /* Unsigned integer colour image sum  */

                                       /* Accumulation operation             */
ItraAccumulator(nSrc, trSum, IPROCESS_MODE_0, 1, 0, NULL);

uSum = rSum;

printf("sum = %u \n", uSum);           /* Print mode zero sum                */
```

■**Example 2:** Accumulation of pixels in each band of a colour image.

```
Idnimage        nSrc;                  /* Source image identifier            */

                                       /* Sum of pixels data structure pointer */
Ipfloat         raSum[3], *traSum = &raSum[0];

                                       /* Unsigned integer band sums         */
unsigned int    uRedSum, uGreenSum, uBlueSum;

                                       /* Accumulation operation             */
ItraAccumulator(nSrc, traSum, IPROCESS_MODE_1, 3, 0, NULL);

uRedSum = raSum[0];

uGreenSum = raSum[1];

uBlueSum = raSum[2];

printf("red sum = %u \n", uRedSum);    /* Print red band sum                 */

printf("green sum = %u \n", uGreenSum); /* Print green band sum              */

printf("blue sum = %u \n", uBlueSum);  /* Print blue band sum                */
```

allocate_histogram

See Section 4.2.1

The *allocate_histogram* mechanism allocates a reference to a histogram object and creates its attributes. Its API is:

```
Idnhist InAllocateHist(                    /* OUT histogram identifier       */
    Ipsattrs_hist      sAttrs              /* histogram attributes           */
);
```

where `Ipsattrs_hist` is the name of the following *piks.h* structure that specifies the histogram attributes.

```
typedef struct{
    Ipuint         uHistSize;              /* histogram size                 */
    Ipfloat        rLowerBound;            /* lower amplitude bound          */
    Ipfloat        rUpperBound;            /* upper amplitude bound          */
} Ipsattrs_hist;
```

■ **Example:**   Allocation of a histogram.

```
Idnhist            nHist;                  /* Histogram identifier           */

Ipsattrs_hist      sAttrsHist;             /* Histogram attributes           */

sAttrsHist.uHistSize = 256;                /* Histogram size                 */

sAttrsHist.rLowerBound = 0.0;              /* Histogram lower amplitude bound */

sAttrsHist.rUpperBound = 255.0;            /* Histogram upper amplitude bound */

nHist = InAllocateHist(sAttrsHist);        /* Histogram allocation           */
```

The *allocate_image* mechanism allocates a reference to an image object and creates its metric and colour descriptor attributes. Its API is:

```
Idnimage InAllocateImage(                    /* OUT image identifier              */
    Ipsattrs_image      sAttrs               /* image attributes                  */
);
```

where `Ipsattrs_image` is the name of the following *piks.h* structure that specifies the image attributes.

```
typedef struct{
    Idntuple        nImageSize;              /* image size ND 5-tuple identifier     */
    Idntuple        nBandType;               /* band data type SD B-tuple id         */
    Idntuple        nBandPrecision;          /* band precision ND B-tuple identifier */
    Ipfloat         rXWhite;                 /* X tristimulus value white point      */
    Ipfloat         rYWhite;                 /* Y tristimulus value white point      */
    Ipfloat         rZWhite;                 /* Z tristimulus value white point      */
    Ipint           iImageStructureOption;   /* image structure option               */
    Ipint           iColourOption;           /* colour space option                  */
} Ipsattrs_image;
```

The following image structure and colour space #define options are provided in *piks.h*.

```
IIMAGE_STRUCTURE_MON              1     /* monochrome                                    */
IIMAGE_STRUCTURE_COLR             4     /* colour                                        */

ICOLOUR_NONE                      1     /* unspecified                                   */
ICOLOUR_NON_STANDARD_RGB          2     /* nonstandard RGB                               */
ICOLOUR_LIN_CCIR_D65_RGB          3     /* linear CCIR illuminant D65 RGB                */
ICOLOUR_LIN_CIE_E_RGB             4     /* linear CIE illuminant E RGB                   */
ICOLOUR_LIN_EBU_C_RGB             5     /* linear EBU illuminant C RGB                   */
ICOLOUR_LIN_EBU_D65_RGB           6     /* linear EBU illuminant D65 RGB                 */
ICOLOUR_LIN_NTSC_C_RGB            7     /* linear NTSC illuminant C RGB                  */
ICOLOUR_LIN_NTSC_D65_RGB          8     /* linear NTSC illuminant D65 RGB                */
ICOLOUR_LIN_SMPTE_D65_RGB         9     /* linear SMPTE illuminant D65 RGB               */
ICOLOUR_GAMMA_CCIR_D65_RGB        10    /* gamma CCIR illuminant C RGB                   */
ICOLOUR_GAMMA_EBU_C_RGB           11    /* gamma EBU illuminant C RGB                    */
ICOLOUR_GAMMA_EBU_D65_RGB         12    /* gamma EBU illuminant D65 RGB                  */
ICOLOUR_GAMMA_NTSC_C_RGB          13    /* gamma NTSC illuminant C RGB                   */
ICOLOUR_GAMMA_NTSC_D65_RGB        14    /* gamma NTSC illuminant D65 RGB                 */
ICOLOUR_GAMMA_SMPTE_D65_RGB       15    /* gamma SMPTE illuminant D65 RGB                */
ICOLOUR_LUM_CHR_EBU_C_YUV         16    /* luminance/chrominance EBU illuminant C YUV    */
ICOLOUR_LUM_CHR_EBU_D65_YUV       17    /* luminance/chrominance EBU illuminant D65 YUV  */
ICOLOUR_LUM_CHR_NTSC_C_YIQ        18    /* luminance/chrominance NTSC ill. C YIQ         */
ICOLOUR_LUM_CHR_NTSC_D65_YIQ      19    /* luminance/chrominance NTSC ill. D65 YIQ       */
ICOLOUR_LUM_CHR_SMPTE_D65_YCBCR   20    /* luminance/chrominance SMPTE ill. D65 YCbCr    */
ICOLOUR_CIE_XYZ                   21    /* CIE XYZ                                       */
ICOLOUR_CIE_UVW                   22    /* CIE UVW                                       */
ICOLOUR_CIE_YXY                   23    /* CIE Yxy                                       */
ICOLOUR_CIE_YUV                   24    /* CIE Yuv                                       */
ICOLOUR_CIE_LAB                   25    /* CIE L*a*b*                                    */
ICOLOUR_CIE_LUV                   26    /* CIE L*u*v*                                    */
ICOLOUR_IHS                       27    /* IHS                                           */
ICOLOUR_CMY                       28    /* CMY                                           */
ICOLOUR_CMYK                      29    /* CMYK                                          */
```

Note The missing image structure options are not supported in PIKS Foundation.

■**Example 1:**   Allocation of a 512×512 pixel, colour, nonnegative integer image.

```
Idnimage              nImage;                 /* Image identifier                  */

Idntuple              nImageSize:             /* Image size ND 5-tuple identifier  */

Idntuple              nBandType;              /* Band data type SD B-tuple identifier */

Idntuple              nBandPrecision;         /* Band precision ND B-tuple identifier */

Ipsattrs_image        sAttrsImage;            /* Image attributes                  */


sAttrsImage.nImageSize = nImageSize;          /* Image size tuple                  */

sAttrsImage.nBandType = nBandType;            /* Band data type tuple              */

sAttrsImage.nBandPrecision = nBandPrecision;  /* Band precision tuple              */

sAttrsImage.rXWhite = 0.981;                  /* X tristimulus value white point   */

sAttrsImage.rYWhite = 1.000;                  /* Y tristimulus value white point   */

sAttrsImage.rZWhite = 1.182;                  /* Z tristimulus value white point   */

                                              /* Colour image                      */
sAttrsImage.iImageStructureOption = IIMAGE_STRUCTURE_COLR;

                                              /* Linear NTSC, Illuminant C, RGB image */
sAttrsImage.iColourOption = ICOLOUR_LIN_NTSC_C_RGB;


nImage = InAllocateImage(sAttrsImage);        /* Image allocation                  */
```

Note   See InCreateTuple for descriptions of tuple allocation and generation.

■**Example 2:**   Allocation of a 512×512 pixel, monochrome, nonnegative integer image using the prepare monochrome image convenience function.

```
Idnimage              nImage;                 /* Image identifier                  */

Ipuint                uHorizontal = 512;      /* Image width                       */

Ipuint                uVertical = 512;        /* Image height                      */

Ipuint                uPrecision = 8;         /* Image band precision              */

                                              /* Image allocation                  */
nImage = InPrepareMonochromeImage(uHorizontal, uVertical, IDATA_TYPE_INTERNAL_ND,
    uPrecision);
```

The *allocate_lookup_table* mechanism allocates a reference to a lookup table object and creates its attributes. Its API is:

```
Idnlut InAllocateLUT(                          /* OUT lookup table identifier    */
    Ipsattrs_lut        sAttrs                 /* lookup table attributes        */
);
```

where `Ipsattrs_lut` is the name of the following *piks.h* structure that specifies the lookup table attributes.

```
typedef struct{
    Ipuint          uTableEntries;         /* number of table entries         */
    Ipuint          uTableBands;           /* number of table bands           */
    Ipint           iInputTypeOption;      /* table input data type option    */
    Ipint           iOutputTypeOption;     /* table output data type option   */
} Ipsattrs_lut;
```

The following lookup table data type #define options are provided in *piks.h*.

```
IDATA_TYPE_INTERNAL_BD          1       /* Boolean                 */
IDATA_TYPE_INTERNAL_ND          2       /* unsigned integer        */
IDATA_TYPE_INTERNAL_SD          3       /* signed integer          */
```

■**Example:**   Allocation of a single band lookup table.

```
Idnlut              nLUT;                   /* LUT identifier        */

Ipsattrs_lut        sAttrsLUT;              /* LUT attributes        */

sAttrsLUT.uTableEntries = 256;              /* LUT to have 256 entries    */

sAttrsLUT.uTableBands = 1;                  /* LUT to have 1 band         */

                                            /* LUT to have ND data type input     */
sAttrsLUT.iInputTypeOption = IDATA_TYPE_INTERNAL_ND;

                                            /* LUT to have ND data type output    */
sAttrsLUT.iOutputTypeOption = IDATA_TYPE_INTERNAL_ND;

nLUT = InAllocateLUT(sAttrsLUT);            /* LUT allocation        */
```

allocate_matrix

See Section 4.2.4

The *allocate_matrix* mechanism allocates a reference to a matrix array object and creates its attributes. Its API is:

```
Idnmatrix InAllocateMatrix(              /* OUT matrix identifier        */
    Ipsattrs_matrix    sAttrs            /* matrix attributes            */
);
```

where Ipsattrs_matrix is the name of the following *piks.h* structure that specifies the matrix attributes.

```
typedef struct{
    Ipuint         uColumnSize;          /* matrix column size           */
    Ipuint         uRowSize;             /* matrix row size              */
    Ipint          iTypeOption;          /* matrix data type option      */
} Ipsattrs_matrix;
```

The following matrix data type #define options are provided in *piks.h*.

```
IDATA_TYPE_INTERNAL_ND      2            /* unsigned integer             */
IDATA_TYPE_INTERNAL_SD      3            /* signed integer               */
IDATA_TYPE_INTERNAL_RD      4            /* real arithmetic              */
```

■**Example:** Allocation of a colour conversion matrix.

```
Idnmatrix            nMatrix;                 /* Matrix identifier            */

Ipsattrs_matrix      sAttrsMatrix;            /* Matrix attributes            */

sAttrsMatrix.uRowSize = 3;                    /* Matrix to have 3 rows        */

sAttrsMatrix.uColumnSize = 3;                 /* Matrix to have 3 columns     */

                                              /* Matrix to contain RD data type */
sAttrsMatrix.iTypeOption = IDATA_TYPE_INTERNAL_RD;

nMatrix = InAllocateMatrix(sAttrsMatrix);     /* Matrix allocation            */
```

allocate_neighbourhood_array
See Section 4.2.5

The *allocate_neighbourhood_array* mechanism allocates a reference to a neighbourhood array object and creates its attributes. Its API is:

```
Idnnbhood InAllocateNbhoodArray(        /* OUT neighbourhood array identifier  */
    Ipsattrs_nbhood    sAttrs           /* neighbourhood array attributes       */
);
```

where `Ipsattrs_nbhood` is the name of the following *piks.h* structure that specifies the neighbourhood array attributes.

```
typedef struct{
    Idntuple        nArraySize;         /* nbhood array size ND 5-tuple id        */
    Idntuple        nKeyPixel;          /* nbhood array key pixel SD 5-tuple id   */
    Ipint           iScaleFactor;       /* nbhood array scale factor              */
    Ipint           iLabelOption;       /* nbhood array semantic label option     */
    Ipint           iTypeOption;        /* nbhood array data type option          */
} Ipsattrs_nbhood;
```

The following neighbourhood array semantic label and array data type #define options are provided in *piks.h*.

```
INBHOOD_LABEL_GENERIC        1          /* generic                */
INBHOOD_LABEL_DITHER         2          /* dither                 */
INBHOOD_LABEL_IMPULSE        3          /* impulse response       */
INBHOOD_LABEL_MASK           4          /* mask                   */
INBHOOD_LABEL_STRUCTURE      5          /* structuring element    */

IDATA_TYPE_INTERNAL_BD       1          /* Boolean                */
IDATA_TYPE_INTERNAL_ND       2          /* unsigned integer       */
IDATA_TYPE_INTERNAL_SD       3          /* signed integer         */
IDATA_TYPE_INTERNAL_RD       4          /* real arithmetic        */
```

■**Example:** Allocation of a 3×3 signed integer impulse response function neighbourhood array with a centered key pixel.

```
Idnnbhood              nImpulse;               /* Impulse array identifier           */

Idntuple               nSizeImpulse;           /* Impulse size ND 5-tuple identifier  */

Idntuple               nKeyImpulse;            /* Impulse key pixel ND 5-tuple id     */

Ipsattrs_nbhood        sAttrsImpulse;          /* Impulse array attributes           */


                                               /* 3x3 impulse array size ND 5-tuple  */
nSizeImpulse = InGenerateND5Tuple(3, 3, 1, 1, 1);

                                               /* Centered key pixel SD 5-tuple      */
nKeyImpulse = InGenerateSD5Tuple(1, 1, 0, 0, 0);

sAttrsImpulse.nArraySize = nSizeImpulse;       /* Impulse size ND 5-tuple            */

sAttrsImpulse.nKeyPixel = nKeyImpulse;         /* Impulse key pixel SD 5-tuple       */

sAttrsImpulse.iScaleFactor = 1;                /* Impulse array scale factor         */

                                               /* Impulse response array             */
sAttrsImpulse.iLabelOption = INBHOOD_LABEL_IMPULSE;

                                               /* Impulse array has SD data type     */
sAttrsImpulse.iTypeOption = IDATA_TYPE_INTERNAL_SD;


nImpulse = InAllocateNbhoodArray(sAttrsImpulse); /* Impulse array allocation         */
```

allocate_roi

See Section 4.2.6

The `allocate_roi` mechanism allocates a reference to a region-of-interest object and creates its attributes. Its API is:

```
Idnroi InAllocateROI(                        /* OUT ROI identifier               */
    Ipsattrs_roi      sAttrs                  /* ROI attributes                   */
);
```

where `Ipsattrs_roi` is the name of the following *piks.h* structure that specifies the region-of-interest attributes.

```
typedef struct{
    Idntuple          nROISize;              /* ROI size ND 5-tuple data identifier */
    Ipint             iStructureOption;      /* ROI structure option             */
    Ipepolarity       ePolarityOption        /* ROI polarity option              */
} Ipsattrs_roi;
```

The following ROI structure #define option is provided in *piks.h*.

```
IROI_RECTANGULAR                  6          /* rectangular ROI structure        */
```

Note: PIKS Foundation only supports two-dimensional, rectangular regions-of-interest.

`Ipepolarity` is the name of the enum that specifies the ROI polarity option:

```
IPOLARITY_TRUE                               /* set TRUE within defined region   */
IPOLARITY_FALSE                              /* set FALSE within defined region  */
```

■**Example 1:** Allocation of a 512×512 rectangular-shaped region-of-interest.

```
Idnroi             nROI;                      /* ROI identifier                   */

Idntuple           nROISize;                  /* ROI size ND 5-tuple              */

Ipsattrs_roi       sAttrsROI;                 /* ROI attributes                   */

                                              /* 512x512 ROI array                */
nROISize = InGenerateND5Tuple(512, 512, 1, 1, 1);

sAttrsROI.nROISize = nROISize;                /* ROI size ND 5-tuple identifier   */

sAttrsROI.iStructureOption = IROI_RECTANGULAR;   /* ROI rectangular               */

sAttrsROI.ePolarityOption = IPOLARITY_TRUE;   /* ROI set TRUE                     */


nROI = InAllocateROI(sAttrsROI);              /* ROI allocation                   */
```

■**Example 2:** Allocation of a 512×512 rectangular-shaped region-of-interest using the prepare two-dimensional rectangular ROI convenience function.

```
Idnroi             nROI;                      /* ROI identifier                   */

                                              /* ROI allocation                   */
nROI = InPrepare2DROIRectangular(512, 512, IPOLARITY_TRUE);
```

206   PIKS C ELEMENT PROTOTYPES   CHAPTER 7

The *allocate_tuple* mechanism allocates a reference to a tuple object and creates its attributes. Its API is:

```
Idntuple InAllocateTuple(                    /* OUT tuple identifier           */
    Ipsattrs_tuple      sAttrs                /* tuple attributes               */
);
```

where `Ipsattrs_tuple` is the name of the following *piks.h* structure that specifies the tuple attributes.

```
typedef struct{
    Ipuint          uTupleSize;               /* tuple size                     */
    Ipint           iTypeOption;              /* tuple data type option         */
} Ipsattrs_tuple;
```

The following tuple data type #define options are provided in *piks.h*.

```
IDATA_TYPE_INTERNAL_BD          1            /* Boolean                        */
IDATA_TYPE_INTERNAL_ND          2            /* unsigned integer               */
IDATA_TYPE_INTERNAL_SD          3            /* signed integer                 */
IDATA_TYPE_INTERNAL_RD          4            /* real arithmetic                */
```

■**Example:** Allocation of tuples that specify the size, data type, and band precision of a monochrome image.

```
Idntuple          nImageSize;              /* Image size ND 5-tuple identifier     */

Idntuple          nBandType;               /* Band data type SD 1-tuple identifier  */

Idntuple          nBandPrecision;          /* Band precision ND 1-tuple identifier  */

Ipsattrs_tuple    sAttrs5NDTuple;          /* Image size ND 5-tuple attributes      */

Ipsattrs_tuple    sAttrsSD1Tuple;          /* Band data type SD 1-tuple attributes  */

Ipsattrs_tuple    sAttrsND1Tuple;          /* Band precision ND 1-tuple attributes  */

sAttrsND5Tuple.uTupleSize = 5;             /* 5-tuple to contain 5 data values      */

                                           /* 5-tuple to contain ND data types      */
sAttrsND5Tuple.iTypeOption = IDATA_TYPE_INTERNAL_ND;

sAttrsSD1Tuple.uTupleSize = 1;             /* 1-tuple to contain 1 data value       */

                                           /* 1-tuple to contain SD data type       */
sAttrsSD1Tuple.iTypeOption = IDATA_TYPE_INTERNAL_SD;

sAttrsND1Tuple.uTupleSize = 1;             /* 1-tuple to contain 1 data values      */

                                           /* 1-tuple to contain ND data type       */
sAttrsND1Tuple.iTypeOption = IDATA_TYPE_INTERNAL_ND;

nImageSize = InAllocateTuple(sAttrsND5Tuple);   /* Image size ND 5-tuple allocation  */

nBandType = InAllocateTuple(sAttrsSD1Tuple);    /* Band data type SD 1-tuple allocation */

                                                /* Band precision ND 1-tuple allocation */
nBandPrecision = InAllocateTuple(sAttrsND1Tuple);
```

Note: In the example above, the entries

```
sAttrsND5Tuple.uTupleSize
sAttrsND5Tuple.iTypeOption
sAttrsSD1Tuple.uTupleSize
sAttrsSD1Tuple.iTypeOption
sAttrsND1Tuple.uTupleSize
sAttrsND1Tuple.iTypeOption
```

can be individually or jointly left unspecified by setting their values to zero. If set to zero during allocation, their values must be specified by the *create_tuple* or *import_tuple* utilities. Otherwise, an error is reported.

alpha_blend_constant
See Section 2.2.1

The *alpha_blend_constant* operator performs alpha blending combination of a pair of images with a constant alpha blend factor. Its API is:

```
Idnimage InAlphaBlendConstant(          /* OUT destination image identifier      */
    Idnimage            nSourceImage1,  /* first input source image identifier   */
    Idnimage            nSourceImage2,  /* second input source image identifier  */
    Idnimage            nDestImage,     /* destination image identifier          */
    Ipfloat             rAlphaFactor    /* alpha factor                          */
);
```

■**Example:**   Alpha blend of a pair of images.

```
Idnimage            nSrc1;              /* First source image identifier       */

Idnimage            nSrc2;              /* Second source image identifier      */

Idnimage            nDst;               /* Destination image identifier        */

Ipfloat             rAlpha = 0.7;       /* Alpha blend factor                  */


                                        /* Alpha blend constant operation      */
InAlphaBlendConstant(nSrc1, nSrc2, nDst, rAlpha);
```

array_to_lut

See Section 3.2.1

The *array_to_lut* tool inserts an external array of values into a lookup table at a specified index offset. Its API is:

```
Idnlut InArrayToLUT(                         /* OUT lookup table identifier       */
    Idnlut               nLUT,               /* lookup table identifier           */
    Ipsparameter_pixel   stArray,            /* lookup table array pointer union  */
    Ipuint               uEntryOffset,       /* lookup table entry offset         */
    Ipuint               uBandOffset,        /* lookup table band offset          */
    Ipuint               uColumns,           /* number of array columns           */
    Ipuint               uRows               /* number of array rows              */
);
```

where `Ipsparameter_pixel` is the name of the following *piks.h* union that specifies the data type and values of the array.

```
typedef union{
    Ipbool       *tbPixel;       /* Boolean pointer           */
    Ipuint       *tuPixel;       /* unsigned integer pointer  */
    Ipint        *tiPixel;       /* signed integer pointer    */
} Ipsparameter_pixel;
```

■**Example:**   Create and copy a one-dimensional scaled square root array to a LUT.

```
Idnlut               nLUT;                   /* Lookup table identifier        */

Ipsparameter_pixel   stExtLUT;               /* LUT data array pointer union   */

Ipuint               uEntryOffset = 0;       /* Lookup table entry offset      */

Ipuint               uBandOffset = 0;        /* Lookup table band offset       */

Ipuint               uColumns = 1;           /* Number of array columns        */

Ipuint               uRows = 256;            /* Number of array rows           */

                                             /* External LUT array             */
Ipuint               uaExtLUTArray[256], *tuaExtLUTArray = &uaExtLUTArray[0];

int                  i;                      /* table index                    */


for(i = 0; i < 256; i++){                    /* Scaled square root table       */
    uaExtLUTArray[i] = (sqrt(255)) * (sqrt(i));
}

stExtLUT.tuPixel = tuaExtLUTArray;           /* Pointer to external LUT array  */

                                             /* Array to LUT operation         */
InArrayToLUT(nLUT, stExtLUT, uEntryOffset, uBandOffset, uColumns, uRows);
```

The *bind_roi* mechanism binds a ROI object and a ROI offset tuple to an image. Its API is:

```
Idnimage InBindROI(                             /* OUT source image identifier        */
    Idnimage        nSourceImage,               /* source image identifier            */
    Idnroi          nROI,                       /* ROI identifier                     */
    Idntuple        nOffset                     /* offset SD 5-tuple identifier       */
);
```

■**Example 1:**   Bind a ROI to an image at a spatial offset of (50, -100) using the allocate and create tuple mechanisms.

```
Idnimage                nSrc;                       /* Source image identifier              */

Idnroi                  nSrcROI;                    /* Source ROI identifier                */

Idntuple                nROIOffset;                 /* ROI offset SD 5-tuple identifier     */

Ipsattrs_tuple          sAttrsROIOffsetTuple;       /* ROI offset SD 5-tuple attributes     */

Ipsparameter_basic      stROIOffsetData             /* ROI offset tuple data pointer union  */

Ipint                   iaROIOffsetData[5];         /* ROI offset data array                */

sAttrsROIOffsetTuple.uTtupleSize = 5;               /* 5-tuple to contain 5 data values     */

                                                    /* 5-tuple to contain SD data types     */
sAttrsROIOffsetTuple.iTypeOption = IDATA_TYPE_INTERNAL_SD;

                                                    /* ROI offset SD 5-tuple allocation     */
nROIOffset = InAllocateTuple(sAttrsROIOffsetTuple);

iaROIOffsetData[0] = 50;                            /* Horizontal ROI offset                */

iaROIOffsetData[1] = -100;                          /* Vertical ROI offset                  */

iaROIOffsetData[2] = 0;                             /* Depth ROI offset                     */

iaROIOffsetData[3] = 0;                             /* Temporal ROI offset                  */

iaROIOffsetData[4] = 0;                             /* Band ROI offset                      */

                                                    /* Pointer to ROI offset data           */
stROIOffsetData.tiParameter = &iaROIOffsetData[0];

                                                    /* Create ROI offset SD 5-tuple         */
InCreateTuple(stROIOffsetData, nROIOffset, sSD5TupleAttrs);

InBindROI(nSrc, nSrcROI, nROIOffset);               /* Bind ROI                             */
```

Note: See InCreateTuple for descriptions of tuple allocation and generation.

■**Example 2:**   Bind a ROI to an image at a spatial offset of (50, -100) using the generate tuple convenience function.

```
Idnimage                nSrc;                       /* Source image identifier              */

Idnroi                  nSrcROI;                    /* Source ROI identifier                */

Idntuple                nROIOffset;                 /* ROI offset SD 5-tuple identifier     */

                                                    /* Generate ROI offset SD 5-tuple       */
nROIOffset = InGenerateSD5Tuple(50, -100, 0, 0, 0);

InBindROI(nSrc, nSrcROI, nROIOffset);               /* Bind ROI                             */
```

bit_shift

See Section 2.1.1

The *bit_shift* operator performs bit shifting of an integer data type pixel image. Its API is:

```
Idnimage InBitShift(                          /* OUT destination image identifier      */
    Idnimage        nSourceImage,             /* source image identifier               */
    Idnimage        nDestImage,               /* destination image identifier          */
    Ipuint          uBits,                    /* number of bits to be shifted          */
    Ipint           iOption                   /* bit shift option                      */
);
```

The following bit shift #define options are provided in *piks.h*.

```
IBIT_SHIFT_LEFT_OVERFLOW        1             /* left overflow shift                   */
IBIT_SHIFT_RIGHT_OVERFLOW       2             /* right overflow shift                  */
IBIT_SHIFT_LEFT_BARREL          3             /* left barrel shift                     */
IBIT_SHIFT_RIGHT_BARREL         4             /* right barrel shift                    */
IBIT_SHIFT_LEFT_ARITH           5             /* left arithmetic shift                 */
IBIT_SHIFT_RIGHT_ARITH          6             /* right arithmetic shift                */
```

The "left" bit of a SD integer is its sign bit. The "left" bit of a ND integer is its most significant bit. The "right" bit of a ND or SD integer is its least significant bit.

■**Example:** Right overflow bit shift

```
IdnImage          nSrc;                       /* Source image identifier               */

IdnImage          nDst;                       /* Destination image identifier          */

Ipuint            uBits = 3;                  /* Bit shift by 3 bits                   */


                                              /* Bit shift operation                   */
InBitShift(nSrc, nDst, ubits, IBIT_SHIFT_RIGHT_OVERFLOW);
```

The *close_piks* mechanism performs normal closure of a PIKS session. Its API is:

```
void IvClosePIKS(                       /* no output return               */
   void                                 /* no input arguments             */
);
```

■**Example:**   Usage of the close PIKS mechanism.

```
fclose(nErrorFile);                     /* Close error file after interrogation  */

IvClosePIKS();                          /* Close PIKS, normal situation   */
```

Note: All previously allocated data objects are automatically deallocated by the *close_piks* mechanism.

close_piks_emergency

See Section 4.1.2

IvClosePIKSEmergency

The *close_piks_emergency* mechanism performs emergency closure of a PIKS session. Its API is:

```
void IvClosePIKSEmergency(          /* no output return              */
   void                             /* no input arguments            */
);
```

■**Example:** Usage of both of the close PIKS mechanisms.

```
fclose(nErrorFile);                 /* Close error file after interrogation  */

if(IbErrorTest()) {
   IvClosePIKSEmergency();          /* Close PIKS, abnormal situation         */
}
else{
   IvClosePIKS();                   /* Close PIKS, normal situation           */
}
```

Note: All previously allocated data objects are automatically deallocated by the *close_piks_emergency* mechanism.

The *colour_conversion_linear* operator performs linear inter-band colour conversion of a trichromatic colour image between colour spaces. Its API is:

```
Idnimage InColourConvLin(                       /* OUT destination image identifier     */
    Idnimage          nSourceImage,             /* source image identifier              */
    Idnimage          nDestImage,               /* destination image identifier         */
    Idnmatrix         nColourMatrix             /* colour conversion matrix identifier  */
)
```

■**Example:**   Linear colour conversion between linear NTSC illuminant D65 and XYZ colour spaces for signed integer colour images.

```
Idnimage            nSrcSD;                     /* Source image identifier              */

Idnimage            nDstSD;                     /* Destination image identifier         */

Idnmatrix           nMatrixId;                  /* Repository entry identifier          */


                                                /* Repository entry identifier output   */
nMatrixId = InReturnRepositoryId(IR_C_LIN_NTSC_D65_RGB_XYZ, IREPOSITORY_COLOUR);

nColourConvLin(nSrcSD, nDstSD, nMatrixId);      /* Linear colour conversion operation   */
```

Note 1:   IR_C_LIN_NTSC_D65_RGB_XYZ is the entry name for a NTSC illuminant C to XYZ colour conversion matrix stored in the data object repository.

Note 2:   IREPOSITORY_COLOUR is the #define name indicating that the repository class is colour conversion matrices.

Note 3:   See the *return_repository_id* manual page for an explanation of its usage.

colour_conversion_matrix   IvColourConvMatrix
See Section 3.2.2

The *colour_conversion_matrix* tool generates 3×3 colour conversion matrices for conversion between XYZ and RGB colour spaces. Its API is:

```
void IvColourConvMatrix(                        /* no output return                      */
    Idnmatrix        nXYZMatrixRGB,             /* XYZ to RGB conversion matrix id       */
    Idnmatrix        nRGBMatrixXYZ,             /* RGB to XYZ conversion matrix id       */
    Ipfloat          rRedXChrom,                /* red primary x chrom coordinate        */
    Ipfloat          rRedYChrom,                /* red primary y chrom. coordinate       */
    Ipfloat          rGreenXChrom,              /* green primary x chrom. coordinate     */
    Ipfloat          rGreenYChrom,              /* green primary y chrom. coordinate     */
    Ipfloat          rBlueXChrom,               /* blue primary x chrom. coordinate      */
    Ipfloat          rBlueYChrom,               /* blue primary y chrom. coordinate      */
    Ipfloat          rWhiteXChrom,              /* white reference x chrom. coordinate   */
    Ipfloat          rWhiteYChrom               /* white reference y chrom. coordinate   */
);
```

■**Example:**   Generation of colour conversion matrices for conversion between linear NTSC D65 and XYZ colour spaces and use of the RGB to XYZ colour conversion matrix.

```
Idnimage         nSrc;                 /* Source image                      */

Idnimage         nDst;                 /* Destination image                 */

Idnmatrix        nXYZ_to_RGB;          /* RGB to XYZ conversion matrix       */

Idnmatrix        nRGB_to_XYZ;          /* RGB to XYZ conversion matrix       */

Ipfloat          rRedx = 0.67;         /* Red primary x chromaticity         */

Ipfloat          rRedy = 0.33;         /* Red primary y chromaticity         */

Ipfloat          rGreenx = 0.21;       /* Green primary x chromaticity       */

Ipfloat          rGreeny = 0.71;       /* Green primary y chromaticity       */

Ipfloat          rBluex = 0.14;        /* Blue primary x chromaticity        */

Ipfloat          rBluey = 0.08;        /* Blue primary y chromaticity        */

Ipfloat          rWhitex = 0.310;      /* White reference x chromaticity     */

Ipfloat          rWhitey = 0.316;      /* White reference y chromaticity     */


                                       /* Colour conversion matrix generation */
IvColourConvMatrix(nXYZ_to_RGB, nRGB_to_XYZ, rRedx, rRedy, rGreenx, rGreeny, rBluex,
    rBluey, rWhitex, rWhitey);

InColourConvLin(nSrc, nDst, nRGB_to_XYZ);       /* RGB to XYZ colour conversion      */
```

colour_conversion_subtractive

The *colour_conversion_subtractive* operator performs a conversion of a colour image between additive nonstandard RGB and subtractive CMY or CMYK colour spaces. Its API is:

```
Idnimage InColourConvSubtractive(          /* OUT destination image identifier   */
    Idnimage            nSourceImage,      /* source image identifier            */
    Idnimage            nDestImage,        /* destination image identifier       */
    Ipfloat             rBlackFactor,      /* blackness factor                   */
    Ipuint              uIntegerSize,      /* maximum integer size               */
    Ipsparameter_arith  stMethod,          /* method param. collection ptr union */
    Ipint               iDirectionOption,  /* colour conversion, direction option */
    Ipint               iMethodOption      /* colour conversion, method option   */
);
```

where `Ipsparameter_arith` is the name of the following *piks.h* union that specifies the arithmetic data types of the implementation-dependent conversion.

```
typedef union{
    Ipuint              *tuArith;          /* unsigned integer value pointer     */
    Ipint               *tiArith;          /* signed integer value pointer       */
    Ipfloat             *trArith;          /* real value pointer                 */
} Ipsparameter_arith;
```

The following colour conversion direction and method #define options are provided in *piks.h*.

```
ICOLOUR_DIRECTION_RGB_CMY      1           /* RGB to CMY option                  */
ICOLOUR_DIRECTION_RGB_CMYK     2           /* RGB to CMYK option                 */
ICOLOUR_DIRECTION_CMY_RGB      3           /* CMY to RGB option                  */
ICOLOUR_DIRECTION_CMYK_RGB     4           /* CMYK to RGB option                 */

ICOLOUR_METHOD_SIMPLE          1           /* Simple conversion                  */
ICOLOUR_METHOD_IMPL_DEPENDENT  2           /* Implementation-dependent conversion */
```

■**Example:** Subtractive colour conversion between RGB and CMYK colour spaces.

```
Idnimage            nSrc;                  /* Source image                       */

Idnimage            nDst;                  /* Destination image                  */

Ipsparameter_arith  stMethod;              /* Dummy method pointer union         */

Ipfloat             f = 0.1;               /* Blackness factor                   */

Ipuint              uIntSize = 255;        /* Maximum integer size               */


stMethod.tuArith = NULL;                   /* Dummy method information           */


                                           /* RGB tp CMYK conversion             */
InColourConvSubtractive(nSrc, nDst, f, uIntSize, stMethod, ICOLOUR_DIRECTION_RGB_CMYK,
    ICOLOUR_METHOD_SIMPLE);
```

complement
See Section 2.1.2

InComplement
InComplement

The complement operator performs the logical complement of a Boolean or integer image. Its API is:

```
Idnimage InComplement(                              /* OUT destination image identifier    */
    Idnimage            nSourceImage,               /* source image identifier             */
    Idnimage            nDestImage                  /* destination image identifier         */
);
```

■**Example:**   Complement of an integer image.

```
Idnimage              nSrc;                         /* Source image identifier             */

Idnimage              nDst;                         /* Destination image identifier         */

InComplement(nSrc, nDst);                           /* Complement image operation           */
```

The *convert_array_to_image* utility converts a matrix or neighbourhood array data object to a monochrome image. Its API is:

```
Idnimage InConvertArrayToImage(        /* OUT destination image identifier  */
    Idnimage         nImage,           /* destination image identifier      */
    Ipsarray_id      snArray           /* array identifier                  */
);
```

where `Ipsarray_id` is the name of the following *piks.h* union that specifies whether the array is a matrix or neighbourhood array and references its identifier.

```
typedef union{
    Idnmatrix        nMatrix;          /* matrix identifier                 */
    Idnnbhood        nNbhood;          /* neighbourhood array identifier    */
} Ipsarray_id;
```

■**Example:**   Convert an impulse response neighbourhood array to a monochrome image.

```
Idnimage            nDst;             /* Destination image identifier      */

Idnnbhood           nImpulse;         /* Impulse response function array   */

Ipsarray_id         snArray;          /* Array identifier                  */


snArray.nNbhood = nImpulse;           /* Array is a neighbourhood object    */


InConvertArrayToImage(nDst, snArray); /* Convert array to image operation   */
```

convert_image_datatype
See Section 5.1.2

InConvertImageDatatype

The *convert_image_datatype* utility converts a PIKS image from one arithmetic data type to another. Its API is:

```
Idnimage InConvertImageDatatype(          /* OUT destination image identifier    */
    Idnimage          nSourceImage,       /* source image identifier             */
    Idnimage          nDestImage          /* destination image identifier        */
);
```

The source and destination data types are implicitly declared by their respective data type attributes.

■**Example:**   Convert an image from ND to SD data type.

```
Idnimage              nSrcND;             /* Source image identifier             */

Idnimage              nDstSD;             /* Destination image identifier        */

InConvertImageDatatype(nSrcND, nDstSD);   /* Data type conversion operation      */
```

convert_image_to_array
See Section 5.1.3

The *convert_image_to_array* utility converts a monochrome image to a matrix or neighbourhood array data object. Its API is:

```
Ipsarray_id IsnConvertImageToArray(     /* OUT array identifier              */
    Idnimage            nImage,         /* source image identifier           */
    Ipsarray_id         snArray         /* array identifier                  */
);
```

where `Ipsarray_id` is the name of the following *piks.h* union that specifies whether the array is a matrix or neighbourhood array and references its identifier.

```
typedef union{
    Idnmatrix           nMatrix;        /* matrix identifier                 */
    Idnnbhood           nNbhood;        /* neighbourhood array identifier    */
} Ipsarray_id;
```

■**Example:**   Convert a Boolean image to a structuring element neighbourhood array.

```
Idnimage            nSrcBD;             /* Source image identifier           */

Idnnbhood           nSel;               /* Structuring element array         */

Ipsarray_id         snArray;            /* Array identifier                  */


snArray.nNbhood = nSel;                 /* Array is a structuring element array */


IsnConvertImageToArray(nSrcBD, snArray); /* Convert image to array operation  */
```

convert_roi_to_image

InConvertROIToImage

See Section 5.1.4

The *convert_roi_to_image* utility converts a region-of-interest data object to a Boolean image. Its API is:

```
Idnimage InConvertROIToImage(        /* OUT destination image identifier    */
    Idnimage        nImage,          /* destination image identifier        */
    Idnroi          nROI             /* source ROI identifier               */
);
```

■**Example:**   Convert a ROI to a Boolean image.

```
Idnimage          nDstBD;            /* Destination image identifier        */

Idnroi            nROI;              /* Region-of-interest identifier        */

InConvertROIToImage(nDstBD, nROI);   /* Convert ROI to Boolean image        */
```

The *convolve_2d* operator performs two-dimensional convolution with an impulse response function array for several image boundary conditions. It API is:

```
Idnimage InConvolve2D(                       /* OUT destination image identifier   */
    Idnimage        nSourceImage,            /* source image identifier            */
    Idnimage        nDestImage,              /* destination image identifier        */
    Idnnbhood       nImpulse,                /* impulse response array identifier   */
    Ipint           iOption                  /* convolution 2D option              */
);
```

The following convolution #define options are provided in *piks.h*.

```
ICONVOLVE_UPPER_LEFT              1           /* upper left corner justified        */
ICONVOLVE_ENCLOSED                2           /* enclosed array                     */
ICONVOLVE_KEY_ZERO                3           /* key pixel, zero exterior           */
ICONVOLVE_KEY_REFLECTED           4           /* key pixel, reflected exterior      */
```

■**Example:** Two-dimensional convolution of a monochrome image with a 3×3 uniform impulse response function array from the data object repository.

```
Idnimage            nSrc;                    /* Source image identifier            */

Idnimage            nDst;                    /* Destination image identifier        */

Idnnbhood           nArrayId;                /* Repository entry identifier         */


                                             /* Repository entry identifier output */
nArrayId = InReturnRepositoryId(IR_UNIFORM_3x3, IREPOSITORY_IMPULSE);


                                             /* Convolution operation              */
InConvolve2D(nSrc, nDst, nArrayId, ICONVOLVE_ENCLOSED);
```

Note 1: IR_UNIFORM_3x3 is the entry name for a 3×3 uniform impulse response function array stored in the data object repository.

Note 2: IREPOSITORY_IMPULSE is the #define name indicating that the repository class is impulse response arrays.

Note 3: See the *return_repository_id* manual page for an explanation of its usage.

copy_window

See Section 5.1.5

InCopyWindow

The *copy_window* utility copies a rectangular-shaped window from a source image into a destination image. Its API is:

```
Idnimage InCopyWindow(                              /* OUT destination image identifier    */
    Idnimage           nSourceImage,                /* source image identifier             */
    Idnimage           nDestImage,                  /* destination image identifier        */
    Idntuple           nSourceOffset,               /* source index offset SD 5-tuple id   */
    Idntuple           nDestOffset,                 /* dest. index offset SD 5-tuple id    */
    Idntuple           nWindowSize                  /* window size ND 5-tuple identifier   */
);
```

■**Example:** Copy a 100×100 window at offset coordinate (50, 100) from a source image to a destination image with no destination offset.

```
Idnimage           nSrc;                    /* Source image identifier          */

Idnimage           nDst;                    /* Destination image identifier     */

Idntuple           nSrcOff;                 /* Source image offset SD 5-tuple id */

Idntuple           nDstOff;                 /* Dest. image offset SD 5-tuple id  */

Idntuple           nSrcWin;                 /* Src image window size ND 5-tuple id */

                                            /* Generate source image offset 5-tuple */
nSrcOff = InGenerateSD5Tuple(50, 100, 0, 0, 0);

nDstOff = InGenerateSD5Tuple(0, 0, 0, 0, 0);    /* Generate dest. image offset 5-tuple */

                                            /* Generate source window size 5-tuple */
nSrcWin = InGenerateND5Tuple(100, 100, 1, 1, 1);

                                            /* Copy image window operation      */
InCopyWindow(nSrc, nDst, nSrcOff, nDstOff, nSrcWin);
```

The *create_tuple* utility creates a tuple data object. Its API is:

```
Idntuple InCreateTuple(                          /* OUT tuple identifier          */
    Ipsparameter_basic stTupleData,              /* tuple data pointer union      */
    Idntuple           nTupleId,                 /* tuple identifier              */
    Ipsattrs_tuple     sAttrsTuple               /* tuple attributes              */
);
```

where `Ipsattrs_tuple` is the name of the following *piks.h* structure that specifies the tuple attributes.

```
typedef struct{
    Ipuint             uTupleSize;               /* tuple size                    */
    Ipint              iTypeOption;              /* tuple data type option        */
} Ipsattrs_tuple;
```

`Ipsparameter_basic` is the name of the following *piks.h* union that specifies the data type and values of the tuple.

```
typedef union{
    Ipbool             *tbParameter;             /* Boolean pointer               */
    Ipuint             *tuParameter;             /* unsigned integer pointer      */
    Ipint              *tiParameter;             /* signed integer pointer        */
    Ipfloat            *trParameterFloat;        /* float pointer                 */
    char               *tcParameter;             /* character pointer             */
} Ipsparameter_basic;
```

■**Example:** Allocation and creation of tuples that specify the size, data type, and band precision of a 512×512 pixel, colour, unsigned integer, 8-bit precision image.

```
Idntuple           nImageSize;                   /* Image size ND 5-tuple identifier   */

Idntuple           nBandType;                    /* Image band data type SD 3-tuple id */

Idntuple           nBandPrecision;               /* Image band precision ND 3-tuple id */

Ipsattrs_tuple     sAttrsND5Tuple;               /* ND 5-tuple attributes              */

Ipsattrs_tuple     sAttrsSD3Tuple;               /* SD 3-tuple attributes              */

Ipsattrs_tuple     sAttrsND3Tuple;               /* ND 3-tuple attributes              */

Ipsparameter_basic stImageSize;                  /* Image size tuple data pointer union */

Ipsparameter_basic stBandType;                   /* Band type tuple data pointer union */

Ipsparameter_basic stBandPrecision;              /* Band precision tuple data ptr union */

Ipuint             uaImageSize[5];               /* Image size data array              */

Ipint              iaBandType[3];                /* Band type data array               */

Ipuint             uaBandPrecision[3];           /* Band precision data array          */

                                                 /* Tuple allocation                   */

sAttrsND5Tuple.uTupleSize = 5;                   /* 5-tuple to contain 5 data values   */

                                                 /* 5-tuple to contain ND data types   */
sAttrsND5Tuple.iTypeOption = IDATA_TYPE_INTERNAL_ND;

sAttrsSD3Tuple.uTupleSize = 3;                   /* 3-tuple to contain 3 data values   */

                                                 /* 3-tuple to contain SD data types   */
sAttrsSD3Tuple.iTypeOption = IDATA_TYPE_INTERNAL_SD;

sAttrsND3Tuple.uTupleSize = 3;                   /* 3-tuple to contain 3 data values   */
```

```
                                         /* 3-tuple to contain ND data types    */
sAttrsND3Tuple.iTypeOption = IDATA_TYPE_INTERNAL_ND;
nImageSize = InAllocateTuple(sAttrsND5Tuple);    /* Image size ND 5-tuple allocation   */

nBandType = InAllocateTuple(sAttrsSD3Tuple);     /* Image data type SD 3-tuple alloc.  */

                                         /* Image precision ND 3-tuple alloc.    */
nBandPrecision = InAllocateTuple(sAttrsND3Tuple);

                                         /* Tuple creation                       */

uaImageSize[0] = 512;                    /* X = 512                              */

uaImageSize[1] = 512;                    /* Y = 512                              */

uaImageSize[2] = 1;                      /* Z = 1                                */

uaImageSize[3] = 1;                      /* T = 1                                */

uaImageSize[4] = 3;                      /* B = 3                                */

iaBandType[0] = IDATA_TYPE_ND;           /* Band 0 is ND data type               */

iaBandType[1] = IDATA_TYPE_ND;           /* Band 1 is ND data type               */

iaBandType[2] = IDATA_TYPE_ND;           /* Band 2 is ND data type               */

uaBandPrecision[0] = 8;                  /* Band 0 has 8-bit precision           */

uaBandPrecision[1] = 8;                  /* Band 1 has 8-bit precision           */

uaBandPrecision[2] = 8;                  /* Band 2 has 8-bit precision           */

stImageSize.tuParameter = &uaImageSize[0];       /* Pointer to image size data    */

stBandType.tiParameter = &iaBandType[0];         /* Pointer to band type data     */

                                         /* Pointer to band precision data       */
stBandPrecision.tuParameter = &uaBandPrecision[0];


                                         /* Create image size ND 5-tuple  .      */
InCreateTuple(stImageSize, nImageSize, sAttrsND5Tuple);
                                         /* Create band data type SD 3-tuple     */
InCreateTuple(stBandType, nBandType, sAttrsSD3Tuple);
                                         /* Create band precision 3-tuple        */
InCreateTuple(stBandPrecision, nBandPrecision, sAttrsND3Tuple);
```

deallocate_data_object
See Section 4.2.8

The *deallocate_data_object* mechanism deallocates physical storage associated with an image or nonimage data object and destroys its attributes. Its API is:

```
void IvDeallocateDataObject(          /* no output return              */
    Ipsobject        snObject         /* object identifier             */
);
```

where Ipsobject is the name of the following *piks.h* union that specifies the data object identifier.

```
typedef union{
    Idnhist          nHist;           /* histogram identifier          */
    Idnimage         nImage;          /* image identifier              */
    Idnlut           nLUT;            /* lookup table identifier       */
    Idnmatrix        nMatrix;         /* matrix identifier             */
    Idnnbhood        nNbhood;         /* neighbourhood identifier      */
    Idnrepository    nRepository;     /* repository identifier         */
    Idnroi           nROI;            /* region of interest identifier */
    Idntuple         nTuple;          /* tuple identifier              */
} Ipsobject;
```

■**Example:**   Deallocation of an image.

```
Idnimage             nSrc;           /* Source image identifier        */

Ipsobject            snObject;       /* Data object identifier         */

snObject.nImage = nSrc;              /* Reference to source image object */


IvDeallocateDataObject(snObject);    /* Deallocate image data object    */
```

Note: Repository data objects cannot be deleted.

define_sub_image

InDefineSubImage

See Section 4.4.2

The *define_sub_image* mechanism creates a reference to a sub-image. Its API is:

```
Idnimage InDefineSubImage(             /* OUT desination sub-image identifier  */
    Idnimage        nSourceImage,      /* source image identifier              */
    Idnimage        nDestImage,        /* destination sub-image identifier     */
    Idntuple        nOffset,           /* index offset ND 5-tuple identifier   */
    Idntuple        nSubImageSize      /* sub-image size ND 5-tuple identifier  */
);
```

■**Example:**   Define a 100×150 sub-image of an image at an offset coordinate (120, 30).

```
Idnimage          nSrc;                        /* Source image identifier              */

Idnimage          nDst;                        /* Destination image identifier         */

Idntuple          nOffset;                     /* Index offset ND 5-tuple identifier   */

Idntuple          nSize;                       /* Sub-image size ND 5-tuple identifier */


nOffset = InGenerateND5Tuple(120, 30, 0, 0, 0);  /* Generate index offset ND 5-tuple    */

nSize = InGenerateND5Tuple(100, 150, 0, 0, 0);   /* Generate sub-image size ND 5-tuple  */


InDefineSubImage(nSrc, nDst, nOffset, nSize);    /* Define sub-image                    */
```

The *diffuse* operator performs error diffusion halftoning on a source image to reduce the number of amplitude levels per pixel. Its API is:

```
Idnimage InDiffuse(                             /* OUT destination image identifier   */
    Idnimage            nSourceImage,           /* source image identifier            */
    Idnimage            nDestImage,             /* destination image identifier       */
    Idntuple            nAmplitudeLevel         /* dest. amplitude level ND B-tuple id */
)
```

■**Example:**   Diffusion rendering of an 8-bit colour image to an 8-bit pseudocolour image with a coding of 3 red bits, 3 green bits, and 2 blue bits.

```
Idnimage                nSrcColour;             /* Source colour image identifier     */

Idnimage                nDstMon;                /* Destination monochrome image id    */

Idntuple                nAmplitudeLevel;        /* Dest. amplitude level ND 3-tuple id */


nAmplitudeLevel = InGenerateND3Tuple(3, 3, 2);  /* Amplitude level ND 3-tuple        */

                                                /* Diffuse operation                  */
InDiffuse(nSrcColour, nDstMon, nAmplitudeLevel);
```

dither

See Section 2.5.2

The *dither* operator performs ordered dither halftoning on a source image to reduce the number of amplitude levels per pixel. Its API is:

```
Idnimage InDither(                              /* OUT destination image identifier      */
    Idnimage         nSourceImage,              /* source image identifier               */
    Idnimage         nDestImage,                /* destination image identifier          */
    Idnnbhood        nDither,                   /* dither array identifier               */
    Idntuple         nAmplitudeLevel            /* dest. amplitude level ND B-tuple id   */
);
```

■**Example:** Dithering rendering of an 8-bit colour image to an 8-bit pseudocolour image with a coding of 3 red bits, 3 green bits, and 2 blue bits using the 4×4 dither array from the data object repository.

```
Idnimage              nSrcColour;           /* Source image identifier               */

Idnimage              nDstMon;              /* Destination image identifier          */

Idntuple              nAmplitudeLevel;      /* Dest. amplitude level ND B-tuple id   */

Idnrepository         nArrayId;             /* Repository entry identifier           */

nAmplitudeLevel = InGenerateND3Tuple(3, 3, 2);   /* Amplitude level ND 3-tuple       */

                                            /* Repository entry identifier output    */
nArrayId = InReturnRepositoryId(IR_DITHER_4x4, IREPOSITORY_DITHER);

                                            /* Dithering operation                   */
InDither(nSrcColour, nDstMon, nArrayId, nAmplitudeLevel);
```

Note 1: IR_DITHER_4x4 is the entry name for a 4×4 dither array stored in the data object repository.

Note 2: IREPOSITORY_DITHER is the #define name indicating that the repository class is dither arrays.

Note 3: See the *return_repository_id* manual page for an explanation of its usage.

The *draw_pixels* operator inserts pixels specified by an external array into an image. Its API is:

```
Idnimage InDrawPixels(                    /* OUT destination image identifier   */
    Ipsdraw_pixels    *tsaPixels,         /* pixel array structure pointer      */
    Idnimage          nDestImage,         /* destination image identifier       */
    Ipuint            uEntries            /* number of array entries            */
);
```

where `Ipsdraw_pixels` is the name of the following *piks.h* structure that specifies the external array size and references the array of pixel values.

```
typedef struct{
    Ipuint            uHorizontal;        /* horizontal coordinate value        */
    Ipuint            uVertical;          /* vertical coordinate value          */
    Ipuint            uDepth;             /* depth coordinate value             */
    Ipuint            uTemporal;          /* temporal coordinate value          */
    Ipuint            uBand;              /* band coordinate value              */
    union {                              /* pixel value union                  */
        Ipbool        bValue;            /* Boolean value                      */
        Ipuint        uValue;            /* unsigned integer value             */
        Ipint         iValue;            /* signed integer value               */
    } sPixel;
} Ipsdraw_pixels;
```

■**Example:** Draw a diagonal line of pixels of amplitude 255 from the origin to the bottom right corner of a 512×512 image.

```
#define IMAGE_SIZE 512                            /* 512x512 pixel image                */

Idnimage              nDst;                       /* Destination image identifier       */

                                                  /* Pixel array structure pointer      */
Ipsdraw_pixels        saDraw[IMAGE_SIZE], *tsaDraw = &saDraw[0];

int                   i;                          /* Array index                        */

/* Create diagonal line of amplitude 255                                                */

for(i = 0; i < IMAGE_SIZE; i++) {
    saDraw[i].uHorizontal = i;
    saDraw[i].uVertical = i;
    saDraw[i].uDepth = saDraw[i].uTemporal = saDraw[i].uBand = 0;
    saDraw[i].sPixel.uValue = 255;
}

InDrawPixels(tsaDraw, nDst, IMAGE_SIZE);          /* Draw pixels operation              */
```

dyadic_arithmetic

InDyadicArith

See Section 2.2.2

The *dyadic_arithmetic* operator performs dyadic arithmetic combination of a pair of integer images. Its API is:

```
Idnimage InDyadicArith(                         /* OUT destination image identifier    */
     Idnimage          nSourceImage1,           /* first source image identifier       */
     Idnimage          nSourceImage2,           /* second source image identifier      */
     Idnimage          nDestImage,              /* destination image identifier        */
     Ipint             iOption                  /* dyadic, arithmetic combination opt. */
);
```

The following dyadic, arithmetic #define options are provided in *piks.h*.

```
IDYADIC_ABSOLUTE_DIFFERENCE      1      /* absolute value difference  */
IDYADIC_ADDITION                 2      /* addition                   */
IDYADIC_ADDITION_SCALED          3      /* addition, scaled           */
IDYADIC_ARCTANGENT               4      /* arctangent                 */
IDYADIC_DIVISION                 5      /* division                   */
IDYADIC_MAXIMUM                  6      /* maximum                    */
IDYADIC_MINIMUM                  7      /* minimum                    */
IDYADIC_MULTIPLICATION           8      /* multiplication             */
IDYADIC_SUBTRACTION              9      /* subtraction                */
IDYADIC_SUBTRACTION_SCALED      10      /* subtraction, scaled        */
```

■**Example:**   Scaled addition of a pair of images.

```
Idnimage          nSrc1;              /* First source image identifier       */

Idnimage          nSrc2;              /* Second source image identifier      */

Idnimage          nDst;              /* Destination image identifier        */


                                      /* Scaled addition of image pair       */
InDyadicArith(nSrc1, nSrc2, nDst, IDYADIC_ADDITION_SCALED);
```

The *dyadic_logical* operator performs dyadic logical combination of a pair of Boolean or integer images. Its API is:

```
Idnimage InDyadicLogical(              /* OUT destination image identifier    */
    Idnimage        nSourceImage1,     /* first source image identifier       */
    Idnimage        nSourceImage2,     /* second source image identifier      */
    Idnimage        nDestImage,        /* destination image identifier        */
    Ipint           iOption            /* dyadic, logical combination option  */
);
```

The following dyadic, logical #define options are provided in *piks.h*.

```
IDYADIC_LOGICAL_AND             1      /* bitwise AND             */
IDYADIC_LOGICAL_NAND            2      /* bitwise NAND            */
IDYADIC_LOGICAL_NOR             3      /* bitwise NOR             */
IDYADIC_LOGICAL_OR              4      /* bitwise OR              */
IDYADIC_LOGICAL_XOR             5      /* bitwise XOR             */
IDYADIC_LOGICAL_INTERSECTION    6      /* Boolean intersection    */
IDYADIC_LOGICAL_UNION           7      /* Boolean union           */
```

■**Example:** Logical OR of a pair of integer images.

```
Idnimage                    nSrc1;     /* First source image identifier     */

Idnimage                    nSrc2;     /* Second source image identifier    */

Idnimage                    nDst;      /* Destination image identifier      */

                                       /* Logical OR of image pair          */
InDyadicLogical(nSrc1, nSrc2, nDst, IDYADIC_LOGICAL_OR);
```

dyadic_predicate

InDyadicPredicate

See Section 2.2.5

The *dyadic_predicate* operator performs dyadic predicate combination of a pair of integer images. Its API is:

```
Idnimage InDyadicPredicate(          /* OUT destination image identifier    */
    Idnimage        nSourceImage1,   /* first source image identifier       */
    Idnimage        nSourceImage2,   /* second source image identifier      */
    Idnimage        nDestImage,      /* destination image identifier        */
    Ipint           iOption          /* dyadic, predicate combination option */
);
```

The following dyadic predicate #define options are provided in *piks.h*.

```
IDYADIC_PREDICATE_GREATER        1    /* greater than             */
IDYADIC_PREDICATE_GREATER_EQUAL  2    /* greater than or equal to */
IDYADIC_PREDICATE_LESS           3    /* less than                */
IDYADIC_PREDICATE_LESS_EQUAL     4    /* less than or equal to    */
IDYADIC_PREDICATE_EQUAL          5    /* equal to                 */
IDYADIC_PREDICATE_NOT_EQUAL      6    /* not equal to             */
```

■**Example:** Less than predicate of a pair of images.

```
Idnimage            nSrc1;          /* First source image identifier    */

Idnimage            nSrc2;          /* Second source image identifier   */

Idnimage            nDst;           /* Destination image identifier     */


                                    /* Less than predicate of image pair */
InDyadicPredicate(nSrc1, nSrc2, nDst, IDYADIC_PREDICATE_LESS);
```

PIKS C ELEMENT PROTOTYPES   CHAPTER 7

The *error_handler* mechanism handles error conditions detected by a PIKS element during execution. Its API is:

```
void IvErrorHandler(                               /* no output return                    */
    Ipint                   iCode,                 /* error identifier code               */
    Ipint                   iElement,              /* identity of element detecting error */
    Idnchain                nChain,                /* error detecting chain identifier    */
    Ipnerror                nError,                /* error file specification identifier */
    Ipesynchronicity_state  eSynchronicityState    /* synchronicity state                 */
);
```

where Ipesynchronicity_state is the name of a *piks.h* enum that specifies the synchronicity state option:

```
ISYNCHRONICITY_STATE_SYNCH                         /* synchronous execution state         */
ISYNCHRONICITY_STATE_ASYNCH                        /* asynchonous state                   */
```

Note: PIKS Foundation only supports synchronous execution.

■**Example:**   Invoke error handler.

```
Ipint              iCode;                  /* Error identifier code             */

Ipint              iElement;               /* PIKS element detecting error      */

Idnchain           nChain = NULL;          /* Chaining not in PIKS Foundation   */

Ipnerror           nErrorFile;             /* Error file specification          */

char               "piks_errors"           /* Error file name                   */


if((nErrorFileFile = (Ipnerror) fopen("piks_errors", "w"))== NULL)
                   exit(2);

iElement = IF_CONVOLVE_2D;                 /* InConvolve2D element 64           */

iCode = IE_IMAGE_ID                        /* Image identifier is invalid, code 11 */

                                           /* Error handler invocation          */
IvErrorHandler(iCode, iElement, nChain, nError, ISYNCHRONICITY_STATE_SYNCH);
```

The *error_logger* mechanism logs detected error conditions in a previously designated error file. Its API is:

```
void IvErrorLogger(                            /* no output return                       */
    Ipint                   iCode,             /* error identifier code                  */
    Ipint                   iElement,          /* identity of element detecting error    */
    Idnchain                nChain,            /* error detecting chain identifier       */
    Ipnerror                nError,            /* error file specification identifier    */
    Ipesynchronicity_state  eSynchronicityState /* synchronicity state                   */
);
```

where Ipesynchronicity_state is the name of a *piks.h* enum that specifies the synchronicity state option:

```
ISYNCHRONICITY_STATE_SYNCH                     /* synchronous execution state            */
ISYNCHRONICITY_STATE_ASYNCH                    /* asynchonous state                      */
```

Note: PIKS Foundation only supports synchronous execution.

■**Example:**   Invoke error logger.

```
Ipint              iCode;                 /* Error identifier code            */

Ipint              iElement;              /* PIKS element detecting error     */

Idnchain           nChain = NULL;         /* Chaining not in PIKS Foundation  */

Ipnerror           nErrorFile;            /* Error file specification         */

char               "piks_errors"          /* Error file name                  */


if((nErrorFile = (Ipnerror) fopen("piks_errors", "w"))== NULL)
            exit(2);

iElement = IF_CONVOLVE_2D;                /* InConvolve2D element 64          */

iCode = IE_IMAGE_ID                       /* Image identifier is invalid, code 11 */

                                          /* Error logger invocation          */
IvErrorLogger(iCode, IElement, nChain, nError, ISYNCHRONICITY_STATE_SYNCH):
```

The *error_test* mechanism tests for the occurrence of a detected error condition since the last *error_test* mechanism was invoked. Its API is:

```
Ipbool IbErrorTest(                      /* OUT error flag                 */
    void                                 /* no input arguments             */
);
```

■**Example:**   Perform error test.

```
if(IbErrorTest()) {                      /* Test for error condition       */
    fclose(nErrorFile);                  /* Close error file               */
    IvClosePIKSEmergency;                /* Abnormal PIKS close            */
}
```

export_histogram

See Section 5.3.1

The *export_histogram* utility exports the array data of a histogram object to an application. Its API is:

```
Ipuint *ItuaExportHist(                    /* OUT external data array pointer   */
    Idnhist              nHist,            /* histogram identifier              */
    Ipuint              *tuaData           /* external data array pointer       */
);
```

■**Example:** Export a 256-bin histogram of a monochrome image to an application.

```
Idnhist              nHist;               /* Histogram identifier              */

                                          /* External histogram array          */
Ipuint               uaExtHistArray[256], *tuaExtHistArray = &uaExtHistArray[0];

ItuaExportHist(nHist, tuaExtHistArray);   /* Export histogram operation        */
```

The *export_image* utility exports a PIKS image to an application and converts the image to the external data type. Its API is:

```
Ipspiks_pixel_types IstExportImage(      /* OUT external data array ptr. union   */
    Idnimage              nSourceImage,  /* source image identifier              */
    Ipspiks_pixel_types   stDestImage,   /* external image data pointer union    */
    Ipuint                uPrecision,    /* number of destination bits per pixel */
    Ipint                 iType,         /* external data type option            */
    Ipint                 iApplBufferSize, /* data transfer buffer size or option */
    Ipuint                uStartPoint,   /* index offset within internal data    */
    Ipuint                *tuDataSize    /* OUT post transfer data size pointer   */
);
```

where `Ipspiks_pixel_types` is the name of the following *piks.h* union that specifies the pixel data type class and the data values of the image to be exported.

```
typedef union{
    Imbool     *tbPixel;        /* external Boolean pixel value pointer  */
    Imuint     *tuPixel;        /* ext. unsigned int pixel value ptr.    */
    Imint      *tiPixel;        /* ext. signed integer pixel pointer     */
    Imfixed    *trPixelFixed;   /* external fixed point pixel pointer    */
} Ipspiks_pixel_types;
```

The following external pixel data type #define options are provided in *piks.h*.

```
IPIXEL_BI_MSB_PLANAR        1   /* Boolean planar ordered from msb       */
IPIXEL_BI_MSB_INTERLEAVED   2   /* Boolean interleaved ordered from msb  */
IPIXEL_BI_LSB_PLANAR        3   /* Boolean planar ordered from lsb       */
IPIXEL_BI_LSB_INTERLEAVED   4   /* Boolean interleaved ordered from lsb  */
IPIXEL_NI_PLANAR            5   /* nonnegative integer planar            */
IPIXEL_NI_INTERLEAVED       6   /* nonnegative integer interleaved       */
IPIXEL_SI_PLANAR            7   /* signed integer planar                 */
IPIXEL_SI_INTERLEAVED       8   /* signed integer interleaved            */
IPIXEL_TI_PLANAR            9   /* fixed point integer planar            */
IPIXEL_TI_INTERLEAVED       10  /* fixed point integer interleaved       */
```

■**Example:** Export a 512×512, nonnegative, monochrome image to an application.

```
#define WIDTH 512                               /* Image width                       */

#define HEIGHT 512                              /* Image height                      */


Idnimage              nSrcND;                   /* Source image identifier           */

Ipspiks_pixel_types   stExtImageArray;          /* External image data pointer union */

Ipuint                uPrecision = 8;           /* Number of destination bits per pixel */

                                                /* noninterleaved NI data type       */
Ipint                 iType = IPIXEL_NI_PLANAR;

                                                /* External image array              */
Imuint                uaExtImageArray[HEIGHT][WIDTH];

                                                /* Data transfer buffer size         */
Ipint                 iApplBufferSize = WIDTH * HEIGHT;

                                                /* Post transfer data size pointer   */
Ipuint                uDataSize, *tuDataSize = &uDataSize;

                                                /* Pointer to external image array   */
stExtImageArray.tuPixel = &uaExtImageArray[0][0];


                                                /* Export image operation            */
IstExportImage(nSrcND, stExtImageArray, uPrecision, iType, iApplBufferSize, 0, tuDataSize);
```

export_lut

See Section 5.3.3

The *export_lut* utility exports the array data of a lookup table object to an application. Its API is:

```
Ipsparameter_pixel IstExportLUT(          /* OUT external data array ptr. union   */
     Idnlut               nLUT,            /* lookup table identifier              */
     Ipsparameter_pixel   stData,          /* external data array pointer union    */
     Ipint                iApplBufferSize, /* data transfer buffer size or option  */
     Ipuint               uStartPoint,     /* index offset within internal data    */
     Ipuint               *tuDataSize      /* OUT post transfer data size pointer   */
);
```

where `Ipsparameter_pixel` is the name of the following *piks.h* union that specifies the data type and values of the array to be exported.

```
typedef union{
     Ipbool            *tbPixel;           /* Boolean pointer            */
     Ipuint            *tuPixel;           /* unsigned integer pointer   */
     Ipint             *tiPixel;           /* signed integer pointer     */
} Ipsparameter_pixel;
```

■**Example:** Export a 256-entry, unsigned integer lookup table to an application.

```
Idnlut              nLUT;                  /* Lookup table identifier              */

Ipsparameter_pixel  stExtLUTArray         /* External data array pointer union    */

Ipuint              uaExtLUTArray[256];    /* External data array                  */
                                           /* Post transfer data size pointer      */
Ipuint              uDataSize, *tuDataSize = &uDataSize;


stExtLUTArray.tuPixel = uaExtLUTArray[0];  /* Pointer to external data array       */

                                           /* Export LUT operation                 */
IstExportLUT(nLUT, stExtLUTArray, 256, 0, tuDataSize);
```

The *export_matrix* utility exports the array data of a matrix object to an application. Its API is:

```
Ipsparameter_numeric IstExportMatrix(      /* OUT external data array ptr. union  */
    Idnmatrix              nMatrix,        /* matrix identifier                   */
    Ipsparameter_numeric stData            /* external data array pointer union   */
);
```

where `Ipsparameter_numeric` is the name of the following *piks.h* union that specifies the numeric data type and values of the external array.

```
typedef union{
    Ipuint              *tuNumeric;        /* unsigned integer pointer            */
    Ipint               *tiNumeric;        /* signed integer pointer              */
    Ipfloat             *trNumericFloat;   /* float pointer                       */
} Ipsparameter_numeric;
```

■**Example:** Export a real, 3×3, colour conversion matrix image to an application.

```
Idnmatrix              nMatrix;            /* Colour matrix identifier            */

Ipsparameter_numeric   stExtMatrixArray;   /* External data array pointer union   */

Ipfloat                raExtMatrixArray[3][3];  /* External data array            */


                                           /* Pointer to external data array      */
stExtMatrixArray.NumericFloat = &raExtMatrixArray[0][0];

IstExportMatrix(nMatrix, stExtMatrixArray);  /* Export matrix operation           */
```

export_neighbourhood_array

See Section 5.3.5

The *export_neighbourhood_array* utility exports the array data of a neighbourhood array object to an application. Its API is:

```
Ipsparameter_pixel IstExportNbhoodArray(    /* OUT external data array ptr. union  */
    Idnnbhood          nNbhood,             /* neighbourhood array identifier      */
    Ipsparameter_pixel stData,              /* external data array pointer union   */
    Ipint             *tiScaleFactor        /* OUT scale factor pointer            */
);
```

where `Ipsparameter_pixel` is the name of the following *piks.h* union that specifies the data type and values of the array to be exported.

```
typedef union{
    Ipbool          *tbPixel;         /* Boolean pointer           */
    Ipuint          *tuPixel;         /* unsigned integer pointer  */
    Ipint           *tiPixel;         /* signed integer pointer    */
    Ipfloat         *trPixelFloat;    /* float pointer             */
} Ipsparameter_pixel;
```

■**Example:** Export an integer, 3×3, impulse response function neighbourhood array to an application.

```
Idnnbhood               nImpulse;                    /* Neighbourhood array identifier  */

Ipsparameter_pixel      sExtImpulseArray;            /* External data array pointer union  */

                                                     /* External data array             */
Ipint                   iaExtImpulseArray[3][3];

                                                     /* Scale factor pointer            */
Ipint                   iScaleFactor, *tiScaleFactor = &iScaleFactor;

                                                     /* Pointer to data array           */
sExtImpulseArray.tiPixel = &iaExtImpulseArray[0][0];

                                                     /* Export neighbourhood array operation  */
IstExportNbhood(nImpulse, stExtImpulseArray, tiScaleFactor);
```

The *export_tuple* utility exports the array data of a tuple object to an application. Its API is:

```
Ipsparameter_basic IstExportTuple(        /* OUT external data array ptr. union   */
    Idntuple           nTuple,            /* tuple identifier                     */
    Ipsparameter_basic stData             /* external data array pointer union    */
);
```

where `Ipsparameter_basic` is the name of the following *piks.h* union that specifies the tuple data type and its values.

```
typedef union{
    Ipbool          *tbParameter;         /* Boolean pointer                       */
    Ipuint          *tuParameter;         /* nonnegative integer pointer           */
    Ipint           *tiParameter;         /* signed integer pointer                */
    Ipfloat         *trParameterFloat;    /* float pointer                         */
    char            *tcParameter          /* character pointer                     */
} Ipsparameter_basic;
```

■**Example:**   Export an image size tuple to an application.

```
Idntuple           nImageSize;            /* ND 5-tuple identifier              */

Ipsparameter_basic stTupleArray;          /* External data array pointer union  */

Ipunint            uaTupleArray[5];       /* External data array                */


stTupleArray.tuParameter = &uaTupleArray[0];  /* Pointer to external data array     */


IstExportTuple(nImageSize, stTupleArray);     /* Export tuple operation             */
```

extract_pixel_plane

See Section 5.1.7

The *extract_pixel_plane* utility extracts a monochrome image from a colour image. Its API is:

```
Idnimage InExtractPixelPlane(              /* OUT destination image identifier    */
    Idnimage          nSourceImage,        /* source image identifier             */
    Idnimage          nDestImage,          /* destination image identifier        */
    Ipuint            uDepth,              /* depth index value                   */
    Ipuint            uTemporal,           /* temporal index value                */
    Ipuint            uBand                /* band index value                    */
);
```

■**Example:**   Extract green band from a colour image.

```
Idnimage          nSrcColour;             /* Source image identifier             */

Idnimage          nDstMon;                /* Destination image identifier        */

Ipuint            uDepth = 0;             /* Depth index value                   */

Ipuint            uTemporal = 0;          /* Temporal index value                */

Ipuint            uBand = 1;              /* Green band index value              */


                                          /* Extract green band                  */
InExtractPixelPlane(nSrcColour, nDstMon, uDepth, uTemporal, uBand);
```

IvExtrema

The *extrema* operator detects the smallest and largest pixels of an image and records their values in an external array. Its API is:

```
void IvExtrema(                                  /* no outout return                        */
    Idnimage           nSourceImage,             /* source image identifier                 */
    Ipfloat            *traMinimum,              /* OUT minimum extrema array pointer        */
    Ipfloat            *traMaximum,              /* OUT maximum extrema array pointer        */
    Ipeprocess         eOption,                  /* processing mode option                  */
    Ipint              iApplBufferSize,          /* data transfer buffer size or option     */
    Ipuint             uStartPoint,              /* index offset within internal data       */
    Ipuint             *tuDataSize               /* OUT post transfer data size pointer      */
);
```

where Ipeprocess is the name of a *piks.h* enum that specifies the processing mode option:

```
IPROCESS_MODE_0                                  /* processing mode zero                    */
IPROCESS_MODE_1                                  /* processing mode one                     */
IPROCESS_MODE_2                                  /* processing mode two                     */
IPROCESS_MODE_3                                  /* processing mode three                   */
IPROCESS_MODE_4                                  /* processing mode four                    */
```

Note: Processing modes one, two, and three give the same results in PIKS Foundation.

■**Example 1:** Determine extrema pixels in a ND data type, colour image.

```
Idnimage           nSrc;                         /* Source image identifier                 */

Ipfloat            rMin, *trMin = &rMin;         /* Minimum extrema value pointer           */

Ipfloat            rMax, *trMax = &rMax;         /* Maximum extrema value pointer           */

unsigned int       uMin, uMax;                   /* Unsigned integer extrema                */


                                                 /* Extrema operation                      */
IvExtrema(nSrc, trMin, trMax, IPROCESS_MODE_0, -1, 0, NULL);

uMin = rMin;                                     /* Colour image minimum                    */

uMax = rMin;                                     /* Colour image maximum                    */

printf("min = %u \n", uMin);                     /* Print minimum extrema value             */

printf("max = %u \n", uMax);                     /* Print maximum extrema value             */
```

■**Example 2:** Determine extrema pixels in each band of a ND data type, colour image.

```
Idnimage           nSrc;                         /* Source image identifier                 */

                                                 /* Minimum extrema array                   */
Ipfloat            raMin[3], *traMin = &raMin[0];

                                                 /* Maximum extrema array                   */
Ipfloat            raMax[3], *traMax = &raMax[0];

                                                 /* Unsigned integer minima                 */
unsigned int       uRedMin, uGreenMin, uBlueMin;

                                                 /* Unsigned integer maxima                 */
unsigned int       uRedMax, uGreenMax, uBlueMax;


                                                 /* Extrema operation                      */
IvExtrema(nSrc, traMin, traMax, IPROCESS_MODE_1, -1, 0, NULL);

uRedMin = raMin[0];

uGreenMin = raMin[1];
```

```
uBlueMin = raMin[2];

uRedMax = raMax[0]

uGreenMax = raMax[1]

uBlueMax = raMax[2];

printf("red min = %u \n", uRedMin);          /* Print red band minimum extrema     */
printf("green min = %u \n", uGreenMin);       /* Print green band minimum extrema   */
printf("blue min = %u \n", uBlueMin);         /* Print blue band minimum extrema    */
printf("red min = %u \n", uRedMax);           /* Print red band maximum extrema     */
printf("green min = %u \n", uGreenMax);       /* Print green band maximum extrema   */
printf("blue min = %u \n", uBlueMax);         /* Print blue band maximum extrema    */
```

The *flip_spin_transpose* operator performs flip, spin, or transpose manipulations on pixel planes of an image. Its API is:

```
Idnimage InFlipSpinTranspose(          /* OUT destination image identifier   */
    Idnimage          nSourceImage,    /* source image identifier            */
    Idnimage          nDestImage,      /* destination image identifier       */
    Ipeflip           eOption          /* flip, spin, transpose option        */
);
```

where Ipeflip is the name of a *piks.h* enum that specifies the following flip, spin, or transpose options:

```
IFLIP_TOP_BOTTOM                   /* top-to-bottom flip                      */
IFLIP_LEFT_RIGHT                   /* left-to-right flip                      */
ISPIN_90_DEGREES_CCW               /* 90 degrees counter clockwise spin       */
ISPIN_180_DEGREES_CCW              /* 180 degrees counter clockwise spin      */
ISPIN_270_DEGREES_CCW              /* 270 degrees counter clockwise spin      */
ITRANSPOSE_UPLEFT_LOWRIGHT         /* transpose, upper left to lower right    */
ITRANSPOSE_LOWLEFT_UPRIGHT         /* transpose, lower left to upper right    */
```

■ **Example:**   Top-to-bottom flip of an image.

```
Idnimage          nSrc;            /* Source image identifier            */

Idnimage          nDst;            /* Destination image identifier       */


                                   /* Top-to-bottom flip operation       */
InFlipSpinTranspose(nSrc, nDst, IFLIP_TOP_BOTTOM);
```

flip_spin_transpose_roi

InFlipSpinTransposeROI

See Section 2.4.2

The *flip_spin_transpose_roi* operator performs flip, spin, or transpose manipulations on a ROI. Its API is:

```
Idnroi InFlipSpinTransposeROI(          /* OUT destination ROI identifier      */
    Idnroi          nSourceROI,         /* source ROI identifier               */
    Idnroi          nDestROI,           /* destination ROI identifier          */
    Ipeflip         eOption             /* flip, spin, transpose option        */
);
```

where `Ipeflip` is the name of a *piks.h* enum that specifies the following flip, spin, or transpose options:

```
IFLIP_TOP_BOTTOM                        /* top-to-bottom flip                  */
IFLIP_LEFT_RIGHT                        /* left-to-right flip                  */
ISPIN_90_DEGREES_CCW                    /* 90 degrees counter clockwise spin   */
ISPIN_180_DEGREES_CCW                   /* 180 degrees counter clockwise spin  */
ISPIN_270_DEGREES_CCW                   /* 270 degrees counter clockwise spin  */
ITRANSPOSE_UPLEFT_LOWRIGHT              /* transpose, upper left to lower right */
ITRANSPOSE_LOWLEFT_UPRIGHT              /* transpose, lower left to upper right */
```

■**Example:**   Top-to-bottom flip of a ROI.

```
Idnroi              nSrcROI;            /* Source ROI identifier               */

Idnroi              nDstROI;            /* Destination ROI identifier          */


                                        /* Top-to-bottom flip operation        */
InFlipSpinTransposeROI(nSrcROI, nDstROI, IFLIP_TOP_BOTTOM);
```

The *get_colour_pixel* utility returns the value of a colour pixel to an application. Its API is:

```
void IvGetColourPixel(                              /* no output return                    */
    Idnimage            nSourceImage,               /* source image identifier             */
    Ipsparameter_colour stBand0,                    /* OUT band 0 pixel value pointer union */
    Ipsparameter_colour stBand1,                    /* OUT band 1 pixel value pointer union */
    Ipsparameter_colour stBand2,                    /* OUT band 2 pixel value pointer union */
    Ipsparameter_colour stBand3,                    /* OUT band 3 pixel value pointer union */
    Ipuint              uHorizontal,                /* horizontal index value              */
    Ipuint              uVertical,                  /* vertical index value                */
    Ipuint              uDepth,                     /* depth index value                   */
    Ipuint              uTemporal                   /* temporal index value                */
);
```

where `Ipsparameter_colour` is the name of the following *piks.h* union that specifies the data type and value of each band of the colour pixel to be exported to the application.

```
typedef union{
    Ipbool  *tbColour                               /* Boolean pointer                     */
    Ipuint  *tuColour;                              /* unsigned integer pointer            */
    Ipint   *tiColour;                              /* signed integer pointer              */
} Ipsparameter_colour;
```

■**Example:**   Get a RGB colour pixel from a colour image at spatial coordinate (150, 240) and print its RGB component values.

```
Idnimage                nSrc;                       /* Source image identifier             */

Ipsparameter_colour     stBand0;                    /* Band 0 pixel value pointer union    */

Ipsparameter_colour     stBand1;                    /* Band 1 pixel value pointer union    */

Ipsparameter_colour     stBand2;                    /* Band 2 pixel value pointer union    */

Ipsparameter_colour     stBand3;                    /* Band 3 pixel value pointer union    */

                                                    /* Pixel values                       */
Ipuint          uBand0, uBand1, uBand2, uBand3;

stBand0.tuColour = &uBand0;

stBand1.tuColour = &uBand1;

stBand2.tuColour = &uBand2;

stBand3.tuColour = &uBand3;

                                                    /* Get colour pixel operation          */
IvGetColourPixel(nSrc, stBand0, stBand1, stBand2, stBand3, 150, 240, 0, 0);

printf("red = %u \n", uBand0);                      /* Print red pixel value               */

printf("green = %u \n", uBand1);                    /* Print green pixel value             */

printf("blue = %u \n", uBand2);                     /* Print blue pixel value              */
```

get_pixel

See Section 5.3.8

The *get_pixel* utility returns the value of a single pixel to an application. Its API is:

```
Ipsparameter_pixel IstGetPixel(          /* OUT pixel value pointer union      */
    Idnimage           nSourceImage,     /* source image identifier            */
    Ipsparameter_pixel stPixel,          /* pixel value pointer union          */
    Ipuint             uHorizontal,      /* horizontal index value             */
    Ipuint             uVertical,        /* vertical index value               */
    Ipuint             uDepth,           /* depth index value                  */
    Ipuint             uTemporal,        /* temporal index value               */
    Ipuint             uBand             /* band index value                   */
)
```

where `Ipsparameter_pixel` is the name of the following *piks.h* union that specifies the data type and value of the pixel to be exported to the application.

```
typedef union{
    Ipbool    *tbPixel;                  /* Boolean pointer                    */
    Ipuint    *tuPixel;                  /* unsigned integer pointer           */
    Ipint     *tPixel;                   /* signed integer pointer             */
} Ipsparameter_pixel;
```

■**Example:** Get a pixel from a RGB colour image at coordinate (460, 123) in the blue band and print its value.

```
Idnimage            nSrc;                     /* Source image identifier      */

Ipsparameter_pixel  stPixel;                  /* Pixel value pointer union    */

Ipuint              uPixel;                   /* Pixel value                  */

Ipuint              uHorizontal = 460;        /* Horizontal index value       */

Ipuint              uVertical = 123;          /* Vertical index value         */

Ipuint              uDepth = 0;               /* Depth index value            */

Ipuint              uTemporal = 0;            /* Temporal index value         */

Ipuint              uBand = 2;                /* Blue band index value        */


stPixel.tuPixel = &uPixel;

                                              /* Get pixel operation          */
stPixel = IstGetPixel(nSrc, stPixel, uHorizontal, uVertical, uDepth, uTemporal, uBand);

printf("pixel value is %u \n", uPixel);       /* Print pixel value            */
```

The *get_pixel_roi* utility returns the value of a single ROI pixel to an application. Its API is:

```
Ipbool IbGetPixelROI(                               /* OUT ROI pixel value             */
    Idnroi          nSourceROI,                     /* source ROI identifier           */
    Ipbool          *tbROIPixel,                    /* ROI pixel value pointer          */
    Ipuint          uHorizontal,                    /* horizontal index value          */
    Ipuint          uVertical,                      /* vertical index value            */
    Ipuint          uDepth,                         /* depth index value               */
    Ipuint          uTime,                          /* temporal index value            */
    Ipuint          uBand                           /* band index value                */
)
```

■**Example:**   Get a pixel from a ROI at spatial coordinate (460, 123) and print its value.

```
Idnroi              nSrcROI;                        /* Source ROI identifier           */

                                                    /* ROI pixel value pointer          */
Ipbool              bROIPixel, *tbROIPixel =&bROIPixel;


                                                    /* Get ROI value                   */
bROIPixel = IbGetPixelROI(nSrcROI, tbROIPixel, 460, 123, 0, 0, 0);

printf("ROI value is %x \n", bROIPixel);/* Print ROI value                             */
```

get_pixel_array

See Section 5.3.10

The *get_pixel_array* utility returns a rectangular array of pixels to an application. Its API is:

```
Ipsparameter_pixel IstGetPixelArray(          /* OUT pixel values array pointer union  */
    Idnimage            nSourceImage,         /* source image identifier               */
    Ipsparameter_pixel  stPixels,             /* pixel values array pointer union       */
    Ipuint              uOffset1,             /* first index offset                    */
    Ipuint              uOffset2,             /* second index offset                   */
    Ipuint              uValue3,              /* third index value                     */
    Ipuint              uValue4,              /* fourth index value                    */
    Ipuint              uValue5,              /* fifth index value                     */
    Ipuint              uColumns,             /* number of array columns               */
    Ipuint              uRows                 /* number of array rows                  */
);
```

where `Ipsparameter_pixel` is the name of the following *piks.h* union that specifies the data type and values of the pixels to be exported to the application.

```
typedef union{
    Ipbool      *tbPixel;            /* Boolean pointer             */
    Ipuint      *tuPixel;            /* unsigned integer pointer    */
    Ipint       *tiPixel;            /* signed integer pointer      */
} Ipsparameter_pixel;
```

■**Example:**   Get a 5 × 10 pixel array from a monochrome image at coordinate (100, 110) and print its elements.

```
#define COLS 10                                   /* Number of array columns      */

#define ROWS 5                                    /* Number of array rows         */


Idnimage            nSrc;                         /* Source image declaration     */

Ipsparameter_pixel  stPixels;                     /* Pixel values array pointer   */

Ipuint              uFirstOff = 100;              /* First index offset           */

Ipuint              uSecondOff = 110;             /* Second index offset          */

                                                  /* Pixel array                  */
Ipuint              uaPixels[ROWS][COLS], *tuaPixels = &uaPixels[0][0];

unsigned int        j, k;                         /* Array indices                */


stPixels.tuPixel = &uaPixels;                     /* Pointer at pixel array       */

                                                  /* Get pixel array              */
IstGetPixelArray(nSrc, stPixels, uFirstOff, uSecondOff, 0, 0, 0, COLS, ROWS);

for(k = 0; k < ROWS; k++) {                       /* Print array elements         */
    for(j = 0; j < COLS; j++) {
                    printf("%5u ", uPixels[k][j]);
    }
    printf("\n");
}
```

The *get_pixel_array_roi* utility returns a rectangular array of ROI pixels to an application. Its API is:

```
Ipbool *ItbaGetPixelArrayROI(        /* OUT pixel array pointer      */
    Idnroi          nSourceROI,      /* source ROI identifier        */
    Ipbool          *tbaPixels,      /* pixel array pointer          */
    Ipuint          uOffset1,        /* first index offset value     */
    Ipuint          uOffset2,        /* second index offset value    */
    Ipuint          uValue3,         /* third index value            */
    Ipuint          uValue4,         /* fourth index value           */
    Ipuint          uValue5,         /* fifth index value            */
    Ipuint          uColumns,        /* number of array columns      */
    Ipuint          uRows            /* number of array rows         */
);
```

■**Example:**   Get a 5×10 pixel array from a ROI at coordinate (100, 110) and print its elements.

```
Idnroi          nROI;                       /* Source ROI identifier        */

                                            /* Pixel array pointer          */
Ipbool          baPixels[5][10], *tbaPixels = &baPixels[0][0];

Ipuint          uFirstOff = 100:            /* First index offset value     */

Ipuint          uSecondOff = 110:           /* Second index offset value    */

Ipuint          uCols = 10:                 /* Number of array columns      */

Ipuint          uRows = 5:                  /* Number of array rows         */

unsigned int    j, k;

                                            /* Get pixel ROI array          */
ItbaGetPixelArrayROI(nROI, tbaPixels, uFirstOff, uSecondOff, 0, 0, 0, uCols, uRows);

for(k = 0; k < ROWS; k++) {                 /* Print array elements         */
    for(j = 0; j < COLS; j++) {
        printf("%3x ", baPixels[k][j]);
    }
    printf("\n");
}
```

histogram_1d

See Section 2.8.3

The *histogram_1d* operator generates a one-dimensional histogram of an image. Its API is:

```
Idnhist InHist1D(                                  /* histogram identifier        */
    Idnimage        nSourceImage,                  /* source image identifier     */
    Idnhist         nHist,                         /* histogram identifier        */
    Ipuint          uBins,                         /* number of histogram bins    */
    Ipfloat         rLowerBound,                   /* lower amplitude bound       */
    Ipfloat         rUpperBound,                   /* upper amplitude bound       */
    Ipint           iOption                        /* histogram computation option */
);
```

The following histogram computation #define options are provided in *piks.h*.

```
IHIST_LIMIT_SPECIFIED            1                 /* specified limits            */
IHIST_LIMIT_EXTREMA              2                 /* image extrema limits        */
```

■**Example:** Histogram of a 256 grey level, monochrome image over the unsigned integer range of 15 to 225.

```
Idnimage           nSrc;                     /* Source image identifier        */

Idnhist            nHist;                    /* Histogram identifier           */

Ipuint             uBins = 256;              /* Number of histogram bins       */

Ipfloat            rLowerBound = 15.0;       /* Lower amplitude bound          */

Ipfloat            rUpperBound = 225.0;      /* Upper amplitude bound          */

                                             /* Histogram computation          */
InHist1D(nSrc, nHist, uBins, rLowerBound, rUpperBound, IHIST_LIMIT_SPECIFIED);
```

image_constant

See Section 3.1.1

The *image_constant* tool creates an image whose pixels are of the same constant value. Its API is:

```
Idnimage InImageConstant(                          /* OUT destination image identifier      */
    Idnimage           nDestImage,                 /* destination image identifier          */
    Idntuple           nSize,                      /* image size ND 5-tuple identifier      */
    Ipsparameter_pixel stValue,                    /* constant value pointer union          */
    Ipint              iType                       /* destination image data type option    */
);
```

where `Ipsparameter_pixel` is the name of the following *piks.h* union that specifies the data type and value of the constant.

```
typedef union{
    Ipbool  *tbPixel;                              /* Boolean pointer                       */
    Ipuint  *tuPixel;                              /* unsigned integer pointer              */
    Ipint   *tiPixel;                              /* signed integer pointer                */
} Ipsparameter_pixel;
```

The following PIKS data type #define options are provided in *piks.h*.

```
IDATA_TYPE_INTERNAL_BD          1                  /* Boolean                               */
IDATA_TYPE_INTERNAL_ND          2                  /* unsigned integer                      */
IDATA_TYPE_INTERNAL_SD          3                  /* signed integer                        */
```

■**Example:** Create a 512×512 nonnegative data type monochrome image of amplitude 120.

```
Idnimage            nDst;                          /* Destination image identifier          */

Idntuple            nSize;                         /* Image size ND 5-tuple identifier      */

Ipsparameter_pixel  stValue;                       /* Constant value pointer union          */

Ipuint              uValue;                        /* Constant value                        */


nSize = InGenerateND5Tuple(512, 512, 1, 1, 1);     /* Image size ND 5-tuple generation      */

stValue.tuPixel = &uValue;                         /* Pointer to pixel value                */

uValue = 120;                                      /* Constant value of 120                 */


                                                   /* Create constant value image          */
InImageConstant(nDst, nSize, stValue, IDATA_TYPE_INTERNAL_ND);
```

The *import_histogram* utility imports an external array of data values from an application and puts it into a histogram object. Its API is:

```
Idnhist InImportHist(                         /* OUT histogram identifier     */
    Ipuint           *tuaData,                /* external data array pointer  */
    Idnhist          nHist,                   /* histogram identifier         */
    Ipsattrs_hist    sAttrs                   /* histogram attributes         */
);
```

where `Ipsattrs_hist` is the name of the following *piks.h* structure that specifies the histogram attributes.

```
typedef struct{
    Ipuint        uHistSize;                  /* histogram size           */
    Ipfloat       rLowerBound;                /* lower amplitude bound    */
    Ipfloat       rUpperBound;                /* upper amplitude bound    */
} Ipsattrs_hist;
```

■ **Example:** Import a 256-bin histogram of a monochrome image from an application.

```
Idnhist           nHist;                      /* Histogram identifier        */

Ipsattrs_hist     sAttrsHist;                 /* Histogram attributes        */

                                              /* External histogram array    */
Ipuint            uaExtHistArray[256], *tuaExtHistArray = &uaExtHistArray[0];

sAttrsHist.uHistSize = 256;                   /* Number of histogram bins    */

sAttrsHist.rLowerBound = 0.0;                 /* Lower amplitude bound       */

sAttrsHist.rUpperBound = 255.0;               /* Upper amplitude bound       */

nHist = IdnAllocateHist(sAttrsHist);          /* Allocate histogram          */


                                              /* Import histogram            */
InImportHist(tuaExtHistArray, nHist, sAttrsHist);
```

The *import_image* utility imports an image from an application and converts it to the internal PIKS data type. Its API is:

```
Idnimage InImportImage(                          /* OUT destination image identifier    */
    Ipspiks_pixel_types   stSourceImage,         /* external source image data ptr union */
    Idnimage              nDestImage,            /* destination image identifier        */
    Ipuint                uPrecision,            /* number of source bits per pixel     */
    Ipint                 iType,                 /* external pixel data type option     */
    Ipint                 iApplBufferSize,       /* data transfer buffer size or option */
    Ipuint                uStartPoint,           /* index offset within internal data   */
    Ipuint                *tuDataSize            /* OUT post transfer data size pointer */
);
```

where `Ipspiks_pixel_types` is the name of the following *piks.h* union that specifies the pixel data type and data values of the image to be imported.

```
typedef union{
    Imbool     *tbPixel;          /* external Boolean pixel value pointer */
    Imuint     *tuPixel;          /* ext. unsigned int pixel value ptr.   */
    Imint      *tiPixel;          /* ext. signed integer pixel pointer    */
    Imfixed    *trPixelFixed;     /* external fixed point pixel pointer    */
} Ipspiks_pixel_types;
```

The following external pixel data type #define options are provided in *piks.h*.

```
IPIXEL_BI_MSB_PLANAR          1     /* Boolean planar ordered from msb      */
IPIXEL_BI_MSB_INTERLEAVED     2     /* Boolean interleaved ordered from msb */
IPIXEL_BI_LSB_PLANAR          3     /* Boolean planar ordered from lsb      */
IPIXEL_BI_LSB_INTERLEAVED     4     /* Boolean interleaved ordered from lsb */
IPIXEL_NI_PLANAR              5     /* nonnegative integer planar           */
IPIXEL_NI_INTERLEAVED         6     /* nonnegative integer interleaved      */
IPIXEL_SI_PLANAR              7     /* signed integer planar                */
IPIXEL_SI_INTERLEAVED         8     /* signed integer interleaved           */
IPIXEL_TI_PLANAR              9     /* fixed point integer planar           */
IPIXEL_TI_INTERLEAVED        10     /* fixed point integer interleaved      */
```

■**Example:**   Create a horizontal ramp image and import it from an application.

```
#define WIDTH 512                              /* Image width                      */

#define HEIGHT 512                             /* Image height                     */

#define ND_PRECISION 8                         /* Band pixel precision             */


Idnimage              nDst;                    /* Destination image identifier     */

Ipspiks_pixel_types   stExtImageArray;         /* External source image data ptr union */

                                               /* Application buffer size          */
Ipint                 iApplBufferSize = WIDTH * HEIGHT;

                                               /* Post transfer data size pointer  */
Ipuint                uDataSize, *tuDataSize = &uDataSize;

                                               /* External image array             */
Imuint                uaExtImageArray[HEIGHT][WIDTH];

                                               /* Prepare monochrome destination   */
nDst = InPrepareMonochromeImage(WIDTH, HEIGHT, IDATA_TYPE_INTERNAL_ND, ND_PRECISION);
```

```
/*  Create horizontal ramp external image array                           */

    for(y = 0; y < HEIGHT; y++)
    {
        for(x = 0; x < WIDTH; x++)
        {
            uaExtImageArray[y][x] = x/2;
        }
    }

                                     /* Pointer to external image array    */
    stExtImageArray.tuPixel = uaExtImageArray[0][0];

                                     /* Import image from application       */
    InImportImage(stExtImageArray, nDst, ND_PRECISION, IPIXEL_NI_PLANAR, iApplBufferSize,
        0, tuDataSize);
```

The *import_lut* utility imports an external array of data values from an application and puts it into a lookup table object. Its API is:

```
Idnlut InImportLUT(                         /* OUT lookup table identifier        */
    Ipsparameter_pixel stData,              /* external data array pointer union  */
    Idnlut             nLUT,                /* lookup table identifier            */
    Ipsattrs_lut       sAttrs,              /* lookup table attributes            */
    Ipint              iApplBufferSize,     /* data transfer buffer size or option */
    Ipuint             uStartPoint,         /* index offset within internal data  */
    Ipuint             *tuDataSize          /* OUT post transfer data size pointer */
);
```

where Ipsparameter_pixel is the name of the following union that specifies the data type and values of the array to be imported.

```
typedef union{
    Ipbool      *tbPixel;       /* Boolean pointer          */
    Ipuint      *tuPixel;       /* unsigned integer pointer */
    Ipint       *tiPixel;       /* signed integer pointer   */
} Ipsparameter_pixel;
```

Ipsattrs_lut is the name of the following *piks.h* structure that specifies the lookup table attributes

```
typedef struct{
    Ipuint      uTableEntries;      /* number of table entries       */
    Ipuint      uTableBands;        /* number of table bands         */
    Ipint       iInputTypeOption;   /* table input data type option  */
    Ipint       iOutputTypeOption;  /* table output data type option */
} Ipsattrs_lut;
```

The following lookup table data type #define options are provided in *piks.h*.

```
IDATA_TYPE_INTERNAL_BD      1       /* Boolean          */
IDATA_TYPE_INTERNAL_ND      2       /* unsigned integer */
IDATA_TYPE_INTERNAL_SD      3       /* signed integer   */
```

■**Example:** Create and import a 256-entry scaled square root lookup table from an application.

```
Idnlut              nLUT;                   /* LUT identifier                 */

Ipsattrs_lut        sAttrsLUT;              /* LUT attributes                 */

Ipsparameter_pixel  saExtLUTArray;          /* LUT data array pointer union   */

Ipunit              uaExtLUTArray[256];     /* LUT data array                 */

                                            /* Post transfer data size pointer */
Ipuint              uDataSize, *tuDataSize = &uDataSize;

Ipint               i;                      /* Array index                    */

sAttrsLUT.uTableEntries = 256;              /* 256 LUT entries                */
sLutAttrs.uTableBands = 1;                  /* One LUT band                   */

                                            /* LUT to have ND data type input */
sLutAttrs.iInputTypeOption = IDATA_TYPE_INTERNAL_ND;

                                            /* LUT to have ND data type output */
sLutAttrs.iOutputTypeOption = IDATA_TYPE_INTERNAL_ND;

nLUT = InAllocateLUT(sAttrsLUT);            /* Allocate LUT                   */
```

```
/*  Create unsigned int scaled square root array for LUT                      */

for (i = 0; i < 256; i++) {
    uaExtLUTArray[i] = (sqrt(255)) * (sqrt(i));
}
stExtLUTArray.tuPixel = &uaExtLUTArray[0];        /* Pointer to external LUT array    */

                                                   /* Import LUT from application      */
InImportLUT(stExtLUTArray, nLUT, sAttrsLUT, 256, 0, tuDataSize);
```

The *import_matrix* utility imports an external array of data values from an application and puts it into a matrix object. Its API is:

```
Idnmatrix InImportMatrix(                          /* OUT matrix identifier              */
    Ipsparameter_numeric        stData,            /* external data array pointer union  */
    Idnmatrix                   nMatrix,           /* matrix identifier                  */
    Ipsattrs_matrix             sAttrs             /* matrix attributes                  */
);
```

where Ipsparameter_numeric is the name of the following *piks.h* union that specifies the numeric data type and values of the external array to be imported.

```
typedef union{
    Ipuint          *tuNumeric;         /* unsigned integer pointer   */
    Ipint           *tiNumeric;         /* signed integer pointer     */
    Ipfloat         *trNumericFloat;    /* float pointer              */
} Ipsparameter_numeric;
```

Ipsattrs_matrix is the name of the following *piks.h* structure that specifies the matrix attributes.

```
typedef struct{
    Ipuint          uColumnSize;        /* matrix column size         */
    Ipuint          uRowSize;           /* matrix row size            */
    Ipint           iTypeOption;        /* matrix data type option    */
} Ipsattrs_matrix;
```

The following matrix data type #define data type options are provided in *piks.h*.

```
IDATA_TYPE_INTERNAL_ND          2       /* unsigned integer   */
IDATA_TYPE_INTERNAL_SD          3       /* signed integer     */
IDATA_TYPE_INTERNAL_RD          4       /* real arithmetic    */
```

■**Example:**   Create and import a real, 3×3, colour conversion matrix from an application.

```
Idnmatrix               nMatrix;                /* Matrix identifier                  */

Ipsparameter_numeric    stExtMatrixArray;       /* External data array pointer union  */

Ipfloat                 raExtMatrixArray[3][3]; /* External matrix data array         */

Ipsattrs_matrix         sAttrsMatrix;           /* Matrix attributes                  */

sAttrsMatrix.uColumnSize = 3;                   /* Number of matrix columns           */

sAttrsMatrix.uRowSize = 3;                      /* Number of matrix rows              */

                                                /* Matrix real data type              */
sAttrsMatrix.iTypeOption = IDATA_TYPE_INTERNAL_RD;

nMatrix = InAllocateMatrix(sAttrsMatrix);       /* Allocate matrix                    */

                                                /* Create colour conversion matrix    */

raExtMatrixArray[0][0] = 0.8;

raExtMatrixArray[0][1] = 0.1;

raExtMatrixArray[0][2] = 0.1;

raExtMatrixArray[1][0] = 0.2;

raExtMatrixArray[1][1] = 0.7;

raExtMatrixArray[1][2] = 0.1;

raExtMatrixArray[2][0] = 0.0;
```

```
raExtMatrixArray[2][1] = 0.1;

raExtMatrixArray[2][2] = 0.9;

                                        /* Pointer to matrix array         */
stExtMatrixArray.trNumericFloat =&raExtMatrixArray[0][0];

                                        /* Import matrix from application   */
InImportMatrix(stExtMatrixArray, nMatrix, sAttrsMatrix);
```

import_neighbourhood_array

The *import_neighbourhood_array* utility imports an external array of data values from an application and puts it into a neighbourhood array object. Its API is:

```
Idnnbhood InImportNbhoodArray(
    Ipsparameter_pixel  stData,         /* OUT neighbourhood array identifier  */
    Idnnbhood           nNbhood,        /* external data array pointer union   */
    Ipsattrs_nbhood     sAttrs          /* neighbourhood array identifier      */
);                                      /* neighbourhood array attributes      */
```

where `Ipsparameter_pixel` is the name of the following union that specifies the data type and values of the array to be imported.

```
typedef union{
    Ipbool       *tbPixel;       /* Boolean pointer             */
    Ipuint       *tuPixel;       /* unsigned integer pointer     */
    Ipint        *tiPixel;       /* signed integer pointer       */
    Ipfloat      *trPixelFloat;  /* float pointer                */
} Ipsparameter_pixel;
```

`Ipsattrs_nbhood` is the name of the following *piks.h* structure that specifies the neighbourhood array attributes.

```
typedef struct{
    Idntuple     nArraySize;     /* nbhood array size ND 5-tuple id      */
    Idntuple     nKeyPixel;      /* nbhood array key pixel SD 5-tuple id  */
    Ipint        iScaleFactor;   /* nbhood array scale factor             */
    Ipint        iLabelOption;   /* nbhood array semantic label option    */
    Ipint        iTypeOption;    /* nbhood array data type option         */
} Ipsattrs_nbhood;
```

The following label and data type #define options are provided in *piks.h*.

```
INBHOOD_LABEL_GENERIC       1    /* generic                */
INBHOOD_LABEL_DITHER        2    /* dither                 */
INBHOOD_LABEL_IMPULSE       3    /* impulse response       */
INBHOOD_LABEL_MASK          4    /* mask                   */
INBHOOD_LABEL_STRUCTURE     5    /* structuring element    */

IDATA_TYPE_INTERNAL_BD      1    /* Boolean                */
IDATA_TYPE_INTERNAL_ND      2    /* unsigned integer       */
IDATA_TYPE_INTERNAL_SD      3    /* signed integer         */
IDATA_TYPE_INTERNAL_RD      4    /* real arithmetic        */
```

■**Example:**   Import a signed integer, 3×3, impulse response function neighbourhood array from an application.

```
Idnnbhood            nImpulse;               /* Neighbourhood array identifier   */

Ipsparameter_pixel   stExtImpulseArray;      /* External data array pointer union */

Ipint                iaExtImpulseArray[3][3]; /* External neighbourhood data array */

Ipsattrs_nbhood      sAttrsNbhood;           /* Neighbourhood attributes          */

Idntuple             nNbhoodSize;            /* Neighbourhood size tuple          */

Idntuple             nNbhoodKey;             /* Neighbourhood key pixel tuple     */


                                             /* 3x3 2D impulse response array     */
nNbhoodSize = InGenerateND5Tuple(3, 3, 1, 1, 1);

nNbhoodKey = InGenerateSD5Tuple(1, 1, 0, 0, 0);  /* Centered key pixel            */

                                             /* Neighbourhood impulse response array */
sAttrsNbhood.iLabelOption = INBHOOD_LABEL_IMPULSE;
```

```
                                          /* Neighbourhood array SD data type   */
sAttrsNbhood.iTypeOption = IDATA_TYPE_INTERNAL_SD;

sAttrsNbhood.nArraySize = nNbhoodSize;    /* Neighbourhood size ND 5-tuple      */

sAttrsNbhood.nKeyPixel = nNbhoodKey;      /* Neighbourhood key pixel SD 5-tuple */

sAttrsNbhood.iScaleFactor = 1;            /* Neighbourhood array scale factor   */

nImpulse = InAllocateNbhoodArray(sAttrsNbhood);  /* Allocate neighbourhood array */

                                          /* Create impulse response array      */

iaExtImpulseArray[0][0] = -1;

iaExtImpulseArray[0][1] = 0;

iaExtImpulseArray[0][2]1 = -1;

iaExtImpulseArray[1][0] = 0;

iaExtImpulseArray[1][1] = 5;

iaExtImpulseArray[1][2] = 0;

iaExtImpulseArray[2][0] = -1;

iaExtImpulseArray[2][1] = 0;

iaExtImpulseArray[2][2] = -1;

                                          /* Pointer to data array              */
stExtImpulseArray.tiPixel = &iaExtImpulseArray[0][0];

                                          /* Import impulse response array      */
InImportNbhoodArray(stExtImpulseArray, nNbhood, sAttrsNbhood);
```

The *import_tuple* utility imports an external array of data values from an application and puts it into a tuple object. Its API is:

```
Idntuple InImportTuple(                    /* OUT tuple identifier              */
    Ipsparameter_basic stData,             /* external data array pointer union */
    Idntuple           nTuple,             /* tuple identifier                  */
    Ipsattrs_tuple     sAttrs              /* tuple attributes                  */
);
```

where `Ipsparameter_basic` is the name of the following *piks.h* union that specifies the data type and values of the tuple to be imported.

```
typedef union{
    Ipbool       *tbParameter;             /* Boolean pointer            */
    Ipuint       *tuParameter;             /* unsigned integer pointer   */
    Ipint        *tiParameter;             /* signed integer pointer     */
    Ipfloat      *trParameterFloat;        /* float pointer              */
    char         *tcParameter;             /* character pointer          */
} Ipsparameter_basic;
```

`Ipsattrs_tuple` is the name of the following *piks.h* structure that specifies the tuple attributes.

```
typedef struct{
    Ipuint       uTupleSize;               /* tuple size             */
    Ipint        iTypeOption;              /* tuple data type option */
} Ipsattrs_tuple;
```

The following data type #define options are provided in *piks.h*.

```
IDATA_TYPE_INTERNAL_BD        1            /* Boolean          */
IDATA_TYPE_INTERNAL_ND        2            /* unsigned integer */
IDATA_TYPE_INTERNAL_SD        3            /* signed integer   */
IDATA_TYPE_INTERNAL_RD        4            /* real arithmetic  */
```

■**Example:**   Create and import an image size 5-tuple from an application.

```
Idntuple                nImageSize;                /* Image size ND 5-tuple identifier   */

Ipsparameter_basic      stExtTupleArray;           /* External data array pointer union  */

Ipuint                  uaExtTupleArray[5];        /* External data array                */

Ipsattrs_tuple          sAttrsTuple;               /* Tuple attributes                   */


sAttrsTuple.uSize = 5;                             /* Tuple size                         */

sAttrsTuple.iType = IDATA_TYPE_INTERNAL_ND;        /* Tuple unsigned integer data type   */

nImageSize = InAllocateTuple(sAttrsTuple);         /* Allocate tuple                     */

uaExtTupleArray[0] = 512;                          /* X = 512                            */

uaExtTupleArray[1] = 512;                          /* Y = 512                            */

uaExtTupleArray[2] = 0;                            /* Z = 0                              */

uaExtTupleArray[3] = 0;                            /* T = 0                              */

uaExtTupleArray[4] = 3;                            /* B = 3                              */

stExtTupleArray.tuParameter = &uaExtTupleArray[0];

                                                   /* Import tuple                       */
InImportTuple(stExtTupleArray, nImageSize, sAttrsTuple);
```

impulse_rectangular

InImpulseRectangular

See Section 3.2.3

The *impulse_rectangular* tool generates a uniform amplitude, rectangular-shaped, two-dimensional impulse response function neighbourhood array object. Its API is:

```
Idnnbhood InImpulseRectangular(          /* OUT impulse response array id       */
    Idnnbhood         nArray,            /* impulse response array identifier   */
    Idntuple          nSize,             /* array size ND 5-tuple identifier    */
    Idntuple          nKey               /* key pixel SD 5-tuple identifier     */
);
```

■**Example:** Create a 5×7 rectangular impulse response function array with a centered key pixel.

```
Idnnbhood            nImpulse;           /* Impulse array identifier            */

Idntuple             nImpulseSize;       /* Impulse array size ND 5-tuple       */

Idntuple             nKeyPixel;          /* Key pixel SD 5-tuple                */

                                         /* Generate impulse array size 5-tuple */
nImpulseSize = InGenerateND5Tuple(5, 7, 1, 1, 1);

nKeyPixel = InGenerateSD5Tuple(2, 3, 0, 0, 0);   /* Generate centered key pixel 5-tuple */

                                         /* Rectangular impulse array creation  */
InImpulseRectangular(nImpulse, nImpulseSize, nKeyPixel);
```

The *inquire_elements* mechanism returns an array of information to an application regarding an implementation's support of implemented elements. Its API is:

```
void IvInquireElements(                           /* no return output                     */
    Ipint          *tiaInput,                     /* registration numbers pointer          */
    Ipbool         *tbaOutput,                    /* OUT registration responses pointer    */
    Ipuint         uSize,                         /* array size                            */
    char           *tzLabel,                      /* OUT private label information         */
    Ipevalidity    *teValid                       /* OUT data validity indicator           */
);
```

where Ipevalidity is the name of the following *piks.h* enum that indicates the availability or nonavailability of the requested information.

```
IVALIDITY_VALID                                   /* data is valid and available           */
IVALIDITY_INVALID                                 /* data is not valid                     */
```

■**Example:**   Inquiry to determine if the three colour conversion elements are supported in a PIKS Foundation implementation.

```
Ipint              iaInput[3] = {                 /* Registration numbers array            */
                   IF_COLOUR_CONV_LIN,
                   IF_COLOUR_CONV_MATRIX,
                   IF_COLOUR_CONV_SUBTRACTIVE};

Ipint              *tiaInput = &iaInput[0];       /* Registration numbers array pointer    */

                                                  /* Registration responses pointer        */
Ipbool             baOutput[3], *tbaOutput = &baOutput[0];

Ipuint             uArraySize = 3;                /* Array Size                            */

                                                  /* Data validity indicator               */
Ipevalidity        eValid, *teValid = &eValid;

                                                  /* Inquire elements                      */
IvInquireElements(tiaInput, tbaOutput, uArraySize, NULL, teValid);

if(eValid == IVALIDITY_VALID) {                   /* Inquiry validity check                */
    If(baOutput[0] == IBOOL_TRUE)
                   printf("colour_conversion_linear is available\n");
    If(baOutput[1] == IBOOL_TRUE)
                   printf("colour_conversion_matrix is available\n");
    If(baOutput[2] == IBOOL_TRUE)
                   printf("colour_conversion_subtractive is available\n");
}
```

inquire_image
See Section 4.3.2

The *inquire_image* mechanism returns image attribute information to an application. Its API is:

```
void IvInquireImage(                        /* no output return                      */
    Idnimage          nSourceImage,         /* source image identifier               */
    Ipsattrs_image    *tsAttrs,             /* OUT image attributes                   */
    Ipsbind_image,    *tsBind,              /* OUT match point, ROI binding pointer   */
    Ipevalidity       *teValid              /* OUT data validity indicator            */
);
```

where `Ipsattrs_image` is the name of the following *piks.h* structure that specifies the image attributes.

```
typedef struct{
    Idntuple    nImageSize;            /* image size ND 5-tuple identifier      */
    Idntuple    nBandType;             /* band data type SD B-tuple identifier  */
    Idntuple    nBandPrecision;        /* band precision ND B-tuple identifier  */
    Ipfloat     rXWhite;               /* X tristimulus value white point       */
    Ipfloat     rYWhite;               /* Y tristimulus value white point       */
    Ipfloat     rZWhite;               /* Z tristimulus value white point       */
    Ipint       iImageStructureOption; /* image structure option                */
    Ipint       iColourOption;         /* colour space option                   */
} Ipsattrs_image;
```

The following image structure and colour space #define options are provided in *piks.h*

```
IIMAGE_STRUCTURE_MON          1     /* monochrome                              */
IIMAGE_STRUCTURE_COLR         4     /* colour                                  */

ICOLOUR_NONE                  1     /* unspecified                             */
ICOLOUR_NON_STANDARD_RGB      2     /* nonstandard RGB                         */
ICOLOUR_LIN_CCIR_D65_RGB      3     /* linear CCIR illuminant D65 RGB          */
ICOLOUR_LIN_CIE_E_RGB         4     /* linear CIE illuminant E RGB             */
ICOLOUR_LIN_EBU_C_RGB         5     /* linear EBU illuminant C RGB             */
ICOLOUR_LIN_EBU_D65_RGB       6     /* linear EBU illuminant D65 RGB           */
ICOLOUR_LIN_NTSC_C_RGB        7     /* linear NTSC illuminant C RGB            */
ICOLOUR_LIN_NTSC_D65_RGB      8     /* linear NTSC illuminant D65 RGB          */
ICOLOUR_LIN_SMPTE_D65_RGB     9     /* linear SMPTE illuminant D65 RGB         */
ICOLOUR_GAMMA_CCIR_D65_RGB   10     /* gamma CCIR illuminant C RGB             */
ICOLOUR_GAMMA_EBU_C_RGB      11     /* gamma EBU illuminant C RGB              */
ICOLOUR_GAMMA_EBU_D65_RGB    12     /* gamma EBU illuminant D65 RGB            */
ICOLOUR_GAMMA_NTSC_C_RGB     13     /* gamma NTSC illuminant C RGB             */
ICOLOUR_GAMMA_NTSC_D65_RGB   14     /* gamma NTSC illuminant D65 RGB           */
ICOLOUR_GAMMA_SMPTE_D65_RGB  15     /* gamma SMPTE illuminant D65 RGB          */
ICOLOUR_LUM_CHR_EBU_C_YUV    16     /* luminance/chrominance EBU illuminant C YUV  */
ICOLOUR_LUM_CHR_EBU_D65_YUV  17     /* luminance/chrominance EBU illuminant D65 YUV */
ICOLOUR_LUM_CHR_NTSC_C_YIQ   18     /* luminance/chrominance NTSC ill. C YIQ   */
ICOLOUR_LUM_CHR_NTSC_D65_YIQ 19     /* luminance/chrominance NTSC ill. D65 YIQ */
ICOLOUR_LUM_CHR_SMPTE_D65_YCBCR 20  /* luminance/chrominance SMPTE ill. D65 YCbCr */
ICOLOUR_CIE_XYZ              21     /* CIE XYZ                                 */
ICOLOUR_CIE_UVW             22     /* CIE UVW                                 */
ICOLOUR_CIE_YXY             23     /* CIE Yxy                                 */
ICOLOUR_CIE_YUV             24     /* CIE Yuv                                 */
ICOLOUR_CIE_LAB             25     /* CIE L*a*b*                              */
ICOLOUR_CIE_LUV             26     /* CIE L*u*v*                              */
ICOLOUR_IHS                 27     /* IHS                                     */
ICOLOUR_CMY                 28     /* CMY                                     */
ICOLOUR_CMYK                29     /* CMYK                                    */
```

Note: The missing image structure options are not supported in PIKS Foundation.

`Ipsbind_image` is the name of the following *piks.h* structure that specifies the match point 5-tuple, ROI identifier and its associated offset 5-tuple.

```
typedef struct{
    Idntuple    nMatch;     /* Match point SD 5-tuple              */
    Idnroi      nROI;       /* ROI identifier                      */
    Idntuple    nOffset;    /* ROI offset SD 5-tuple identifier    */
} Ipsbind_image;
```

Ipevalidity is the name of the following *piks.h* enum that indicates the availability or non-availability of the requested information.

```
IVALIDITY_VALID                          /* data is valid and available      */
IVALIDITY_INVALID                        /* data is not valid                */
```

■**Example:**   Inquiry of a monochrome image. Print image size and check that an ROI is bound to the image.

```
Idnimage            nSrc;                    /* Image identifier             */

                                             /* Image attributes             */
Ipsattrs_image      sAttrs, *tsAttrs = &sAttrs;

                                             /* ROI binding information      */
Ipsbind_image       sBind, *tsBind = &sBind;

                                             /* Data validity indicator      */
Ipevalidity         eValid, *teValid = &eValid;

IvInquireImage(nSrc, tsAttrs, tsBind, teValid);  /* Inquire image           */

if(eValid != IVALIDITY_VALID) {              /* Inquiry validity check       */
    printf("error: PIKS not open\n");
    exit(1);
}

                                             /* Print horizontal image size  */
printf("horizontal size = %u \n", sAttrs.nImageSize[0]);

                                             /* Print vertical image size    */
printf("vertical size = %u \n", sAttrs.nImageSize[1]);

if(sBind.nROI == NULL)                       /* Check if ROI is bound        */
    printf("error: ROI is not bound\n");
```

inquire_non_image_object

IvInquireNonImageObject

See Section 4.3.3

The *inquire_non_image_object* mechanism returns nonimage data object information to an application. Its API is:

```
void IvInquireNonImageObject(          /* no return output            */
    Ipsnon_image_object  snObject,     /* nonimage object identifier  */
    Ipsattrs_non_image   stData,       /* OUT nonimage attributes     */
    Ipint                iType,        /* object type option          */
    Ipevalidity          *teValid      /* OUT data validity indicator */
);
```

where `Ipsnon_image_object` is the name of the following *piks.h* union that specifies the non-image data object identifier.

```
typedef union{
    Idnhist          nHist;        /* histogram identifier          */
    Idnlut           nLUT;         /* lookup table identifier       */
    Idnmatrix        nMatrix;      /* matrix identifier             */
    Idnnbhood        nNbhood;      /* neighbourhood identifier      */
    Idnroi           nROI;         /* region of interest identifier */
    Idntuple         nTuple;       /* tuple identifier              */
} Ipsnon_image_object;
```

`Ipsattrs_non_image` is the name of the following *piks.h* union that specifies the nonimage data object attributes

```
typedef union{
    Ipattrs_hist         *tsHist;         /* histogram attributes pointer    */
    Ipattrs_lut          *tsLUT;          /* lookup table attributes pointer */
    Ipattrs_matrix       *tsMatrix;       /* matrix attributes pointer       */
    Ipattrs_nbhood       *tsNbhood;       /* nbhood array attributes pointer */
    Ipattrs_roi_rectangular
                         *tsROIRectangular; /* ROI attributes pointer        */
    Ipattrs_tuple        *tsTuple;        /* tuple attributes pointer        */
} Ipsattrs_non_image;
```

The following object type #define options are provided in *piks.h*.

```
IOBJECT_HIST            2        /* histogram            */
IOBJECT_LUT             6        /* lookup table         */
IOBJECT_MATRIX          7        /* matrix               */
IOBJECT_NBHOOD          8        /* neighbourhood array  */
IOBJECT_ROI_RECTANGULAR 15       /* ROI, rectangular     */
IOBJECT_TUPLE           17       /* tuple                */
```

Note: The missing options are not supported in PIKS Foundation.

`Ipevalidity` is a pointer to a *piks.h* enum that indicates the availability or nonavailability of the requested information

```
IVALIDITY_VALID                  /* data is valid and available */
IVALIDITY_INVALID                /* data is not valid           */
```

■**Example:** Inquiry of the number of entries of a lookup table.

```
Ipsnon_image_object    snObject;                          /* Object identifier            */

Idnlut                 nLookup;                            /* LUT identifier               */

Ipsattrs_non_image     stData;                             /* Nonimage object attributes   */

                                                           /* LUT inquiry attributes       */
Ipsattrs_lut           sLUTOutput, *tsLUTOutput = &sLUTOutput;

                                                           /* Data validity indicator      */
Ipevalidity            eValid, *teValid = &eValid;
```

```
snObject.nLUT = nLookup;                              /* Reference to LUT object              */

stData.tsAttrsLUT = tsLUTOutput;                      /* Pointer to LUT inquiry data          */

                                                      /* Inquire lookup table                 */
IvInquireNonImageObject(snObject, stData, IOBJECT_LUT, teValid);

if(eValid != IVALIDITY_VALID) {                       /* Inquiry validity check               */
    printf("error: PIKS not open\n");
    exit(1);
}

                                                      /* Print LUT entries                    */
printf("LUT entries = %u\n", sLUTOutput.uTableEntries);
```

inquire_piks_implementation   IvInquirePIKSImpl
See Section 4.3.4

The *inquire_piks_implementation* mechanism returns information about a PIKS implementation. Its API is:

```
void IvInquirePIKSImpl(                   /* no return output                  */
    Ipspiks_impl    *tsData,              /* implementation information        */
    Ipevalidity     *teValid,             /* OUT data validity indicator       */
    Ipint            iApplBufferSize,     /* data transfer buffer size or option */
    Ipuint           uStartPoint,         /* index offset within internal data */
    Ipuint          *tuDataSize           /* post transfer data size pointer   */
);
```

where `Ipspiks_impl` is the name of the following *piks.h* structure that specifies the implementation information.

```
typedef struct
  char            zProfile[IL_PROFILE];   /* conformance profile label         */
    Idntuple      nDimensionLimit;        /* maximum dimension sizes identifier */
    Ipint         iNDPrecision;           /* storage precision of ND data type  */
    Ipint         iSDPrecision;           /* storage precision of SD data type  */
    Ipint         iRDPrecision;           /* storage precision of RD data type  */
    char          zRD[IL_REAL];           /* implementation method RD data type */
    char         *tzInformation;          /* implementation information pointer */
    Ipebinary_event eAsynch;              /* asynchronous support               */
} Ipspiks_impl;
```

where `IL_PROFILE` and `IL_REAL` are defined as 15 and 3, respectively.

`Ipevalidity` is the name of the following *piks.h* enum that indicates the availability or non-availability of the requested information.

```
IVALIDITY_VALID                           /* data is valid and available       */
IVALIDITY_INVALID                         /* data is not valid                 */
```

■**Example:** Inquiry of PIKS implementation.

```
                                          /* Implementation information pointer */
Ipspiks_impl        sData, *tsData = &sData;

                                          /* Data validity indicator           */
Ipevalidity         eValid, *teValid = &eValid;

                                          /* Inquire PIKS implemenation         */
IvInquirePIKSImpl(tsData, teValid, -1, 0, NULL);

if(eValid != IVALIDITY_VALID) {           /* Inquiry validity check            */
    printf("error: PIKS not open\n");
    exit(1);
}

                                          /* Print ND precision                */
printf("ND precision = %d\n", sData.iNDPrecision);
```

The *inquire_piks_status* mechanism returns information about PIKS state and global control mode status. Its API is:

```
void IvInquirePIKSStatus(                    /* no output return              */
    Ipspiks_states    *tsStates,             /* OUT inquire PIKS states pointer */
    Ipspiks_modes     *tsModes,              /* OUT inquire PIKS modes pointer  */
    Ipevalidity       *teValid               /* OUT data validity indicator     */
);
```

Ipspiks_states is the name of the following *piks.h* structure that specifies the PIKS operational, chain, error, and synchronicity states.

```
typedef struct{
    Ipepiks_operation_state eOperationState;     /* PIKS operational state    */
    Ipechain_state          eChainState;         /* PIKS chain state          */
    Ipeerror_state          eErrorState;         /* PIKS error state          */
    Ipesynchronicity_state  eSynchronicity_state;/* PIKS synchronicity state  */
} Ipspiks_states;
```

Ipepiks_operation_state is the name of the following enum that indicates whether PIKS is open or closed.

```
IPIKS_OPERATION_CLOSED                        /* PIKS closed                  */
IPIKS_OPERATION_OPEN                          /* PIKS open                    */
```

Ipechain_state is the name of the following enum that indicates whether PIKS is in the chain build, execute, or nonchain state.

```
ICHAIN_BUILD                                  /* building chain state         */
ICHAIN_EXECUTE                                /* executing chain state        */
ICHAIN_NOT                                    /* not in any chain state       */
```

Note: PIKS Foundation does not support element chaining.

Ipeerror_state is the name of the following enum that indicates whether PIKS is in an error or nonerror substate.

```
IERROR_SUBSTATE                               /* error substate condition exists */
IERROR_NO                                     /* no error condition           */
```

Ipesynchronicity_state is the name of the following enum that indicates whether PIKS is operating synchronously or asynchronously.

```
ISYNCHRONICITY_STATE_SYNCH                    /* synchronous state            */
ISYNCHRONICITY_STATE_ASYNCH                   /* asynchronous state           */
```

Note: PIKS Foundation only supports synchronous processing.

Ipspiks_modes is the name of the following *piks.h* structure that specifies the PIKS operational modes.

```
typedef struct{
    Iperoi_control_mode       eROIControlMode;     /* ROI control mode              */
    Iperoi_process_mode       eROIProcessMode;     /* ROI processing mode           */
    Ipematch_mode             eMatchPointMode;     /* match point control mode      */
    Ipeindex_mode             eIndexAssignmentMode;/* index assignment mode         */
    Ipesynchronicity_mode     eSynchronicityMode;  /* sychronicity mode             */
    Ipeerror_report_mode      eErrorReportMode;    /* error report mode             */
    Ipint                     iImageResampleMode;  /* image resampling selection mode */
    Ipint                     iROIResampleMode;    /* ROI resampling selection mode */
} Ipspiks_modes;
```

`Iperoi_control_mode` is the name of the following enum that indicates whether ROI control is on or off.

```
IROI_CONTROL_ON                          /* ROI control operative              */
IROI_CONTROL_OFF                         /* ROI control inoperative            */
```

`Iperoi_process_mode` is the name of the following enum that indicates whether ROIs are automatically processed along with images.

```
IROI_PROCESS_ON                          /* ROI processing operative           */
IROI_PROCESS_OFF                         /* ROI processing inoperative         */
```

Note: PIKS Foundation does not support automatic ROI processing.

`Ipematch_mode` is the name of the following enum that indicates whether match point control is invoked or not invoked.

```
IMATCH_POINT_ON                          /* match point control operative      */
IMATCH_POINT_OFF                         /* match point control inoperative    */
```

Note: PIKS Foundation does not support match point control.

`Ipeindex_mode` is the name of the following enum that indicates whether index assignment is invoked or not invoked.

```
IINDEX_ASSIGNMENT_ON                     /* index assignment operative         */
IINDEX_ASSIGNMENT_OFF                    /* index assignment inoperative       */
```

Note: PIKS Foundation does not support index assignment.

`Ipesynchronicity_mode` is the name of the following enum that indicates whether PIKS is operating synchronously or asynchronously.

```
ISYNCHRONICITY_MODE_SYNCH                /* synchronous mode                   */
ISYNCHRONICITY_MODE_ASYNCH               /* asynchronous mode                  */
```

Note: PIKS Foundation only supports synchronous processing.

`Ipeerror_report_mode` is the name of the following enum that indicates whether error reporting is active or inactive.

```
IERROR_REPORT_ACTIVE                     /* error reporting active             */
IERROR_REPORT_INACTIVE                   /* error reporting inactive           */
```

The following image resampling #define options are provided in *piks.h*.

```
#define     IRESAMPLE_NEAREST_NEIGHBOUR   1    /* nearest neighbour             */
#define     IRESAMPLE_2_BILINEAR          2    /* support 2 bilinear            */
```

The following ROI resampling #define options is provided in *piks.h*.

```
#define     IRESAMPLE_NEAREST_NEIGHBOUR1       /* nearest neighbour             */
```

`Ipevalidity` is the name of the following *piks.h* enum that indicates the availability or non-availability of the requested information.

```
IVALIDITY_VALID                          /* data is valid and available        */
IVALIDITY_INVALID                        /* data is not valid                  */
```

■**Example:**   Inquiry of PIKS ROI control mode status.

```
                                        /* PIKS states pointer           */
Ipspiks_states          sStates, *tsStates = &sStates;

                                        /* PIKS modes pointer            */
Ipspiks_modes           sModes, *tsModes = &sModes;

                                        /* Data validity indicator       */
Ipevalidity             eValid, *teValid = &eValid;


                                        /* Inquire PIKS status           */
IvInquirePIKSStatus(tsStates, tsModes, teValid);

if(eValid != IVALIDITY_VALID) {         /* Inquiry validity check        */
    printf("error: PIKS not open\n");
    exit(1);
}


                                        /* Print PIKS ROI control mode   */
if(sModes.eROIControlMode == IROI_CONTROL_ACTIVE)
    printf("ROI control mode is active \n");
else
    printf("ROI control mode is inactive \n");
```

inquire_repository

See Section 4.3.6

The *inquire_repository* mechanism returns an array of information to an application regarding an implementation's support of data object repository entries. Its API is:

```
void IvInquireRepository(              /* no return output                   */
    Ipint          *tiaInput,          /* rep. registration numbers pointer  */
    Ipbool         *tbaOutput,         /* OUT rep. registration responses ptr */
    Ipuint          uSize,             /* array size                         */
    char           *tzLabel,           /* OUT private label information ptr  */
    Ipint           iClassOption,      /* repository class option            */
    Ipevalidity    *teValid            /* OUT data validity indicator        */
);
```

where `Ipevalidity` is the following *piks.h* enum that indicates the availability or nonavailability of the requested information.

```
IVALIDITY_VALID                        /* data is valid and available        */
IVALIDITY_INVALID                      /* data is not valid                  */
```

■**Example:**   Inquiry to determine if the three Laplacian impulse response function arrays are in the data object repository of a PIKS implementation.

```
Ipint              iaInput[3] = {              /* Registration numbers array          */
                     IR_LAPLACE_1,
                     IR_LAPLACE_2,
                     IR_LAPLACE_3};

                                               /* Registration numbers array pointer  */
Ipint              *tiaInput = &iaInput[0];

                                               /* Registration responses array pointer */
Ipbool             baOutput[3], *tbaOutput = &baOutput[0];

Ipuint             uArraySize = 3;             /* Array Size                          */

                                               /* Data validity indicator             */
Ipedata_validity   eValid, *teValid = &eValid;

                                               /* Inquire repository                  */
IvInquireRepository(tiaInput, tbaOutput, uArraySize, NULL, IREPOSITORY_IMPULSE, teValid);

if(eValid == IVALIDITY_VALID) {                /* Inquiry validity check              */
    If(baOutput[0] == IBOOL_TRUE)
        printf("Laplacian 1 is available\n);
    If(baOutput[1] == IBOOL_TRUE)
        printf("Laplacian 2 is available\n);
    If(baOutput[2] == IBOOL_TRUE)
        printf("Laplacian 3 is available\n);
}
```

The *inquire_resampling* mechanism returns information to an application regarding an implementation's support of resampling options. Its API is:

```
void IvInquireResampling(                    /* no return output                   */
    Ipint           *tiaInput,               /* resampling registration numbers    */
    Ipbool          *tbaOutput,              /* OUT resampling reg. responses       */
    Ipuint          uSize,                   /* array size                          */
    char            *tzLabel,                /* OUT private label information        */
    Ipevalidity     *teValid,                /* OUT data validity indicator         */
);
```

where `Ipevalidity` is the following *piks.h* enum that indicates the availability or nonavailability of the requested information.

```
IVALIDITY_VALID                              /* data is valid and available         */
IVALIDITY_INVALID                            /* data is not valid                   */
```

■**Example:**   Inquiry to determine if bilinear interpolation resampling is supported by a PIKS Foundation implementation

```
Ipint           iInput = {                   /* Registration number                 */
                    IRESAMPLE_2_BILINEAR};

Ipint           *tiaInput = &iaInput;        /* Registration number pointer         */

                                             /* Registration response pointer       */
Ipbool          baOutput, *tbaOutput = &baOutput;

Ipuint          uDataSize = 1;               /* Data Size                           */

                                             /* Data validity indicator             */
Ipevalidity     eValid, *teValid = &eValid;

                                             /* Inquire resampling option           */
IvInquireResampling(tiaInput, tbaOutput, uDataSize, NULL, teValid);

if(eValid == IVALIDITY_VALID) {              /* Inquiry validity check              */
    If(baOutput == IBOOL_TRUE)
        printf("Bilinear resampling is available\n);
    else
        printf("Bilinear resampling is not available\n);
}
```

insert_pixel_plane   `InInsertPixelPlane`
See Section 5.1.7

The *insert_pixel_plane* utility inserts a monochrome image into a colour image band. Its API is:

```
Idnimage InInsertPixelPlane(              /* OUT destination image identifier  */
    Idnimage        nSourceImage,         /* source image identifier           */
    Idnimage        nDestImage,           /* destination image identifier      */
    Ipuint          uDepth,               /* depth index value                 */
    Ipuint          uTemporal,            /* temporal index value              */
    Ipuint          uBand                 /* band index value                  */
);
```

■**Example:**   Inserts a replacement of the green band into a colour image.

```
Idnimage            nSrcMon;                /* Source image identifier          */

Idnimage            nDstColour;             /* Destination image idnetifier     */

Ipuint              uDepth = uTemporal = 0; /* Depth and temporal index values  */

Ipuint              uBand = 1:              /* Green band index value           */

                                            /* Insert green band                */
InInsertPixelPlane(nSrcMon, nDstColour, uDepth, uTemporal, uBand);
```

The *lookup* operator performs a lookup table manipulation of an image. Its API is:

```
Idnimage InLookup(                              /* OUT destination image identifier    */
    Idnimage        nSourceImage,               /* source image identifier             */
    Idnimage        nDestImage,                 /* destination image identifier         */
    Idnlut          nLUT,                       /* lookup table identifier              */
    Ipuint          uOffset,                    /* source offset entry                  */
    Ipint           iOption                     /* lookup table option                  */
);
```

The following lookup table mode #define options are provided in *piks.h*.

```
ILOOKUP_1D          1                           /* one-dimensional lookup table         */
ILOOKUP_2D          2                           /* two-dimensional lookup table         */
```

■**Example:**   Lookup table conversion of a monochrome image to a colour image.

```
Idnimage            nSrcMon;                    /* Source image identifier             */

Idnimage            nDstColour;                 /* Destination image identifier        */

Idnlut              nLUT;                       /* Lookup table identifier             */

Ipuint              uOffset = 0;                /* Source offset entry is zero         */

                                                /* Lookup table operation              */
InLookup(nSrcMon, nDstColour, nLUT, uOffset, ILOOKUP_2D);
```

luminance_generation

See Section 2.6.3

The *luminance_generation* operator generates a luminance image from a trichromatic colour image. Its API is:

```
Idnimage InLumGeneration(              /* OUT destination image identifier  */
    Idnimage        nSourceImage,      /* source image identifier           */
    Idnimage        nDestImage,        /* destination image identifier      */
    Ipint           iOption            /* luminance RGB colour option       */
);
```

The following RGB colour to luminance conversion options are provided in *piks.h*.

```
ILUM_LIN_CCIR_D65_RGB        1     /* linear CCIR illuminant D65 RGB   */
ILUMR_LIN_CIE_E_RGB          2     /* linear CIE illuminant E RGB      */
ILUM_LIN_EBU_C_RGB           3     /* linear EBU illuminant C RGB      */
ILUM_LIN_EBU_D65_RGB         4     /* linear EBU illuminant D65 RGB    */
ILUM_LIN_NTSC_C_RGB          5     /* linear NTSC illuminant C RGB     */
ILUM_LIN_NTSC_D65_RGB        6     /* linear NTSC illuminant D65 RGB   */
ILUM_LIN_SMPTE_D65_RGB       7     /* linear SMPTE illuminant D65 RGB  */
ILUM_GAMMA_EBU_C_RGB         8     /* gamma EBU illuminant C RGB       */
ILUM_GAMMA_EBU_65_RGB        9     /* gamma EBU illuminant D65 RGB     */
ILUM_GAMMA_NTSC_C_RGB       10     /* gamma NTSC illuminant C RGB      */
ILUM_GAMMA_NTSC_D65_RGB     11     /* gamma NTSC illuminant D65 RGB    */
ILUM_GAMMA_SMPTE_D65_RGB    12     /* gamma SMPTE illuminant D65 RGB   */
```

■**Example:**   Luminance generation from NTSC illuminant D65 RGB colour space image.

```
Idnimage          nSrcColour;          /* Source image identifier        */

Idnimage          nDstMon;             /* Destination image identifier   */

                                       /* Luminance generation operation */
InLumGeneration(nSrcColour, nDstMon, ILUM_LIN_NTSC_D65_RGB);
```

The *moments* operator computes the mean and standard deviation moments of an image. Its API is:

```
void IvMoments(                              /* no return output                    */
    Idnimage           nSourceImage,         /* source image identifier             */
    Ipfloat            *trMean,              /* OUT mean value                      */
    Ipfloat            *trDeviation          /* OUT standard deviation value        */
);
```

■**Example:**   Computation of image moments.

```
Idnimage              nSrc;                  /* Source image                        */

                                             /* Mean value                          */
Ipfloat               rMean, *trMean = &rMean;

                                             /* Standard deviation value            */
Ipfloat               rDeviation, *trDeviation = &rDeviation;

IvMoments(nSrc, trMean, trDeviation);        /* Moments operation                   */

printf("mean = %f \n", rMean);               /* Print mean value                    */

printf("deviation = %f \n", rDeviation);     /* Print standard deviation value      */
```

monadic_arithmetic
See Section 2.1.4

InMonadicArith

The *monadic_arithmetic* operator performs a monadic arithmetic combination of an integer image and an integer constant. Its API is:

```
Idnimage InMonadicArith(                    /* OUT destination image identifier      */
    Idnimage             nSourceImage,       /* source image identifier               */
    Idnimage             nDestImage,         /* destination image identifier          */
    Ipsparameter_arith   stConstant,         /* constant value pointer union          */
    Ipint                iOption             /* monadic, arithmetic combination opt. */
);
```

where `Ipsparameter_arith` is the name of the following *piks.h* union that specifies the data type and value of the constant.

```
typedef union{
    Ipuint               *tuArith;           /* unsigned integer pointer              */
    Ipint                *tiArith;           /* signed integer pointer                */
} Ipsparameter_arith;
```

The following monadic, arithmetic combination #define options are provided in *piks.h*.

```
IMONADIC_ADDITION_BY              1     /* addition by constant              */
IMONADIC_ADDITION_BY_SCALED       2     /* addition by constant, scaled      */
IMONADIC_DIVISION_BY              3     /* division by constant              */
IMONADIC_DIVISION_OF              4     /* division of constant              */
IMONADIC_MAXIMUM                  5     /* maximum with constant             */
IMONADIC_MINIMUM                  6     /* minimum with constant             */
IMONADIC_MULTIPLICATION           7     /* multiplication by constant        */
IMONADIC_SUBTRACTION_BY           8     /* subtraction by constant           */
IMONADIC_SUBTRACTION_BY_SCALED    9     /* subtraction by constant, scaled   */
IMONADIC_SUBTRACTION_OF          10     /* subtraction of constant           */
IMONADIC_SUBTRACTION_OF_SCALED   11     /* subtraction of constant, scaled   */
```

■**Example:**   Addition of an unsigned integer constant to an image.

```
Idnimage             nSrcND;                /* Source image identifier           */

Idnimage             nDstND;                /* Destination image identifier      */

Ipsparameter_arith   stConstant;            /* Constant value pointer union      */

Ipuint               uConstant;             /* Constant value                    */


stConstant.tuArith = &uConstant;            /* Pointer to constant value         */

uConstant = 50;                             /* Unsigned integer constant of 50   */

                                            /* Scaled addition of constant       */
InMonadicArith(nSrcND, nDstND, stConstant, IMONADIC_ADDITION_BY);
```

282   PIKS C ELEMENT PROTOTYPES   CHAPTER 7

The *monadic_logical* operator performs a monadic logical combination of a Boolean or integer image and a constant. Its API is:

```
Idnimage InMonadicLogical(              /* OUT destination image identifier   */
    Idnimage            nSourceImage,   /* source image identifier            */
    Idnimage            nDestImage,     /* destination image identifier       */
    Ipsparameter_logical stConstant,    /* constant value pointer union       */
    Ipint               iOption         /* monadic, logical combination option */
);
```

where `Ipsparameter_logical` is the name of the following *piks.h* union that specifies the data type and value of the constant.

```
typedef union{
    Ipbool              *tbLogical;     /* Boolean pointer                    */
    Ipuint              *tuLogical;     /* unsigned integer pointer           */
    Ipint               *tiLogical;     /* signed integer pointer             */
} Ipsparameter_logical;
```

The following monadic, logical combination #define options are provided in *piks.h*.

```
IMONADIC_LOGICAL_AND          1         /* bitwise AND                        */
IMONADIC_LOGICAL_NAND         2         /* bitwise NAND                       */
IMONADIC_LOGICAL_NOR          3         /* bitwise NOR                        */
IMONADIC_LOGICAL_OR           4         /* bitwise OR                         */
IMONADIC_LOGICAL_XOR          5         /* bitwise XOR                        */
IMONADIC_LOGICAL_INTERSECTION 6         /* Boolean intersection               */
IMONADIC_LOGICAL_UNION        7         /* Boolean union                      */
```

■**Example:** Bitwise AND of an unsigned integer constant and an image.

```
Idnimage                nSrcND;         /* Source image identifier            */

Idnimage                nDstND;         /* Destination image identifier       */

Ipsparameter_logical    stConstant;     /* Constant value pointer union       */

Ipuint                  uConstant;      /* Constant value                     */


stConstant.tuLogical = &uConstant;      /* Pointer to constant value          */

uConstant = 128;                        /* Unsigned integer constant of 128   */

                                        /* AND with constant operation        */
InMonadicLogical(nSrcND, nDstND, stConstant, IMONADIC_LOGICAL_AND);
```

morphic_processor

See Section 2.3.2

InMorphicProcessor

The *morphic_processor* operator performs morphological processing on a Boolean image using a 3×3 hit or miss transformation with a specified transformation table. Its API is:

```
Idnimage InMorphicProcessor(            /* OUT destination image identifier    */
    Idnimage        nSourceImage,       /* source image identifier             */
    Idnimage        nDestImage,         /* destination image identifier        */
    Idnlut          nLUT,               /* hit or miss lookup table identifier  */
    Ipint           iIterations,        /* number of iterations                */
    Ipuint          *tuCycles           /* OUT number of cycles                */
);
```

■**Example:**   Dilation of a Boolean image.

```
Idnimage            nSrcBD;                         /* Source image identifier           */

Idnimage            nDstBD;                         /* Destination image identifier      */

Idnlut              nLUTDilate;                     /* Dilation LUT identifier           */

Ipsattrs_lut        sAttrsLUT;                      /* Lookup table attributes           */

Ipint               iIterations = 3:                /* Three iterations                  */

                                                    /* Number of cycles returned         */
Ipuint              uCycles, *tuCycles = &uCycles;

Ipsparameter_pixel  stExtLUTArray;                  /* LUT data array pointer union      */

                                                    /* Post transfer data size pointer    */
Ipuint              uDataSize, *tuDataSize = &uDataSize;

                                                    /* LUT data array                    */
Ipuint              uaExtLUTArray[256], *tuaExtLUTArray = &uaExtLUTArray[0];


/* Allocate lookup table                                                                 */

sAttrsLUT.uTableEntries = 512;                      /* 512 entries                       */

sAttrsLUT.uTableBands = 1;                          /* One band                          */

                                                    /* SD input data type                */
sAttrsLUT.iInputTypeOption = IDATA_TYPE_INTERNAL_SD;

                                                    /* BD output data type               */
sAttrsLUT.iOutputTypeOption = IDATA_TYPE_INTERNAL_BD;

nLUTDilate = InAllocLUT(sAttrsLUT);                 /* LUT allocation                    */


/* Create dilation lookup table data in import buffer and import it                      */

uaExtLUTArray[0] = 0x0;

for(i = 1; i < 512; i++)
{
    uaExtLUTArray[i] = 0x1;
}

stExtLUTArray.tuPixel = tuaExtLUTArray;             /* Pointer to external LUT array     */

                                                    /* Import LUT operation              */
InImportLUT(stExtLUTArray, nLUTDilate, sAttrsLUT, 512, 0, tuDataSize);

                                                    /* Morphic processor dilation operation */
InMorphicProcessor(nSrcBD, nDstBD, nLUTDilate, iIterations, tuCycles);
```

The *open_piks* mechanism initiates a PIKS session. Its API is:

```
void IvOpenPIKS(                              /* no return output             */
    Ipnerror          nFile                   /* error file identifier        */
);
```

■**Example:**   Opening of a PIKS session.

```
Ipnerror              nErrorFile;             /* PIKS error file designation  */

char                  "piks_errors"           /* Error file name              */

if((nErrorFile = (Ipnerror) fopen("piks_errors", "w"))== NULL)
              exit(2);

IvOpenPIKS(nErrorFile);                        /* Open PIKS session            */
```

Note: The *open_piks* mechanism sets the PIKS default states and modes:

- ROI control disengaged
- Errors reported
- Nearest neighbour image resampling
- Nearest neighbour ROI resampling

put_colour_pixel

See Section 5.2.7

InPutColourPixel

The *put_colour_pixel* utility inserts a colour pixel into a colour image. Its API is:

```
Idnimage InPutColourPixel(                      /* OUT destination image identifier    */
    Idnimage            nDestImage,             /* destination image identifier        */
    Ipsparameter_colour stBand0,                /* band 0 pixel value pointer union    */
    Ipsparameter_colour stBand1,                /* band 1 pixel value pointer union    */
    Ipsparameter_colour stBand2,                /* band 2 pixel value pointer union    */
    Ipsparameter_colour stBand3,                /* band 3 pixel value pointer union    */
    Ipuint              uHorizontal,            /* horizontal index value              */
    Ipuint              uVertical,              /* vertical index value                */
    Ipuint              uDepth,                 /* depth index value                   */
    Ipuint              uTemporal               /* temporal index value                */
);
```

where Ipsparameter_colour is the name of the following *piks.h* structure that specifies the data type and value of each band of the colour pixel to be imported from an application.

```
typedef union{
    Ipbool  *tbColour                           /* Boolean pointer             */
    Ipuint  *tuColour;                          /* unsigned integer pointer    */
    Ipint   *tiColour;                          /* signed integer pointer      */
} Ipsparameter_colour;
```

■**Example:** Put a RGB colour pixel with values (113, 35, 206) into a tri-chromatic, nonnegative colour image at coordinate (150, 250).

```
Idnimage            nDstND;                     /* Destination image identifier        */

Ipsparameter_colour stBand0;                    /* Band 0 pixel value pointer union     */

Ipsparameter_colour stBand1;                    /* Band 1 pixel value pointer union     */

Ipsparameter_colour stBand2;                    /* Band 2 pixel value pointer union     */

Ipsparameter_colour stBand3;                    /* Band 3 pixel value pointer union     */

Ipuint              uRedPixel = 113;            /* Red pixel value                      */

Ipuint              uGreenPixel = 35;           /* Green pixel value                    */

Ipuint              uBluePixel = 206;           /* Blue pixel value                     */

Ipuint              uDummyPixel = 0;            /* Band 3 dummy pixel value             */


stBand0.tuColour = &uRedPixel;                  /* Pointer to red pixel value           */

stBand1.tuColour = &uGreenPixel;                /* Pointer to green pixel value         */

stBand2.tuColour = &uBluePixel;                 /* Pointer to blue pixel value          */

stBand3.tuColour = &uDummyPixel;                /* Pointer to band 3 dummy pixel value  */

                                                /* Put colour pixel operation           */
InPutColourPixel(nDstND, stBand0, stBand1, stBand2, stBand3, 150, 250, 0, 0);
```

The *put_pixel* utility inserts a pixel into an image. Its API is:

```
Idnimage InPutPixel(                       /* OUT destination image identifier   */
    Idnimage          nDestImage,          /* destination image identifier       */
    Ipsparameter_pixel stPixel,            /* pixel value pointer union          */
    Ipuint            uHorizontal,         /* horizontal index value             */
    Ipuint            uVertical,           /* vertical index value               */
    Ipuint            uDepth,              /* depth index value                  */
    Ipuint            uTemporal,           /* temporal index value               */
    Ipuint            uBand                /* band index value                   */
);
```

where `Ipsparameter_pixel` is the name of the following *piks.h* union that specifies the data type and value of the pixel to be imported from an application.

```
typedef union{
    Ipbool            *tbPixel;            /* Boolean pointer                    */
    Ipuint            *tuPixel;            /* unsigned integer pointer           */
    Ipint             *tiPixel;            /* signed integer pointer             */
} Ipsparameter_pixel;
```

■**Example:** Put a pixel of value 222 into a nonnegative, monochrome image at coordinate (150, 250).

```
Idnimage              nDstND;             /* Destination image identifier       */

Ipsparameter_pixel    stPixel;            /* Pixel value pointer union          */

Ipuint                uPixel = 222;       /* Pixel value                        */

stPixel.tuPixel = &uPixel;                /* Pointer to pixel value             */

InPutPixel(nDstND, stPixel, 150, 250, 0, 0, 0);  /* Put pixel operation        */
```

put_pixel_array

See Section 5.2.9

put_pixel_array

InPutPixelArray

See Section 5.2.9

The *put_pixel_array* utility inserts an array of pixels into an image. Its API is:

```
Idnimage InPutPixelArray(               /* OUT destination image identifier    */
    Idnimage            nDestImage,     /* destination image identifier        */
    Ipsparameter_pixel  stPixels,       /* pixel values array pointer union    */
    Ipuint              uOffset1,        /* first index offset value            */
    Ipuint              uOffset2,        /* second index offset value           */
    Ipuint              uValue3,         /* third index value                   */
    Ipuint              uValue4,         /* fourth index value                  */
    Ipuint              uValue5,         /* fifth index value                   */
    Ipuint              uColumns,        /* number of array columns             */
    Ipuint              uRows            /* number of array rows                */
);
```

where `Ipsparameter_pixel` is the name of the following *piks.h* union that specifies the data type and value of the pixels to be imported from an application.

```
typedef union{
    Ipbool      *tbPixel;       /* Boolean pointer              */
    Ipuint      *tuPixel;       /* unsigned integer pointer     */
    Ipint       *tiPixel;       /* signed integer pointer       */
} Ipsparameter_pixel;
```

■**Example:** Create and put a 5×10 pixel array of constant value 50 into an unsigned integer, monochrome image at coordinate (250, 300).

```
#define COLS 10                             /* Number of array columns              */

#define ROWS 5                              /* Number of array rows                 */


Idnimage            nDstND;                 /* Destination image                    */

Ipsparameter_pixel  stPixels;              /* Pixel values array pointer union     */

Ipuint              uFirstOff = 250:        /* First index offset value             */

Ipuint              uSecondOff = 300:       /* Second index offset value            */

                                            /* Pixel array                          */
Ipuint              uaPixels[ROWS][COLS], *tuaPixels = &uaPixels[0][0];

unsigned int        j, k;                   /* Array indices                        */


/* Create external unsigned integer pixel array of constant value 50               */

for(k = 0; k < ROWS; k++) {
    for(j = 0; j < COLS; j++) {
        uaPixels[k][j] = 50;
    }
}

stPixels.tuPixel = &uaPixels;               /* Pointer to pixel array               */

                                            /* Put pixel array                      */
InPutPixelArray(nDstND, stPixels, uFirstOff, uSecondOff, 0, 0, 0, COLS, ROWS);
```

The *rescale* operator performs size rescaling of a window of an image. Its API is:

```
Idnimage InRescale(                        /* OUT destination image identifier    */
    Idnimage          nSourceImage,        /* source image identifier             */
    Idnimage          nDestImage,          /* destination image identifier        */
    Idntuple          nScale,              /* scale factor RD 5-tuple identifier   */
    Idntuple          nUpper,              /* upper value RD 5-tuple identifier    */
    Idntuple          nLower               /* lower value RD 5-tuple identifier    */
);
```

■**Example:** Rescaling of an image. The image window between (100, 100) and (200, 200) is rescaled to an image of 200 × 200 pixels.

```
Idnimage          nSrc;          /* Source image identifier             */

Idnimage          nDst;          /* Destination image identifier        */

Idntuple          nScale;        /* Scale factor RD 5-tuple identifier   */

Idntuple          nUpper;        /* Upper value RD 5-tuple identifier    */

Idntuple          nLower;        /* Lower value RD 5-tuple identifier    */


                                 /* Generate scale factor RD 5-tuple    */
nScale = InGenerateRD5Tuple(2.0, 2.0, 1.0, 1.0, 1.0);

                                 /* Generate upper value RD 5-tuple     */
nUpper = InGenerateRD5Tuple(200.0, 200.0, 0.0, 0.0, 0.0);

                                 /* Generate lower value RD 5-tuple     */
nLower = InGenerateRD5Tuple(100.0, 100.0, 0.0, 0.0, 0.0);

InRescale(nSrc, nDst, nScale, nUpper, nLower);   /* Rescale image operation     */
```

rescale_roi

InRescaleROI

See Section 2.4.4

The *rescale_roi* operator performs size rescaling of a window of a ROI. Its API is:

```
Idnroi InRescaleROI(                                /* OUT destination ROI identifier      */
    Idnroi          nSourceROI,                     /* source ROI identifier               */
    Idnroi          nDestROI,                       /* destination ROI identifier          */
    Idntuple        nScale,                         /* scale factor RD 5-tuple identifier  */
    Idntuple        nUpper,                         /* upper value RD 5-tuple identifier   */
    Idntuple        nLower                          /* lower value RD 5-tuple identifier   */
);
```

■**Example:** Rescaling of a ROI. The ROI window between (100, 100) and (200, 200) is re-scaled to a ROI of 200 × 200 pixels.

```
Idnroi          nSrcROI;                /* Source ROI identifier                 */

Idnroi          nDstROI;                /* Destination ROI identifier            */

Idntuple        nScale;                 /* Scale factor RD 5-tuple identifier    */

Idntuple        nUpper;                 /* Upper value RD 5-tuple identifier     */

Idntuple        nLower;                 /* Lower value RD 5-tuple identifier     */


                                        /* Generate scale factor RD 5-tuple      */
nScale = InGenerateRD5Tuple(2.0, 2.0, 1.0, 1.0, 1.0);

                                        /* Generate upper value RD 5-tuple       */
nUpper = InGenerateRD5Tuple(200.0, 200.0, 0.0, 0.0, 0.0);

                                        /* Generate lower value RD 5-tuple       */
nLower = InGenerateRD5Tuple(100.0, 100.0, 0.0, 0.0, 0.0);

                                        /* Rescale ROI operation                 */
InRescaleROI(nSrcROI, nDstROI, nScale, nUpper, nLower);
```

The *resize* operator performs resizing of an image by reducing or enlarging its coordinate sizes. Its API is:

```
Idnimage InResize(                              /* OUT destination image identifier   */
    Idnimage        nSourceImage,              /* source image identifier            */
    Idnimage        nDestImage,                /* destination image identifier       */
    Idntuple        nDestSize                  /* destination size ND 5-tuple id     */
);
```

■**Example:** Resizing of an image to produce a destination image of 200 × 300 pixels.

```
Idnimage            nSrc;                       /* Source image identifier            */

Idnimage            nDst;                       /* Destination image identifier       */

Idntuple            nDstSize;                   /* Destination size ND 5-tuple id     */

                                                /* Generate destination size ND 5-tuple  */
nDstSize = InGenerateND5Tuple(200, 300, 1, 1, 1);

InResize(nSrc, nDst, nDstSize);                 /* Resize image operation             */
```

Note 1:   The size of the source image is minified or magnified to produce a destination image with 300 rows and 200 columns.

Note 2:   The destination image is resampled by nearest neighbour or bilinear interpolation according to the global resampling mode in effect at the time of execution of the resize operator.

resize_roi

InResizeROI

See Section 2.4.6

The *resize_roi* operator performs resizing of a ROI by reducing or enlarging its coordinate sizes. Its API is:

```
Idnroi InResizeROI(                              /* OUT destination ROI identifier    */
    Idnroi          nSourceROI,                  /* source ROI identifier             */
    Idnroi          nDestROI,                    /* destination ROI identifier        */
    Idntuple        nDestSize                    /* destination size ND 5-tuple id    */
);
```

■**Example:**   Resizing of a ROI to produce a destination ROI of 200 × 300 pixels.

```
Idnroi          nSrcROI;             /* Source ROI identifier            */

Idnroi          nDstROI;             /* Destination ROI identifier       */

Idntuple        nDstSize;            /* Destination size ND 5-tuple id   */

                                     /* Generate destination size ND 5-tuple */
nDstSize = InGenerateND5Tuple(200, 300, 1, 1, 1);

InResizeROI(nSrcROI, nDstROI, nDstSize);         /* Resize ROI operation   */
```

Note 1:   The size of the source ROI is minified or magnified to produce a destination ROI with 300 rows and 200 columns.

Note 2:   The destination ROI is resampled by nearest neighbour interpolation.

The *return_repository_id* mechanism returns the identifier of a data object repository entry to an application. Its API is:

```
Idnrepository InReturnRepositoryId(      /* OUT repository identifier         */
    Ipint            iIndex,             /* repository index within class     */
    Ipint            iClassOption        /* repository class option           */
);
```

The following repository class #define options are provided in *piks.h*.

```
IREPOSITORY_IMPULSE          1           /* impulse response array            */
IREPOSITORY_DITHER           2           /* dither array                      */
IREPOSITORY_COLOUR           3           /* colour conversion matrix          */
```

■**Example 1:**   Return repository identifier of Laplacian 3 impulse response function array with access by integer index.

```
Idnrepository        nRepId;            /* Repository identifier              */

Ipint                iIndex = 68;       /* Repository index within class      */

Ipint                iClassOption = 1;  /* Repository class                   */

                                        /* Return repository identifier output */
nRepId = InReturnRepositoryId(iIndex, iClassOption);
```

■**Example 2:**   Return repository identifier of Laplace 3 impulse response function array with access by array name and class name.

```
Idnrepository        nRepId;            /* Repository identifier              */


                                        /* Return repository identifier output */
nRepId = InReturnRepositoryId(IR_LAPLACE_3, IREPOSITORY_IMPULSE);
```

Appendix B contains the #define names of the data object repository entries.

roi_rectangular

See Section 3.1.2

InROIRectangular

The *roi_rectangular* tool generates a two-dimensional, rectangular-shaped region-of-interest. Its API is:

```
Idnroi InROIRectangular(                            /* OUT destination ROI identifier      */
    Idnroi          nDestROI,                       /* destination ROI identifier          */
    Idntuple        nSize,                          /* ROI size ND 5-tuple                 */
    Idntuple        nStart,                         /* start position ND 5-tuple           */
    Idntuple        nEnd,                           /* end position ND 5-tuple             */
    Idntuple        nIndexManipulation,             /* index manipulation CS 5-tuple       */
    Ipedimension    eDimensionOption,               /* rectangle dimension option          */
    Ipepolarity     ePolarityOption                 /* ROI polarity option                 */
);
```

where Ipedimension is the name of the *piks.h* enum that specifies the dimension of the rectangular ROI:

```
IDIMENSION_1D                                       /* one dimension                       */
IDIMENSION_2D                                       /* two dimension                       */
IDIMENSION_3D                                       /* three dimension                     */
IDIMENSION_4D                                       /* four dimension                      */
IDIMENSION_5D                                       /* five dimension                      */
```

Ipepolarity is the name of the enum that specifies the ROI polarity option:

```
IPOLARITY_TRUE                                      /* set TRUE                            */
IPOLARITY_FALSE                                     /* set FALSE                           */
```

Note 1:   PIKS Foundation only supports the generation of one and two-dimenional ROIs.

Note 2:   PIKS Foundation does not support index manipulation.

■**Example:** Create a rectangular ROI which is TRUE in the region of (100, 200) to (300, 400) in a 512 × 512 pixel ROI.

```
Idnroi          nROI;                       /* ROI identifier                      */

Idntuple        nSize;                      /* ROI size ND 5-tuple                 */

Idntuple        nStart;                     /* Start position ND 5-tuple           */

Idntuple        nEnd;                       /* End position ND 5-tuple             */


nSize = InGenerateND5Tuple(512, 512, 1, 1, 1);   /* Generate ROI size ND 5-tuple        */

nStart = InGenerateND5Tuple(100, 200, 0, 0, 0);  /* Generate start position ND 5-tuple  */

nEnd = InGenerateND5Tuple(300, 400, 0, 0, 0);    /* Generate end position ND 5-tuple    */

                                                 /* Rectangular ROI generation          */
InROIRectangular(nROI, nSize, nStart, nEnd, NULL, IDIMENSION_2D, IPOLARITY_TRUE);
```

The *rotate* operator performs two-dimensional rotation of an image about a point. Its API is:

```
Idnimage InRotate(                                  /* OUT destination image identifier   */
    Idnimage        nSourceImage,                   /* source image identifier            */
    Idnimage        nDestImage,                     /* destination image identifier       */
    Ipfloat         rCentre1,                       /* x index source rotation centre     */
    Ipfloat         rCentre2,                       /* y index source rotation centre     */
    Ipfloat         rCentre3,                       /* z index source rotation centre     */
    Ipfloat         rAngleFirstSecond,              /* x-y plane rotation angle           */
    Ipfloat         rAngleFirstThird,               /* x-z plane rotation angle           */
    Ipfloat         rAngleSecondThird,              /* y-z plane rotation angle           */
    Ipint           iOption                         /* rotation option                    */
);
```

The following rotation #define option is provided in *piks.h*.

```
IROTATION_SPACE_2D      1                           /* 2D rotation                        */
```

Note: PIKS Foundation only supports two-dimensional rotation of a monochrome or colour image about its *x-y* plane centre of rotation. The parameters rCentre3, rAngleFirstThird, and rAngleSecondThird are ignored.

■**Example:** Rotation of an image about coordinate (250.0, 100.0) by an angle of 0.5 radians.

```
Idnimage            nSrc;                       /* Source image identifier           */

Idnimage            nDst;                       /* Destination image identifier      */

Ipfloat             rxCentre = 250.0;           /* x index source rotation centre    */

Ipfloat             ryCentre = 100.0;           /* y index source rotation centre    */

Ipfloat             rAngle = 0.5;               /* Rotation angle                    */

                                                /* Rotation operation                */
InRotate(nSrc, nDst, rxCentre, ryCentre, 0.0, rAngle, 0.0, 0.0, IROTATION_SPACE_2D);
```

set_error_handler

See Section 4.5.4

The *set_error_handler* mechanism replaces error handlers. Its API is:

```
Iptferror_function ItfSetErrorHandler(          /* OUT old error handler pointer    */
    Iptferror_function tfNewErrorHandler        /* new error handler pointer        */
);
```

where `Iptferror_function` is the name of the following *piks.h* function pointer prototype that specifies the replacement error handler.

```
typedef void (*Iptferror_function)              /* error handler function pointer   */
    (Ipint                      iCode,
     Ipint                      iElement,
     Idnchain                   nChain,
     Ipnerror                   nError,
     Ipesynchronicity_state     eSynchronicityState);
```

■**Example:** Replace default error handler with application-defined error handler.

```
extern                      vApplicationErrorHandler(
    Ipint                   iCode,
    Ipint                   iElement,
    Idnchain                nChain,
    Ipnerror                nError,
    Ipesynchronicity        eSynchronicityState);

Ipnerror                    nError              /* Error file                   */

Ipesynchronicity            eSynchronicityState);   /* Synchronicity state      */

Iptferror_function          tfStandardErrorHandler  /* Standard error handler pointer   */

                                                /* Set new error handler        */
tfStandardErrorHandler = ItfSetErrorHandler(vApplicationErrorHandle);
```

The *set_globals* mechanism sets PIKS global modes. Its API is:

```
void IvSetGlobals(                                /* no return output            */
   Ipspiks_modes        sModes                    /* mode settings               */
);
```

where `Ipspiks_modes` is the name of the following *piks.h* structure that specifies the PIKS modes.

```
typedef struct{
   Iperoi_control_mode    eROIControlMode;         /* ROI control mode            */
   Iperoi_process_mode    eROIProcessMode;         /* ROI processing mode         */
   Ipematch_mode          eMatchPointMode;         /* match point control mode    */
   Ipeindex_mode          eIndexAssignmentMode;    /* index assignment mode       */
   Ipesynchronicity_mode  eSynchronicityMode;      /* sychronicity mode           */
   Ipeerror_report_mode   eErrorReportMode;        /* error report mode           */
   Ipint                  iImageResampleMode;      /* image resampling selection mode */
   Ipint                  iROIResampleMode;        /* ROI resampling selection mode   */
} Ipspiks_modes;
```

`Iperoi_control_mode` is the name of the following enum that indicates whether ROI control is on or off.

```
IROI_CONTROL_ON                                   /* ROI control operative       */
IROI_CONTROL_OFF                                  /* ROI control inoperative     */
```

`Iperoi_process_mode` is the name of the following enum that indicates whether ROIs are automatically processed along with images.

```
IROI_PROCESS_ON                                   /* ROI processing operative    */
IROI_PROCESS_OFF                                  /* ROI processing inoperative  */
```

Note: PIKS Foundation does not support automatic ROI processing.

`Ipematch_mode` is the name of the following enum that indicates whether match point control is invoked or not invoked.

```
IMATCH_POINT_ON                                   /* match point control operative   */
IMATCH_POINT_OFF                                  /* match point control inoperative */
```

Note: PIKS Foundation does not support index assignment.

`Ipeindex_mode` is the name of the following enum that indicates whether index assignment is invoked or not invoked.

```
IINDEX_ASSIGNMENT_ON                              /* index assignment operative      */
IINDEX_ASSIGNMENT_OFF                             /* index assignment inoperative    */
```

Note: PIKS Foundation does not support index assignment.

`Ipesynchronicity_mode` is the name of the following enum that indicates whether PIKS is operating synchronously or asynchronously.

```
ISYNCHRONICITY_MODE_SYNCH                         /* synchronous mode            */
ISYNCHRONICITY_MODE_ASYNCH                        /* asynchronous mode           */
```

Note: PIKS Foundation only supports synchronous processing.

`Ipeerror_report_mode` is the name of the following enum that indicates whether error reporting is active or inactive.

```
IERROR_REPORT_ACTIVE                              /* error reporting active      */
IERROR_REPORT_INACTIVE                            /* error reporting inactive    */
```

set_globals

IvSetGlobals

See Section 4.4.4

The following image resampling #define options are provided in *piks.h*.

```
#define   IRESAMPLE_NEAREST_NEIGHBOUR   1   /* nearest neighbour        */
#define   IRESAMPLE_2_BILINEAR          2   /* support 2 bilinear       */
```

The following ROI resampling #define options is provided in *piks.h*.

```
#define   IRESAMPLE_NEAREST_NEIGHBOUR   1   /* nearest neighbour        */
```

■**Example 1:** Set PIKS globals to engage ROI control, report errors, support 2 bilinear image resampling, nearest neighbour ROI resampling, and all other mandatory PIKS Foundation modes.

```
Ipspiks_modes          sModes;                     /* Mode settings            */

sModes.eROIControlMode = IROI_CONTROL_ON;       /* ROI control operative        */

sModes.eROIProcessMode = IROI_PROCESS_ON;       /* ROI processing inoperative   */

sModes.eMatchPointMode = IMATCH_POINT_OFF;      /* Match point control inoperative */

                                                /* Index assignment inoperative */
sModes.eIndexAssignmentMode = IINDEX_ASSIGNMENT_OFF;

                                                /* Synchronous mode             */
sModes.eSynchronicityMode = ISYNCHRONICITY_MODE_SYNCH;

sModes.eErrorReportMode = IERROR_REPORT_ACTIVE; /* Error reporting active        */

                                                /* Support 2 bilinear image resampling */
sModes.iImageResampleMode = IRESAMPLE_2_BILINEAR;

                                                /* Nearest neighbour ROI resampling */
sModes.iROIResampleMode = IRESAMPLE_NEAREST_NEIGHBOUR;

IvSetGlobals(sModes);                           /* Set globals                  */
```

■**Example 2:** Inquire PIKS ROI control status and change to ROI control inactive if status was previously active.

```
                                                /* PIKS modes pointer           */
Ipspiks_modes          sModes, *tsModes = &sModes;

                                                /* Data validity indicator      */
Ipevalidity            eValid, *teValid = &eValid;

IvInquirePIKSStatus(NULL, tsModes, teValid);    /* Inquire PIKS status          */

if(eValid != IVALIDITY_VALID) {                 /* Inquiry validity check       */
    printf("error: PIKS not open\n");
    exit(1);
}

if(sModes.eROIControlMode == IROI_CONTROL_ON) {
    printf("ROI control mode was active \n");   /* Print PIKS ROI control mode  */
    sModes.eROIControlMode = IROI_CONTROL_OFF); /* Change ROI control to inactive */
}
else {
    printf("ROI control mode is inactive \n");  /* Print PIKS ROI control mode  */
}

IvSetGlobals(sModes);                           /* Set ROI control to inactive  */
```

The *set_image_attributes* mechanism sets image attributes of a previously allocated image. Its API is:

```
Idnimage InSetImageAttrs(              /* OUT destination image identifier   */
    Idnimage          nDestImage,      /* destination image identifier       */
    Ipsattrs_image    sAttrs           /* image attributes                   */
);
```

where `Ipsattrs_image` is the name of the following *piks.h* structure that specifies the image attributes.

```
typedef struct{
    Idntuple    nImageSize;            /* image size ND 5-tuple identifier      */
    Idntuple    nBandType;             /* band data type SD B-tuple identifier  */
    Idntuple    nBandPrecision;        /* band precision ND B-tuple identifier  */
    Ipfloat     rXWhite;               /* X tristimulus value white point       */
    Ipfloat     rYWhite;               /* Y tristimulus value white point       */
    Ipfloat     rZWhite;               /* Z tristimulus value white point       */
    Ipint       iImageStructureOption; /* image structure option                */
    Ipint       iColourOption;         /* colour space option                   */
} Ipsattrs_image;
```

The image structure and colour space options provided in *piks.h* are described in the *allocate_image* mechanism manual page.

■**Example:**   Inquire image attributes and set only colour image white point attributes.

```
Idnimage            nDst;                              /* Image identifier               */

                                                       /* Image attributes               */
Ipsattrs_image      sAttrsImage, *tsAttrsImage = &sAttrsImage;

                                                       /* ROI binding information        */
Ipsbind_image       sImageBind, *tsImageBind = &sImageBind;

                                                       /* Data validity indicator        */
Ipevalidity         eValid, *teValid = &eValid;


                                                       /* Inquire image                  */
IvInquireImage(nSrc, tsAttrsImage, tsImageBind, teValid);

if(eValid != IVALIDITY_VALID) {                        /* Inquiry validity check         */
    printf("error: PIKS not open\n");
    exit(1);
}

sAttrsImage.rXWhite = 0.981;                           /* X tristimulus value white point */

sAttrsImage.rYWhite = 1.000;                           /* Y tristimulus value white point */

sAttrsImage.rZWhite = 1.182;                           /* Z tristimulus value white point */


InSetImageAttrs(nDst, tsAttrsImage);                   /* Set white point                */
```

split_image

See Section 2.2.5

The *split_image* operator generates split image views of a pair of monochrome or colour images. Its API is:

```
Idnimage InSplitImage(                              /* OUT destination image identifier    */
    Idnimage          nSourceImage1,                /* first source image identifier       */
    Idnimage          nSourceImage2,                /* second source image identifier      */
    Idnimage          nDestImage,                   /* destination image identifier        */
    Ipuint            uSplitPosition,               /* split position                      */
    Ipint             iOption                       /* split image option                  */
);
```

The following split image #define options are provided in *piks.h*.

```
ISPLIT_LEFT-LEFT            1            /* split left 1 - left 2        */
ISPLIT_RIGHT_RIGHT          2            /* split right 1 - right 2      */
ISPLIT_TOP_TOP              3            /* split top 1 - top 2          */
ISPLIT_BOTTOM_BOTTOM        4            /* split bottom 1 - bottom 2    */
ISPLIT_LEFT_RIGHT           5            /* split left 1 - right 2       */
ISPLIT_TOP_BOTTOM           6            /* split top 1 - bottom 2       */
```

■**Example:** Top 1 – top 2 split image of a pair of images at vertical position of 100 pixels.

```
Idnimage          nSrc1;                     /* Source image identifier      */

Idnimage          nSrc2;                     /* Source image identifier      */

Idnimage          nDst;                      /* Destination image identifier */

Ipuint            uSplitPosition = 100;      /* Split position, 100 pixels   */

                                             /* Split image operation        */
InSplitImage(nSrc1, nSrc2, nDst, uSplitPosition, ISPLIT_TOP_TOP);
```

The *subsample* operator performs spatial subsampling of an image. Pixels are extracted from a source window offset with respect to the source origin and placed in a destination image window offset with respect to the destination origin. Its API is:

```
Idnimage InSubsample(                          /* OUT destination image identifier   */
    Idnimage        nSourceImage,              /* source image identifier            */
    Idnimage        nDestImage,                /* destination image identifier        */
    Ipuint          uFactor1,                  /* source first index subsample factor  */
    Ipuint          uFactor2,                  /* source second index subsample factor */
    Ipuint          uSourceOffset1,            /* source first index offset            */
    Ipuint          uSourceOffset2,            /* source second index offset           */
    Ipuint          uDestOffset1,              /* destination first index offset        */
    Ipuint          uDestOffset2,              /* destination second index offset       */
    Ipuint          uSourceWindow1,            /* Source first index window             */
    Ipuint          uSourceWindow2             /* Source second index window            */
);
```

■**Example:** Subsampling of an image. Every second pixel along the *x* index and every third pixel along the *y* index is extracted from the source image in a 200×200 window at a spatial offset coordinate (225, 350) and inserted in the destination image at a spatial offset coordinate (300, 275).

```
Idnimage            nSrc;                      /* Source image identifier            */

Idnimage            nDst;                      /* Destination image identifier        */

Ipuint              uxFactor = 2;              /* x index subsampling factor          */

Ipuint              uyFactor = 3;              /* y index subsampling factor          */

Ipuint              uxSrcOff = 225;            /* x index source offset                */

Ipuint              uySrcOff = 350;            /* y index source offset                */

Ipuint              uxDstOff = 300;            /* x index destination offset           */

Ipuint              uyDstOff = 275;            /* y index destination offset           */

Ipuint              uxSrcWind = 200;           /* x index source window                */

Ipuint              uySrcWind = 200;           /* y index source window                */

                                               /* Subsample operation                 */
InSubsample(nSrc, nDst, uxFactor, uyFactor, uxSrcOff, uySrcOff, uxDstOff, uyDstOff,
    uxSrcWind, uySrcWind);
```

threshold

InThreshold

See Section 2.1.6

The *threshold* operator performs pixel amplitude thresholding of an image. Its API is:

```
Idnimage InThreshold(                      /* OUT destination image identifier    */
    Idnimage           nSourceImage,       /* source image identifier             */
    Idnimage           nDestImage,         /* destination image identifier        */
    Ipsparameter_pixel stAbove,            /* above threshold clip value ptr union */
    Ipsparameter_pixel stBelow,            /* below threshold clip value ptr union */
    Ipsparameter_arith stThreshold         /* threshold value pointer union       */
);
```

where `Ipsparameter_pixel` is the name of the following *piks.h* union that specifies the data type and values of the clip parameters.

```
typedef union{
    Ipbool         *tbPixel;       /* Boolean pointer             */
    Ipuint         *tuPixel;       /* unsigned integer pointer    */
    Ipint          *tiPixel;       /* signed integer pointer      */
} Ipsparameter_pixel;
```

`Ipsparameter_arith` is the name of the following *piks.h* union that specifies the data type and value of the threshold parameter.

```
typedef union{
    Ipuint         *tuArith;       /* unsigned integer pointer    */
    Ipint          *tiArith;       /* signed integer pointer      */
} Ipsparameter_arith;
```

■**Example:**   Thresholding of a nonnegative source image such that the destination Boolean image is TRUE if a source pixel is greater than the threshold value, 135, and is FALSE otherwise.

```
Idnimage           nSrcND;                 /* Source image                         */

Idnimage           nDstBD;                 /* Destination image                    */

Ipsparameter_pixel stAbove;                /* Above threshold clip value ptr union */

Ipsparameter_pixel stBelow;                /* Below threshold clip value ptr union */

Ipsparameter_arith stThreshold;            /* Threshold value pointer union        */

Ipbool             bAbove = IBOOL_TRUE;    /* Above threshold clip value           */

Ipbool             bBelow = IBOOL_FALSE;   /* Below threshold clip value           */

Ipuint             uThreshold = 135;       /* Threshold value                      */


stAbove.tbPixel = &bAbove;                 /* Boolean above threshold value        */

stBelow.tbPixel = &bBelow;                 /* Boolean below threshold value        */

stThreshold.tuPixel = &uThreshold;         /* Unsigned integer threshold value     */

                                           /* Threshold operation                  */
InThreshold(nSrcND, nDstBD, stAbove, stBelow, stThreshold);
```

PIKS C ELEMENT PROTOTYPES   CHAPTER 7

The *translate* operator performs a spatial translation of an image with respect to its origin. Its API is:

```
Idnimage InTranslate(                         /* OUT destination image identifier    */
   Idnimage         nSourceImage,             /* source image identifier             */
   Idnimage         nDestImage,               /* destination image identifier        */
   Idntuple         nOffset                   /* index offset RD 5-tuple identifier   */
);
```

■**Example:** Translation of an image by the spatial coordinate (50.3, –60.5).

```
Idnimage            nSrc;                     /* Source image identifier             */

Idnimage            nDst;                     /* Destination image identifier        */

Idntuple            nOffset;                  /* Index offset RD 5-tuple identifier  */


                                              /* Generate index offset RD 5-tuple    */
nOffset = InGenerateRD5Tuple(50.3, -60.5, 0.0, 0.0, 0.0);


InTranslate(nSrc, nDst, nOffset);            /* Translate image operation           */
```

Note: PIKS Foundation supports nearest neighbour and bilinear interpolation resampling of the source image according to the global resampling option in effect.

translate_roi

InTranslateROI

See Section 2.4.10

The *translate_roi* operator performs a spatial translation of a ROI with respect to its origin. Its API is:

```
Idnroi InTranslateROI(                              /* OUT destination ROI identifier      */
    Idnroi          nSourceROI,                     /* source ROI identifier               */
    Idnroi          nDestROI,                       /* destination ROI identifier          */
    Idntuple        nOffset                         /* index offset RD 5-tuple identifier  */
);
```

■**Example:** Translation of a ROI by the spatial coordinate (50.3, –60.5).

```
Idnroi          nSrcROI;                    /* Source ROI identifier               */

Idnroi          nDstROI;                    /* Destination ROI identifier          */

Idntuple        nOffset;                    /* Index offset RD 5-tuple identifier  */


                                            /* Generate index offset RD 5-tuple    */
nOffset = InGenerateRD5Tuple(50.3, -60.5, 0.0, 0.0, 0.0);


InTranslateROI(nSrcROI, nDstROI, nOffset);  /* Translate ROI operation             */
```

Note: PIKS Foundation supports only nearest neighbour resampling of the source ROI.

The *unary_integer* operator performs unary point conversion of pixels of an integer data type image. Its API is:

```
Idnimage InUnaryInteger(              /* OUT destination image identifier   */
    Idnimage         nSourceImage,    /* source image identifier            */
    Idnimage         nDestImage,      /* destination image identifier       */
    Ipint            iOption          /* unary integer conversion option    */
);
```

The following unary integer conversion #define options are provided in *piks.h*.

```
IUNARY_INTEGER_ABSOLUTE       1       /* absolute value                     */
IUNARY_INTEGER_CUBE           2       /* cube                               */
IUNARY_INTEGER_NEGATIVE       3       /* negative                           */
IUNARY_INTEGER_SQUARE         4       /* square                             */
```

■**Example:**   Negative of a signed integer image.

```
Idnimage          nSrcSD;              /* Source image identifier           */

Idnimage          nDstSD;              /* Destination image identifier      */

                                       /* Negative operation                */
InUnaryInteger(nSrcSD, nDstSD, IUNARY_INTEGER_NEGATIVE);
```

The *window_level* operator performs window-level point scaling of an image. Its API is:

```
Idnimage InWindowLevel(              /* OUT destination image identifier   */
    Idnimage            nSourceImage,    /* source image identifier        */
    Idnimage            nDestImage,      /* destination image identifier   */
    Ipsparameter_arith  stAbove,         /* above window clip value ptr union */
    Ipsparameter_arith  stBelow,         /* below window clip value ptr union */
    Ipsparameter_arith  stWidth,         /* window width value pointer union  */
    Ipsparameter_arith  stLevel          /* window level value pointer union  */
);
```

where `Ipsparameter_arith` is the name of the following *piks.h* union that specifies the data type and values of the four operator input parameters.

```
typedef union{
    Ipuint    *tuArith;    /* unsigned integer pointer    */
    Ipint     *tiArith;    /* signed integer pointer      */
} Ipsparameter_arith;
```

■**Example:** Window-level operation on an image. Source image pixels in the range of 100 to 200 are linearly rescaled in the destination over the range of 0 to 255. Source image pixels of value less than 100 are clipped to value 0 in the destination image and source image pixels of value greater than 200 are clipped to value 255 in the destination image.

```
Idnimage            nSrcND;          /* Source image identifier           */

Idnimage            nDstND;          /* Destination image identifier      */

Ipsparameter_arith  stAbove;         /* Above window clip value ptr union */

Ipsparameter_arith  stBelow;         /* Below window clip value ptr union */

Ipsparameter_arith  stWidth;         /* Window width value pointer union  */

Ipsparameter_arith  stLevel;         /* Window level value pointer union  */

Ipuint              uAbove = 255;    /* Above window clip value           */

Ipuint              uBelow = 0;      /* Below window clip value           */

Ipuint              uWidth = 100;    /* Window width value                */

Ipuint              uLevel = 150;    /* Window level value value          */


stAbove.tuArith = &uAbove;           /* Pointer to above window clip value */

stBelow.tuArith = &uBelow;           /* Pointer to below window clip value */

stWidth.tuArith = &uWidth;           /* Pointer to window width value      */

stLevel.tuArith = &uLevel;           /* Pointer to window level value      */
                                     /* Window-level operation             */
InWindowLevel(nSrcND, nDstND, stAbove, stBelow, stWidth, stLevel);
```

The *zoom* operator performs zooming of an image by magnifying its pixel planes by integer scale factors. Its API is:

```
Idnimage InZoom(                            /* OUT destination image identifier    */
    Idnimage          nSourceImage,         /* source image identifier             */
    Idnimage          nDestImage,           /* destination image identifier        */
    Idntuple          nScale                /* zoom scale factor ND 5-tuple         */
);
```

■**Example:**   Zoom of an image by a factor of 2 to 1 along the *x* index and by a factor of 1 to 1 along the *y* index.

```
Idnimage              nSrc;                 /* Source image identifier             */

Idnimage              nDst;                 /* Destination image identifier        */

Idntuple              nScale;               /* Zoom scale factor ND 5-tuple id     */

nScale = InGenerateND5Tuple(2, 1, 1, 1, 1); /* Generate scale factor ND 5-tuple   */

InZoom(nSrc, nDst, nScale);                 /* Zoom operation                      */
```

The *zoom_roi* operator performs zooming of a ROI by magnifying its pixel plane by integer scale factors. Its API is:

```
Idnroi InZoomROI(                              /* OUT destination ROI identifier    */
    Idnroi          nSourceROI,                /* source ROI identifier             */
    Idnroi          nDestROI,                  /* destination ROI identifier        */
    Idntuple        nScale                     /* zoom scale factor ND 5-tuple      */
);
```

■**Example:**   Zoom of a ROI by a factor of 2 to 1 along the *x* index and by a factor of 1 to 1 along the *y* index

```
Idnroi              nSrcROI;               /* Source ROI identifier             */

Idnroi              nDstROI;               /* Destination ROI identifier        */

Idntuple            nScale;                /* Zoom scale factor ND 5-tuple id   */

nScale = InGenerateND5Tuple(2, 1, 1, 1, 1);  /* Generate scale factor ND 5-tuple  */

InZoomRoi(nSrcROI, nDstROI, nScale);       /* Zoom ROI operation                */
```

8

PIKS C Language Convenience Function and PixelSoft Utility Prototypes

The following pages of this chapter contain the syntactical C language binding definitions of the standardized PIKS Foundation convenience function prototypes. The chapter also contains the syntactical C language bindings of the PixelSoft, Inc. file, window, and display utilities. These utilities are not part of the PIKS standard because utilities of this nature tend to be operating system and implementation dependent. However, such utilities are necessary to create complete PIKS-based programs. The program examples of Chapter 6 use many of these PixelSoft utilities.

This chapter lists the PIKS convenience function and PixelSoft utility prototypes in alphabetical order by their prototype name, i.e., the name following the sentinel I and the compound prefix. A "functional specification" name, analogous to the Functional Specification name of a PIKS element is also listed for each prototype.

boolean_display

The PixelSoft *boolean_display* utility displays a Boolean image in a monochrome display window. Its API is:

```
Idnimage InBooleanDisplay(               /* OUT image identifier          */
    Idnimage            nSourceImage,    /* image identifier              */
    void                *tDisplay        /* pointer to display window      */
);
```

This nonstandard utility converts a Boolean image to an unsigned integer image for display. Logically FALSE pixels are converted to integer value zero and logically TRUE pixels are converted to the maximum integer display value, typically 255.

A display window must be opened by the *open_window* utility prior to invocation of the *boolean_display* utility. If the *key_delay* utility is invoked after the *boolean_display* utility is invoked, program execution will be halted and the display will be maintained in the window until a key is pressed while the cursor is within the display window.

■**Example:**   Display of a 512×512 Boolean image.

```
Idnimage            nSrcBD;              /* Boolean image identifier      */

void                *tDisplay;           /* Pointer to display window     */

unsigned int        uWidth = 512;        /* Image width of 512 pixels     */

unsigned int        uHeight = 512;       /* Image height of 512 pixels    */

unsigned int        uBands = 1;          /* One display band              */

                                         /* Open a 512x512 monochrome window */
tDisplay = ItOpenWindow(uWidth, uHeight, uBands);

InBooleanDisplay(nSrcBD, tDisplay);      /* Display Boolean image         */

IvKeyDelay(tDisplay);                    /* Press key to continue         */

IvCloseWindow(tDisplay);                 /* Close window                  */
```

Note: The display may show colour artifacts if the system cursor is not placed within the display window.

close_window   IvCloseWindow

The PixelSoft *close_window* utility closes a previously opened display window. Its API is:

```
void IvCloseWindow(                    /* no output return            */
void                *tDisplay         /* pointer to display window    */
);
```

■**Example:**   Sequential display of 512×512, ND data type, monochrome images in a single window.

```
Idnimage            nSrcMon1;          /* First monochrome image identifier    */

Idnimage            nSrcMon2;          /* Second monochrome image identifier   */

void                *tDisplay;         /* Pointer to display window            */

unsigned int        uWidth = 512;      /* Image width of 512 pixels            */

unsigned int        uHeight = 512;     /* Image height of 512 pixels           */

unsigned int        uBands = 1;        /* One display band                     */

                                       /* Open a 512x512 monochrome window     */
tDisplay = ItOpenWindow(uWidth, uHeight, uBands);

InMonochromeDisplay(nSrcMon1, tDisplay);   /* Display first monochrome image   */

IvKeyDelay(tDisplay);                  /* Press key to continue                */

InMonochromeDisplay(nSrcMon2, tDisplay);   /* Display second monochrome image  */

IvKeyDelay(tDisplay);                  /* Press key to continue                */

IvCloseWindow(tDisplay);               /* Close window                         */
```

The PixelSoft *colour_display* utility displays an ND data type, RGB colour image in a display window. Its API is:

```
Idnimage InColourDisplay(                    /* OUT image identifier        */
Idnimage              nSourceImage,          /* colour image identifier     */
void                  *tDisplay              /* pointer to display window    */
```

This nonstandard utility converts a PIKS colour image with a PIKS implementation's internal precision to the precision of a colour display frame buffer. If the frame buffer supports full colour display, typically 8 bits per pixel for each red, green, and blue component, the utility converts each source image component to the precision of the corresponding colour display component. If the frame buffer supports pseudocolour display, typically 3 bits per pixel for the red and green components and 2 bits per pixel for the blue component, the utility performs dithering and passes the display buffer pixels through a colour map for display. See the dither man page.

A display window must be opened by the *open_window* utility prior to invocation of the *colour_display* utility. If the *key_delay* utility is invoked after the *colour_display* utility is invoked, program execution will be halted and the display will be maintained in the window until a key is pressed while the cursor is within the display window.

■**Example:**   Display of a 512×512, ND data type, RGB colour image.

```
Idnimage              nSrcColour;            /* Colour image identifier     */

void                  *tDisplay;             /* Pointer to display window    */

unsigned int          uWidth = 512;          /* Image width of 512 pixels   */

unsigned int          uHeight = 512;         /* Image height of 512 pixels  */

unsigned int          uBands = 3;            /* Three display bands         */

                                             /* Open a 512x512 colour window */
tDisplay = ItOpenWindow(uWidth, uHeight, uBands);

InColourDisplay(nSrcColour, tDisplay);       /* Display colour image        */

IvKeyDelay(tDisplay);                        /* Press key to continue       */

IvCloseWindow(tDisplay);                     /* Close window                */
```

Note: The display may show colour artifacts if the system cursor is not placed within the display window.

generate_nd_1_tuple InGenerateND1Tuple

The *generate_nd_1_tuple* convenience function creates a tuple containing a single ND data type value. Its API is:

```
Idntuple InGenerateND1Tuple(              /* OUT ND data type 1-tuple identifier  */
   Ipuint          uValue                 /* value                                */
);
```

This convenience function is the one-step equivalent of allocating and creating an ND data type tuple containing a single data value. See the *allocate_tuple* man page.

■**Example:** Generation of a tuple that specifies the precision of an SD data type, monochrome image to be 16 bits per pixel.

```
Idntuple              nBandPrecision;         /* Band precision ND 1-tuple        */

unsigned int          uBandPrecision = 16;    /* 16-bit SD data type band precision */


                                              /* Generate image precision tuple   */
nBandPrecision = InGenerateND1Tuple(uBandPrecision);
```

generate_nd_3_tuple

The *generate_nd_3_tuple* convenience function creates a tuple containing three ND data type values. Its API is:

```
Idntuple InGenerateND3Tuple(              /* OUT ND data type 3-tuple identifier  */
    Ipuint          uValue1,              /* first value                          */
    Ipuint          uValue2,              /* second value                         */
    Ipuint          uValue3               /* third value                          */
);
```

This convenience function is the one-step equivalent of allocating and creating an ND data type tuple containing three data values.

■**Example:**   Generation of a tuple that specifies the precision of an ND data type, RGB colour image to be 8 bits per pixel.

```
Idntuple          nBandPrecision;         /* Band precision ND 3-tuple        */

nBandPrecision = InGenerateND3Tuple(8, 8, 8);   /* Generate RGB image precision tuple    */
```

generate_nd_4_tuple   InGenerateND4Tuple

The *generate_nd_4_tuple* convenience function creates a tuple containing four ND data type values. Its API is:

```
Idntuple InGenerateND4Tuple(            /* OUT ND data type 4-tuple identifier   */
    Ipuint          uValue1,            /* first value                           */
    Ipuint          uValue2,            /* second value                          */
    Ipuint          uValue3,            /* third value                           */
    Ipuint          uValue4             /* fourth value                          */
);
```

This convenience function is the one-step equivalent of allocating and creating an ND data type tuple containing four data values.

■**Example:**   Generation of a tuple that specifies the precision of an ND data type, CMYK colour image to be 8 bits per pixel.

```
Idntuple            nBandPrecision;         /* Band precision ND 4-tuple        */

                                            /* Generate CMYK image precision tuple   */
nBandPrecision = InGenerateND4Tuple(8, 8, 8, 8);
```

generate_nd_5_tuple

The *generate_nd_5_tuple* convenience function creates a tuple containing five ND data type values. Its API is:

```
Idntuple InGenerateND5Tuple(          /* OUT ND data type 5-tuple identifier  */
    Ipuint            uValue1,        /* first value                          */
    Ipuint            uValue2,        /* second value                         */
    Ipuint            uValue3,        /* third value                          */
    Ipuint            uValue4,        /* fourth value                         */
    Ipuint            uValue5         /* fifth value                          */
);
```

This convenience function is the one-step equivalent of allocating and creating an ND data type tuple containing five data values.

■**Example:** Generation of a tuple that specifies the size of a ND data type, RGB colour to be 512 × 512 pixels.

```
Idntuple            nSize;              /* Image size 5-tuple                    */

nSize = InGenerateND5Tuple(512, 512, 1, 1, 3);  /* Generate image size tuple     */
```

generate_rd_5_tuple

InGenerateRD5Tuple

The *generate_rd_5_tuple* convenience function creates a tuple containing five RD data type values. Its API is:

```
Idntuple InGenerateRD5Tuple(          /* OUT RD data type 5-tuple identifier  */
    Ipfloat         rValue1,          /* first value                          */
    Ipfloat         rValue2,          /* second value                         */
    Ipfloat         rValue3,          /* third value                          */
    Ipfloat         rValue4,          /* fourth value                         */
    Ipfloat         rValue5           /* fifth value                          */
);
```

This convenience function is the one-step equivalent of allocating and creating an RD data type tuple containing five data values.

■**Example:**   Generation of a tuple that specifies the translation values of an image to be 50.3 pixels horizontally and –60.5 pixels vertically.

```
Idntuple            nOffset;          /* Index offset 5-tuple                 */

                                      /* Generate index offset tuple          */
nOffset = InGenerateRD5Tuple(50.3, -60.5, 0.0, 0.0, 0.0);
```

The *generate_sd_1_tuple* convenience function creates a tuple containing a single SD data type value. Its API is:

```
Idntuple InGenerateSD1Tuple(              /* OUT SD data type 1-tuple identifier  */
    Ipuint            iValue              /* value                                */
);
```

This convenience function is the one-step equivalent of allocating and creating an SD data type tuple containing a single data value.

■**Example:** Generation of a tuple that specifies the data type of a monochrome image to be of ND data type.

```
Idntuple               nBandType;              /* Band data type SD 1-tuple        */

                                               /* Generate band data type tuple    */
    nBandType = InGenerateSD1Tuple(IDATA_TYPE_INTERNAL_ND);
```

generate_sd_3_tuple InGenerateSD3Tuple

The *generate_sd_3_tuple* convenience function creates a tuple containing three SD data type values. Its API is:

```
Idntuple InGenerateSD3Tuple(          /* OUT SD data type 3-tuple identifier  */
    Ipuint          iValue1,          /* first value                          */
    Ipuint          iValue2,          /* second value                         */
    Ipuint          iValue3           /* third value                          */
);
```

This convenience function is the one-step equivalent of allocating and creating an SD data type tuple containing three data values.

■**Example:** Generation of a tuple that specifies the data type of a RGB colour image to be of SD data type.

```
Idntuple            nBandType;                /* Band data type SD 3-tuple           */

                                              /* Generate band data type tuple       */
nBandType = InGenerateSD3Tuple(IDATA_TYPE_INTERNAL_SD, IDATA_TYPE_INTERNAL_SD,
            IDATA_TYPE_INTERNAL_SD);
```

Note: In PIKS Foundation, all bands must be of the same data type.

The *generate_sd_4_tuple* convenience function creates a tuple containing four SD data type values. Its API is:

```
Idntuple InGenerateSD4Tuple(          /* OUT SD data type 4-tuple identifier  */
    Ipint          iValue1,           /* first value                          */
    Ipint          iValue2,           /* second value                         */
    Ipint          iValue3,           /* third value                          */
    Ipint          iValue4            /* fourth value                         */
);
```

This convenience function is the one-step equivalent of allocating and creating an SD data type tuple containing four data values.

■**Example:** Generation of a tuple that specifies the data type of a CMYK colour image to be of SD data type.

```
Idntuple          nBandType;          /* Band data type SD 4-tuple            */

                                      /* Generate band data type tuple        */
nBandType = InGenerateSD4Tuple(IDATA_TYPE_INTERNAL_SD, IDATA_TYPE_INTERNAL_SD,
          IDATA_TYPE_INTERNAL_SD, IDATA_TYPE_INTERNAL_SD);
```

Note: In PIKS Foundation, all bands must be of the same data type.

generate_sd_5_tuple InGenerateSD5Tuple

The *generate_sd_5_tuple* convenience function creates a tuple containing five SD data type values. Its API is:

```
Idntuple InGenerateSD5Tuple(            /* OUT SD data type 5-tuple identifier  */
    Ipint           iValue1,            /* first value                          */
    Ipint           iValue2,            /* second value                         */
    Ipint           iValue3,            /* third value                          */
    Ipint           iValue4,            /* fourth value                         */
    Ipint           iValue5             /* fifth value                          */
);
```

This convenience function is the one-step equivalent of allocating and creating an SD data type tuple containing five data values.

■**Example:**   Generation of a tuple that specifies the offset of a ROI to be 50 pixels horizontally and −100 pixels vertically.

```
Idntuple            nROIOffset;         /* ROI offset SD 5-tuple        */

                                        /* Generate ROI offset tuple    */
nROIOffset = InGenerateSD5Tuple(50, -100, 0, 0, 0);
```

generate_2d_roi_rectangular

The *generate_2d_roi_rectangular* convenience function creates a ROI identifier that specifies the attributes of a two-dimensional rectangular region-of-interest object. Its API is:

```
Idnroi InGenerate2DROIRectangular(          /* OUT ROI identifier              */
    Ipuint          uHorizontal,            /* ROI width                       */
    Ipuint          uVertical,              /* ROI height                      */
    Ipuint          uStartHorizontal,       /* rectangle horizontal start index */
    Ipuint          uStartVertical,         /* rectangle vertical start index  */
    Ipuint          uEndHorizontal,         /* rectangle width                 */
    Ipuint          uEndVertical,           /* rectangle height                */
    Ipepolarity     ePolarityOption         /* polarity of ROI content         */
);
```

This convenience function is the one-step equivalent of allocating and creating the size, start, and end 5-tuples of a rectangular ROI, and then creating it using the *roi_rectangular* tool. See the *roi_rectangular* manpage.

■**Example:**   Generation of a 2D rectangular ROI which is logically TRUE in the region of (100, 200) to (300, 400) in a 512×512 ROI.

```
Idnroi              nROI;                   /* ROI identifier                  */

                                            /* Generate 2D rectangular ROI     */
nROI = InGenerate2DROIRectangular(512, 512, 100, 200, 300, 400, IPOLARITY_TRUE);
```

get_file

The PixelSoft *get_file* utility copies the contents of a file to an application buffer. Its API is:

```
Ipspiks_pixel_types IstGetFile(          /* OUT external data array pointer    */
    char                *tzName          /* File name pointer                  */
);
```

where `Ipspiks_pixel_types` is the name of the following piks.h union that specifies the pixel data type class and the data values of the image to be exported.

```
typedef union{
    Imbool          *tbPixel;        /* external Boolean pixel value pointer  */
    Imuint          *tuPixel;        /* ext. unsigned int pixel value ptr.    */
    Imint           *tiPixel;        /* ext. signed integer pixel pointer     */
    Imfixed         *trPixelFixed;   /* external fixed point pixel pointer    */
} Ipspiks_pixel_types;
```

The contents of the file specified by the file name are copied to an application buffer. This is usually followed by an import of the buffer to PIKS.

■**Example:** Copy a 512×512, ND data type, monochrome image from a file named brainscan and import it to PIKS.

```
#define WIDTH 512                              /* Image width                     */

#define HEIGHT 512                             /* Image height                    */

#define PRECISION 8                            /* Pixel precision                 */

Idnimage            nSrc;                      /* Source image identifier         */

Ipspiks_pixel_types stExtImageArray            /* External image array pointer union */

                                               /* External image array            */
Imuint              uaExtImageArray[HEIGHT][WIDTH],

                    *tuaExtImageArray = &uaExtImageArray[0][0];

                                               /* Application buffer size         */
Ipint               iApplBufferSize = HEIGHT * WIDTH;

                                               /* Post transfer data size pointer */
Ipuint              uDataSize, *tuDataSize = &uDataSize;

stExtImageArray.tuPixel = tuaExtImageArray;    /* Pointer to external image array */

                                               /* Copy file to buffer             */
stExtImageArray.tuPixel = IstGetFile("brainscan").tuPixel;

                                               /* Import image to PIKS from buffer */
nSrc = InImportImage(stExtImageArray, nSrc, PRECISION, IPIXEL_NI_PLANAR,
        iApplBufferSize, 0, tuDataSize);
```

The PixelSoft *key_delay* utility causes program execution to continue after an image is displayed. Its API is:

```
void IvKeyDelay(                            /* no output return            */
void                    *tDisplay           /* pointer to display window   */
);
```

After an image display utility has been invoked, pressing any key while the cursor is within the active display window causes program execution to continue.

■**Example:**   Display of a 512×512, ND data type, monochrome image.

```
Idnimage            nSrcMon;                /* Monochrome image identifier     */

void                *tDisplay;              /* Pointer to display window       */

unsigned int        uWidth = 512;           /* Image width of 512 pixels       */

unsigned int        uHeight = 512;          /* Image height of 512 pixels      */

unsigned int        uBands = 1;             /* One display band                */

                                            /* Open a 1512x512 monochrome window  */
tDisplay = ItOpenWindow(uWidth, uHeight, uBands);

InMonochromeDisplay(nSrcMon, tDisplay);     /* Display monochrome image        */

                                            /* Press key to continue message   */
printf("Press any key in window to continue \n");

IvKeyDelay(tDisplay);                       /* Key delay                       */

IvCloseWindow(tDisplay);                    /* Close window                    */
```

monochrome_display InMonochromeDisplay

The PixelSoft *monochrome_display* utility displays an ND data type, monochrome image in a display window. Its API is:

```
Idnimage InMonochromeDisplay(          /* OUT image identifier          */
Idnimage            nSourceImage,      /* monochrome image identifier   */
void                *tDisplay          /* pointer to display window      */
);
```

This nonstandard utility converts a PIKS monochrome image with a PIKS implementation's internal precision to the precision of a monochrome display frame buffer, typically 8 bits per pixel.

A display window must be opened by the *open_window* utility prior to invocation of the *monochrome_display* utility. If the *key_delay* utility is invoked after the *monochrome_display* utility is invoked, program execution will be halted and the display will be maintained in the window until a key is pressed while the cursor is within the display window.

■**Example:**   Display of a 1024×512, ND data type, monochrome image.

```
Idnimage            nSrcMon;          /* Monochrome image identifier    */

void                *tDisplay;        /* Pointer to display window      */

unsigned int        uWidth = 1024;    /* Image width of 1024 pixels     */

unsigned int        uHeight = 512;    /* Image height of 512 pixels     */

unsigned int        uBands = 1;       /* One display band               */

                                      /* Open a 1024x512 monochrome window */
tDisplay = ItOpenWindow(uWidth, uHeight, uBands);

InMonochromeDisplay(nSrcMon, tDisplay);   /* Display monochrome image   */

IvKeyDelay(tDisplay);                 /* Press key to continue          */

IvCloseWindow(tDisplay);              /* Close window                   */
```

open_window

The PixelSoft *open_window* utility opens a monochrome or colour display window. Its API is:

```
void *ItOpenWindow(                        /* no output return          */
    Ipuint          uWidth,                /* window width              */
    Ipuint          uHeight,               /* window height             */
    Ipuint          uBands                 /* window bands              */
);
```

This nonstandard utility opens a display window of a frame buffer. For a monochrome display, the number of window bands is one. For a colour or pseudocolour display, the number of display bands is three.

The display window consists of a window frame around the image to be displayed. The screen contents prior to invocation of the *open_window* utility will be seen until an image is caused to be displayed. If the *key_delay* utility is invoked after the *monochrome_display* or *colour_display* utility is invoked, program execution will be halted and the display will be maintained in the window until a key is pressed while the cursor is within the display window.

■**Example:** Display of 512×512, ND data type, monochrome and colour images in separate windows.

```
Idnimage            nSrcMon;               /* Monochrome image identifier        */

Idnimage            nSrcColour;            /* Colour image identifier            */

void                *tDisplayMon;          /* Pointer to monochrome display window */

void                *tDisplayColour;       /* Pointer to colour display window    */

unsigned int        uWidth = 512;          /* Image width of 512 pixels          */

unsigned int        uHeight = 512;         /* Image height of 512 pixels         */

unsigned int        uMonBands = 1;         /* One monochrome display band        */

unsigned int        uColourBands = 3;      /* Three colour display bands         */


                                           /* Open a 512x512 monochrome window   */
tDisplayMon = ItOpenWindow(uWidth, uHeight, uMonBands);

InMonochromeDisplay(nSrcMon, tDisplayMon); /* Display monochrome image           */

IvKeyDelay(tDisplayMon);                   /* Press key to continue              */

                                           /* Open a 512x512 colour window       */
tDisplayColour = ItOpenWindow(uWidth, uHeight, uColourBands);

InColourDisplay(nSrcColour, tDisplayColour); /* Display colour image             */

IvKeyDelay(tDisplayColour);                /* Press key to continue              */

IvCloseWindow(tDisplayMon);                /* Close monochrome window            */

IvCloseWindow(tDisplayColour);             /* Close colour window                */
```

prepare_colour_image

The *prepare_colour_image* convenience function allocates a colour image and specifies its attributes. Its API is:

```
Idnimage InPrepareColourImage(          /* OUT image identifier             */
Ipuint          uHorizontal,            /* image width                     */
Ipuint          uVertical,              /* image height                    */
Ipuint          uBands,                 /* image bands                     */
Ipint           iType,                  /* image data type                 */
Ipuint          uPrecision,             /* image precision                 */
Ipfloat         rXWhite,                /* X tristimulus value white point */
Ipfloat         rYWhite,                /* Y tristimulus value white point */
Ipfloat         rZWhite,                /* Z tristimulus value white point */
Ipint           iColourOption           /* image colour space code         */
);
```

This convenience function is a one-step equivalent of allocating and creating the image size, band data type, and band precision tuples, specifying the white point and colour option, and then allocating the image using the *allocate_image* mechanism. See the *allocate_image* manpage.

■**Example:**   Allocation of a 512 × 512 pixel, linear NTSC illuminant C RGB colour, ND data type image.

```
Idnimage        nImage;                 /* Image identifier                */

Ipfloat         rXWhite = 0.981;        /* X tristimulus value white point */

Ipfloat         rYWhite = 1.000;        /* Y tristimulus value white point */

Ipfloat         rZWhite = 1.182;        /* Z tristimulus value white point */

Ipuint          uPrecision = 8;         /* Band precision of 8 bits per pixel */

                                        /* Prepare colour image            */
nImage = InPrepareColourImage(512, 512, 3, IDATA_TYPE_INTERNAL_ND, uPrecision, rXWhite,
        rYWhite, rZWhite, ICOLOUR_LIN_NTSC_C_RGB);
```

prepare_monochrome_image

The *prepare_monochrome_image* convenience function allocates a monochrome image and specifies its attributes. Its API is:

```
Idnimage InPrepareMonochromeImage(      /* OUT image identifier    */
Ipuint              uHorizontal,        /* image width             */
Ipuint              uVertical,          /* image height            */
Ipint               iType,              /* image data type         */
Ipuint              uPrecision          /* image precision         */
);
```

This convenience function is a one-step equivalent of allocating and creating the image size, band data type, and band precision tuples, and then allocating the image using the *allocate_image* mechanism. See the *allocate_image* manpage.

■**Example:** Allocation of a 1024×1024 monochrome, SD data type image.

```
Idnimage            nImage;             /* Image identifier              */

Ipuint              uPrecision = 16;    /* Image precision of 16 bits per pixel */

                                        /* Prepare monochrome image      */
nImage = InPrepareMonochromeImage(1024, 1024, IDATA_TYPE_INTERNAL_SD, uPrecision);
```

prepare_2d_roi_rectangular

InPrepare2DROIRectangular

The *prepare_2d_roi_rectangular* convenience function allocates a two-dimensional rectangular region-of-interest object and specifies its attributes. Its API is:

```
Idnroi InPrepare2DROIRectangular(      /* OUT ROI identifier        */
Ipuint             uHorizontal,        /* ROI width                 */
Ipuint             uVertical,          /* ROI height                */
Ipepolarity        ePolarityOption     /* ROI polarity option       */
);
```

This convenience function is a one-step equivalent of allocating and creating the ROI size tuple and its polarity option, and then allocating the ROI using the *allocate_roi* mechanism. See the *allocate_roi* manpage.

■**Example:** Allocation of a 512×512 rectangular ROI that is logically FALSE within a rectangle.

```
Idnroi             nROI;              /* ROI identifier            */

                                      /* Prepare 2D rectangular ROI */
nROI = InPrepare2DROIRectangular(512, 512, IPOLARITY_FALSE);
```

pseudocolour_display

The PixelSoft *pseudocolour_display* utility displays an ND data type, monochrome image in a colour display window. Its API is:

```
Idnimage InPseudocolourDisplay(        /* OUT image identifier            */
Idnimage              nSourceImage,    /* monochrome image identifier     */
void                  *tDisplay        /* pointer to display window       */
);
```

This nonstandard utility converts a PIKS monochrome image with a PIKS implementation's internal precision to the precision of a pseudocolour display frame buffer, typically 3 bits per pixel for the red and green components and 2 bits per pixel for the blue component. The utility passes the display buffer pixels through a pseudocolour map for display.

A display window must be opened by the *open_window* utility prior to invocation of the *pseudocolour_display* utility. If the *key_delay* utility is invoked after the *pseudocolour_display* utility is invoked, program execution will be halted and the display will be maintained in the window until a key is pressed while the cursor is within the display window.

■**Example:** Display of a 512×512, ND data type, monochrome image as a pseudocolour image.

```
Idnimage              nSrcMon;           /* Monochrome image identifier      */

void                  *tDisplay;         /* Pointer to display window        */

unsigned int          uWidth = 512;      /* Image width of 512 pixels        */

unsigned int          uHeight = 512;     /* Image height of 512 pixels       */

unsigned int          uBands = 3;        /* Three display bands              */


                                         /* Open a 512x512 colour window     */
tDisplay = ItOpenWindow(uWidth, uHeight, uBands);

InPseudocolourDisplay(nSrcMon, tDisplay);  /* Display pseudocolour image     */

IvKeyDelay(tDisplay);                      /* Press key to continue          */

IvCloseWindow(tDisplay);                   /* Close window                   */
```

Note: The display may show colour artifacts if the system cursor is not placed within the display window.

put_file

The PixelSoft *put_file* utility copies the contents of an application buffer to a file. Its API is:

```
void IvPutFile(                                /* no output return                  */
    Ipspiks_pixel_types stPixels,              /* external image data pointer union */
    char                *tzName,               /* file name                         */
    Ipuint              uHorizontal,           /* image width                       */
    Ipuint              uVertical,             /* image height                      */
    Ipuint              uPrecision,            /* band precision                    */
    Ipuint              uBands                 /* number of bands                   */
);
```

where `Ipspiks_pixel_types` is the name of the following piks.h union that specifies the pixel data type class and the data values of the image to be exported.

```
typedef union{
Imbool               *tbPixel;                 /* external Boolean pixel value pointer */
Imuint               *tuPixel;                 /* ext. unsigned int pixel value ptr.   */
Imint                *tiPixel;                 /* ext. signed integer pixel pointer    */
Imfixed              *trPixelFixed;            /* external fixed point pixel pointer   */
} Ipspiks_pixel_types;
```

The contents of an application buffer containing an image are copied to a specified file.

■**Example:** Export a 512×512, ND data type, monochrome image and copy it to a file named "test_image."

```
#define WIDTH 512                              /* Image width                       */

#define HEIGHT 512                             /* Image height                      */

#define BANDS 1                                /* Image bands                       */

#define PRECISION 8                            /* Pixel precision                   */

Idnimage            nDst;                      /* Image identifier                  */


Ipspiks_pixel_types stExtImageArray            /* External image array pointer union */

                                               /* External image array              */
Imuint              uaExtImageArray[HEIGHT][WIDTH],
                    *tuaExtImageArray = &uaExtImageArray[0][0];

                                               /* Application buffer size           */
Ipint               iApplBufferSize = HEIGHT * WIDTH;

                                               /* Post transfer data size pointer   */
Ipuint              uDataSize, *tuDataSize = &uDataSize;

stExtImageArray.tuPixel = tuaExtImageArray;    /* Pointer to external image array   */

                                               /* Export image to buffer            */
IstExportImage(nDst, stExtImageArray, PRECISION, IPIXEL_NI_PLANAR,
    iApplBufferSize, 0, tuDataSize);

                                               /* Copy buffer to file               */
IvPutFile(stExtImageArray, "test_image", WIDTH, HEIGHT, PRECISION, BANDS);
```

APPENDIX A

Definitions of Mathematical Symbols and Functions

This appendix provides a notational guide and reference to common mathematical symbols and functions used within this Guide. Appendix A also provides notation and definitions for special mathematical symbols functions used to define PIKS.

A.1 Conventional Mathematical Symbols

+	Plus or positive symbol
−	Minus or negative symbol
×	Multiply symbol
/	Divide symbol
÷	Integer divide symbol
<	Less than symbol
≤	Less than or equal to symbol
>	Greater than symbol
≥	Greater than or equal to symbol
I[.]I	Magnitude of argument symbol
∪	Boolean union symbol
∩	Boolean intersection symbol
$\overline{[.]}$	Complement overbar symbol
⊕	Logical AND symbol
⊖	Logical OR symbol
⊗	Logical XOR symbol

A.2 Mathematical Functions

ATAN2   Arc tangent ratio function

$$\text{ATAN } 2 \{ a, b \} = \arctan \left[\frac{a}{b} \right] \quad 0 \leq \text{ATAN } 2\{a, b\} < 2\pi$$

CHOICE   Choice function

$$j = \text{CHOICE}\{x, y, y, z, t, b\}$$

The variable j is equated to $x, y, z, t,$ or b.

COS   Cosine function

$$\text{COS}\{a\} = \cos(a)$$

LIV   lowest integer value function

$$\text{LIV}\{a\} = p \quad\quad \text{if } p \leq a < p + 1$$

where a is a real number and p is an integer number

LOOK   Lookup table function

$$d(b) = \text{LOOK}\{s, f, b, \text{id}\}$$

The lookup table referenced by the table identifier, id, has E entries and B cells per entry. The unsigned integer input to the lookup table, s, is biased negatively by the table offset, f, where $f \geq 0$, to form the lookup table entry cell index

$$e = s - f$$

The content of the lookup table cell, $T(b,e)$, for $0 \leq b \leq B - 1$ and $0 \leq e \leq E - 1$ is assigned to the table output, $d(b)$.

MAX   Maximum of sequence function

$$\text{MAX}\{s(1), s(2), \dots, s(q), \dots, s(Q)\} = s(p)$$

where $s(p)$ is an element of the sequence for which $s(p) \geq s(q)$ for all q.

MIN   Minimum of sequence function

$$\text{MIN}\{s(1), s(2), \dots, s(q), \dots, s(Q)\} = s(p)$$

where $s(p)$ is an element of the sequence for which $s(p) \leq s(q)$ for all q.

MOD   Modulus function

$$\text{MOD}\{p, q\} = p - q \times (p - q)$$

where p and q are integer numbers.

NIV   Nearest integer value function

$\text{NIV}\{a\} = p$ if $p \le a < p + 1/2$

$\text{NIV}\{a\} = p + 1$ if $p + 1/2 \le p < p + 1$

where a is a real number and p is an integer number.

RES_2 Two-dimensional resampling function

$D(x, y, 0, 0, b) = \text{RES}_2\{S, x', y', 0, 0, b\}$

The function RES_2 is defined indirectly by the following computational steps.

$D(x, y, 0, 0, b) = S(x', y', 0, 0, b)$

where for support 1, nearest neighbour resampling

$S(x', y', 0, 0, b) = S(x'', y'', 0, 0, b)$

and

$x' = G_x\{x, y, 0, 0, b\}$
$y' = G_y\{x, y, 0, 0, b\}$
$x'' = \text{LIV}\{x\}$
$y'' = \text{LIV}\{y\}$

The functions $G_x\{.\}$ and $G_y\{.\}$ represent the geometrical transformation equations of a particular geometric operation, e.g., rotate.

For support 2, bilinear interpolation resampling

$$S(x', y', 0, 0, b) = \sum_{x_o = 0}^{1} \sum_{y_o = 0}^{1} S(x'' + x_o, y'' + y_o, 0, 0, b) \, R(x' - x'' - x_o) \, R(y' - y'' - y_o)$$

where

$R(u) = u + 1$ $-1 \le u < 0$

$R(u) = 1 - u$ $0 \le u \le 1$

SIN   Sine function

$\text{SIN}\{a\} = \sin(a)$

APPENDIX B

PIKS Header

The following sections describe the content of the *piks.h* PIKS Foundation header file that is relevant to an application writer.

B.1 External Physical Image Data Types

The following are the typedef declarations of the piks.h external physical image data types.

```
typedef         unsigned char      Imbool;      /*  BI data type                */
typedef         unsigned char      Imuint;      /*  NI data type                */
typedef         int                Imint;       /*  SI data type                */
typedef         int                Imfixed;     /*  TI data type                */
```

B.2 Parameter Data Types

The following are the typedef declarations of the *piks.h* parameter data types.

```
typedef         unsigned char      Ipbool;      /*  BP data type                */
typedef         unsigned long int  Ipuint;      /*  NP data type                */
typedef         int                Ipint;       /*  SP data type                */
typedef         float              Ipfloat;     /*  RP data type                */
```

B.3   Data Object Identifiers

The following are the typedef declarations of the piks.h data objects.

```
typedef          void        *Idnchain;         /* PIKS internal chain object    */

typedef          void        *Idnhist;          /* PIKS histogram               */

typedef          void        *Idnimage;         /* PIKS image                   */

typedef          void        *Idnlut;           /* PIKS lookup table            */

typedef          void        *Idnmatrix;        /* PIKS matrix                  */

typedef          void        *Idnnbhood;        /* PIKS neighbourhood array     */

typedef          void        *Idnrepository;    /* PIKS repository              */

typedef          void        *Idnroi;           /* PIKS region of interest      */

typedef          void        *Idntuple;         /* PIKS tuple                   */

typedef          FILE         *Ipnerror;         /* external error file          */
```

B.4   Enumerated Type Definitions

The following are the enumerated data type definitions in *piks.h*.

Binary Event Option

```
typedef enum {
    IBINARY_EVENT_ON,                    /* yes or on                     */
    IBINARY_EVENT_OFF                    /* no or off                     */
} Ipebinary_event;
```

Chain States

```
typedef enum {
    ICHAIN_BUILD,                        /* building chain state          */
    ICHAIN_EXECUTE,                      /* executing chain state         */
    ICHAIN_NOT                           /* not in any chain state        */
} Ipechain_state;
```

Dimension Option

```
typedef enum{
    IDIMENSION_1D,                       /* one dimension                 */
    IDIMENSION_2D,                       /* two dimension                 */
    IDIMENSION_3D,                       /* three dimension               */
    IDIMENSION_4D,                       /* four dimension                */
    IDIMENSION_5D                        /* five dimension                */
} Ipedimension;
```

Error Report Modes

```
typedef enum{
    IERROR_REPORT_ACTIVE,                /* error reporting active        */
    IERROR_REPORT_INACTIVE               /* error reporting inactive      */
} Ipeerror_report_mode;
```

Error States

```
typedef enum{
    IERROR_SUBSTATE,                     /* error substate condition exists */
    IERROR_NO                            /* no error condition            */
} Ipeerror_state;
```

Flip, Spin, Transpose Options

```
typedef enum{
    IFLIP_TOP_BOTTOM,                       /* top-to-bottom flip                    */
    IFLIP_LEFT_RIGHT,                       /* left-to-right flip                    */
    ISPIN_90_DEGREES_CCW,                   /* 90 degrees counterclockwise spin      */
    ISPIN_180_DEGREES_CCW,                  /* 180 degrees counterclockwise spin     */
    ISPIN_270_DEGREES_CCW,                  /* 270 degrees counterclockwise spin     */
    ITRANSPOSE_UPLEFT_LOWRIGHT,             /* transpose, upper left to lower right  */
    ITRANSPOSE_LOWLEFT_UPRIGHT              /* transpose, lower left to upper right  */
} Ipeflip;
```

Index Assignment Modes

```
typedef enum {
    IINDEX_ASSIGNMENT_ON,                   /* index assignment operative            */
    IINDEX_ASSIGNMENT_OFF                   /* index assignment inoperative          */
} Ipeindex_mode;
```

Match Point Modes

```
typedef enum {
    IMATCH_POINT_ON,                        /* match point adjustment operative      */
    IMATCH_POINT_OFF                        /* match point adjustment inoperative    */
} Ipematch_mode;
```

Operational States

```
typedef enum{
    IPIKS_OPERATION_CLOSED,                 /* PIKS closed                           */
    IPIKS_OPERATION_OPEN                    /* PIKS open                             */
} Ipepiks_operation_state;
```

Polarity Option

```
typedef enum{
    IPOLARITY_TRUE,                         /* TRUE state                            */
    IPOLARITY_FALSE                         /* FALSE state                           */
} Ipepolarity;
```

Processing Mode Option

```
typedef enum{
    IPROCESS_MODE_0,                        /* processing mode zero                  */
    IPROCESS_MODE_1,                        /* processing mode one                   */
    IPROCESS_MODE_2,                        /* processing mode two                   */
    IPROCESS_MODE_3,                        /* processing mode three                 */
    IPROCESS_MODE_4                         /* processing mode four                  */
} Ipeprocess;
```

ROI Control Modes

```
typedef enum{
    IROI_CONTROL_ON,                        /* ROI control operative                 */
    IROI_CONTROL_OFF                        /* ROI control inoperative               */
} Iperoi_control_mode;
```

ROI Process Modes

```
typedef enum {
    IROI_PROCESS_ON,                        /* ROI process operative                 */
    IROI_PROCESS_OFF                        /* ROI process inoperative               */
} Iperoi_process_mode;
```

Synchronicity Modes

```
typedef enum{
    ISYNCHRONICITY_MODE_SYNCH,              /* synchronous mode                      */
    ISYNCHRONICITY_MODE_ASYNCH              /* asynchronous mode                     */
} Ipesynchronicity_state;
```

Synchronicity State

```
typedef enum {
    ISYNCHRONICITY_STATE_SYNCH,          /* synchonous state        */
    ISYNCHRONICITY_STATE_ASYNCH          /* asynchonous state       */
} Ipesynchronicity_state;
```

Validity Indicator

```
typedef enum{
    IVALIDITY_VALID,                     /* data is valid and available  */
    IVALIDITY_INVALID                    /* data is not valid            */
} Ipevalidity;
```

B.5   Data Type Union Definitions

The following are the typedef declarations of the piks.h data type unions.

Array Identifier

```
typedef union{
    Idnmatrix          nMatrix;          /* matrix identifier            */
    Idnnbhood          nNbhood;          /* neighbourhood array identifier */
} Ipsarray_id;
```

Nonimage Attributes

```
typedef union{
    Ipattrs_hist       *tsHist;          /* histogram attributes pointer    */
    Ipattrs_lut        *tsLUT;           /* lookup table attributes pointer */
    Ipattrs_matrix     *tsMatrix;        /* matrix attributes pointer       */
    Ipattrs_nbhood     *tsNbhoods;       /* nbhood array attributes pointer */
    Ipattrs_roi_rectangular
                       *tsROIRectangular; /* ROI rectangular attributes pointer */
    Ipattrs_tuple      *tsTuple;         /* tuple attributes pointer        */
} Ipsattrs_non_image;
```

Internal Nonimage Object Identifiers

```
typedef union{
    Idnhist            nHist;            /* histogram identifier            */
    Idnlut             nLUT;             /* lookup table identifier         */
    Idnmatrix          nMatrix;          /* matrix identifier               */
    Idnnbhood          nNbhood;          /* neighbourhood identifier        */
    Idnroi             nROI;             /* region of interest identifier   */
    Idntuple           nTuple;           /* tuple identifier                */
} Ipsnon_image_object;
```

Internal Object Identifiers

```
typedef union{
    Idnhist            nHist;            /* histogram identifier            */
    Idnimage           nImage;           /* image identifier                */
    Idnlut             nLUT;             /* lookup table identifier         */
    Idnmatrix          nMatrix;          /* matrix identifier               */
    Idnnbhood          nNbhood;          /* neighbourhood identifier        */
    Idnrepository      nRepository;      /* repository identifier           */
    Idnroi             nROI;             /* region of interest identifier   */
    Idntuple           nTuple;           /* tuple identifier                */
} Ipsobject;
```

Arithmetic Parameter

```
typedef union{
    Ipuint             *tuArith;         /* unsigned integer pointer        */
    Ipint              *tiArith;         /* signed integer pointer          */
    Ipfloat            *trArithFloat;    /* float pointer                   */
} Ipsparameter_arith;
```

Basic Parameter

```
typedef union{
    Ipbool          *tbParameter;          /* Boolean pointer                     */
    Ipuint          *tuParameter;          /* nonnegative integer pointer         */
    Ipint           *tiParameter;          /* signed integer pointer              */
    Ipfloat         *trParameterFloat;     /* float pointer                       */
    char            *tcParameter;          /* character pointer                   */
} Ipsparameter_basic;
```

Colour Parameter

```
typedef union {
    Ipbool          *tbColour;             /* Boolean pointer                     */
    Ipuint          *tuColour;             /* nonnegative integer pointer         */
    Ipint           *tiColour;             /* signed integer pointer              */
    Ipfloat         *trColourFloat;        /* float pointer                       */
} Ipsparameter_colour;
```

Logical Parameter

```
typedef union{
    Ipbool          *tbLogical;            /* Boolean pointer                     */
    Ipuint          *tuLogical;            /* unsigned integer pointer            */
    Ipint           *tiLogical;            /* signed integer pointer              */
} Ipsparameter_logical;
```

Numeric Parameter

```
typedef union{
    Ipuint          *tuNumeric;            /* unsigned integer pointer            */
    Ipint           *tiNumeric;            /* signed integer pointer              */
    Ipfloat         *trNumericFloat;       /* float pointer                       */
} Ipsparameter_numeric;
```

Pixel Parameter

```
typedef union{
    Ipbool          *tbPixel;              /* Boolean pointer                     */
    Ipuint          *tuPixel;              /* nonnegative integer pointer         */
    Ipint           *tiPixel;              /* signed integer pointer              */
    Ipfloat         *trPixelFloat;         /* float pointer                       */
} Ipsparameter_pixel;
```

External Physical Image Data Types

```
typedef union{
    Imbool          *tbPixel;              /* external Boolean pixel value pointer */
    Imuint          *tuPixel;              /* ext unsigned int pixel value pointer */
    Imint           *tiPixel;              /* ext signed integer pixel pointer     */
    Imfixed         *trPixelFixed;         /* external fixed point pixel pointer   */
} Ipspiks_pixel_types;
```

B.6   Structure Type Definitions

The following are the typedef declarations of the piks.h structures.

Attributes, Histogram

```
typedef struct{
    Ipuint          uHistSize;             /* histogram size                      */
    Ipfloat         rLowerBound;           /* lower amplitude bound               */
    Ipfloat         rUpperBound;           /* upper amplitude bound               */
} Ipsattrs_hist;
```

Attributes, Image

```
typedef struct{
    Idntuple        nImageSize;              /* image size 5-tuple identifier      */
    Idntuple        nBandType;               /* band data types B-tuple identifier */
    Idntuple        nBandPrecision;          /* band precision B-tuple identifier  */
    Ipfloat         rXWhite;                 /* X tristimulus value white point    */
    Ipfloat         rYWhite;                 /* Y tristimulus value white point    */
    Ipfloat         rZWhite;                 /* Z tristimulus value white point    */
    Ipint           iImageStructureOption;   /* image structure option             */
    Ipint           iColourOption;           /* colour space option                */
} Ipsattrs_image;
```

Attributes, Lookup Table

```
typedef struct{
    Ipuint          uTableEntries;           /* table entries                      */
    Ipuint          uTableBands;             /* table bands                        */
    Ipint           iInputTypeOption;        /* table input data type option code  */
    Ipint           iOutputTypeOption;       /* table output data type option code */
} Ipsattrs_lut;
```

Attributes, Matrix

```
typedef struct{
    Ipuint          uColumnSize;             /* matrix column size                 */
    Ipuint          uRowSize;                /* matrix row size                    */
    Ipint           iTypeOption;             /* matrix data type option code       */
} Ipsattrs_matrix;
```

Attributes, Neighbourhood Array

```
typedef struct{
    Idntuple        nArraySize;              /* nbhood array size 5-tuple identifier */
    Idntuple        nKeyPixel;               /* nbhood array key pixel 5-tuple id.   */
    Ipint           iScaleFactor;            /* nbhood array scale factor            */
    Ipint           iLabelOption;            /* nbhood array semantic label option   */
    Ipint           iTypeOption;             /* nbhood array data type option        */
} Ipsattrs_nbhood;
```

Attributes, ROI

```
typedef struct{
    Idntuple        nROISize;                /* ROI size 5-tuple identifier        */
    Ipint           iStructureOption;        /* ROI structure option               */
    Ipepolarity     ePolarityOption;         /* ROI polarity option                */
} Ipsattrs_roi;
```

Attributes, ROI Rectangular

```
typedef struct{
    Idntuple        nROISize;                /* ROI size 5-tuple                   */
    Idntuple        nRectangleStart;         /* rectangle start position 5-tuple   */
    Idntuple        nRectangleEnd;           /* rectangle end position 5-tuple     */
    Idntuple        nIndexManipulation;      /* manipulation 5-tuple               */
    Ipedimension    eDimensionOption;        /* dimension option                   */
    Ipepolarity     ePolarityOption;         /* polarity option                    */
} Ipsattrs_roi_rectangular;
```

Attributes, Tuple

```
typedef struct{
    Ipuint          uTupleSize;              /* tuple size                         */
    Ipint           iTypeOption;             /* tuple data type option             */
} Ipsattrs_tuple;
```

Bindings, Image

```
typedef struct{
    Idntuple            nMatch;                 /* match point 5-tuple            */
    Idnroi              nROI;                   /* ROI identifier                 */
    Idntuple            nOffset;                /* ROI offset 5-tuple             */
} Ipsbind_image;
```

Draw Pixels Image Collection Element

```
typedef struct{
    Ipuint              uHorizontal;            /* horizontal coordinate value    */
    Ipuint              uVertical;              /* vertical coordinate value      */
    Ipuint              uDepth;                 /* depth coordinate value         */
    Ipuint              uTemporal;              /* temporal coordinate value      */
    Ipuint              uBand;                  /* band coordinate value          */
    union {                                     /* pixel value union              */
            Ipbool      bValue;                 /* Boolean value                  */
            Ipuint      uValue;                 /* unsigned integer value         */
            Ipint       iValue;                 /* signed integer value           */
    } sPixel;
} Ipsdraw_pixels;
```

Inquire PIKS Implementation Information

```
typedef struct
    char                zProfile[IL_PROFILE];   /* conformance profile label        */
    Idntuple            nDimensionLimit;        /* maximum dimension sizes identifier */
    Ipint               iNDPrecision;           /* storage precision of ND data type */
    Ipint               iSDPrecision;           /* storage precision of SD data type */
    Ipint               iRDPrecision;           /* storage precision of RD data type */
    char                zRD[IL_REAL];           /* implementation method RD data type */
    char                *tzInformation;         /* implementation information pointer */
    Ipebinary_event     eAsynch;                /* asynchronous support             */
} Ipspiks_impl;
```

PIKS Modes

```
typedef struct{
    Iperoi_control_mode     eROIControlMode;        /* ROI control mode              */
    Iperoi_process_mode     eROIProcessMode;        /* ROI processing mode           */
    Ipematch_mode           eMatchPointMode;        /* match point control mode      */
    Ipeindex_mode           eIndexAssignmentMode;   /* index assignment mode         */
    Ipesynchronicity_mode   eSynchronicityMode;     /* sychronicity mode             */
    Ipeerror_report_mode    eErrorReportMode;       /* error report mode             */
    Ipint                   iImageResampleMode;     /* image resampling selection mode */
    Ipint                   iROIResampleMode;       /* ROI resampling selection mode */
} Ipspiks_modes;
```

PIKS States

```
typedef struct{
    Ipepiks_operation_state eOperationState;        /* operational state             */
    Ipechain_state          eChainState;            /* chain state                   */
    Ipeerror_state          eErrorState;            /* error state                   */
    Ipesynchronicity_state  eSynchronicity_state;   /* synchronocity state           */
} Ipspiks_states;
```

B.7   Macro Definitions

The following are the definitions of the piks.h #define macros. Some of the #define options are not allowed in PIKS Foundation, but are supported in other PIKS profiles. The element manual pages indicate the nonallowed options.

Bit Shift Options

```
#define    IBIT_SHIFT_LEFT_OVERFLOW        1    /* left overflow shift        */
#define    IBIT_SHIFT_RIGHT_OVERFLOW       2    /* right overflow shift       */
#define    IBIT_SHIFT_LEFT_BARREL          3    /* left barrel shift          */
#define    IBIT_SHIFT_RIGHT_BARREL         4    /* right barrel shift         */
#define    IBIT_SHIFT_LEFT_ARITH           5    /* left arithmetic shift      */
#define    IBIT_SHIFT_RIGHT_ARITH          6    /* right arithmetic shift     */
```

Boolean Values

```
#define    IBOOL_FALSE                     0    /* FALSE Boolean value        */
#define    IBOOL_TRUE                      1    /* TRUE Boolean value         */
```

Colour Conversion Subtractive, Direction Options

```
#define    ICOLOUR_DIRECTION_RGB_CMY       1    /* RGB to CMY option          */
#define    ICOLOUR_DIRECTION_RGB_CMYK      2    /* RGB to CMYK option         */
#define    ICOLOUR_DIRECTION_CMY_RGB       3    /* CMY to RGB option          */
#define    ICOLOUR_DIRECTION_CMYK_RGB      4    /* CMYK to RGB option         */
```

Colour Conversion Subtractive, Method Options

```
#define    ICOLOUR_METHOD_SIMPLE           1    /* Simple conversion          */
#define    ICOLOUR_METHOD_IMPL_DEPENDENT   2    /* Implementation dep. conv.  */
```

Colour Space Options

```
#define    ICOLOUR_NONE                    1    /* unspecified                */
#define    ICOLOUR_NON_STANDARD_RGB        2    /* nonstandard RGB            */
#define    ICOLOUR_LIN_CCIR_D65_RGB        3    /* linear CCIR illuminant D65 RGB  */
#define    ICOLOUR_LIN_CIE_E_RGB           4    /* linear CIE illuminant E RGB */
#define    ICOLOUR_LIN_EBU_C_RGB           5    /* linear EBU illuminant C RGB */
#define    ICOLOUR_LIN_EBU_D65_RGB         6    /* linear EBU illuminant D65 RGB  */
#define    ICOLOUR_LIN_NTSC_C_RGB          7    /* linear NTSC illuminant C RGB   */
#define    ICOLOUR_LIN_NTSC_D65_RGB        8    /* linear NTSC illuminant D65 RGB */
#define    ICOLOUR_LIN_SMPTE_D65_RGB       9    /* linear SMPTE illuminant D65 RGB */
#define    ICOLOUR_GAMMA_CCIR_D65_RGB     10    /* gamma CCIR illuminant D65 RGB  */
#define    ICOLOUR_GAMMA_EBU_C_RGB        11    /* gamma EBU illuminant C RGB  */
#define    ICOLOUR_GAMMA_EBU_D65_RGB      12    /* gamma EBU illuminant D65 RGB   */
#define    ICOLOUR_GAMMA_NTSC_C_RGB       13    /* gamma NTSC illuminant C RGB */
#define    ICOLOUR_GAMMA_NTSC_D65_RGB     14    /* gamma NTSC illuminant D65 RGB  */
#define    ICOLOUR_GAMMA_SMPTE_D65_RGB    15    /* gamma NTSC illuminant D65 RGB  */
#define    ICOLOUR_LUM_CHR_EBU_C_YUV      16    /* lum/chr EBU illuminant C YUV   */
#define    ICOLOUR_LUM_CHR_EBU_D65_YUV    17    /* lum/chr EBU illuminant D65 YUV */
#define    ICOLOUR_LUM_CHR_NTSC_C_YIQ     18    /* lum/chr NTSC illuminant C YIQ  */
#define    ICOLOUR_LUM_CHR_NTSC_D65_YIQ   19    /* lum/chr NTSC illuminant D65 YIQ */
#define    ICOLOUR_LUM_CHR_SMPTE_D65_YCBCR 20   /* lum/chr SMPTE illuminant D65 YCbCr */
#define    ICOLOUR_CIE_XYZ                21    /* CIE XYZ                    */
#define    ICOLOUR_CIE_UVW               22    /* CIE UVW                    */
#define    ICOLOUR_CIE_YXY              23    /* CIE Yxy                    */
#define    ICOLOUR_CIE_YUV              24    /* CIE Yuv                    */
#define    ICOLOUR_CIE_LAB             25    /* CIE L*a*b*                 */
#define    ICOLOUR_CIE_LUV             26    /* CIE L*u*v*                 */
#define    ICOLOUR_IHS                 27    /* IHS                        */
#define    ICOLOUR_CMY                 28    /* CMY                        */
#define    ICOLOUR_CMYK                29    /* CMYK                       */
```

Convolve, 2D Options

```
#define    ICONVOLVE_UPPER_LEFT            1    /* upper left corner justified */
#define    ICONVOLVE_ENCLOSED              2    /* enclosed array             */
#define    ICONVOLVE_KEY_ZERO              3    /* key pixel, zero exterior   */
#define    ICONVOLVE_KEY_REFLECTED         4    /* key pixel, reflected exterior */
```

Data Type (Internal) Options

```
#define    IDATA_TYPE_INTERNAL_BD          1    /* Boolean                    */
#define    IDATA_TYPE_INTERNAL_ND          2    /* unsigned integer           */
#define    IDATA_TYPE_INTERNAL_SD          3    /* signed integer             */
#define    IDATA_TYPE_INTERNAL_RD          4    /* real arithmetic            */
```

Dyadic, Arithmetic Combination Options

```
#define    IDYADIC_ABSOLUTE              1     /* absolute value difference      */
#define    IDYADIC_ADDITION              2     /* addition                       */
#define    IDYADIC_ADDITION_SCALED       3     /* addition, scaled               */
#define    IDYADIC_ARCTANGENT            4     /* arctangent                     */
#define    IDYADIC_DIVISION              5     /* division                       */
#define    IDYADIC_MAXIMUM               6     /* maximum                        */
#define    IDYADIC_MINIMUM               7     /* minimum                        */
#define    IDYADIC_MULTIPLICATION        8     /* multiplication                 */
#define    IDYADIC_SUBTRACTION           9     /* subtraction                    */
#define    IDYADIC_SUBTRACTION_SCALED    10    /* subtraction, scaled            */
```

Dyadic, Logical Combination Options

```
#define    IDYADIC_LOGICAL_AND           1     /* bitwise AND                    */
#define    IDYADIC_LOGICAL_NAND          2     /* bitwise NAND                   */
#define    IDYADIC_LOGICAL_NOR           3     /* bitwise NOR                    */
#define    IDYADIC_LOGICAL_OR            4     /* bitwise OR                     */
#define    IDYADIC_LOGICAL_XOR           5     /* bitwise XOR                    */
#define    IDYADIC_LOGICAL_INTERSECTION  6     /* Boolean intersection           */
#define    IDYADIC_LOGICAL_UNION         7     /* Boolean union                  */
```

Dyadic Predicate Combination Options

```
#define    IDYADIC_PREDICATE_GREATER        1  /* greater than                   */
#define    IDYADIC_PREDICATE_GREATER_EQUAL  2  /* greater than or equal to       */
#define    IDYADIC_PREDICATE_LESS           3  /* less than                      */
#define    IDYADIC_PREDICATE_LESS_EQUAL     4  /* less than or equal to          */
#define    IDYADIC_PREDICATE_EQUAL          5  /* equal to                       */
#define    IDYADIC_PREDICATE_NOT_EQUAL      6  /* not equal to                   */
```

Histogram Computation Options

```
#define    IHIST_LIMIT_SPECIFIED         1     /* specified limits               */
#define    IHIST_LIMIT_EXTREMA           2     /* image extrema limits           */
```

Image Structure Options

```
#define    IIMAGE_STRUCTURE_MON          1     /* monochrome                     */
#define    IIMAGE_STRUCTURE_COLR         4     /* colour                         */
```

Lookup Table Modes

```
#define    ILOOKUP_1D                    1     /* one dimension                  */
#define    ILOOKUP_2D                    2     /* two dimensions                 */
```

Luminance RGB Color Options

```
#define    ILUM_LIN_CCIR_D65_RGB         1     /* linear CCIR illuminant D65 RGB */
#define    ILUM_LIN_CIE_E_RGB            2     /* linear CIE illuminant E RGB    */
#define    ILUM_LIN_EBU_C_RGB            3     /* linear EBU illuminant C RGB    */
#define    ILUM_LIN_EBU_D65_RGB          4     /* linear EBU illuminant D65 RGB  */
#define    ILUM_LIN_NTSC_C_RGB           5     /* linear NTSC illuminant C RGB   */
#define    ILUM_LIN_NTSC_D65_RGB         6     /* linear NTSC illuminant D65 RGB */
#define    ILUM_LIN_SMPTE_D65_RGB        7     /* linear SMPTE illuminant D65 RGB*/
#define    ILUM_GAMMA_EBU_C_RGB          8     /* gamma EBU illuminant C RGB     */
#define    ILUM_GAMMA_EBU_D65_RGB        9     /* gamma EBU illuminant D65 RGB   */
#define    ILUM_GAMMA_NTSC_C_RGB         10    /* gamma NTSC illuminant C RGB    */
#define    ILUM_GAMMA_NTSC_D65_RGB       11    /* gamma NTSC illuminant D65 RGB  */
#define    ILUM_GAMMA_SMPTE_D65_RGB      12    /* gamma SMPTE illuminant D65 RGB */
```

Monadic, Arithmetic Options

```
#define    IMONADIC_ADDITION_BY          1     /* addition by constant           */
#define    IMONADIC_ADDITION_BY_SCALED   2     /* addition by constant, scaled   */
#define    IMONADIC_DIVISION_BY          3     /* division by constant           */
#define    IMONADIC_DIVISION_OF          4     /* division of constant           */
#define    IMONADIC_MAXIMUM              5     /* maximum with constant          */
#define    IMONADIC_MINIMUM              6     /* minimum with constant          */
```

```
#define    IMONADIC_MULTIPLICATION              7    /* multiplication by constant            */
#define    IMONADIC_SUBTRACTION_BY              8    /* subtraction by constant               */
#define    IMONADIC_SUBTRACTION_BY_SCALED       9    /* subtraction by constant, scaled       */
#define    IMONADIC_SUBTRACTION_OF             10    /* subtraction of constant               */
#define    IMONADIC_SUBTRACTION_OF_SCALED      11    /* subtraction of constant, scaled       */
```

Monadic, Logical Options

```
#define    IMONADIC_LOGICAL_AND                 1    /* bitwise AND                           */
#define    IMONADIC_LOGICAL_NAND                2    /* bitwise NAND                          */
#define    IMONADIC_LOGICAL_NOR                 3    /* bitwise NOR                           */
#define    IMONADIC_LOGICAL_OR                  4    /* bitwise OR                            */
#define    IMONADIC_LOGICAL_XOR                 5    /* bitwise XOR                           */
#define    IMONADIC_LOGICAL_INTERSECTION        6    /* Boolean intersection                  */
#define    IMONADIC_LOGICAL_UNION               7    /* Boolean union                         */
```

Neighbourhood Array Semantic Label Options

```
#define    INBHOOD_LABEL_GENERIC                1    /* generic                               */
#define    INBHOOD_LABEL_DITHER                 2    /* dither                                */
#define    INBHOOD_LABEL_IMPULSE                3    /* impulse response                      */
#define    INBHOOD_LABEL_MASK                   4    /* mask                                  */
#define    INBHOOD_LABEL_STRUCTURE              5    /* structuring element                   */
```

Object Type Options

```
#define    IOBJECT_IMAGE                        1    /* image                                 */
#define    IOBJECT_HIST                         2    /* histogram                             */
#define    IOBJECT_LUT                          6    /* lookup table                          */
#define    IOBJECT_MATRIX                       7    /* matrix                                */
#define    IOBJECT_NBHOOD                       8    /* neighbourhood array                   */
#define    IOBJECT_ROI_RECTANGULAR             15    /* ROI, rectangular type                 */
#define    IOBJECT_TUPLE                       17    /* tuple                                 */
```

Pixel Data Type (External) Options

```
#define    IPIXEL_BI_MSB_PLANAR                 1    /* Boolean planar ordered from msb       */
#define    IPIXEL_BI_MSB_INTERLEAVED            2    /* Boolean interleaved ordered from msb  */
#define    IPIXEL_BI_LSB_PLANAR                 3    /* Boolean planar ordered from lsb       */
#define    IPIXEL_BI_LSB_INTERLEAVED            4    /* Boolean interleaved ordered from lsb  */
#define    IPIXEL_NI_PLANAR                     5    /* nonnegative integer planar            */
#define    IPIXEL_NI_INTERLEAVED                6    /* nonnegative integer interleaved       */
#define    IPIXEL_SI_PLANAR                     7    /* signed integer planar                 */
#define    IPIXEL_SI_INTERLEAVED                8    /* signed integer interleaved            */
#define    IPIXEL_TI_PLANAR                     9    /* fixed point integer planar            */
#define    IPIXEL_TI_INTERLEAVED               10    /* fixed point integer interleaved       */
```

Repository Class Choices

```
#define    IREPOSITORY_IMPULSE                  1    /* impulse response array                */
#define    IREPOSITORY_DITHER                   2    /* dither array                          */
#define    IREPOSITORY_COLOUR                   3    /* colour conversion matrix              */
```

Resampling Options

```
#define    IRESAMPLE_NEAREST_NEIGHBOUR          1    /* nearest neighbour                     */
#define    IRESAMPLE_2_BILINEAR                 2    /* support 2 bilinear                    */
```

ROI Type Option

```
#define    IROI_RECTANGULAR                     6    /* rectangular ROI type                  */
```

Rotation Space Options

```
#define IROTATION_SPACE_2D                      1    /* 2D rotation                           */
```

Split Image Options

```
#define   ISPLIT_LEFT_LEFT        1    /* split left 1 - left 2       */
#define   ISPLIT_RIGHT_RIGHT      2    /* split right 1 - right 2     */
#define   ISPLIT_TOP_TOP          3    /* split top 1 - top 2         */
#define   ISPLIT_BOTTOM_BOTTOM    4    /* split bottom 1 - bottom 2   */
#define   ISPLIT_LEFT_RIGHT       5    /* split left 1 - right 2      */
#define   ISPLIT_TOP_BOTTOM       6    /* split top 1 - bottom 2      */
```

Unary Integer Conversion Options

```
#define   IUNARY_INTEGER_ABSOLUTE   1    /* absolute value   */
#define   IUNARY_INTEGER_CUBE       2    /* cube             */
#define   IUNARY_INTEGER_NEGATIVE   3    /* negative         */
#define   IUNARY_INTEGER_SQUARE     4    /* square           */
```

Array Lengths

```
#define   IL_PROFILE    15    /* Conformance profile label string
                                 length                              */

#define   IL_REAL        3    /* Implementation method of RD data type
                                 string length                       */
```

B.8   Element Designaters

The following are listings of the piks.h #define element designaters. They are arranged alphabetically by macro name.

```
#define   IF_ACCUMULATOR                2    /* accumulator                  */
#define   IF_ALLOCATE_HIST              8    /* allocate_histogram           */
#define   IF_ALLOCATE_IMAGE             9    /* allocate_image               */
#define   IF_ALLOCATE_LUT              10    /* allocate_lookup_table        */
#define   IF_ALLOCATE_MATRIX           11    /* allocate_matrix              */
#define   IF_ALLOCATE_NBHOOD_ARRAY     12    /* allocate_neighbourhood_array */
#define   IF_ALLOCATE_ROI              14    /* allocate_roi                 */
#define   IF_ALLOCATE_TUPLE            16    /* allocate_tuple               */
#define   IF_ALPHA_BLEND_CONSTANT      19    /* alpha_blend_constant         */
#define   IF_ARRAY_TO_LUT              21    /* array_to_lut                 */
#define   IF_BIND_ROI                  23    /* bind_roi                     */
#define   IF_BIT_SHIFT                 24    /* bit_shift                    */
#define   IF_CLOSE_PIKS                34    /* close_piks                   */
#define   IF_CLOSE_PIKS_EMERGENCY      35    /* close_piks_emergency         */
#define   IF_COLOUR_CONV_LIN           36    /* colour_conversion_linear     */
#define   IF_COLOUR_CONV_MATRIX        37    /* colour_conversion_matrix     */
#define   IF_COLOUR_CONV_SUBTRACTIVE   39    /* colour_conversion_subtractive */
#define   IF_COMPLEMENT                41    /* complement                   */
#define   IF_CONV_ARRAY_TO_IMAGE       59    /* convert_array_to_image       */
#define   IF_CONV_IMAGE_DATATYPE       60    /* convert_image_datatype       */
#define   IF_CONV_IMAGE_TO_ARRAY       61    /* convert_image_to_array       */
#define   IF_CONV_ROI_TO_IMAGE         63    /* convert_roi_to_image         */
#define   IF_CONVOLVE_2D               64    /* convolve_2d                  */
#define   IF_COPY_WINDOW               66    /* copy_window                  */
#define   IF_CREATE_TUPLE              68    /* create_tuple                 */
#define   IF_DEALLOCATEATE_DATA_OBJECT 70    /* deallocate_data_object       */
#define   IF_DEFINE_SUB_IMAGE          71    /* define_sub_image             */
#define   IF_DIFFUSE                   73    /* diffuse                      */
#define   IF_DITHER                    74    /* dither                       */
#define   IF_DRAW_PIXELS               75    /* draw_pixels                  */
#define   IF_DYADIC_ARITH              77    /* dyadic_arithmetic            */
#define   IF_DYADIC_LOGICAL            79    /* dyadic_logical               */
#define   IF_DYADIC_PREDICATE          81    /* dyadic_predicate             */
#define   IF_ERROR_HANDLER             90    /* error_handler                */
#define   IF_ERROR_LOGGER              91    /* error_logger                 */
#define   IF_ERROR_TEST                92    /* error_test                   */
#define   IF_EXPORT_HIST               93    /* export_histogram             */
#define   IF_EXPORT_IMAGE              94    /* export_image                 */
#define   IF_EXPORT_LUT                95    /* export_lut                   */
#define   IF_EXPORT_MATRIX             96    /* export_matrix                */
#define   IF_EXPORT_NBHOOD_ARRAY       97    /* export_neighbourhood_array   */
#define   IF_EXPORT_TUPLE             100    /* export_tuple                 */
```

```
#define   IF_EXTRACT_PIXEL_PLANE        102   /* extract_pixel_plane          */
#define   IF_EXTREMA                    104   /* extrema                      */
#define   IF_FLIP_SPIN_TRANSPOSE        119   /* flip_spin_transpose          */
#define   IF_FLIP_SPIN_TRANSPOSE_ROI    120   /* flip_spin_transpose_roi      */
#define   IF_GET_COLOUR_PIXEL           122   /* get_colour_pixel             */
#define   IF_GET_PIXEL                  123   /* get_pixel                    */
#define   IF_GET_PIXEL_ROI              124   /* get_pixel_roi                */
#define   IF_GET_PIXEL_ARRAY            125   /* get_pixel_array              */
#define   IF_GET_PIXEL_ARRAY_ROI        126   /* get_pixel_array_roi          */
#define   IF_HIST_1D                    133   /* histogram_1d                 */
#define   IF_IMAGE_CONSTANT             139   /* image_constant               */
#define   IF_IMPORT_HIST                143   /* import_histogram             */
#define   IF_IMPORT_IMAGE               144   /* import_image                 */
#define   IF_IMPORT_LUT                 145   /* import_lut                   */
#define   IF_IMPORT_MATRIX              146   /* import_matrix                */
#define   IF_IMPORT_NBHOOD_ARRAY        147   /* import_neighbourhood_array   */
#define   IF_IMPORT_TUPLE               150   /* import_tuple                 */
#define   IF_IMPULSE_RECTANGULAR        159   /* impulse_rectangular          */
#define   IF_INQUIRE_ELEMENTS           164   /* inquire_elements             */
#define   IF_INQUIRE_IMAGE              165   /* inquire_image                */
#define   IF_INQUIRE_NON_IMAGE_OBJECT   167   /* inquire_non_image_object     */
#define   IF_INQUIRE_PIKS_IMPL          168   /* inquire_piks_implementation  */
#define   IF_INQUIRE_PIKS_STATUS        169   /* inquire_piks_status          */
#define   IF_INQUIRE_REPOSITORY         170   /* inquire_repository           */
#define   IF_INQUIRE_RESAMPLING         171   /* inquire_resampling           */
#define   IF_INSERT_PIXEL_PLANE         172   /* insert_pixel_plane           */
#define   IF_LOOKUP                     178   /* lookup                       */
#define   IF_LUM_GENERATION             180   /* luminance_generation         */
#define   IF_MOMENTS                    182   /* moments                      */
#define   IF_MONADIC_ARITH              183   /* monadic_arithmetic           */
#define   IF_MONADIC_LOGICAL            185   /* monadic_logical              */
#define   IF_MORPHIC_PROCESSOR          187   /* morphic_processor            */
#define   IF_OPEN_PIKS                  195   /* open_piks                    */
#define   IF_PUT_COLOUR_PIXEL           203   /* put_colour_pixel             */
#define   IF_PUT_PIXEL                  204   /* put_pixel                    */
#define   IF_PUT_PIXEL_ARRAY            206   /* put_pixel_array              */
#define   IF_RESCALE                    210   /* rescale                      */
#define   IF_RESCALE_ROI                211   /* rescale_roi                  */
#define   IF_RESIZE                     212   /* resize                       */
#define   IF_RESIZE_ROI                 213   /* resize_roi                   */
#define   IF_RETURN_REPOSITORY_ID       214   /* return_repository_id         */
#define   IF_ROI_RECTANGULAR            218   /* roi_rectangular              */
#define   IF_ROTATE                     219   /* rotate                       */
#define   IF_SET_ERROR_HANDLER          269   /* set_error_handler            */
#define   IF_SET_GLOBALS                225   /* set_globals                  */
#define   IF_SET_IMAGE_ATTRS            226   /* set_image_attributes         */
#define   IF_SPLIT_IMAGE                231   /* split_image                  */
#define   IF_SUBSAMPLE                  232   /* subsample                    */
#define   IF_THRESHOLD                  236   /* threshold                    */
#define   IF_TRANSLATE                  241   /* translate                    */
#define   IF_TRANSLATE_ROI              242   /* translate_roi                */
#define   IF_UNARY_INTEGER              243   /* unary_integer                */
#define   IF_WINDOW_LEVEL               263   /* window_level                 */
#define   IF_ZOOM                       266   /* zoom                         */
#define   IF_ZOOM_ROI                   267   /* zoom_roi                     */
```

B.9   Convenience Function Designaters

The following are listings of the piks.h #define convenience function designaters.

```
#define   IC_GENERATE_2D_ROI_RECTANGULAR  1001  /* generate 2D ROI rectangular  */
#define   IC_GENERATE_ND_1_TUPLE          1006  /* generate ND 1-tuple          */
#define   IC_GENERATE_ND_3_TUPLE          1007  /* generate ND 3-tuple          */
#define   IC_GENERATE_ND_4_TUPLE          1008  /* generate ND 4-tuple          */
#define   IC_GENERATE_ND_5_TUPLE          1009  /* generate ND 5-tuple          */
#define   IC_GENERATE_RD_5_TUPLE          1012  /* generate RD 5-tuple          */
#define   IC_GENERATE_SD_1_TUPLE          1013  /* generate SD 1-tuple          */
#define   IC_GENERATE_SD_3_TUPLE          1014  /* generate SD 3-tuple          */
#define   IC_GENERATE_SD_4_TUPLE          1015  /* generate SD 4-tuple          */
#define   IC_GENERATE_SD_5_TUPLE          1016  /* generate SD 5-tuple          */
#define   IC_PREPARE_COLOUR_IMAGE         1017  /* prepare colour image         */
#define   IC_PREPARE_MONOCHROME_IMAGE     1018  /* prepare monochrome image     */
#define   IC_PREPARE_2D_ROI_RECTANGULAR   1019  /* prepare 2D rectangular ROI   */
```

B.10 Impulse Response Array Repository Entry Designaters

The following are listings of the *piks.h* #define designaters of the impulse response function arrays in the PIKS data object repository. identifiers. They are arranged alphabetically by macro name.

```
#define    IR_BOXCAR_5x5_HORIZONTAL           90
#define    IR_BOXCAR_5x5_VERTICAL             91
#define    IR_CHEBYSHEV_1                     69
#define    IR_CHEBYSHEV_2                     70
#define    IR_CHEBYSHEV_3                     71
#define    IR_CHEBYSHEV_4                     72
#define    IR_CHEBYSHEV_5                     73
#define    IR_CHEBYSHEV_6                     74
#define    IR_CHEBYSHEV_7                     75
#define    IR_CHEBYSHEV_8                     76
#define    IR_CHEBYSHEV_9                     77
#define    IR_CORNER_NBR_AVERAGE             7
#define    IR_DECORRELATE                    65
#define    IR_DELTA_3x3                       1
#define    IR_EIGHT_NBR_AVERAGE              5
#define    IR_FOUR_NBR_AVERAGE               6
#define    IR_FREI_HORIZONTAL               21
#define    IR_FREI_VERTICAL                 22
#define    IR_HIGH_PASS_1_3x3                8
#define    IR_HIGH_PASS_2_3x3                9
#define    IR_HIGH_PASS_3_3x3               10
#define    IR_KIRSCH_EAST                   31
#define    IR_KIRSCH_NORTH                  33
#define    IR_KIRSCH_NORTHEAST              32
#define    IR_KIRSCH_NORTHWEST              34
#define    IR_KIRSCH_SOUTH                  37
#define    IR_KIRSCH_SOUTHEAST             38
#define    IR_KIRSCH_SOUTHWEST            36
#define    IR_KIRSCH_WEST                   35
#define    IR_LAPLACE_1                     66
#define    IR_LAPLACE_2                     67
#define    IR_LAPLACE_3                     68
#define    IR_LAWS_1                        78
#define    IR_LAWS_2                        79
#define    IR_LAWS_3                        80
#define    IR_LAWS_4                        81
#define    IR_LAWS_5                        82
#define    IR_LAWS_6                        83
#define    IR_LAWS_7                        84
#define    IR_LAWS_8                        85
#define    IR_LAWS_9                        86
#define    IR_LOW_PASS_3x3                   4
#define    IR_NEVATIA_0                     94
#define    IR_NEVATIA_120                   98
#define    IR_NEVATIA_150                   99
#define    IR_NEVATIA_180                  100
#define    IR_NEVATIA_210                  101
#define    IR_NEVATIA_240                  102
#define    IR_NEVATIA_270                  103
#define    IR_NEVATIA_30                    95
#define    IR_NEVATIA_300                  104
#define    IR_NEVATIA_330                  105
#define    IR_NEVATIA_60                    96
#define    IR_NEVATIA_90                    97
#define    IR_PIXEL_DIFF_HORIZONTAL         11
#define    IR_PIXEL_DIFF_VERTICAL           12
#define    IR_PIXEL_STACK                   87
#define    IR_PREWITT_COMPASS_EAST          23
#define    IR_PREWITT_COMPASS_NORTH         25
#define    IR_PREWITT_COMPASS_NORTHEAST     24
#define    IR_PREWITT_COMPASS_NORTHWEST     26
#define    IR_PREWITT_COMPASS_SOUTH         29
#define    IR_PREWITT_COMPASS_SOUTHEAST     30
#define    IR_PREWITT_COMPASS_SOUTHWEST     28
#define    IR_PREWITT_COMPASS_WEST          27
#define    IR_PREWITT_HORIZONTAL            17
#define    IR_PREWITT_VERTICAL              18
```

```
#define    IR_PYRAMID_3x3                      3
#define    IR_PYRAMID_5x5                      89
#define    IR_ROBERTS_3_LEVEL_EAST             39
#define    IR_ROBERTS_3_LEVEL_NORTH            41
#define    IR_ROBERTS_3_LEVEL_NORTHEAST        40
#define    IR_ROBERTS_3_LEVEL_NORTHWEST        42
#define    IR_ROBERTS_3_LEVEL_SOUTH            45
#define    IR_ROBERTS_3_LEVEL_SOUTHEAST        46
#define    IR_ROBERTS_3_LEVEL_SOUTHWEST        44
#define    IR_ROBERTS_3_LEVEL_WEST             43
#define    IR_ROBERTS_5_LEVEL_EAST             47
#define    IR_ROBERTS_5_LEVEL_NORTH            49
#define    IR_ROBERTS_5_LEVEL_NORTHEAST        48
#define    IR_ROBERTS_5_LEVEL_NORTHWEST        50
#define    IR_ROBERTS_5_LEVEL_SOUTH            53
#define    IR_ROBERTS_5_LEVEL_SOUTHEAST        54
#define    IR_ROBERTS_5_LEVEL_SOUTHWEST        52
#define    IR_ROBERTS_5_LEVEL_WEST             51
#define    IR_ROBERTS_HORIZONTAL               15
#define    IR_ROBERTS_VERTICAL                 16
#define    IR_SEP_PIXEL_DIFF_HORIZONTAL        13
#define    IR_SEP_PIXEL_DIFF_VERTICAL          14
#define    IR_SOBEL_HORIZONTAL                 19
#define    IR_SOBEL_VERTICAL                   20
#define    IR_SPOT_4_CONNECTED                 63
#define    IR_SPOT_8_CONNECTED                 64
#define    IR_TRUNC_PYRAMID_5x5_HORIZONTAL     92
#define    IR_TRUNC_PYRAMID_5x5_VERTICAL       93
#define    IR_UNIFORM_3x3                      2
#define    IR_UNIFORM_5x5                      88
#define    IR_UNWEIGHTED_LINE_1                55
#define    IR_UNWEIGHTED_LINE_2                56
#define    IR_UNWEIGHTED_LINE_3                57
#define    IR_UNWEIGHTED_LINE_4                58
#define    IR_WEIGHTED_LINE_1                  59
#define    IR_WEIGHTED_LINE_2                  60
#define    IR_WEIGHTED_LINE_3                  61
#define    IR_WEIGHTED_LINE_4                  62
```

B.11 Dither Array Repository Entry Designaters

The following are listings of the piks.h #define designaters of the dither arrays in the PIKS data object repository. identifiers. They are arranged alphabetically by macro name.

```
#define    IR_DITHER_2x2                       1
#define    IR_DITHER_4x4                       2
#define    IR_DITHER_8x8                       3
#define    IR_DITHER_16x16                     4
```

B.12 Colour Conversion Matrix Repository Entry Designaters

The following are listings of the piks.h #define designaters of the colour conversion matrices in the PIKS data object repository. They are arranged alphabetically by macro name.

```
#define    IR_A_LIN_CCIR_D65_CIE_E_RGB         73
#define    IR_A_LIN_CCIR_D65_EBU_C_RGB         74
#define    IR_A_LIN_CCIR_D65_NTSC_C_RGB        75
#define    IR_A_LIN_CIE_E_CCIR_D65_RGB         76
#define    IR_A_LIN_CIE_E_EBU_C_RGB            77
#define    IR_A_LIN_CIE_E_EBU_D65_RGB          78
#define    IR_A_LIN_CIE_E_NTSC_C_RGB           79
#define    IR_A_LIN_CIE_E_NTSC_D65_RGB         80
#define    IR_A_LIN_CIE_E_SMPTE_D65_RGB        81
#define    IR_A_LIN_EBU_C_CCIR_D65_RGB         82
#define    IR_A_LIN_EBU_C_CIE_E_RGB            83
#define    IR_A_LIN_EBU_C_EBU_D65_RGB          84
#define    IR_A_LIN_EBU_C_NTSC_D65_RGB         85
```

```
#define    IR_A_LIN_EBU_C_SMPTE_D65_RBG          86
#define    IR_A_LIN_EBU_D65_CIE_E_RGB            87
#define    IR_A_LIN_EBU_D65_EBU_C_RGB            88
#define    IR_A_LIN_EBU_D65_NTSC_C_RGB           89
#define    IR_A_LIN_NTSC_C_CCIR_D65_RGB          90
#define    IR_A_LIN_NTSC_C_CIE_E_RGB             91
#define    IR_A_LIN_NTSC_C_EBU_D65_RGB           92
#define    IR_A_LIN_NTSC_C_NTSC_D65_RGB          93
#define    IR_A_LIN_NTSC_C_SMPTE_D65_RGB         94
#define    IR_A_LIN_NTSC_D65_CIE_E_RGB           95
#define    IR_A_LIN_NTSC_D65_EBU_C_RGB           96
#define    IR_A_LIN_NTSC_D65_NTSC_C_RGB          97
#define    IR_A_LIN_SMPTE_D65_CIE_E_RGB          98
#define    IR_A_LIN_SMPTE_D65_EBU_C_RGB          99
#define    IR_A_LIN_SMPTE_D65_NTSC_C_RGB         100
#define    IR_C_LIN_CCIR_D65_CIE_E_RGB           1
#define    IR_C_LIN_CCIR_D65_EBU_C_RGB           2
#define    IR_C_LIN_CCIR_D65_EBU_D65_RGB         3
#define    IR_C_LIN_CCIR_D65_NTSC_C_RGB          4
#define    IR_C_LIN_CCIR_D65_NTSC_D65_RGB        5
#define    IR_C_LIN_CCIR_D65_RGB_UVW             7
#define    IR_C_LIN_CCIR_D65_RGB_XYZ             8
#define    IR_C_LIN_CCIR_D65_SMPTE_D65_RGB       6
#define    IR_C_LIN_CIE_E_CCIR_D65_RGB           9
#define    IR_C_LIN_CIE_E_EBU_C_RGB              10
#define    IR_C_LIN_CIE_E_EBU_D65_RGB            11
#define    IR_C_LIN_CIE_E_NTSC_C_RGB             12
#define    IR_C_LIN_CIE_E_NTSC_D65_RGB           13
#define    IR_C_LIN_CIE_E_RGB_UVW                15
#define    IR_C_LIN_CIE_E_RGB_XYZ                16
#define    IR_C_LIN_CIE_E_SMPTE_D65_RGB          14
#define    IR_C_LIN_EBU_C_CCIR_D65_RGB           17
#define    IR_C_LIN_EBU_C_CIE_E_RGB              18
#define    IR_C_LIN_EBU_C_EBU_D65_RGB            19
#define    IR_C_LIN_EBU_C_NTSC_C_RGB             20
#define    IR_C_LIN_EBU_C_NTSC_D65_RGB           21
#define    IR_C_LIN_EBU_C_RGB_UVW                23
#define    IR_C_LIN_EBU_C_RGB_XYZ                24
#define    IR_C_LIN_EBU_C_SMPTE_D65_RGB          22
#define    IR_C_LIN_EBU_D65_CCIR_D65_RGB         25
#define    IR_C_LIN_EBU_D65_CIE_E_RGB            26
#define    IR_C_LIN_EBU_D65_EBU_C_RGB            27
#define    IR_C_LIN_EBU_D65_NTSC_C_RGB           28
#define    IR_C_LIN_EBU_D65_NTSC_D65_RGB         29
#define    IR_C_LIN_EBU_D65_RGB_UVW              31
#define    IR_C_LIN_EBU_D65_RGB_XYZ              32
#define    IR_C_LIN_EBU_D65_SMPTE_D65_RGB        30
#define    IR_C_LIN_NTSC_C_CCIR_D65_RGB          33
#define    IR_C_LIN_NTSC_C_CIE_E_RGB             34
#define    IR_C_LIN_NTSC_C_EBU_C_RGB             35
#define    IR_C_LIN_NTSC_C_EBU_D65_RGB           36
#define    IR_C_LIN_NTSC_C_NTSC_D65_RGB          37
#define    IR_C_LIN_NTSC_C_RGB_UVW               39
#define    IR_C_LIN_NTSC_C_RGB_XYZ               40
#define    IR_C_LIN_NTSC_C_SMPTE_D65_RGB         38
#define    IR_C_LIN_NTSC_D65_CCIR_D65_RGB        41
#define    IR_C_LIN_NTSC_D65_CIE_E_RGB           42
#define    IR_C_LIN_NTSC_D65_EBU_C_RGB           43
#define    IR_C_LIN_NTSC_D65_EBU_D65_RGB         44
#define    IR_C_LIN_NTSC_D65_NTSC_C_RGB          45
#define    IR_C_LIN_NTSC_D65_RGB_UVW             47
#define    IR_C_LIN_NTSC_D65_RGB_XYZ             48
#define    IR_C_LIN_NTSC_D65_SMPTE_D65_RGB       46
#define    IR_C_LIN_SMPTE_D65_CCIR_D65_RGB       49
#define    IR_C_LIN_SMPTE_D65_CIE_E_RGB          50
#define    IR_C_LIN_SMPTE_D65_EBU_C_RGB          51
#define    IR_C_LIN_SMPTE_D65_EBU_D65_RGB        52
#define    IR_C_LIN_SMPTE_D65_NTSC_C_RGB         53
#define    IR_C_LIN_SMPTE_D65_NTSC_D65_RGB       54
#define    IR_C_LIN_SMPTE_D65_RGB_UVW            55
#define    IR_C_LIN_SMPTE_D65_RGB_XYZ            56
#define    IR_C_UVW_LIN_CCIR_D65_RGB             57
#define    IR_C_UVW_LIN_CIE_E_RGB                58
#define    IR_C_UVW_LIN_EBU_C_RGB                59
#define    IR_C_UVW_LIN_EBU_D65_RGB              60
#define    IR_C_UVW_LIN_NTSC_C_RGB               61
```

```
#define    IR_C_UVW_LIN_NTSC_D65_RGB          62
#define    IR_C_UVW_LIN_SMPTE_D65_RGB         63
#define    IR_C_UVW_XYZ                       64
#define    IR_C_XYZ_LIN_CCIR_D65_RGB          65
#define    IR_C_XYZ_LIN_CIE_E_RGB             66
#define    IR_C_XYZ_LIN_EBU_C_RGB             67
#define    IR_C_XYZ_LIN_EBU_D65_RGB           68
#define    IR_C_XYZ_LIN_NTSC_C_RGB            69
#define    IR_C_XYZ_LIN_NTSC_D65_RGB          70
#define    IR_C_XYZ_LIN_SMPTE_D65_RGB         71
#define    IR_C_XYZ_UVW                       72
#define    IR_GAMMA_EBU_C_RGB_YUV            101
#define    IR_GAMMA_EBU_D65_RGB_YUV          102
#define    IR_GAMMA_NTSC_C_RGB_YIQ           103
#define    IR_GAMMA_NTSC_D65_RGB_YIQ         104
#define    IR_GAMMA_SMPTE_D65_RGB_YCBCR      105
#define    IR_ILLUMINANT_C_D50              111
#define    IR_ILLUMINANT_C_D65              112
#define    IR_ILLUMINANT_C_E                113
#define    IR_ILLUMINANT_D50_C              114
#define    IR_ILLUMINANT_D50_D65            115
#define    IR_ILLUMINANT_D50_E              116
#define    IR_ILLUMINANT_D65_C              117
#define    IR_ILLUMINANT_D65_D50            118
#define    IR_ILLUMINANT_D65_E              119
#define    IR_ILLUMINANT_E_C                120
#define    IR_ILLUMINANT_E_D50              121
#define    IR_ILLUMINANT_E_D65              122
#define    IR_YCBCR_GAMMA_SMPTE_D65_RGB     110
#define    IR_YIQ_GAMMA_NTSC_C_RGB          108
#define    IR_YIQ_GAMMA_NTSC_D65_RGB        109
#define    IR_YUV_GAMMA_EBU_C_RGB           106
#define    IR_YUV_GAMMA_EBU_D65_RGB         107
```

B.13 Error Code Designaters

The following are listings of the *piks.h* #define error code designaters. They are arranged by error number. Error codes absent in sequence are either unspecified or not used in PIKS Foundation.

```
#define    IE_NO_ERROR               0    /* No error.                          */

#define    IE_PARAMETER_DATA_TYPE    1    /* Elementary input data parameter is
                                             incorrect data type.               */

#define    IE_ENUM_PARAMETER_RANGE   2    /* Enumerated option parameter is out of
                                             range                              */

#define    IE_OPTION                 3    /* Signed integer option parameter is out
                                             of range.                          */

#define    IE_IMAGE_ID              11    /* Image identifier is invalid.       */

#define    IE_NON_ID                12    /* Nonimage identifier is invalid.    */

#define    IE_ID_NOT_IMAGE          13    /* Identifier is not to an image.     */

#define    IE_ID_NOT_NON            14    /* Identifier is not to a nonimage.   */

#define    IE_SOURCE_IMAGE_EMPTY    15    /* Source image does not contain data. */

#define    IE_SOURCE_NON_EMPTY      16    /* Source nonimage does not contain data. */

#define    IE_SUB_IMAGE_REASSIGN    17    /* Attempt to change source image
                                             identifier of existing sub image   */
```

```
#define    IE_SUB_IMAGE_ROI_BIND            18    /* Attempt to bind a ROI to a sub image.
                                                                                              */
#define    IE_SOURCE_IMAGE_INPUT_STRUCTURE  21    /* Mismatch between source image and
                                                     element input structure.                */
#define    IE_SOURCE_NON_INPUT_STRUCTURE    22    /* Mismatch between source nonimage and
                                                     element input structure.                */
#define    IE_DEST_IMAGE_OUTPUT_STRUCTURE   23    /* Mismatch between destination image and
                                                     element output structure.               */
#define    IE_DEST_NON_OUTPUT_STRUCTURE     24    /* Mismatch between destination nonimage
                                                     and element output structure.           */
#define    IE_SOURCE_DEST_IMAGE_STRUCTURE   25    /* Mismatch between source and destination
                                                     image structure.                        */
#define    IE_SOURCE_DEST_NON_STRUCTURE     26    /* Mismatch between source and destination
                                                     nonimage structures.                    */
#define    IE_SOURCE_IMAGE_STRUCTURES       27    /* Mismatch between multiple source image
                                                     structures.                             */
#define    IE_SOURCE_NON_STRUCTURES         28    /* Mismatch between source nonimage
                                                     structures.                             */
#define    IE_DEST_NON_STRUCTURES           30    /* Mismatch between multiple destination
                                                     nonimage structures.                    */
#define    IE_SOURCE_IMAGE_DEST_NON         31    /* Mismatch between image and destination
                                                     nonimage structures                     */
#define    IE_SOURCE_NON_DEST_IMAGE         32    /* Mismatch between source nonimage and
                                                     dest. nonimage image structures         */
#define    IE_SOURCE_IMAGE_DEST_NON_TYPE    40    /* Mismatch between source image and
                                                     destination nonimage type               */
#define    IE_SOURCE_IMAGE_INPUT_TYPE       41    /* Mismatch between source image and
                                                     element input data type.                */
#define    IE_SOURCE_NON_INPUT_TYPE         42    /* Mismatch between source nonimage and
                                                     element input data type.                */
#define    IE_DEST_IMAGE_OUTPUT_TYPE        43    /* Mismatch between destination image and
                                                     element output data type.               */
#define    IE_DEST_NON_OUTPUT_TYPE          44    /* Mismatch between destination nonimage
                                                     and element output data type.           */
#define    IE_SOURCE_DEST_IMAGE_TYPE        45    /* Mismatch between source and destination
                                                     image data types.                       */
#define    IE_SOURCE_DEST_NON_TYPE          46    /* Mismatch between source and nonimage
                                                     data types                              */
#define    IE_SOURCE_IMAGE_TYPES            47    /* Mismatch between multiple source image
                                                     data types.                             */
#define    IE_SOURCE_NON_TYPES              50    /* Mismatch between multiple nonimage
                                                     data types.                             */
#define    IE_SOURCE_IMAGE_NON_TYPE         52    /* Mismatch between source image and
                                                     source nonimage data types.             */
#define    IE_DEST_IMAGE_SOURCE_NON_TYPE    53    /* Mismatch between destination image and
                                                     source nonimage data type.              */
#define    IE_SOURCE_IMAGE_INPUT_COLOUR     54    /* Mismatch between source image and
                                                     element input colour space              */
#define    IE_DEST_IMAGE_OUTPUT_COLOUR      55    /* Mismatch between destination image and
                                                     element output colour space             */
#define    IE_HETEROGENEOUS_BANDS           61    /* Element does not support heterogeneous
                                                     bands                                   */
```

```
#define    IE_INT_EXCESS                71    /* Specified integer size exceeds
                                                 implementation integer size.       */

#define    IE_REAL_EXCESS               72    /* Specified real arithmetic size exceeds
                                                 implementation real arithmetic size */

#define    IE_IMAGE_EXCESS              73    /* Specified image size exceeds
                                                 implementation image size.          */

#define    IE_ARRAY_EXCESS              74    /* Specified array size exceeds
                                                 implementation array size.          */

#define    IE_INPUT_PARAMETER_RANGE     101   /* Element input data parameter is out of
                                                  range.                             */

#define    IE_UPPER_LOWER_PARAMETER     102   /* Upper parameter bound is smaller than
                                                 lower parameter bound               */

#define    IE_SOURCE_NEGATIVE           104   /* Source image contains pixel of negative
                                                 amplitude.                          */

#define    IE_LUT_INDEX_RANGE           122   /* Lookup table index is out of range   */

#define    IE_LUT_SIZE                  123   /* Lookup table size is insufficient.   */

#define    IE_IMPORT_TYPE_CONV          152   /* Illegal import data type conversion. */

#define    IE_EXPORT_TYPE_CONV          153   /* Illegal export data type conversion  */

#define    IE_HIST_OVERFLOW             171   /* Histogram bin overflow.              */

#define    IE_DIVISION_BY_ZERO          172   /* Attempted division by zero-valued
                                                 constant.                           */

#define    IE_PIKS_OPEN                 301   /* State is PIKS_OPEN when PIKS_CLOSED is
                                                 expected.                           */

#define    IE_PIKS_CLOSED               302   /* State is PIKS_CLOSED when PIKS_OPEN is
                                                 expected.                           */

#define    IE_PIKS_INITIALIZATION       303   /* PIKS initialization failure.         */

#define    IE_PIKS_CLOSURE              304   /* PIKS closure failure.                */

#define    IE_POINTER                   1001  /* Pointer out of range                 */

#define    IE_ID                        1002  /* Identifier not assigned              */

#define    IE_STORE                     1003  /* Storage overflow                     */

#define    IE_INPUT_OUTPUT              1004  /* Input/output failure                 */

#define    IE_ALTERATION                1005  /* Attempt to alter permanent object    */

#define    IE_DEALLOCATION              1006  /* Attempt to deallocate a permanent
                                                 object                              */

#define    IE_START_POINT_INVALID       2201  /* Start index is out of range of data
                                                 available                           */

#define    IE_ENUM_TYPE_INVALID         2202  /* Enumerated type out of range         */

#define    IE_REPOSITORY_UNAVAILABLE    2203  /* No identifier points to nonexistent
                                                 repository                          */
```

APPENDIX C

Program Examples

This appendix contains the C language listings of three PIKS example programs:

- roi_complement.c
- histogram.c
- unsharp_mask.c

C.1   roi_complement.c

```
/*** Program:
 ***
 ***  roi_complement.c
 ***
 *** Function:
 ***
 ***   Image complement under source ROI control
 ***
 ***
 *** Operational steps:
 ***
 ***   Allocate monochrome source and destination images
 ***   Generate source image ROI
 ***   Read source image from file to buffer
 ***   Import source image from buffer
 ***   Copy source image into destination image
 ***   Display destination image
 ***   Enable ROI control
 ***   Bind source ROI to source image
 ***   Complement source image into destination image
 ***   Display destination image
 ***   Export destination image to buffer
 ***   Write destination image in buffer to file
 ***
 ***
 *** History:
 ***
 ***   Created        28 September 1994        W. K. Pratt
 ***
 ***/

 /*    Includes                                                */
```

```
#include <stdio.h>
#include <stdlib.h>
#include <sys/types.h>
#include <sys/stat.h>
#include <fcntl.h>
#include <piks.h>


/*      Defines                                                          */

#define HEIGHT 512
#define WIDTH 512
#define BANDS 1
#define ND_PRECISION 8


/*      Main                                                             */

main(int argc, char **argv)
{

/*      Local entities                                                   */

        char                  err_name[] ="piks_errs";

        void                  *tDisplay;


/*      PIKS entities                                                    */

        Idnimage              nSrcND, nDstND;

        Idnroi                nSrcROI;

        Idntuple              nROIOffset;

        Idntuple              nSrcOff, nDstOff, nSrcWin;

        Ipnerror              nErrorFile;

        Ipspiks_pixel_types   stExtImageArray;

        Ipspiks_modes         sModes, *tsModes = &sModes;

        Ipevalidity           eValid, *teValid = &eValid;

        Ipint                 iApplBufferSize;

        Ipuint                uDataSize, *tuDataSize = &uDataSize;


/*      Open PIKS session                                                */

        if((nErrorFile = (Ipnerror)fopen(err_name, "w")) == NULL)
            exit(1);

        InOpenPIKS(nErrorFile);


/*      Allocate monochrome images                                       */

        nSrcND = InPrepareMonochromeImage(WIDTH, HEIGHT, IDATA_TYPE_INTERNAL_ND,
                ND_PRECISION);

        nDstND = InPrepareMonochromeImage(WIDTH, HEIGHT, IDATA_TYPE_INTERNAL_ND,
                ND_PRECISION);


/*      Create rectangular ROI                                           */

        nROIOffset = InGenerateSD5Tuple(0, 0, 0, 0, 0);

        nSrcROI = InGenerate2DROIRectangular(WIDTH, HEIGHT, 50, 100, 300, 250,
                IPOLARITY_TRUE);
/*      Read source image file into buffer                               */
```

```
                stExtImageArray.tuPixel = IstGetFile("brainscan").tuPixel;

    /*      Import source image from buffer                                      */

            iApplBufferSize      = WIDTH * HEIGHT;

            InImportImage(stExtImageArray, nSrcND, ND_PRECISION, IPIXEL_NI_PLANAR,
                iApplBufferSize, 0, tuDataSize);

    /*      Copy source image into destination image                            */

            nSrcOff = InGenerateSD5Tuple(0, 0, 0, 0, 0);

            nDstOff = InGenerateSD5Tuple(0, 0, 0, 0, 0);

            nSrcWin = InGenerateND5Tuple(WIDTH, HEIGHT, 1, 1, 1);

            InCopyWindow(nSrcND, nDstND, nSrcOff, nDstOff, nSrcWin);

    /*      Open X display window and display destination image                 */

            tDisplay = ItOpenWindow(WIDTH, HEIGHT, BANDS);

            InMonochromeDisplay(nDstND, tDisplay);

            printf("Destination image: copied source image \n");
            printf("            Press any key in window to continue \n");

            IvKeyDelay(tDisplay);

    /*      Enable ROI processing                                               */

            IvInquirePIKSStatus(NULL, tsModes, teValid);

            if(eValid == IVALIDITY_VALID) {
                    sModes.eROIControlMode = IROI_CONTROL_ON;
                    IvSetGlobals(sModes);
            }
            else
                    printf ("Error: PIKS reports not open\n");

    /*      Bind source ROI to source image                                     */

            InBindROI(nSrcND, nSrcROI, nROIOffset);

    /*      Complement source image into destination image                      */

            InComplement(nSrcND, nDstND);

    /*      Display destination image and close window                          */

            InMonochromeDisplay(nDstND, tDisplay);

            printf("Destination image: complemented source window inlay \n");
            printf("            Press any key in window to continue \n");

            IvKeyDelay(tDisplay);

            IvCloseWindow(tDisplay);

    /*      Export destination image to buffer                                  */

            IstExportImage(nDstND, stExtImageArray, ND_PRECISION, IPIXEL_NI_PLANAR,
                    iApplBufferSize, 0, tuDataSize);

    /*      Write buffer to image file                                          */
```

```
        IvPutFile(stExtImageArray, "roi_inlay", WIDTH, HEIGHT, ND_PRECISION, BANDS);

/*      Check for errors                                                        */

        fclose(nErrorFile);

        if(IbErrorTest())
                printf("Error exists, check log\n");

/*      Close PIKS session                                                      */

        IvClosePIKS();

        free(stExtImageArray.tuPixel);
}
```

C.2   histogram.c

```
/*** Program:
 ***
 *** histogram.c
 ***
 *** Operational steps:
 ***
 *** Allocate colour source image and monochrome green band subimage
 *** Import source image from file
 *** Display source image
 *** Define green band subimage
 *** Display green band subimage
 *** Compute histogram of green band
 *** Export histogram
 *** Print histogram
 ***
 ***
 *** History:
 ***
 *** Created          28 September 1994    W. K. Pratt
 ***
 ***/


/*      Includes                                                                */

#include <stdio.h>
#include <stdlib.h>
#include <sys/types.h>
#include <sys/stat.h>
#include <fcntl.h>
#include <piks.h>


/*      Defines                                                                 */

#define HEIGHT 512
#define WIDTH 512
#define COLOUR_BANDS 3
#define MON_BANDS 1
#define ND_PRECISION 8


/*      Main                                                                    */

main(int argc, char **argv)
{


/*      Local entities                                                          */

        char            err_name[] ="piks_errors";
        int             i, sum;
```

```
        void            *tDisplay;

/*      PIKS entities                                                          */
        Idnimage        nSrc, nSubSrc;

        Idnhist         nHist;

        Idntuple        nOffset, nSubSize;

        Ipnerror        nErrorFile;

        Ipspiks_pixel_types  stExtImageArray;

        Ipsattrs_hist   sAttrsHist;

        Ipuint          uaExtHistArray[16], *tuaExtHistArray = &uaExtHistArray[0];

        Ipuint          uBins;

        Ipfloat         rLower, rUpper;

        Ipint           iApplBufferSize;

        Ipuint          uDataSize, *tuDataSize = &uDataSize;

/*      Open PIKS session                                                      */
        if((nErrorFile = (Ipnerror)fopen(err_name, "w")) == NULL)
                exit(1);

        InOpenPIKS(nErrorFile);

/*      Allocate images                                                        */
        nSrc = InPrepareColourImage(WIDTH, HEIGHT, COLOUR_BANDS, IDATA_TYPE_INTERNAL_ND,
                ND_PRECISION, 1.0, 1.0, 1.0, ICOLOUR_NON_STANDARD_RGB);

        nSubSrc = InPrepareMonochromeImage(WIDTH, HEIGHT, IDATA_TYPE_INTERNAL_ND,
                ND_PRECISION);

/*      Allocate histogram                                                     */
        sAttrsHist.uHistSize = 16;

        sAttrsHist.rLowerBound = 0.0;

        sAttrsHist.rUpperBound = 255.0;

        nHist = InAllocateHist(sAttrsHist);

/*      Read image file into buffer and import image from buffer*/
        stExtImageArray.tuPixel = IstGetFile("toys").tuPixel;

        iApplBufferSize = WIDTH * HEIGHT * COLOUR_BANDS;

        InImportImage(stExtImageArray, nSrc, ND_PRECISION, IPIXEL_NI_PLANAR,
        iApplBufferSize, 0, tuDataSize);

/*      Open X display window                                                  */
        tDisplay = ItOpenWindow(WIDTH, HEIGHT, COLOUR_BANDS);




/*      Display source colour image                                            */
```

```
        InColourDisplay(nSrc, tDisplay);

        printf("Source colour image \n");
        printf("              Press any key in window to continue \n");

        IvKeyDelay(tDisplay);

/*      Close X display window                                              */

        IvCloseWindow(tDisplay);

/*      Define green band subimage                                         */

        nOffset = InGenerateND5Tuple(0, 0, 0, 0, 1);

        nSubSize = InGenerateND5Tuple(WIDTH, HEIGHT, 1, 1, 1);

        InDefineSubImage(nSrc, nSubSrc, nOffset, nSubSize);

/*      Open X display window                                              */

        tDisplay = ItOpenWindow(WIDTH, HEIGHT, MON_BANDS);

/*      Display source green band monochrome subimage                      */

        InMonochromeDisplay(nSubSrc, tDisplay);

        printf("Source green band subimage \n");
        printf("              Press any key in window to continue \n");

        IvKeyDelay(tDisplay);

/*      Close X display window                                              */

        IvCloseWindow(tDisplay);

/*      Compute histogram for 0 to 255 amplitude limits                    */

        uBins = 16;

        rLower = 0.0;

        rUpper = 255.0;

        InHist1D(nSubSrc, nHist, uBins, rLower, rUpper, IHIST_LIMIT_SPECIFIED);

/*      Export histogram and print results                                 */

        ItuaExportHist(nHist, tuaExtHistArray);

        printf("Histogram printout\n");

        sum = 0;
        for(i = 0; i < uBins; i++) {
                sum += tuaExtHistArray[i];
                printf("h[%d] = %u\n", i, tuaExtHistArray[i]);
        }
        printf("sum = %d\n", sum);

/*      Check for errors                                                   */

        fclose(nErrorFile);

        if(IbErrorTest())
                printf("Error exists, check log\n");

/*      Close PIKS session                                                 */
```

```
      IvClosePIKS();

      free(stExtImageArray.tuPixel);
}
```

C.3   unsharp_mask.c

```
/*** Program:
 ***
 *** unsharp_mask.c
 ***
 *** Function:
 ***
 ***   Unsharp masking.
 ***
 ***
 *** Operational steps:
 ***
 ***   Allocate colour source and destination images
 ***   Generate 5x5 uniform amplitude impulse response array
 ***   Import source image
 ***   Display source image
 ***   Convolve source image with impulse response array to create blurred image
 ***   Display blurred image
 ***   Weight source and blurred image
 ***   Add weighted images to obtain unsharp masked destination image
 ***   Display destination image
 ***
 ***
 *** History:
 ***
 *** Created           28 September 1994    W. K. Pratt
 ***
 ***/


/*     Includes                                                           */

#include <stdio.h>
#include <stdlib.h>
#include <sys/types.h>
#include <sys/stat.h>
#include <fcntl.h>
#include <piks.h>


/*     Defines                                                            */

#define HEIGHT 512
#define WIDTH 512
#define BANDS 3
#define ND_PRECISION 8
#define SD_PRECISION 16


/*     Main                                                               */

main(int argc, char **argv)
{

/*     Local entities                                                     */

      char              err_name[] ="piks_errors";

      void              *tDisplay1, *tDisplay2, *tDisplay3;

      float             p;



/*     PIKS entities                                                      */
```

```
            Idnimage              nSrcND, nDstND, nWrkND;

            Idnimage              nSrcSD, nDstSD, nWrk1SD, nWrk2SD;

            Idnnbhood             nImpulse;

            Idntuple              nImpulseSize, nKeyPixel;

            Ipsattrs_nbhood       sAttrsNbhood;

            Ipnerror              nErrorFile;

            Ipspiks_pixel_types   stExtImageArray;

            Ipsparameter_arith    stw1_numerator, stw2_numerator, stw_denominator;

            Ipsparameter_arith    stAbove, stBelow, stWidth, stLevel;

            Ipint                 iw1_numerator, iw2_numerator, iw_denominator;

            Ipuint                uAbove, uBelow, uWidth, uLevel;

            Ipint                 iApplBufferSize;

            Ipuint                uDataSize, *tuDataSize = &uDataSize;


    /*      Open PIKS session                                                   */

            if((nErrorFile = (Ipnerror)fopen(err_name, "w")) == NULL)
                    exit(1);

            InOpenPIKS(nErrorFile);


    /*      Allocate colour images                                              */

            nSrcND = InPrepareColourImage(WIDTH, HEIGHT, BANDS, IDATA_TYPE_INTERNAL_ND,
                    ND_PRECISION, 1.0, 1.0, 1.0, ICOLOUR_NON_STANDARD_RGB);

            nDstND = InPrepareColourImage(WIDTH, HEIGHT, BANDS, IDATA_TYPE_INTERNAL_ND,
                    ND_PRECISION, 1.0, 1.0, 1.0, ICOLOUR_NON_STANDARD_RGB);

            nWrkND = InPrepareColourImage(WIDTH, HEIGHT, BANDS, IDATA_TYPE_INTERNAL_ND,
                    ND_PRECISION, 1.0, 1.0, 1.0, ICOLOUR_NON_STANDARD_RGB);

            nSrcSD = InPrepareColourImage(WIDTH, HEIGHT, BANDS, IDATA_TYPE_INTERNAL_SD,
                    SD_PRECISION, 1.0, 1.0, 1.0, ICOLOUR_NON_STANDARD_RGB);

            nDstSD = InPrepareColourImage(WIDTH, HEIGHT, BANDS, IDATA_TYPE_INTERNAL_SD,
                    SD_PRECISION, 1.0, 1.0, 1.0, ICOLOUR_NON_STANDARD_RGB);

            nWrk1SD = InPrepareColourImage(WIDTH, HEIGHT, BANDS, IDATA_TYPE_INTERNAL_SD,
                    SD_PRECISION, 1.0, 1.0, 1.0, ICOLOUR_NON_STANDARD_RGB);

            nWrk2SD = InPrepareColourImage(WIDTH, HEIGHT, BANDS, IDATA_TYPE_INTERNAL_SD,
                    SD_PRECISION, 1.0, 1.0, 1.0, ICOLOUR_NON_STANDARD_RGB);


    /*      Allocate and create 5x5 impulse response neighbourhood array         */

            nImpulseSize = InGenerateND5Tuple(5, 5, 1, 1, 1);

            nKeyPixel = InGenerateSD5Tuple(2, 2, 0, 0, 0);

            sAttrsNbhood.iLabelOption = INBHOOD_LABEL_IMPULSE;

            sAttrsNbhood.iTypeOption = IDATA_TYPE_INTERNAL_SD;

            sAttrsNbhood.nArraySize = nImpulseSize;

            sAttrsNbhood.nKeyPixel = nKeyPixel;

            sAttrsNbhood.iScaleFactor = 1;
```

```
        nImpulse = InAllocateNbhoodArray(sAttrsNbhood);

        InImpulseRectangular(nImpulse, nImpulseSize, nKeyPixel);

/*      Read image file into buffer and import image from buffer          */

        stExtImageArray.tuPixel = IstGetFile("toys").tuPixel;

        iApplBufferSize     = WIDTH * HEIGHT * BANDS;

        InImportImage(stExtImageArray, nSrcND, ND_PRECISION, IPIXEL_NI_PLANAR,
        iApplBufferSize, 0, tuDataSize);

/*      Open X display window and display source image                    */

        tDisplay1 = ItOpenWindow(WIDTH, HEIGHT, BANDS);

        InColourDisplay(nSrcND, tDisplay1);

        printf("Source image \n");
        printf("            Press any key in window to continue \n");

        IvKeyDelay(tDisplay1);

/*      Convert ND source image to SD data type                          */

        InConvertImageDatatype(nSrcND, nSrcSD);

/*      Blur source image                                                */

        InConvolve2D(nSrcSD, nWrk2SD, nImpulse, ICONVOLVE_ENCLOSED);

/*      Convert SD blurred image to ND data type and display it          */

        InConvertImageDatatype(nWrk2SD, nWrkND);

        tDisplay2 = ItOpenWindow(WIDTH, HEIGHT, BANDS);

        InColourDisplay(nWrkND, tDisplay2);

        printf("Work image:  blurred source image \n");
        printf("            Press any key in window to continue \n");

        IvKeyDelay(tDisplay2);

/*      Weight source image                                              */
        p = 0.6;

        iw1_numerator = 100.0 * p;

        iw_denominator = 100.0 * (2.0 * p - 1.0);

        stw1_numerator.tiArith = &iw1_numerator;

        stw_denominator.tiArith = &iw_denominator;

        InMonadicArith(nSrcSD, nWrk1SD, stw1_numerator, IMONADIC_MULTIPLICATION);

        InMonadicArith(nWrk1SD, nWrk1SD, stw_denominator, IMONADIC_DIVISION_BY);

/*      Weight blurred image                                             */
        iw2_numerator = 100.0 * (1.0 - p);

        stw2_numerator.tiArith = &iw2_numerator;

        InMonadicArith(nWrk2SD, nWrk2SD, stw2_numerator, IMONADIC_MULTIPLICATION);
```

```
        InMonadicArith(nWrk2SD, nWrk2SD, stw_denominator, IMONADIC_DIVISION_BY);

/*      Subtract weighted blurred image from weighted source image              */
        InDyadicArith(nWrk1SD, nWrk2SD, nDstSD, IDYADIC_SUBTRACTION);

/*      Clip unsharp mask image                                                 */
        uAbove = 255;
        uBelow = 0;
        uWidth = 256;
        uLevel = 127;
        stAbove.tuArith = &uAbove;
        stBelow.tuArith = &uBelow;
        stWidth.tuArith = &uWidth;
        stLevel.tuArith = &uLevel;
        InWindowLevel(nDstSD, nDstSD, stAbove, stBelow, stWidth, stLevel);

/*      Convert SD unsharp mask image to ND data type and display it*/
        InConvertImageDatatype(nDstSD, nDstND);

/*      Display unsharp mask image                                              */
        tDisplay3 = ItOpenWindow(WIDTH, HEIGHT, BANDS);

        InColourDisplay(nDstND, tDisplay3);

        printf("Work image:  unsharp mask image \n");
        printf("             Press any key in window to continue \n");

        IvKeyDelay(tDisplay3);

/*      Close windows                                                           */
        IvCloseWindow(tDisplay1);
        IvCloseWindow(tDisplay2);
        IvCloseWindow(tDisplay3);

/*      Check for errors                                                        */
        fclose(nErrorFile);

        if (IbErrorTest())
                printf("Error exists, check log\n");

/*      Close PIKS session                                                      */
        IvClosePIKS();

        free(stExtImageArray.tuPixel);
}
```

INDEX

A

accumulator   103, 199
allocate_histogram   118, 200
allocate_image   15, 119, 201, 299, 328, 329
allocate_lookup_table   122, 203
allocate_matrix   123, 204
allocate_neighbourhood_array   123, 205
allocate_roi   125, 206, 330
allocate_tuple   126, 207, 314
Allocation mechanisms   18, 19, 118
alpha_blend_constant   49, 209
American National Standards Institute
        (ANSI)   viii
Analysis operators   16, 17, 103
Application interface   25
Application Program Interface (API)   viii,
        xiii
array_to_lut   112, 210
ATAN2   334

B

Band   5
BD   (*See* Boolean)
BI   (*See* Boolean)
bind_roi   120, 136, 211
bit_shift   33, 213
Boolean
    BD   8, 25
    BI   26
    BP   25, 26
boolean_display   311
BP   (*See* Boolean)

C

C language binding   x
C programming language   ix
Channel attribute   4, 5
Character string (CS)   9, 26
CHOICE   9, 334
Chromaticity coordinates   7, 114
Chrominance   8
Class A object   15
Class B object   15
Class C object   15
close_piks   27, 117, 213
close_piks_emergency   27, 117, 214
close_window   312
CMY   7
CMYK   7
Colour (COLR)   6
Colour operators   16, 17, 96
Colour, spelling of   x
Colour
    attribute   4, 5
    conversion matrices   15
    index, *b*   5
    pixel   159
    spaces   7, 96
colour_conversion_linear   96, 215
colour_conversion_matrix   113, 216
colour_conversion_subtractive   97, 217
colour_display   313, 327
Colourimetry   96
Common Architecture for Imaging
        (CAI)   viii
complement   35

Control
  attribute   5
  mechanisms   18, 19, 117
convert_array_to_image   145, 219
convert_image_datatype   146, 220
convert_image_to_array   147, 221
convert_roi_to_image   147, 222
Convolution   60
convolve_2d   60, 224
copy_window   148, 224
COS   324
create_tuple   149, 208, 225

D

Data object identifier (ID), (IP)   26
Data object repository   15
Data objects   3
Data type codes   26
deallocate_data_object   127, 227
Deallocation mechanisms   18, 19, 118
define_sub_image   137, 228
Definition   31
Depth index, *z*   5
Destination image   6, 20
Deutsches Institut für Normung
       (DIN)   viii
diffuse   92, 229
Dilation   69
dither   94, 230
Dither arrays (DL)   11, 15
draw_pixels   102, 231
dyadic_arithmetic   50, 232
dyadic_logical   52, 233
dyadic_predicate   55, 234

E

Elements   16, 29
  input parameters   30
  output parameters   31
  specification name   30
  specification template   30
Ensemble operators   16, 17, 20, 49
Enumerated (EP)   26
Erosion   69
Error
  diffusion halftoning   92
  flag   143

  handler   27
  mechanisms   18, 19, 141
  reporting   26
error_handler   27, 141, 235
error_logger   143, 236
error_test   143, 237
Example   32
Export   3
Export from PIKS utilities   18, 19, 161
export_histogram   162, 238
export_image   162, 240
export_lut   163, 240
export_matrix   164, 241
export_neighbourhood_array   165, 242
export_tuple   165, 243
External data types   25
extract_pixel_plane   150, 244
extrema   104, 245

F

Filtering operators   16, 17, 60
Fixed point integer (TI)   26
flip_spin_transpose   70, 247
flip_spin_transpose_roi   72, 248
Frame buffer   92

G

Gamma corrected   8
generate_2d_roi_rectangular   323
generate_nd_1_tuple   314
generate_nd_3_tuple   315
generate_nd_4_tuple   316
generate_nd_5_tuple   317
generate_rd_5_tuple   318
generate_sd_1_tuple   319
generate_sd_3_tuple   320
generate_sd_4_tuple   321
generate_sd_5_tuple   322
Generic array (GA)   11
Geometric operators   16, 17, 22, 69
get_colour_pixel   166, 249
get_file   324
get_pixel   167, 250
get_pixel_array   169, 252
get_pixel_array_roi   170, 253
get_pixel_roi   168, 251
Global control mode   133

H

High-level operators   16
Histogram   152, 162
Histogram (HIST)   12
histogram_1d   106, 254
Horizontal space index, *x*   5

I

IbErrorTest   143, 237
IbGetPixelROI   168, 251
Iconic Kernel System (IKS)   viii
ID (*See* Data object indentifier)
IHS   7
Illuminants   8
   C   7
   D65   7
   E   7
Image array   5, 6
   attributes   4
   data objects   3, 4
Image
   generation   17
   Interchange Facility (IIF)   viii
   Processing and Interchange (IPI)   viii
   structure   6
image_constant   109, 255
imaging model   3
Image generation tools   16, 17, 109
Import   3
Import to PIKS utilities   18, 19, 152
import_histogram   152, 256
import_image   153, 257
import_lut   154, 259
import_matrix   155, 261
import_neighbourhood_array   156, 263
import_tuple   158, 208, 265
Impulse
   response array (IL)   11
   function   60, 115
   function array generation tool   16, 17, 115
   function arrays   15
impulse_rectangular   115, 266
InAllocateHist   118, 200
InAllocateImage   119, 201
InAllocateLUT   122, 203
InAllocateMatrix   123, 204
InAllocateNbhoodArray   123, 205
InAllocateROI   125, 206

InAllocateTuple   126, 207
InAlphaBlendConstant   49, 209
InArrayToLUT   112, 210
InBindROI   136, 211
InBitShift   33, 212
InBooleanDisplay   311
InColourConvLin   96, 215
InColourConvSubtractive   97, 217
InColourDisplay   313
InComplement   35, 218
InConvertArrayToImage   145, 219
InConvertImageDatatype   146, 220
InConvertROIToImage   147, 222
InConvolve2D   60, 223
InCopyWindow   148, 224
InCreateTuple   149, 225
InDefineSubImage   137, 228
InDiffuse   92, 229
InDither   94, 230
InDrawPixels   102, 231
InDyadicArith   50, 232
InDyadicLogical   52, 233
InDyadicPredicate   55, 234
InExtractPixelPlane   150, 244
InFlipSpinTranspose   70, 247
InFlipSpinTransposeROI   72, 248
InGenerate2DROIRectangular   323
InGenerateND1Tuple   314
InGenerateND3Tuple   315
InGenerateND4Tuple   316
InGenerateND5Tuple   317
InGenerateRD5Tuple   318
InGenerateSD1Tuple   319
InGenerateSD3Tuple   320
InGenerateSD4Tuple   321
InGenerateSD5Tuple   322
InHist1D   106, 254
InImageConstant   109, 255
InImportHist   152, 256
InImportImage   153, 257
InImportLUT   154, 259
InImportMatrix   155, 261
InImportNbhoodArray   156, 263
InImportTuple   158, 265
InImpulseRectangular   115, 266
InInsertPixelPlane   151, 278
InLookup   36, 279
InLumGeneration   99, 280

InMonadicArith   39, 282
InMonadicLogical   42, 283
InMonochromeDisplay   326
InMorphicProcessor   68, 284
InPrepare2DROIRectangular   330
InPrepareColourImage   328
InPrepareMonochromeImage   329
InPseudocolourDisplay   331
InPutColourPixel   159, 286
InPutPixel   160, 287
InPutPixelArray   160, 288
inquire_elements   127, 267
inquire_image   128, 268
inquire_non_image_object   130, 270
inquire_piks_implementation   132, 272
inquire_piks_status   133, 273
inquire_repository   134, 276
inquire_resampling   135, 277
Inquiry   18
Inquiry mechanisms   18, 19, 127
InRescale   74, 289
InRescaleROI   76, 290
InResize   78, 291
InResizeROI   80, 292
InReturnRepositoryId   139, 293
InROIRectangular   110, 294
InRotate   82, 295
insert_pixel_plane   151, 278
InSetImageAttrs   140, 299
InSplitImage   59, 300
InSubsample   84, 301
Internal
    data types   25
    utilities   18, 19, 145
International Electrotechnical Commission
        (IEC)   viii
International Organization for Standardiza-
        tion (ISO)   viii
Intersection   55, 333
InThreshold   43, 302
InTranslate   85, 303
InTranslateROI   87, 304
InUnaryInteger   46, 305
InWindowLevel   47, 306
InZoom   89, 307
InZoomROI   90, 308
Ipsattrs_matrix   204, 341
IP (*See* Data object identifier)

Ipsattrs_lut   203, 341
Ipsattrs_nbhood   205, 341
Ipsattrs_roi   206, 341
Ipsattrs_tuple   207, 341
Ipsparameter_pixel   252, 340
Ipspiks_pixel_types   324, 332, 340
IsnConvertImageToArray   147, 221
ISO registration authority   26
IstExportImage   162, 239
IstExportLUT   163, 240
IstExportMatrix   164, 241
IstExportNbhoodArray   165, 242
IstExportTuple   165, 243
IstGetFile   324
IstGetPixel   167, 250
IstGetPixelArray   169, 252
ItbaGetPixelArrayROI   170, 253
ItfSetErrorHandler   144, 296
ItOpenWindow   327
ItraAccumulator   103, 199
ItuaExportHist   162, 238
IvClosePIKS   117, 213
IvClosePIKSEmergency   117, 214
IvCloseWindow   312
IvColourConvMatrix   113, 216
IvDeallocateDataObject   127, 227
IvErrorHandler   141, 235
IvErrorLogger   143, 236
IvExtrema   104, 245
IvGetColourPixel   166, 249
IvInquireElements   127, 267
IvInquireImage   128, 268
IvInquireNonImageObject   130, 270
IvInquirePIKSImpl   132, 272
IvInquirePIKSStatus   133, 273
IvInquireRepository   134, 276
IvInquireResampling   135, 277
IvKeyDelay   325
IvMoments   108, 281
IvOpenPIKS   117, 285
IvPutFile   332
IvSetGlobals   139, 297

K

Key pixel   11, 21, 62, 64, 65, 115, 125
Key point   23
key_delay   311, 313, 325, 326, 327, 331

L

LIV   334
LOOK   334
lookup   36, 279
Lookup table (LUT)   12, 36, 112, 154, 163
Lookup table generation tool   18, 19, 112
Luminance   8
luminance_generation   99, 280

M

Management mechanisms   18, 19, 136
Mask array (ML)   11
Matrix   155, 164
Matrix generation tool   18, 19, 113
MAX   334
Mean   108
Mechanisms   18, 19, 117
MIN   334
MOD   334
moments   108, 281
monadic_arithmetic   39, 282
monadic_logical   42, 283
Monochrome (MON)   6
monochrome_display   326, 327
Morphic processor   69
morphic_processor   68, 284
Morphological operators   16, 17, 60

N

NBHOOD_ARRAY   10
ND   (*See* Nonnegative integer)
Neighbourhood array   115, 156, 165
Neighbourhood operators   21
NIV   335
Nomenclature   32
Nonimage data objects   3, 9
Nonnegative integer
   ND   8, 25, 26
   NI   26
   NP   25, 26
NP (*See* Nonnegative integer)
Null (NULL)   22, 26

O

Object restrictions   31
open_piks   117, 285
open_window   311, 313, 326, 327, 331

Operators   3, 16, 17
   input image   20
   model   18, 20, 24
   output image   20

P

PIKS
   Foundation   ix
   Full   ix
   Imaging Model   3
   Scientific   ix
   Technical   ix
PIKS_OPEN   118
Pixel modification operator   16, 17, 102
Pixel stacker   69
Point operators   16, 17, 20, 33
prepare_2d_roi_rectangular   330
prepare_colour_image   328
prepare_monochrome_image   329
Presentation operators   92
Primitive operators   16
Private identifier   4
Programmer's Imaging Kernel (PIK)   viii
Programmer's Imaging Kernel System
            (PIKS)   viii, xiii
pseudocolour_display   331
put_colour_pixel   159, 286
put_file   332
put_pixel   160, 287
put_pixel_array   160, 288

R

RD (*See* Real arithmetic)
Real arithmetic
   RD   9, 25, 26
   RP   25, 26
Region-of-interest (ROI)   5, 14
   control   22, 23
   control object   22, 23
   data object   23
   generation tool   18, 19, 110
   ROI_RECT   14, 110
   virtual array   14
Remark   31
Representation attribute   4
RES_2 335
Resampling   75, 135, 335
rescale   74, 289

rescale_roi   76, 290
resize   78, 291
resize_roi   80, 292
return_repository_id   139, 223, 230, 293
RGB   7
ROI   (*See* Region-of-interest)
roi_rectangular   110, 294, 323
rotate   82, 295
RP (*See* Real arithmetic)

S

SD   (*See* Signed integer)
set_error_handler   144, 296
set_globals   139, 297
set_image_attributes   140, 299
Signed integer
   SD   8, 25, 26
   SI   26
   SP   26
SIN   335
Source image   6, 20
SP   (*See* Signed integer)
Spectral band index, *b*   5
split_image   59, 300
Standard deviation   108
Structuring element array (SL)   11
subsample   84, 301
System management mechanisms   136
System mechanisms   3

T

Temporal index, *t*   5
threshold   43, 302
Tools   3, 16, 17, 109
translate   85, 303
translate_roi   87, 304
Tuple (TUPLE)   5, 9, 126, 158, 165
Tuple specification   32

U

unary_integer   46, 305
Union   55, 333
Utilities   3, 18, 19, 145

V

Vertical space index, *y*   5
Video   8, 96

W

White reference   7
White point tristimulus values   8
window_level   47, 306

Z

zoom   89, 307
zoom_roi   90, 308

PixelSoft, Inc. Software

Implementations of the PIKS Application Program Interface standard are available from:

PixelSoft, Inc.
Suite 429
101 First Street
Los Altos, CA 94022

(415) 948-5757